Social Psychology
Sociological Perspectives

Social Psychology
Sociological Perspectives

David E. Rohall
Western Illinois University

Melissa A. Milkie
University of Maryland

Jeffrey W. Lucas
University of Maryland

PEARSON

Boston   New York   San Francisco
Mexico City   Montreal   Toronto   London   Madrid   Munich   Paris
Hong Kong   Singapore   Tokyo   Cape Town   Sydney

Senior Series Editor: Jeff Lasser
Series Editorial Assistant: Erikka Adams
Senior Marketing Manager: Kelly May
Production Supervisor: Karen Mason
Editorial Production Service: Pine Tree Composition, Inc.
Composition Buyer: Linda Cox
Manufacturing Buyer: Debbie Rossi
Electronic Composition: Pine Tree Composition, Inc.
Interior Design: Joyce Weston
Photo Researcher: Pine Tree Composition, Inc.
Cover Administrator: Joel Grendon

For related titles and support materials, visit our online catalog at www.ablongman.com.

Between the time website information is gathered and then published, it is not unusual for some sites to have closed. Also, the transcription of URLs can result in typographical errors. The publisher would appreciate notification where these errors occur so that they may be corrected in subsequent editions.

Library of Congress Cataloging-in-Publication Data
Rohall, David E.
  Social psychology: sociological perspectives/David E. Rohall, Melissa A. Milkie, Jeffrey W. Lucas.
      p. cm.
  Includes bibliographical references and index.
  ISBN 0-205-44004-5
  1. Social psychology.   I. Milkie, Melissa A.   II. Lucas, Jeffrey W. III. Title.

HM1033.R64 2007
302—dc22

2006034441

Printed in the United States of America

10 9 8 7 6 5 4 3 2 1   [RRD-VA]   11   10   09   08   07

PHOTO CREDITS: p. 5, Ancil Nance/Stone/Getty Images; 017, Michael Prince/Corbis; 034, Corbis RF; 039, Kayte M. Deioma/PhotoEdit; 065, Bob Daemmrich/The Image Works; 067, David Young-Wolff/PhotoEdit; 089, Cameron/Corbis; 104, Artiga Photo/Corbis; 128, Jose Luis Pelaez/Corbis; 137, James Nubile/The Image Works; 148, Esbin/Anderson/Omni-Photo Communications; 151, David Young-Wolff/PhotoEdit; 181, Joe Sohm/Chromosohm/The Stock Connection; 197, Mark Wilson/Getty Images; 209, John Neubauer/PhotoEdit; 220, Ashley Cooper/Corbis; 237, AP Images; 249, Michael Goldman/Taxi/Getty Images; 256, Cindy Charles/PhotoEdit; 268, Amy Etra/PhotoEdit; 282, Phillipe Crochet/Liaison/Getty Images; 297, C. Niklas Hill/Liaison/Getty Images

To Molly, Michael, Jeremiah, and Virginia
—DR

To Mom for building mastery through my life; to Christopher, Aaron, Kathryn, and Daniel for the amazing sense of mattering you create.
—MM

To Jeremy
—JL

Contents

Part 1   Perspectives and Methods   1

Boxes

Tables

Figures

Preface

Social psychology is the study of how the behaviors, thoughts, and emotions of individuals are created and modified by the social and cultural conditions in which they live. The field of social psychology includes psychologists who emphasize how social conditions affect individual psychology and sociologists who focus on the effects of larger social-structural conditions on individuals and groups. Sociologists also bring a wealth of theories and perspectives from macrosociology into their social psychological research. The goal of this book is to provide you with an extensive review of the *sociological* approach to social psychology.

A number of social psychology textbooks incorporate theories and research in social psychology from *both* the fields of psychology and sociology. Our goal is to provide students with a social psychology textbook that emphasizes sociological work. By emphasizing sociological social psychology, we hope to provide a more complete coverage of the breadth and depth of the work of sociologists than do other textbooks. We also try to emphasize issues most important to sociologists, notably, topics related to inequality in society.

As a heuristic device, we have divided the field of sociological social psychology into three major dimensions or "faces" (House 1977; Smith-Lovin and Molm 2000). The first perspective is called symbolic interactionism. *Symbolic interactionism* examines the effects of face-to-face interaction processes in the social construction of society and the self. Symbolic interaction is a popular area of sociological social psychology. It is so popular that there is at least one journal dedicated solely to the study of symbolic interactionist social psychology, and a number of textbooks emphasize this perspective in the study of social behavior. We keep this tradition in our text but also include other perspectives in the field of social psychology, especially the social structure and personality and group processes perspectives.

The *social structure and personality perspective*, the second "face" of sociological social psychology focuses on the effects of larger social structural conditions on individual psychology, such as the impact of social class on self-image or the effect of urban residence on behavior (House 1992).

The third perspective in sociological psychology that we incorporate in this book is called *group processes* (Smith-Lovin and Molm 2000). Group processes theory and research focuses on the fundamental processes that occur in group settings. It also examines the role of groups in society, that is, how groups interact with one another.

Although there is some overlap in the theories and research in each of these faces, using them as distinct "faces" in this text will help to structure the larger field of sociological social psychology. Thus, we try to combine theories and research into their respective faces within each chapter. In most chapters we will examine important research and theories under each of these three headings. At the end of each chapter we will discuss how these perspectives help to answer important questions in the field.

The three faces of sociological social psychology are unified by their focus on how larger societal conditions affect individual and group dynamics. Therefore, we believe that it is important to understand the parent field of sociology before reviewing research in sociological social psychology. The first section of this book includes three chapters introducing the larger field of sociology, discussing sociological social psychology itself and the methods that social psychologists use to study social behavior. Specifically, Chapter 1, Introduction to Sociological Social Psychology, reviews the general field of sociology and how it relates to social psychology. We review the nature of society and the major macro-level perspectives in the field. We also briefly review the three major perspectives in sociological social psychology and how they apply to the study of micro-level behavior.

In chapter 2, Perspectives in Sociological Social Psychology, we provide a detailed review of the three major perspectives in sociological social psychology as well as the general concepts associated with each perspective. Chapter 3, Studying People, then reviews the major ways that sociologists conduct research. Although this chapter does not explicitly follow the three faces paradigm found in the later chapters, we discuss ways in which researchers from the different perspectives typically apply different methods to study social behavior.

The second section of the book examines micro-level foundations of society and the impact of society on the individual once it has been constructed. Here, we follow the "three faces" paradigm, examining research and theory within each of the major perspectives. We start with the social psychology of stratification because we believe that it is a major way that the larger field of sociology influences sociological social psychology. Specifically, we are trying to answer the question, "How does society affect our sense of self and our social relationships over time?" Chapter 4, The Social Psychology of Stratification, explicitly examines research and theories on how social inequalities develop between people and how they influence relationships. We then examine the self-concept in Chapter 5, Self and Identity. Finally, in Chapter 6, Socialization over the Life Course, we focus on how individuals develop senses of self and social conditions that change the self over time.

The last section of our text reviews sociological theories and research on different aspects of social life. Chapter 7, The Social Psychology of Deviance, emphasizes interactionist perspectives on the study of deviance in society, how we construct the meaning of what is normal or deviant in a given group or society, and the effects of labeling processes on the perpetuation of deviance. Our approach takes an interactionist perspective that focuses on the variety of ways that people can deviate—not just as a reflection of criminal behavior. Hence, our treatment of deviance views it as a social psychological product and a normal part of interaction processes.

Chapter 8, Mental Health and Illness, follows our discussion of deviance by emphasizing the ways that mental health is stigmatized and treated as a form of deviance in society. We also focus on the stress process model of mental health that incorporates socioeconomic characteristics and social resources to explain why people from different social strata have different mental health outcomes.

The next two chapters of our text emphasize the influence of society on our thoughts, feelings, and behaviors. Chapter 9, Attitudes, Values, and Behaviors, examines the current understanding of the meaning of attitudes—how people measure and assess them, and how people use their time—a unique way of assessing human behaviors today. Chapter 10, The Sociology of Sentiment and Emotion, reviews current sociological understanding of how people construct "socially" appropriate emotions under different social conditions.

We end our book by moving from interactions between individuals to the study of large-group behavior. Chapter 11, Collective Behavior, includes research and theories about how groups transform their members. We believe that this review will help students see the complex circle of connection from society to the individual and back to society. The chapter does this by explaining how individuals are linked to groups and by examining large-group behavior.

Most of the subject areas included in this book rely on multiple perspectives to help answer similar research questions. Symbolic interactionists, social structure and personality, and group processes scholars, for instance, are interested in how inequalities develop and affect individuals in society. They approach this topic, however, using different theories and research methods. Our goal is to provide readers with an extensive review of how social psychologists from all these traditions create and answer these and other research questions. In addition, we want to bring the larger field of sociology into the study of social psychology by emphasizing how social and cultural factors affect individuals and groups in society. The result, we hope, will give students a more complete understanding of the diversity of sociological theories and research in social psychology.

Acknowledgments

This book reflects a tradition of writing that includes the works of Morris Rosenberg, Ralph Turner, and countless other sociologists who helped to highlight the role of sociologists in the broader field of social psychology over many decades. We especially thank Timothy Owens (Purdue University) and Karen Hegtvedt (Emory University) for their insights into the structure of our book, and David Miller (Western Illinois University) for his significant contributions to our chapter on collective behavior. We also thank Bill Faulkner and Lora Ebert Wallace (both Western Illinois University) for their insights into our chapters covering Deviance and Mental Health. We thank our mentors in social psychology including Bill Corsaro, Donna Eder, Lee Hamilton, David Heise, Michael Lovaglia, Barry Markovsky, Barbara Meeker, Leonard Pearlin, Bernice Pescosolido, Brian Powell, Stanley Presser, John Robinson, Mady Wechsler Segal, Sheldon Stryker, and Lisa Troyer.

We also want to thank the following colleagues for their comments and suggestions in the development of our manuscript: Jeffrey Chin (Le Moyne College), Jessica Collete (University of Arizona), Brett Harger (University of Indiana at Bloomington), Lynette Hoelter (University of Michigan at Ann Arbor), Elaine McDuff (Truman State University), Douglas Clayton Smith (Western Kentucky State University), and Clovis White (Oberlin College).

We want to acknowledge the staff at Allyn & Bacon/Longman publishers for all of their help in developing and producing this book. We especially thank Jeff Lasser for having the vision for a social psychology textbook that focuses on the work of sociologists, and Judy Ashkenaz for her insights and guidance in the development of our manuscript.

Perspectives and Methods

The first section of this book is designed to give you a basic review of sociological social psychology, the way that we approach research, and the larger field of sociology. The first chapter will review concepts in sociology that sociological social psychologists use in developing theories and research. We will also provide a basic overview of the three major perspectives in social psychology: Symbolic interaction, social structure and personality, and group processes. Chapter 2 will review these perspectives extensively, providing detailed information about the theories and research that employ these perspectives. The third chapter will examine the major methods used in the field to study people.

At the beginning of each chapter you will find a series of questions that we will address; at the end of each section of the chapter, we review how we have tried to answer these questions in that particular section. We end each chapter with a section titled "Bringing It All Together," where we examine the chapter as a whole, summarizing the ways that each section of the chapter relates to the other sections. We also include a series of discussion questions at the end of the chapter to provoke additional thinking about the material. Finally, we provide a list of key words used in each chapter and summaries of them. We believe that these tools will help you to learn the most salient concepts, theories, and research in the field of sociological social psychology.

Introduction to Sociological Social Psychology

I guess you could say that I became obsessed with the man. He was so rude to me in the classroom that day, basically telling me that I had no business in college. I just had to know what this guy was about. Was he just a jerk? Did he have a bad day? I just wanted to know why he was so mean to me. I started asking around and everyone said that he was a great guy. Then I wondered if I might have been the problem—maybe I said something to set him off. I tried to ask him but he did not want to talk about it. The professor later told me that the guy was going through some hard times. Maybe that was it. . . .

—Krystal, sophomore English major

Trying to understand the behaviors of other people can be puzzling. Although social psychologists take numerous approaches to looking at the social world, we all have an interest in understanding the thoughts, feelings, and behaviors of people. You are probably reading this book because you also share this desire to learn about people. You may even have developed some personal theories about human behaviors. Some of these views may focus on a particular person—for example, a "theory" about why one of your friends has difficulty in dating relationships. But you may also have come up with larger-scale explanations to account for the behaviors of many people in various situations—for example, explaining behavior by saying, "It's all about the money," reflecting your belief that most actions are driven by material interests.

Although these personal opinions do not meet a social scientist's criteria for "theory," the general idea is the same: Social scientists seek to develop explanations for the often complex ways that people act.

In the vignette that opens this chapter, we see a student trying to make sense of another student's behavior. Apparently the second student has done something to her that makes her wonder what might have caused the behavior. At first she relies on the nature or personality of the other person: "Is he just a jerk?" Because the man will not tell her why he was rude, she has to rely on information from other people. She discovers that other people think highly of him and realizes that she probably does not have the whole picture. Gradually, she begins to put together a story about the man and how his current life circumstances may have contributed to his poor behavior.

Most of us engage in similar efforts to gather and use available information about people to have enough data to reach conclusions about them. In this way, we are all social scientists, searching the world around us for clues as to how and why people act in the ways they do. But two crucial things separate social science from personal theories of human behavior. First, social scientists do not rely on speculation. They systematically test theories and often revise them based on what they learn by testing. Second, social scientists do not develop theories about the behavior of a single individual. Rather, social scientists seek to develop theories that explain how and why very different people will tend to behave in similar ways when facing similar situations or placed in similar roles. Social psychologists develop theories and then test them using observations, surveys, experiments, and other forms of research. Unlocking these social forces can be very powerful because seeing them helps us to predict others' behavior.

Social psychology is the systematic study of people's thoughts, feelings, and behavior in social contexts. Social psychologists approach the study of human behavior in different ways. Some social psychologists focus on the impact of our immediate social environments on our thoughts, feelings, and behavior. But they soon find that even these immediate contexts are influenced by larger social forces and conditions. In the opening vignette, for example, Krystal could continue her social investigation by incorporating additional levels of analysis. She might investigate what kind of behavior leads someone to be defined as a "jerk" in a given society. In addition, she might try to determine the larger social conditions that may be exacerbating this individual's immediate social problems. Maybe he recently lost his job as part of a large-scale downsizing at his workplace, causing additional stresses in his life that lead him to be more irritable on a day-to-day basis.

When sociologists study social psychology, they emphasize the ways in which society shapes the meaning of social interactions, while also assessing the effects of broad social conditions on our thoughts, feelings, and behaviors. Sociological social psychologists study many of the same topics as psychological social psychologists—emotions, identity, and attitudes, for example—but they use theories and perspectives that tend to place emphasis on the role of society in social processes.

The goal of this book is to provide you with an extensive review of the theories and research developed by sociological social psychologists. In this chapter, we

Sociological social psychologists study the nexus between the individual and society.

will offer a brief overview of the field of sociology and the ways that sociological social psychologists incorporate the larger field of sociology into their work. Specifically, we will address the following questions:

- What is sociology? How does macrosociology differ from microsociology?
- What are the differences in the ways sociologists and psychologists approach social psychology?
- What are the major perspectives in sociological social psychology?
- What do I need to know to study the impact of society in my day-to-day life?

Sociology, Psychology, and Social Psychology

Sociology first came alive to me after watching the film Fahrenheit 9/11. *I didn't agree with everything Michael Moore had to say about President Bush but his film made me wonder how much power other people had over me. It's amazing that the president can send a bunch of troops to war, but I can't even get the local government to fix the potholes down the street! I can't even get the restaurant owner I work for to give me more time off when I want it. It just doesn't seem fair! Those guys are no smarter than me!*

—Steve, junior Political Science major

Sociology is the systematic study of society. Society is a broad term that includes many levels of social interaction, from interactions among individuals to relationships among nations. Sociologists analyze social life across these levels of analysis (Aron 1965; Collins 1985). We usually think of society as a larger entity that exists above and beyond its individual members. Until something bad happens to us, we may not think much about the impact of society on our lives. If a downturn in the economy leads to a job loss, for instance, we may blame the government or get angry at "the direction the country is going." But what do we mean by "society," beyond government rules and regulations? In what other ways can society affect our lives? Sociologists try to elaborate the specific ways that societal processes work to influence people's lives.

In the previous vignette, we see "society" come alive for a student after he watches a controversial film about the American presidency. Steve notices that some people in society have more power than others, and he questions whether those with power are actually any better than him. He seems to think that he is no different than the people in power: He believes he has the same abilities as politicians or business owners, so he should have some of the same control over others and over the way things work. Finally, Steve begins to question where that power comes from and who has the right to exercise power.

Steve's experience helps him realize that some people in society have power over other people through the positions they hold. When sociologists study social life, their goals often include examining how people's positions—for example, being married, being a woman, or being wealthy—affect their thoughts, feelings, and behaviors and their power over others. This section will review the different levels of analysis found in sociology—including social psychology or "microsociology"—as well as differences in how psychologists and sociologists approach the study of social psychology. Finally, we will review the history of sociological social psychology.

Macrosociology and Microsociology

Our society and culture influence us in many ways; to understand these influences, sociologists study social phenomena at different levels of analysis. Suppose you are interested in studying racial discrimination. One way to explore this interest would be to collect societal-level statistics on income and wealth. The U.S. Census, for instance, regularly reports the distribution of income by race. Whites, on average, report higher levels of income than African Americans and Latino Americans (Nelson 2005). You also might study discrimination by examining how people experience racial stratification on a day-to-day basis, more specifically, in the lives and interactions of people from different racial and ethnic backgrounds (e.g., May 2001; Nash 2000). For example, you might find that minority group members, on average, are treated with more hostility in retail stores than are members of the majority group. Both of these examples demonstrate the same basic social phenomena—discrimination that favors majority group members and disadvantages minority group members. The studies, however, approach the issue from different levels of analysis.

Macrosociology focuses on the analysis of large-scale social processes. (See Boxes 1.1 and 1.2.) Instead of researching individual thoughts, feelings, and behavior, macrosociology looks at larger groups and social institutions (Nolan and Lenski 2004). Macrosociologists use societal-level data to examine phenomena such as poverty rates, incidence of violence, or large-scale social change. For instance, C. Wright Mills (2002, originally 1951) traced patterns of change in the American economy from the late eighteenth into the early nineteenth centuries, showing the fall of independent farming and concurrent rise of white-collar professions. He went on to explain the long-term effects of the early American economy on the society and culture of the United States in the 1950s. Mills showed that companies in the bureaucratic age of the 1950s exerted a great deal of control over people's lives, despite the emphasis that U.S. culture placed on independence and freedom converting the American middle-classes from independent entrepreneurs to a group alienated from their own labor.

Macrosociologists also conduct studies across societies and cultures. There are currently 191 members of the United Nations (www.un.org), representing almost all countries in the world today. Sociologists, especially demographers, examine differences in such parameters as fertility, mortality, and immigration rates across the world. For example, when researchers study how resource levels relate to trends in fertility and mortality, they find that some of the richest nations in the world—those with the most resources to raise children—have the lowest fertility and mortality rates (Pampel 2001).

The subject of this book is **microsociology** (what we call *sociological social psychology*), the study of the effects of larger society on social psychological processes. In addition to studying the impact of larger social factors on individuals and their interactions, microsociologists are concerned with the role of the individual in the creation and maintenance of society.

As you can see, both macrosociologists and microsociologists study society, but they do it at different levels and in different ways. Consider divorce as a social phenomenon. Macrosociologists are typically interested in rates of divorce and in how changing divorce rates affect the institution of the family. They may also compare divorce rates by region or across nations in an effort to understand the conditions that affect the rate of divorce in each country (see, for example, Diekmann and Schmidheiny 2004; Wilde 2001; Yi and Deqing 2000). In contrast, microsociologists (or sociological social psychologists) would be more interested in the perceived causes and outcomes of divorces than in the divorce rates. A microsociologist might conduct a study in which a number of divorced men and women talk about the factors that influenced their decisions to divorce their spouses. Or, a microsociologist might study the mental health consequences of going through a divorce and whether these consequences are different for women than for men. Both macrosociological and microsociological approaches contribute to our understanding of the social aspects of divorce. One involves societal-level factors, and the other involves the connection of society to the individual and individual-level perceptions—the sense people make of their divorces.

| Box 1.1 | **Macro-Level Sources of Information** |

Social psychological information is all around us. Macrosociologists, who use information that applies to whole societies, rely on a number of sources of data in particular. For example, the U.S. Census Bureau (www.census.gov) is the hub of a great deal of demographic information about the United States today. In addition to conducting a count of the U.S. population every ten years, the Census Bureau maintains current population estimates for the United States and the world. Census Bureau data is a valuable resource for sociologists interested in studying the U.S. population. It includes detailed information about Americans' income levels, health, education, and housing, among many other topics. Sociologists regularly use census data to track important social issues such as poverty and to examine broad societal conditions associated with those issues—for example, comparing poverty rates by region, race, or gender.

The United Nations (www.un.org) and the World Bank (www.worldbank.org) provide extensive sets of data on nations across the world. Like the Census Bureau, these organizations allow researchers to examine basic demographic information for all the countries on the planet. Researchers can also use these data to study poverty, conflicts, and other important social issues. Macrosociologists use these and other sources of data to track large-scale social processes.

Although macro-level data may not directly relate to our day-to-day lives, it provides a context for understanding individuals' thoughts, feelings, and behavior. Macro-level data, including population size and literacy and unemployment rates, provide an understanding of the social and economic context of people's lives and the types of problems people face in their daily lives.

Both levels of analysis require some understanding of the effects of the larger society on divorce. Social conditions provide a context for understanding interactions between individuals. In one study, a researcher examined divorce rates across 22 countries, finding that the rates are associated with marital equality (Yodanis 2005). That is, countries in which divorce is more accepted (represented by rates of divorce) also have more equal distribution of work between men and women in the household. Hence, a "divorce culture" may affect men's and women's personal relationships in a direct way, giving women more leverage in their marriages. However, individuals may not be aware of how larger social conditions impact their decision-making processes, making it challenging to understand links between macro- and micro-level processes.

Sociological and Psychological Social Psychology

We have defined *microsociology* or sociological social psychology as the study of how the larger society influences basic social psychological processes. Some social psychologists come from the field of **psychology,** the study of human thought processes

Box 1.2   **Theoretical Perspectives in Macrosociology**

Macrosociology includes two major perspectives: structural functionalism and conflict theory. The *structural functionalist perspective* emphasizes how elements of society interact in ways that help society maintain order. Important sociologists linked to structural functionalism include Emile Durkheim (1858–1917) and Talcott Parsons (1902–1979). From the functionalist perspective, society resembles a biological organism in which each part of the body has a function that promotes the survival of the whole. In society, similarly, different groups and individuals function to keep society alive—accountants, teachers, and garbage collectors are all needed to keep things going in the world. However, not all parts of this system are of equal value. (The heart, for instance, is more important for survival than a big toe.) From a functionalist perspective, this specialization leads to differentiation and the establishment of a hierarchy, with some people contributing more toward the functioning of society than others. Medical doctors may be perceived as contributing more to the maintenance and stability of society, for instance, than street cleaners. The result is a class system in which some people gain more money and prestige than others. Change in society occurs when environmental conditions make new roles necessary. Hence, computer programmers have become an important part of Western economies in just the last 30 or 40 years, leading to higher salaries and prestige than some other professions.

The *social conflict perspective* focuses on inequalities in society, especially those associated with class differences. Important conflict theorists include Karl Marx (1818–1883) and C. Wright Mills (1916–1962). In contrast to the functionalist emphasis on maintaining overall harmony in a society, conflict theorists see society as made up of members—both individuals and groups—who are constantly battling over limited resources. Conflict theorists differ from functionalists in their view of what keeps society together, and they focus on different elements of society in explaining social phenomena.

Although these perspectives are often applied to understanding macrosociological processes, functional and conflict theorists have also emphasized the social-psychological relevance of their ideas (House 1977). For instance, Marx employed the concept of "alienation," a psychological state in which people feel disconnected from their work, to describe one of the impacts of capitalist economies on individuals in society. Hence, macrosociological perspectives can be applied to understand some aspects of microsociological phenomenon. Can you think of ways to apply these perspectives to everyday interactions between people?

and behavior. There is some overlap between sociology and psychology. Scholars in sociology, particularly microsociology, like those in psychology, look at how the behaviors, thoughts, and emotions of individuals are created and modified by the social conditions in which they live. However, sociological social psychology, as we discussed earlier, is an extension of the larger field of sociology that emphasizes the

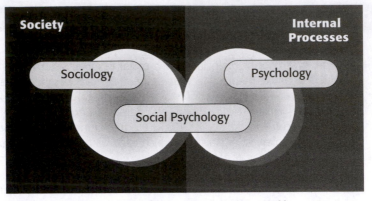

Figure 1.1   Social Psychology Merges Elements of Two Fields

impact of societal forces—in addition to immediate social contexts—on individuals' lives.

Social contexts can range from a small group of people to the larger culture and social conditions manifested in a society as a whole. In a sense, social psychology serves as a natural bridge between the fields of *sociology* (which focuses on the social aspect) and *psychology* (which studies the individual) (see Figure 1.1). However, sociologists are more likely than psychologists to take into account the effects of larger structural forces on individual thoughts, feelings, and behavior. For instance, sociologists are more likely than psychologists to compare the self-esteem levels of different racial and ethnic groups (Rosenberg 1986; Schieman, Pudrovska, and Milkie 2005). Conversely, psychologists are more likely than sociologists to study the thinking processes associated with self-esteem (Crocker and Park 2003). In a sense merging these approaches, sociological social psychology examines the relationship between the larger society and interactions between individuals within that society.

As a subfield of sociology, sociological social psychology brings sociological perspectives to the study of social psychology. Early scholars like William James (1842–1910), George Herbert Mead (1863–1931), and W. E. B. DuBois (1868–1963) became well known for their ability to articulate how social forces influence our day-to-day interactions, as we will discuss in more detail throughout this book. During the same time period, as seen in Box 1.3, many psychologists were developing some of the prominent research and theories associated with individual behaviors and internal thought processes.

Historical Context of Sociological Social Psychology

The term *sociology* was coined by French social philosopher August Comte (1798–1857). Comte first defined the field of sociology in 1838, later than other sciences such as economics and biology. Comte was a staunch positivist. Positivism is the belief that the scientific method is the best approach to the production of knowledge. Comte attempted to place sociology in the context of more

| Box 1.3 | Psychoanalysis in Psychology |

Psychologists generally are interested in internal processes. The German psychologist Sigmund Freud (1856–1939) popularized the idea of the unconscious mind and the development of personality over time. Freud's psychoanalytic method was designed as a means of gaining access to an individual's subconscious thoughts. Psychoanalysis emphasizes the role of conscious and unconscious processes that manifest themselves in everyday life. The role of the psychoanalyst is to access all these inner thoughts and feelings in an effort to liberate the individual from his or her problems by resolving the internal conflicts that have evolved over time. Hence, the analyst must often reconstruct life events and childhood experiences—a process that may take years of analysis to accomplish (Cockerham 2003). The impact of larger social conditions does enter into the psychoanalytic perspectives, but they tend to focus primarily on internal dynamics. Sociologists, by contrast, are less likely to draw a dividing line between internal and external worlds; rather, we view thoughts and feelings as a continual exchange of information between internal and external sources.

traditional scientific fields. In his view, the complexities of social dynamics would make sociology the most challenging scientific field. Think about all the factors that influence what you do on a daily basis—the biological, situational, and historical conditions that lead you to do the things that you do. Although some people believe that social behavior is too complex to understand using the scientific method, we believe that the same features that make sociology a most challenging discipline also make it a most interesting one.

The generation of sociologists who followed August Comte began to make keen observations about the connection of society to the individual. Sociologists such as George Herbert Mead (1863–1931) and William Thomas (1863–1947) helped found a uniquely American school of social psychology at the University of Chicago. Mead studied how social conditions affect our sense of self. Thomas (Thomas and Znaniecki 1958) focused on the role of life histories as a way of assessing the effects of social and historical changes on individuals' lives over time. This research led to the classic book, *The Polish Peasant in Europe and America* (originally published in intervals between 1918 and 1920). The ideas of these early sociologists helped in the creation of *symbolic interactionism*, a perspective in sociological social psychology that will be reviewed in detail in this and subsequent chapters.

Other major contributors to the development of sociological social psychology include Charles Horton Cooley (1864–1929) and Georg Simmel (1858–1918). Cooley (1909) contributed to the development of sociological social psychology with his theoretical formulation of primary and secondary groups. Primary groups refer to small groups of people with whom we have face-to-face contact, such as our friends and family, whereas secondary groups are larger and less intimate. Cooley argued that primary and secondary groups produce fundamentally different types of interactions (see chapter 2). Simmel, a German sociologist at the University of Berlin, viewed society as a complex network of interactions between dyads (two-person groups) and triads (three-person groups) (Simmel 1950) (see also chapter 2).

These sociological social psychologists helped to lay the foundation for the perspectives and theories that modern social psychologists use to study human behavior in a social context. The next section will elaborate on the perspectives that they helped to create.

Section Summary

In this section of the chapter, we answered the questions: What is sociology? How does macrosociology differ from microsociology? What are the differences in the ways sociologists and psychologists study social psychology? We defined sociology as the systematic study of society. Some sociologists focus on macro-level processes in society, the study of societies as a whole. Other sociologists focus on micro-level processes or social psychology, the systematic study of people's thoughts, feelings, and behavior in social context. Although both sociologists and psychologists study social psychology, sociological social psychologists emphasize the impact of large social forces in our lives. Important historical figures in sociological social psychology include George Herbert Mead, Charles Horton Cooley, and Georg Simmel, among others.

Perspectives in Sociological Social Psychology

Johnny and I got along really well when we worked together at the copy shop. Then he got a promotion—he became my boss! All of a sudden, he started ordering me around and wouldn't joke with me anymore. In fact, he stopped hanging around with me—he got new friends in management, I guess. I say his position went to his head, making him act the way he did. My friends say that it is natural for people to change when they hang around new people (management).

—Susan, junior Management major

There are many different ways to investigate the role of society in people's day-to-day lives. You may decide to focus on your immediate social surroundings, or you may try to understand the impact of larger social institutions—for example, the economy—on people's lives. In this vignette, Susan is trying to understand how a promotion could lead to such dramatic changes in the behavior of her friend—now her boss. Could a simple promotion really lead a person to such an abrupt change in personality?

Susan's friends answer the question somewhat differently than her. They analyze Johnny's behavior differently, based on their perspectives. Similarly, sociological social psychologists work within broad perspectives that reflect their orientations, though social psychologists are usually interested in constructing general explanations for behaviors across people, time, and place. The three perspectives most used to characterize sociological social psychology are *symbolic interaction*, *social structure and personality*, and *group processes* (House 1977; Smith-Lovin and Molm 2000). We review the basic tenants of each of these perspectives in this chapter and will elaborate on them in chapter 2. (See also Table 1.1.)

Symbolic Interactionism

Symbolic interactionism, a central perspective in social psychology, merges elements of psychology with macrosociology in an attempt to explain the relationship between the individual and society. **Symbolic interactionism** is the study of how people negotiate the meaning of social life during their interactions with other people. George Herbert Mead is often credited as the father of symbolic interactionism. In a compiled volume of his works, *Mind, Self, and Society from the Standpoint of a Social Behaviorist*, Mead (1934) argued that we create meaning through our interactions with the people around us. Once agreed on, that meaning becomes our social reality. The meanings we attach to ourselves, other people, and objects are negotiated over time.

We use language to give *meaning* to everything in our lives and in the world around us. As one example, consider the concept of motherhood. What does it mean to be a mother? You may define *mother* as a woman who gives birth to a child. But what about women who adopt children? Wouldn't they be considered mothers? In fact, we quickly see that motherhood includes a myriad of meanings, expectations of care and loving that go far beyond the biological connections between people.

We also use language to give *value* to the objects around us. Are mothers good or bad? Although we cannot say that motherhood, in itself, is good or bad, we may define a specific mother as good or bad, depending on whether she meets our criteria for a mother. If a mother is supposed to feed and clothe her children, then a mother who does not do this may be deemed a "bad mother." Finally, we attach emotions to our images of a person, object, or identity. For example, a mother playing with her children may be associated with warm feelings.

From the interactionist perspective, the important connection between society and our inner experiences lies in our interactions with other people. These interactions provide information about the world, which we then accept or modify for our own use (Heise 1999; Mead 1934; Rosenberg 1990). In terms of motherhood, people are continuously negotiating its meaning. The meaning may change over time as we interact with different people with varied backgrounds and experiences, giving us new information about motherhood. A new baby, too, may alter meanings.

Social Structure and Personality

The **social structure and personality** perspective in social psychology focuses on the connections between larger societal conditions and the individual—specifically, on the influence of social structure on individuals. **Social structure** refers to "persisting patterns of behavior and interaction between people or social positions" (House 1992, p. 526). Because there is stability among relationships and positions, sociologists study these patterns and their effects on individuals' thoughts, feelings, and behavior.

The social structure and personality perspective can potentially explain the vignette that opens this section. One of the characters, Johnny, is promoted to a new position and starts acting differently. His new position may require that he order people around, regardless of his feelings toward his coworkers. From the social structure and personality perspective, our position in society dictates, to some degree, the way we are expected to think, feel, and behave. Perhaps the change in position caused him to rethink his relationship to his former coworkers. Other elements of social structure that can affect our lives will be reviewed in chapter 2.

Group Processes

The third face of sociological social psychology, **group processes,** studies how basic social processes operate in group contexts (Smith-Lovin and Molm 2000). Groups are an important part of society and a significant area of social psychological research in both sociology and psychology. Because it takes only two people to make a group, and because humans are inherently social, we all spend a considerable amount of time in our lives in group settings, including family, friends, and coworkers. Those in the group processes perspective study how our interactions and positions within these groups influence our meaning-making processes and other outcomes.

Group processes scholars are particularly interested in *processes* that come into play when groups form. Status is an example. When you form into groups in your classes, you might notice that some people talk more and have their opinions

Table 1.1	Three Perspectives in Sociological Social Psychology: A Comparison	
Perspective	**View of the Role of Individual in Society**	**Area of Focus**
Symbolic interaction	Individual is active participant in construction of society	Meaning-making processes
Social structure and personality	The nature of interaction is based on adherence to roles that people play	Emphasizes process of how larger social structures influence individuals
Group processes	When individuals form into social groups, certain basic processes regularly emerge in interactions	Processes that occur in group contexts

solicited more often than others. How are these differences determined? Power is another group process. When you negotiate the price of a car, certain features of the setting give you or the other person more power to set the final price. What are these situational characteristics that confer power? Justice is another example. When you decide whether the money you earn at your job is fair, you do so by comparing yourself to other people. What groups do we compare ourselves to in these situations, and how do we come to decide that things are fair or unfair? In short, group processes scholars are interested in answering these sorts of questions by studying the processes—such as status, power, and justice—that occur in group contexts.

Section Summary

The goal of this section was to answer the question: What are the major perspectives in sociological social psychology? We define three major perspectives or "faces" in social psychology: symbolic interaction, social structure and personality, and group processes. The symbolic interaction face examines how people negotiate the meaning of social life through interactions with other people. The social structure and personality face of sociological social psychology focuses on the connections between larger societal conditions and the individual. Finally, the group processes perspective emphasizes how basic social processes develop in group contexts. These three faces of social psychology will be used to structure how we present research and theories throughout this book.

Your Social Psychological Tool Kit

I remember my first social psychology course. There is so much to know—so many different topics and chapters. I am never really sure how to bring it all together. Human life is so complex. . . .

—Jamal, sophomore Psychology major

Jamal's story is probably a familiar one for many students who are just starting to study the social sciences. Understanding the social contexts of human behavior means that you must be able to incorporate almost all the elements of both the macro and the micro levels of society—how the influence of society plays out in larger social structures as well as in interactions with other individuals. On your journey through social psychology there are a few essential tools that you can take with you: the concepts and terms that sociologists employ in developing and describing their theories and research. We will be using these concepts throughout this text to help you understand how sociologists develop and interpret social psychological work.

The Sociological Imagination

The impact of society in our lives is often complex. How do we develop the ability to "see" society in our daily lives? Peter Berger (1973) says that we can see social forces in everyday life through individuals' expressions and behavior. We make choices every day without much conscious thought—such as purchasing food and clothing, spending time with friends and family, and the like. How do these choices reflect larger cultural values and norms? Berger argues that we need to develop the ability to see how what you do in your day-to-day life reflects larger social forces.

An important tool for seeing such forces in your life is the **sociological imagination**—the ability to see our personal lives in the context of the history, culture, and social structure of the larger society within which we live. C. Wright Mills (1959) argued that sociologists must understand the larger cultural, structural, and historical conditions influencing individuals before arriving at any conclusions about the causes of their decisions or experiences. Specifically, Mills said, "The sociological imagination enables its possessor to understand the larger historical scene in terms of its meaning for the inner life and the external career of a variety of individuals" (p. 5).

The sociological imagination gives social psychologists the vision necessary to assess all the possible social conditions that may influence individuals' thoughts, feelings, and behavior. If we limit our perspective on the social world to explanations that do not take social factors into consideration, we will miss some of the possible causal explanations for behavior. In a classic example, Durkheim (1951, originally 1897) questioned the traditional approach to understanding suicide, which focused on the mental health of the individual. He proposed that suicide rates are influenced by societal conditions, above and beyond personal problems. Durkheim first examined his ideas by comparing suicide rates over time and in different countries. He found that both time and place affected suicide rates—something that would not be true if suicide simply reflected a response to individual problems. Durkheim concluded that suicide had to be, in part, a manifestation of social issues as well as personal problems. His research showed that groups that are better integrated into society have lower suicide rates than groups with fewer social connections. For instance, married people, who are presumably better integrated into society as part of a social unit, were less susceptible to suicide than singles.

Other Tools in Your Kit

The sociological imagination is a tool that social psychologists can use to understand the influence of society on individuals. What exactly are we looking for? From a social psychological perspective, society exists both *within* and *between* individuals. It also takes the form of our positions in society and the expectations associated with those positions, which give us different levels of power and access to resources. When we try to see the larger influence of society, we must consider our relative positions in groups as well as how our culture views those relationships and positions. Society, from this perspective, is only as stable as the people, positions, and relationships it comprises. In a sense, society exists amid both stability and change, as people either accept existing rules or try to change them to meet the needs of contemporary life. The following concepts will help you know what to look for as you are trying to identify "society" as an influence in your day-to-day life.

Social Norms and Values

Social norms are behavioral guidelines—the rules that regulate our behavior in relationships. If society exists through our relationships with one another, then it is guided by the rules of conduct that apply to those relationships. One of the first things we learn about a society is its rules of conduct. **Values** differ from social norms in that they refer to deeply held ideals and beliefs. The laws of a given society codify many of its shared values and norms. For example, murder is considered such a destructive behavior that we impose large penalties for committing such an act. Other, lesser violations of norms, such as doing something inappropriate in front of a crowd, may be met only with public embarrassment. You will not go to jail for putting a lampshade on your head, but you may be the target of ostracism from others. Society, then, can influence people's behaviors by establishing both formal and informal rules of conduct.

We can discover a society's formal rules by examining its laws. But the process of identifying informal rules is more complex (see Box 1.4). People may not even be aware that they are following norms on a day-to-day basis. In *Tally's Corner*,

Children learn technical and social skills in their interactions with adults and other children.

Box 1.4   **Ethnomethodology**

Harold Garfinkel (b. 1917) proposed a method of studying society as reflected in our typical, day-to-day interactions that he called **ethnomethodology** (Garfinkel 1967). Ethnomethodology is both a theory and a method of inquiry. That is, it is a theoretical understanding of the linkages between the individual and society, and it is also a methodological approach to studying the relationship between the individual and society. One way that ethnomethodologists study informal social norms is through breaching experiments.

Breaching experiments include any method of violating social order to assess how people construct social reality (Ritzer 1996). Garfinkel was famous for asking students to perform breaching acts and report on reactions to these events. In a classic example, students were instructed to engage in a conversation and insist that their partner explain commonplace remarks. The following excerpt comes from Garfinkel's (1967) book, *Studies in Ethnomethodology.*

> SUBJECT: I had a flat tire.
>
> EXPERIMENTER: What do you mean, you had a flat tire?
>
> SUBJECT (appears momentarily stunned and then replies in a hostile manner): What do you mean, "What do you mean?" A flat tire is a flat tire. That is what I meant. Nothing special. What a crazy question.

This interaction demonstrates that there are implicit rules that should not be questioned during an exchange. When those rules are broken, there is an emotional reaction (note the hostility of the subject), followed by an attempt to restore order (restating the comment about the flat tire) and explain the interruption; in this case, the subject explains the experimenter's question as simply crazy. Such interactions are essential to the appearance of social order in everyday life. However, we may not be aware of such rules until they are broken in some way. Breaching experiments provide a way of finding and assessing informal norms and values.

Elliot Liebow (1967) observed a group of poor men living in Washington, D.C., during the 1960s. The men's lives revolved around a corner carryout restaurant, where some men were waiting for work or just "hanging out." Every man had a different reason for hanging out at the corner—some were waiting for someone to offer a part-time job, others were avoiding their families, and still others were just socializing. Despite their different reasons for being on the corner, all of them converged there on a regular basis, and this served as a norm of street corner life, although the norm guiding behavior was not driven by the same motivations for each individual. Relationships set up expectations of behavior that can operate above and beyond our thought processes. Alternatively, these norms can serve as a script, offering us a limited set of behavioral options from which we can choose.

Roles and Statuses

Another aspect of society consists of the roles and statuses that people occupy. **Status** refers to a person's position in a group or society that is associated with varying levels of esteem and power. Statuses are often formalized so that the relative standings of group members can be easily identified. In a workplace setting, for instance, a supervisor is paid to manage a group of people and may be given the right to tell people what to do. Other times, status develops more informally.

Our status usually includes a set of expectations about how to behave in a group. These expectations refer to our **roles** in society. Roles and statuses are related but distinct concepts. For instance, medical doctors have relatively high status in Western society. Expectations associated with their roles include looking after the health of their patients. Some business leaders also have high status in society, but expectations for these leaders are quite different. In other words, top business leaders and medical doctors may occupy similar status positions, but they hold noticeably different roles in society. Statuses, then, refer to our positions in a group or society, whereas roles refer to the specific expectations about how to behave in those positions.

Organizations and Institutions

Society is also reflected in the regular patterns of behavior and relationships between people. Norms of behavior may include regular work schedules (for example 9:00 to 5:00) and sleep patterns. Much of this regulation exists within **organizations**—groups that share a common purpose and contain a formal set of rules and authority structure. Our work and school lives revolve around meeting the demands of our superiors within the rules of those organizations. At work, we are paid to produce a product or service, but we must do so within certain guidelines and procedures. At school, we must turn papers and tests in to our teachers to be judged worthy of a passing grade.

When the accumulation of both formal and informal norms produces patterns of behavior for an entire group or even a whole society, these norms, collectively, are often referred to as an institution. A **social institution** consists of patterns of interaction in which the behavior of a large group is guided by the same norms and roles (Jary and Jary 1991) (see Box 1.5). Traditionally, sociologists have divided society into five major institutions: family, economy, religion, education, and government. Although the norms and rules that govern these institutions may vary by society, almost all human societies have some way of raising children (family), systems of exchange (economy), and an education system. In addition to being found in most or all of the countries in the world today, these institutions have been found to have existed in societies dating back as far as 12,000 years ago.

Institutions are different from other sets of relationships in life because they involve complex sets of rules or laws that serve to guide behaviors. For instance, there are many formal and informal rules governing the family institution in the United States. Laws restrict the number of spouses that are allowed in a family and

Most of our lives can be studied in the context of social institutions—stable patterns of behavior guided by norms and roles. Institutions provide a context for studying individuals' thoughts, feelings, and behavior. Most societies around the world contain at least the following five institutions:

- Economy and work: Ways of coordinating and facilitating the process of gathering resources and converting them into goods and commodities needed in the society

- Politics, government, and the military: System for preserving order in society

- Family: An institution for regulating sexual relations and child rearing

- Religion: Rituals and beliefs regarding sacred things in society

- Education: The institution devoted to the creation and dissemination of knowledge and information about the larger world

All these institutions help define our roles in society. For instance, our position in the economy, defined by our job and income, has a significant impact on how we live. Our position also affects the types of people with whom we interact and the ways in which we interact.

---

other behaviors such as spouse or child abuse. There are also informal rules of conduct in the family. For instance, it is not necessarily illegal to have affairs outside of marriage, but opinion polls continually show that most Americans frown on such behavior (Saad 2006). Individuals usually learn the rules associated with a given institution through their interactions with other people in society.

Culture

Each society has its own **culture**—its unique patterns of behavior and beliefs. The norms, roles, and relationships that make up social institutions vary from one society to another, giving each society its own "personality." For example, two societies may have very different sets of expectations associated with being a father. Hence, to study people from different places, we must examine the ways that these people's lives reflect their cultures. Researchers must also recognize that a given group or society has its own unique set of institutions—different from those that may exist in the researcher's own culture. For example, the media may be a significant institution in American life, but it is probably less important in countries with little access to television, newspapers, and the Internet.

The components of culture include language, symbols, values and beliefs, norms, and material artifacts (see Box 1.6). Differences in language are often most immediately apparent between societies. We use different words and symbols to represent some of the same objects and ideas. Even subtle differences between

Box 1.6   **Elements of Culture**

Sociological social psychologists must be aware of elements of culture that have an impact on our thoughts, feelings, and behavior. These include symbols, values and beliefs, language, norms, and material culture.

- Symbols: Anything that carries a particular meaning recognized by people who share the same culture

- Values and beliefs: Standards by which people assess desirability, goodness, and beauty; serve as both guidelines for living (values) and specific statements that people hold to be true (beliefs)

- Language: A system of symbols that allows people to communicate

- Norms: Rules and expectations for people's behavior within a society

- Material culture: The tangible artifacts of culture—for example, cars, houses, clothing, and computers

The various elements of culture often interact to help us interpret a social situation and decide how to react to other people. People from different cultures may understand the meaning of an action differently and, as a result, may respond with different sets of feelings and actions. To an American, for example, the gesture of raising the middle finger is likely to produce feelings of anger, perhaps leading to an aggressive response. In England, the same gesture may produce no feelings or even be interpreted in a positive manner. Such cultural variations are important to understanding social psychological phenomena.

---

cultures can have large implications for how people live their lives. In a classic example, "The Body Ritual of the Nacerima," Horace Miner (1956) described a "foreign" culture in which the primary belief is that the body is ugly and has a natural tendency toward disease. As a result, the "tribe members" visit "magical practitioners" for the mouth and body on a regular basis. Eventually, readers discover that the "Nacirema" are simply "Americans" (*Nacirema* is *American* spelled backward)!

Miner's point is that it is hard to understand our own culture unless we step outside it enough to see how what we consider "normal" may look to outsiders. Although we can think independently of the people around us, we often make our choices within cultural limitations. In a simple example, when you are thirsty, you may choose to buy bottled water because it is valued as "pure" in your culture; however, this may not be something that people would do in a society that is more critical of marketers' claims about pureness. Rather, they might see such a purchase as wasteful of money and contributing to environmental degradation from leftover plastic bottles.

In similar fashion, society provides both formal and informal rules for making more important decisions—for example, about marriage and intimate partnership. Some cultures limit marital relationships to a single man and woman. Some

Western cultures have recently extended legal marriage to couples of the same sex. Other cultures allow for multiple spouses, but only in the context of marriage. Sociologists try to understand the societal and cultural guidelines that influence the behavior of individuals in a given society.

The social psychological study of culture also emphasizes the ways in which individuals contribute to the development and maintenance of culture in everyday life. How are the formal and informal rules that guide behaviors transmitted from one group to another? How do they change over time? These processes can be studied in the context of socialization among small groups of family members and friends. For instance, Gary Alan Fine (1979) studied a group of youth baseball teams over time by observing the culture of each group and the changes in those cultures over time. He found that the culture of the group changed as new people entered and left the group but that some consistency was maintained as new members learned the ways of the group from older, more senior team members. These processes, however, were stratified—some children, new or old, had more control over creation and maintenance of culture than others.

Section Summary

The final section of this chapter answered the question: What do I need to know to study the impact of society in my day-to-day life? Here, we introduce an important concept in the field of sociology, the sociological imagination, a tool to help you see the larger context of people's decisions and behaviors. In addition, we have given you a tool kit to help you develop the sociological imagination, a kit that includes important concepts that sociologists use in research, including norms, values, statuses, roles, institutions, and culture. All these concepts help to illuminate the effects of society on individuals' thoughts, feelings, and behaviors.

Bringing It All Together

There is so much to study in social psychology. I feel like I can't take it all in sometimes. I look forward to signing up for classes because I know that each one represents another aspect of human life to be studied. I just wish I had the time to take more classes!

—Jacky, senior Sociology major

Jacky's attitude toward social psychology is reasonable given the size and scope of the field. Social psychologists study many aspects of human life—everything from the social factors influencing feelings of love to studies of behaviors in small groups. You will probably find some of those areas more interesting than others, and you may also find that some areas of social life are not covered in this or any other textbook. Perhaps you will even be inspired to develop a new area of social psychological inquiry.

Our goal in this book is to provide you with an overview of sociological social psychology—its perspectives, theories, and concepts—along with the skills necessary to evaluate theories and judge research in the social sciences more broadly. After several introductory chapters, we will review various areas of sociological research. Think of each chapter as a sociological journey into a new area of social life!

As you begin your investigation of sociological social psychology, you should be ready to use your sociological imagination to see how society influences individuals' thoughts, feelings, and behavior. The theories and research we review in this text should help you develop your imagination. The first part of the book will introduce you to the major perspectives and methods used by sociological social psychologists. The next section applies these perspectives to the studies of self and society, with a discussion of social psychological perspectives on the construction of stratification and our sense of identity. The final section considers applications of social psychological research to the study of different aspects of social life, including deviance, mental health, and emotions.

One primary goal of this text is to make the social psychological theories, concepts, and research findings applicable to your daily life. We encourage you to try to apply what you read to your own life, to your interactions at home, at work, and among friends, and to the things you see and hear in the media. Think about this book both as an introduction to the field of sociological social psychology and as the start of a larger journey into the study of social life.

Summary

1. Sociology is the study of society. Sociologists look at society at both the macro and the micro level of analysis. Microsociology is also known as sociological social psychology.

2. Both psychological and sociological social psychologists study the social contexts of human thoughts, feelings, and behaviors. Sociologists, however, also apply the perspectives and methods of the field of sociology to the study of social psychology.

3. Sociology was first defined in 1838 by French social philosopher August Comte, who applied the principles of the scientific method to society. Some of the founders of sociological social psychology include George Herbert Mead, William Thomas, Charles Horton Cooley, and Georg Simmel.

4. Three major perspectives in sociological social psychology include symbolic interactionism, social structure and personality, and group processes.

5. Sociologists use a tool kit consisting of methods and concepts for studying the role of society in social psychological processes. Their tools include such concepts as statuses, roles, norms and values, culture, and social institutions, which they apply to the study of human thoughts, feelings, and behavior.

Breaching experiments: Experiments that violate the established social order to assess how people construct social reality.

Culture: A society's set of unique patterns of behavior and beliefs.

Ethnomethodology: A method of studying society through observation of people's typical day-to-day interactions.

Group processes: A perspective within sociological social psychology that examines how basic social processes operate in group contexts.

Macrosociology: The study of societies as a whole.

Microsociology: The study of the effects of society on socia-psychological processes, also known as sociological social psychology.

Organizations: Groups that share a common purpose and contain a formal set of rules and authority structure.

Psychology: The study of human thought processes and behaviors.

Roles: A set of expectations about how to behave in a group.

Social institution: Patterns of interactions in which behavior within a large group is guided by a common set of norms and roles.

Social psychology: The systematic study of people's thoughts, feelings, and behavior in social contexts.

Social structure: Persisting patterns of behavior and interaction between people within identified social positions.

Social structure and personality: A perspective within sociological social psychology that focuses on the connections between larger societal conditions and the individual.

Sociological imagination: The ability to see personal lives in the context of the larger society—its history, culture, and social structure.

Social norms: The rules that regulate our behavior in relationships.

Sociology: The systematic study of society.

Status: A person's position in a group or society that is associated with varying levels of esteem and power.

Symbolic interactionism: A perspective within sociological social psychology that emphasizes the study of how people negotiate the meaning of social life during their interactions with other people.

Values: Deeply held ideals and beliefs.

1. How would you define society from your personal perspective? How do you picture the role of society in your life?

2. In this chapter, we reviewed a number of perspectives on human behavior. Can you think of any other ways of understanding social interaction?

3. Can you think of any other ways that society may affect people that are not addressed in the tool kit described in this chapter?

4. How can you employ the sociological imagination in your own life?

Perspectives in Sociological Social Psychology

I first got involved with the College Environmentalists—the CE group—because the group met in my dorm building and I overheard an interesting discussion about the worsening conditions of the drinking water in our area. The people were really nice to me. They greeted me when I entered the informational meeting and I got free soda and snacks. Over time, I started caring less about drinking water than the ever-expanding ozone layer. I never knew that the problem was so bad! I really didn't have any money to contribute to help stop the problem, so I decided to participate in a few protests at the state capitol building, just a few hours away from campus. I became one of the group's officers in no time. Even though I had never done this before, I skipped some classes and dropped all of my other sports and club activities in order to keep up with the CE. I really think the decision was worth it. Our work has doubled the size of the group in the last year and a recent petition got signatures from over half of the students on campus.

—Franklin, junior Communications major

The vignette that opens this chapter describes a complex series of events that led a student to change his views on the environment—to move from a somewhat casual focus on water-quality issues to global warming to becoming a leader in working for a cause he had come to see as worthy. To make room for this new role as an "environmentalist," Franklin even began to drop his other activities and identities. Joining the environmental group influenced his role as a student, the way he behaved toward others, and how he thought of himself. Franklin's attitudes toward some aspects of the world and his sense of self came to reflect his new group membership; his decision to join the environmentalist group had larger ramifications for his life than he originally expected.

Social psychologists do not try to predict the conditions under which a particular individual decides on a certain behavior. Rather, we study why people *generally* do the things they do or how they experience certain emotions or problems. Hence, we would not try to understand why Franklin changed, specifically, but the processes by which group membership influences individuals' senses of self more broadly. To do this, we adopt a variety of perspectives. In chapter 1, we reviewed the three major perspectives of sociological social psychology: symbolic interaction, social structure and personality, and group processes. In this chapter, we will elaborate on each of those perspectives. Specifically, we will address the following questions:

- What are the major principles of the symbolic interaction perspective? How does this perspective help us to understand the relationship between the individual and society? What does it mean to "construct" the world around us?
- What is the social structure and personality perspective? How do researchers in this field study the impact of society on the individual?
- What is the group processes perspective? What are some of the basic social processes that play out in group contexts? What are elements of group structure?

The Symbolic Interaction Perspective

> *I never really liked to dance. Even as a kid, I would never dance with my friends. But when I came to college, something changed. I met this guy that was so good to me—and of course, as luck would have it, he really liked to dance! He didn't mind if I sat at the table with some other people as he hit the dance floor, but I always felt awkward about that. Then I decided to take dance lessons. I am finding myself liking it more and more as I get better at it! My boyfriend was so happy to dance with me . . . we have become very close.*
>
> —Vanessa, junior English major

In chapter 1, we defined the *symbolic interaction perspective* as the study of how people negotiate the meaning of social life during their interactions with other people. In the vignette that opens this section, we meet a young woman, Vanessa, who is learning that dancing is not boring, difficult, or embarrassing. Through her interactions with some new people, Vanessa begins to negotiate a new meaning for dancing—"fun." It begins when she meets someone who loves to dance, and to win his approval, she starts rethinking her attitude toward dancing. But she does not change immediately. It takes time, and she continually reevaluates her situation as she talks with and observes her boyfriend and other people. For instance, she chooses to take dance lessons, giving her better skills. As a result of these interactions and decisions, she begins to enjoy the activity more, and her relationship with her boyfriend begins to change.

Symbolic interactionism helps us understand the social processes that influence our understanding of the world (Reynolds and Herman-Kinney 2003; Stryker 2002; Stryker and Vryan 2003). We construct meaning about things that are important in our own lives and in our society. We begin this chapter with an overview of the history and tenets of symbolic interactionism. We then review the two major schools of symbolic interaction.

Society and Agency

In chapter 1, we defined *sociology* as the systematic study of society. How we define *society* depends on the perspective of the researcher. From an interactionist perspective, **society** exists as the network of interactions between people (Blumer 1969; Stryker 2002; Stryker and Vryan 2003). This means that the individual and society cannot be separated from each other: Individuals continually create and are molded by society. Symbolic interactionists also assume that individuals have some control of their social worlds; **agency** refers to our ability to act and think independently from the constraints imposed by social conditions (Musolf 2003a). In other words, we have the ability to make choices and decisions on our own.

Interactionist researchers start by assuming that it is impossible to study the individual without incorporating the study of society or, conversely, to study society without accounting for the individual. Society comprises a complex series of relationships (Blumer 1969; Stryker 2002; Stryker and Vryan 2003). We analyze and negotiate these relationships internally and externally. In the case of Franklin, in the opening vignette, his beliefs about the environment are connected to his group affiliation with the College Environmentalists. At the same time, by interacting with others both inside and outside the organization, Franklin also affects what the CE is and how it is viewed. In the interactionist view, society works the same way: When enough individuals in society begin to change the way they think or feel about an issue, society as a whole changes.

Basic Principles of Symbolic Interactionism

The development of symbolic interactionist thought stems from eighteenth-century Scottish moral philosophers such as Adam Smith (1723–1790) and David Hume (1711–1776), as well as from the American social philosophy of pragmatism (Reynolds 2003; Stryker 1992, 2002). These traditions generally emphasize applied, practical applications of social theory and research. Unlike traditional philosophy that separates our physical environments from our cognitive and spiritual lives, pragmatists view intellectual and social lives as linked together (Reynolds 2003). Hence, psychological and physical worlds produce a constant dialectic, similar to the way that evolutionary theory proposes organisms change to meet the needs of their physical environments over time. Humans adapt to

The social behaviorist perspective in psychology assumes that the best way to scientifically study people is to examine their behaviors because they are the only "observable" aspects of human life. Behaviorism follows the research of psychologists such as B. F. Skinner (1904–1990), who studied the effects of positive and negative stimulation on animals' behavior, called "operant conditioning." The premise deriving from this paradigm is that most human thoughts, feelings, and behavior are a result of a series of rewards and punishments. Hence, babies learn how to become functioning adults by being rewarded for those behaviors and attitudes that are likely to produce good citizens and punished for those behaviors that are not deemed important to proper functioning, such as rude manners. Albert Bandura (b. 1925) extended Skinner's work. He developed a social learning theory that incorporates the concept of imitation in the study of operant conditioning among humans. Imitation assumes that people will adapt new behaviors not only because of rewards to oneself but also when they see other people being rewarded for their behaviors. Social behaviorism and social learning theory both focus on external causes of our thoughts, feelings, and behavior.

Much work in social behaviorism consists of examining the outcomes of rewards and punishments for animals other than humans. Sociologists rarely study animals to understand human behavior. From an interactionist perspective, the ability to create and manipulate meaning is uniquely human. Although the basic idea of rewards and punishments may be applicable to humans, it is very difficult to know how individuals give meaning and values to objects and behaviors. A reward for one person may be a punishment or simply unimportant to another person. Your grade in a course may be very important to you, motivating you to work hard. Your friend may not see much value in grades, leaving her to decide to miss class and study less. Hence, it is difficult to use conditioning to predict thoughts, feelings, and behavior if you do not understand how people give meaning to the world around them. Nevertheless, sociological social psychologists have successfully adopted some elements of the behaviorist approach to study, for instance, exchange relationships between people (see Homans 1974; Molm and Cook 1995).

---

their physical environments as well as to their social worlds. That is, they negotiate their physical and cognitive (i.e., intellectual and emotional) lives with other people, adapting to new situations as they come along. (See also Box 2.1.)

The implication of pragmatism for interactionist theory is that our physical and internal environments cannot be separated in our development of social theory. We derive meaning through interaction with others and intenval thought processes. Hence, interaction is the primary way that we come to any sort of knowledge about ourselves, other people, and the rest of the universe. Herbert Blumer (1900–1987), an important symbolic interactionist, argued that we can study social processes by focusing on three core principles (Blumer 1969):

1. Meanings arise through social interaction among individuals.

2. People use the meanings they derive from interaction to guide their own behavior.

3. People employ an interpretive process regarding these interactions.

We will review each of these principles in more detail in the following sections.

Symbols, Language, and the Development of Meaning

The first principle of symbolic interactionism is that meaning is derived from social interaction. How does this process unfold? Mead (1934) believed that the study of human gestures is at the center of social psychology. To have meaning, according to Mead, individuals need an exchange of **symbols,** where a *symbol* refers to anything that has a similar meaning for two or more individuals. A symbol may derive its meaning from producing similar images in two people or from eliciting the same emotional reaction from both. Any act can be "symbolic" if it produces similar outcomes for two or more people.

Language refers to a series of symbols that can be combined in various ways to provide new meanings. Most of what we call *consciousness* is achieved through the use of language (Hewitt 2003b). Symbols and language may be verbal or nonverbal in nature. Grunts, hand signals, or posture may provide a host of information regarding an individual's thoughts or feelings in a given situation. "Mixed signals" refer to situations in which a person's words convey one meaning of a situation while their behaviors (say posture or intonation) display another meaning. (See also Box 2.2.)

The process by which we use symbols and language to give meaning and value to objects and people is known as the **social construction of reality.** Berger and Luckmann (1967), in *The Social Construction of Reality,* outlined the basic tenets of this perspective. They argued that humans come to understand their reality in the "here and now"—through day-to-day experiences. Language provides a bridge between our private understanding of the world and other people. That is, once we are able to objectify and label objects or people, we can share our assessment of the world with others. If we call a certain four-legged creature by the name "dog," we are now able to show other people the animal and agree on the label—"dog."

Beyond our ability to identify things, it is the way humans take in and analyze information that makes the symbolic process possible. In the book, *The Man Who Mistook His Wife for a Hat and Other Clinical Tales,* neurologist Oliver Sacks (1985) described patients with a variety of neurological disorders, including those who have lost their memory, individuals with perceptual problems, and people unable to recognize common objects. The book's title refers to a patient who, among other things, would misidentify parking meters and fire hydrants as small children and mistake his own shoe for his foot. Upon leaving his first visit with Sacks, this man reached over to his wife's head and tried to put it on his own head—he had mistaken his wife for a hat!

Sacks argued that this patient was capable of thinking like a computer, using pieces of information around him to draw conclusions, but that he lacked judgment

Box 2.2 **Language and Consciousness in Psychology**

Psychologists recognize the importance of language in the development of consciousness. Lev Vygotsky (1896–1934) was a psychologist in the early twentieth century, writing at a time when human development was a major focus of psychology. He (and other psychologists) examined children's "egocentric" thoughts and speech. Egocentric speech refers to the way children verbalize their thoughts without necessarily trying to communicate with someone else. It usually occurs during free play as children apply names to objects, such as when a toddler puts a teddy bear on a couch and says: "There's a bear. He is sitting." In a typical child, this speech starts after the age of one and ends by the age of eight. The question was whether egocentric speech was derived internally or externally. Vygotsky's research showed that egocentric speech serves as a (externalized) thinking process. Children use egocentric speech to "practice" problem solving. Egocentric speech is an intermediate stage for learning inner speech, called self-indication in symbolic interactionist language. Hence, Vygotsky argued, egocentric speech does not disappear at the age of eight—as many psychologists believed at the time—but simply goes "underground" as it becomes part of our consciousness. Egocentric speech goes from external to internal thinking processes. Vygotsky's work showed how children "learn" consciousness by verbalizing their thoughts early on. This research applies to the study of symbolic interaction, the exchange and development of symbols through interaction, by indicating that meaning-making is an external process that develops the interior life, not the other way around.

about those things. It is not enough simply to identify and give meaning to aspects of our lives—we must also process that information in the context of other meanings. In the case of the patient who mistook his wife for a hat, Sacks noted that when the patient watched a romantic film, he was unable to figure out the emotional dialogue between the characters or even their sexes. Hence, these human relationships lacked any real meaning for the patient.

Sacks's research shows that meaning is deep, complex, and subtle. Language is the most precise form of symbolic exchange, but humans also exchange slight movements, gestures, and emotions that convey a host of additional meanings, whether the sender consciously chooses to send such messages to another person or not. We can "read" a situation based on how people act in it, perceiving feelings of stress or anger, without using any verbal language at all. People rely on such subtle forms of communication for meaning as much as on the explicit use of language.

People reared in different cultures and environments will almost certainly have different ideas of reality, because each of us undergoes unique construction processes. You may have heard that comedy does not translate well between cultures—a popular comedian from the United States may find no fans in another country. Even if the cultures share the same language, subtle differences in the meanings associated with the words in a joke may render it humorless in the new environment. Try to imagine your favorite joke being translated into another language or told in another language—would it be just as funny, or would it return blank stares?

Most of us recognize this point, to some degree, when we interact with people from different countries. In a study of Russian professionals interviewing for jobs in the United States, for instance, one researcher found that poor language fluency had both positive and negative effects on interpersonal dynamics (Molinsky 2005). Poor language fluency was associated with lower professional evaluations on the job; however, it also shielded nonnative speakers when they made a "faux pas," a socially unacceptable comment or behavior. That is, natives perceived nonnative speakers as less impolite and more sympathetic than native candidates, probably because the natives generally understood that the nonnative speakers lacked the cultural understandings of how other people interpret their behaviors.

The Use of Meaning Once Derived

The second principle of symbolic interactionism focuses on the *value* of the interaction process. Specifically, why do we engage in the social construction of reality in the first place? According to symbolic interactionism, we are motivated to do so to overcome problems and achieve goals (Blumer 1969; Stryker and Vryan 2003). In short, to get the things we want in life, we must negotiate with other people. According to the second principle of symbolic interactionism, we use information derived from an interaction as a guide for our own behavior. The information tells us how to think, feel, or act.

We are motivated to change our behavior when we must do so to maintain order or, sometimes, to get what we want out of a situation. As a simple example, suppose you want to ask a professor if you can make up a missed exam. You may make the request to take a makeup exam using a series of simple gestures and language to get what you want. But if the professor appears reluctant for some reason, you may change your tone—the way you ask for the assignment—perhaps in an effort to make the professor believe that you are a good student who is worthy of such help. Hence, although you initially entered the interaction with a simple goal, you have now revised your original set of behaviors to incorporate new information—in this case, the professor's reluctant attitude. In short, you may have to modify both your goals and the methods you use to achieve those goals to meet the new social conditions.

This process can be complex because the meaning of a single object may vary depending on social conditions. For instance, Schweingruber and Berns (2003) studied the meaning of money in a door-to-door sales company. The company recruited college students for door-to-door sales of educational books. During training sessions, money was defined as a necessary evil, and students were encouraged to focus on the nonmonetary benefits (e.g., developing managerial skills) of doing the work. However, money was also used as a motivating force—as a way to get people to sell in the first place and as a topic of concern when the sales representatives were alone. Thus, the importance and meaning of money varied depending on the group of people involved and the context of the discussion. Here we see people constructing and manipulating the meaning of a single object in different groups.

Subjective Experience

The last principle of symbolic interactionism is the idea that different people will often come away from an interaction with different interpretations of it. Further, these varying interpretations are what people use to guide their behavior (Blumer 1969). All of us bring different values and beliefs, abilities, and perspectives into a given interaction. As a result, we may interpret the same situation quite differently than others do.

Think about a situation in which two students are investigating a new club on campus by going to an informational meeting. Both of the students have the same experiences—they meet the same people, participate in the same activities, and

People can leave an interaction or event with very different interpretations of it.

see the same literature about the club. But on leaving the meeting, one student feels very happy with the experience, whereas the other one says that she was bored. These two students will likely choose different paths regarding their future affiliations with the club.

The important point of this principle is that people base future behavior on their subjective interpretations of a present situation. Because it is very difficult to know how someone else interprets a situation, we are limited in our ability to predict how people will react to it. In the example given here, if the two friends do not discuss the meeting afterward, each may assume that the other came away with an impression similar to her own—leaving the one who was happy with her experience to wonder why her friend did not show up to the next meeting.

This principle is the basis for the **Thomas theorem,** which states that when people define situations as real, those situations become real in their consequences (Thomas and Thomas 1928; see also Merton 1995; Thomas 1966). As long as we think that our understanding is real, we will act on it. For instance, if you are hit by someone while walking down the hall and assume it was done on purpose, you will likely react more aggressively than if you assume it was an accident. In another example, consider how important the definition of the situation is to sustaining interaction related to romantic relationships. If someone asks you to come over "to study" but really has romance in mind, you may find yourselves with two conflicting definitions of the situation. Ultimately, if two people cannot agree on a definition, the interaction may come to a quick end. Thus, how we define a situation guides our reaction to it and will facilitate or inhibit further interaction.

Two Schools of Symbolic Interactionism

The birthplace of symbolic interactionism is usually considered to be the University of Chicago, where both George Herbert Mead and Herbert Blumer worked in the early to mid twentieth century. Although sociologists from the University of Chicago employed a variety of methods in the study of human interaction, symbolic interactionists clearly moved away from a deterministic approach toward scientific inquiry (Musolf 2003a). If social reality is constantly being negotiated over time, they asked, then how can research predict future behavior? A second school of thought, sometimes called "structural symbolic interactionism" and associated with researchers at the University of Iowa and Indiana University, varies from the traditional view in its emphasis on the idea that interpretations of social reality are, in fact, generally stable and long-lasting.

The Chicago School

The traditional school of symbolic interactionism associated with Blumer and the University of Chicago contends that social reality is fluid and ever changing (Musolf 2003a; Stryker and Vryan 2003). As a result, according to traditional symbolic interactionists, social reality cannot be quantified and predicted in the same way as other aspects of the physical world. This is the perspective of the **Chicago school of symbolic interactionism,** which states that the primary goal of symbolic interactionism is to understand the social processes involved in a given situation—not to quantify those processes or try to predict future behavior.

The Chicago school can be divided into two historical periods (Musolf 2003a). The first Chicago school, before World War II, included the early work of George Herbert Mead and W. I. Thomas, one of the sociologists associated with the Thomas theorem. The second Chicago school, in the post–World War II era, is associated with the work of Herbert Blumer, a student of Mead and, in 1937, the person to coin the term *symbolic interaction*. Blumer was also important in keeping the focus of symbolic interaction on the individual level away from macro-level definitions of society. In this view, society is based on interactions between people, and as a result, people—rather than structures existing outside human interaction—have the ability to maintain or change society. From this perspective, society is a reflection of the shared meanings exchanged during social interaction, which produce a sense of solidarity that is the essence of society. This process is inherently a "minded activity"—based on individual thoughts and feelings in a given social interaction—in which people's interactions and identities are too fluid to study using traditional scientific methods that assume similarity between elements of a sample.

The Indiana and Iowa Schools

The second school of symbolic interactionism is associated with researchers and theorists from the University of Iowa (such as Manford Kuhn) and from Indiana University (such as Sheldon Stryker). Sometimes called "structural symbolic interactionism," it varies from the traditional view in its emphasis on the stable nature of social reality. That is, once an interpretation or "definition of the situation" has been made, it tends to remain for a period of time. Meanings change, but not that quickly. The **Indiana and Iowa schools of symbolic interactionism** argue that, as a result, social reality can be quantified and studied using the scientific method.

These two schools of symbolic interaction developed after World War II, at the time of the second Chicago school. Manford Kuhn, who had joined the University of Iowa faculty in the 1940s, shared with Chicago school interactionists a concern with the reliability of the strictly quantitative studies found in sociological and psychological research at the time. However, unlike his colleagues at the University of Chicago, Kuhn wanted to develop ways of testing symbolic-interactionist principles. These efforts led him to develop the Twenty Statements Test for assessing the self-concept (see chapter 5). In later years, at Indiana University, symbolic interactionists such as Sheldon Stryker conducted research on the self that led to the creation of identity theory (also discussed in chapter 5). Researchers at Iowa and Indiana attempted to develop empirical applications of the symbolic interactionist principles discussed earlier in this chapter.

Both schools of symbolic interactionism see social reality as fluid, but they disagree about the speed with which it changes over time, and they have developed different methods for studying people. Chicago school symbolic interactionists are likely to use observational methods, whereas those in the Iowa and Indiana tradition typically use surveys that quantify individuals' thoughts, feelings, and behaviors, particularly about the self. Despite these differences, researchers and theorists from these varying perspectives continue to emphasize the importance of the self in the maintenance and construction of society.

Section Summary

The first section of this chapter answered the questions: What are the major principles of the symbolic interaction perspective? How does this perspective help us to understand the relationship between the individual and society? What does it mean to "construct" the world around us? The symbolic interaction paradigm is based on three basic principles: That meanings arise through social interaction among individuals, individuals use the meanings they derive from interaction to guide their own behavior, and people act toward objects on the basis of the meanings that those objects have for them. These principles emphasize the importance of agency in day-to-day life, that we have the ability to make choices in the social world around us. As a result, this perspective is essential to understanding individuals' ability to negotiate and construct their social worlds with other people.

The Social Structure and Personality Perspective

I always knew that our positions in life affect us, but it really did not hit home till I joined the army. Corporal Bain was a fun guy. He had been in the service awhile, but he always made fun of the army. He would make fun of the leaders and always had a wisecrack. He was great to have around. I found out that his games cost him a promotion and he had been demoted at least once. Then one day I learned that he'd been promoted to sergeant—a noncommissioned officer. That meant that he would become our supervisor. Finally, I thought, someone who was going to look out for us. Was I surprised! The next day, he started barking orders at us. No jokes, no goofy attitude, just orders. In fact, he was the meanest supervisor I have ever had in the Army! I tried to ask him what was going on, but he stopped talking informally with the rest of the crew. It's amazing how quickly people can change.

—Nancy, junior Education major

The *social structure and personality perspective* focuses on the connections between larger societal conditions and the individual. These social conditions are measured in terms of what we defined in chapter 1 as *social structure*, or persisting patterns of behavior and interaction between people or social positions (House 1992). The idea of "persistent patterns of behavior" suggests that there is some stability to the social world: People tend to develop rules and norms that govern almost every aspect of social life. Patterns typically include regular rules of behavior—that is, how people are expected to act in different social contexts. Such rules serve as guidelines for our behavior and allow us to predict what other people will do. Like structural symbolic interactionists, those who take the social structural and personality perspective view society as stable, making it easier to predict individuals' thoughts, feelings, and behavior.

The idea that social structure affects individuals' thoughts, feelings, and behaviors relates to the macro-level sociological theories outlined in chapter 1. Karl Marx (conflict perspective), for instance, generally believed that the economic systems we live in affect both our social relations and individual thinking processes (conflict theory). Notably, he believed that capitalist economies lead individuals to a sense of alienation or separation from their work and other workers. Similarly, Emile Durkheim (1951, originally 1897) (a structural functionalist) showed that the decision to commit suicide is affected by our location in society. For instance, he found that Protestants kill themselves at higher rates than do Catholics or Jewish people; Durkheim argued that the Protestant religion created less integration, leading people to commit suicide at higher rates than individuals from other religious traditions.

In the opening vignette, Nancy begins to see the effects that structural conditions can have on people. Corporal (now Sergeant) Bain changed dramatically immediately after attaining a leadership position in the group. Not only did his attitudes and identity change, but his relationships with other people changed as well. Examining classes of situations like Nancy's, theories and research based on the social structure and personality perspective try to understand how the larger society affects individuals within it (House 1977, 1992).

James House (1992) argued that our ability to study the effects of larger structural forces on the individual involves three key principles:

1. **Components principle:** We must be able to identify the elements or components of society most likely to affect a given attitude or behavior.

2. **Proximity principle:** We need to understand the aspects of social structure that most affect us—those that are part of our immediate social environment.

3. **Psychology principle:** We need to understand how individuals internalize proximal experiences.

We review each of these principles in this section.

The Components Principle

Traditional research using the social structure and personality paradigm focuses on the components of social structure most likely to affect individuals in a given context: statuses, roles, networks, and institutions. Most of these components were included in the "tool kit" provided in chapter 1. Knowing these dimensions of social life helps us to better predict how social structure affects individuals' lives. We review some of the major components in detail next.

Status

In chapter 1, we defined *status* as a person's position in a group or society that is associated with varying levels of esteem and prestige. Typically, social structure and personality theorists examine such statuses as socioeconomic status (social class), race or ethnicity, gender, age, and sexuality. Although socioeconomic status is often associated with income level, it also reflects level of prestige. Some individuals—for example, religious leaders—may have jobs that pay only a relatively modest income but offer high occupational prestige.

Roles

Another part of your tool kit introduced in chapter 1 is the concept of roles, defined as a set of expectations for how one should behave in a given position or status (see Box 2.3). Roles provide rules or guidelines for our behavior. For example, the professor's role includes teaching courses and giving grades to students,

Individuals are given statuses and roles in society that are associated with differing levels of power.

| Box 2.3 | Role Theory |

Role theory has been an important part of sociological theory. This theory argues that individuals take on social positions and the expectations for their behaviors in those positions (Biddle 1986). Society provides both the basis for all or most social positions and the roles (expectations) associated with those positions. For instance, when we accept a job, we take on the assumptions and expectations of that job. Accountants are expected to calculate numbers and do it well if they are to keep such a job. According to role theory, we can predict individual thoughts, feelings, and behavior by knowing someone's range of available roles. Knowing that someone is a CEO of a large corporation gives us a lot of information about her lifestyle and attitudes. We can probably predict that she lives very well—driving the best cars, eating the finest food, and supporting political candidates that help her industry prosper. We can predict these things without meeting the person or having any other background information.

Individuals can alter the expectations of a given position over time while maintaining its basic nature. Students in the 1950s both dressed and acted very differently than modern students. However, the role of student still conjures expectations to study. Thus, although roles may change over time, many of the basic expectations remain the same. Some symbolic interactionists and social structure and personality researchers continue to incorporate elements of role theory; the components principle within the social structure and personality perspective is one notable example.

whereas the student's role includes attending class, taking notes, and studying for exams. Those who fail to meet the expectations of these roles may receive a formal reprimand. For students, this would take the form of bad grades; for teachers, of unsatisfactory teaching evaluations. In contrast, individuals who live up to most or all role expectations are generally rewarded (with good grades or high evaluations) and, less formally, are deemed "good" at their respective roles.

Social Networks

The importance of statuses and roles in our interactions with other people is highlighted in the opening vignette by Nancy's portrayal of the changes in Corporal Bain after his promotion—he changed dramatically, probably to meet role demands of his status in the military. But society can also exist in the relationships between people. **Social networks** (see Figure 2.1) refer to a series of relationships between individuals and groups. We hold certain positions in society, each of which connects us with other people. Even if we know only one or two people in a network, those people connect us to other people in the network with whom we are not directly acquainted. From this perspective, it is not enough to know about an individual's status and roles because our networks connect us to other people with various levels of resources. For instance, a student may have relatively low status

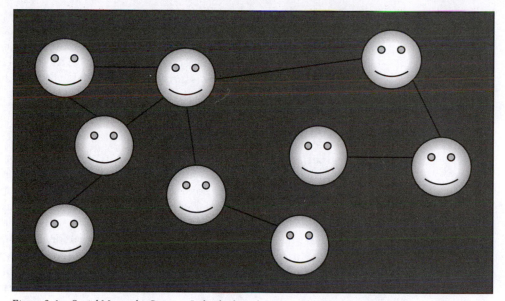

Figure 2.1   Social Networks Connect Individuals and Groups in Society

in society and not be expected to make a lot of money, but her access to family networks may provide the food and income she needs while studying. Ultimately, her network provides the resources she needs while she prepares for a new status in the economy.

The Proximity Principle

The proximity principle states that we often feel the effects of society through interpersonal interaction and communication with people around us (House 1992). Sometimes, larger societal trends affect people directly, but the impact is often indirect. For instance, a high unemployment rate in your city or country is not likely to lead you to experience depression. But if some of your friends or family members lose their jobs as a result of layoffs, you may be affected in that way. Thus, social-structural forces tend to affect individual people through events in their immediate social and physical environments.

Most research on the proximity principle has focused on family and work contexts (McLeod and Lively 2003). We spend a significant part of our waking life at work and about a third of it with friends and family. According to the proximity principle, most of society's impact on us comes through the institutions of work and family.

A number of research projects have attempted to assess the relative effects of structural and personal economic conditions on individual health and well-being. Dooley and Prause (1995), for instance, found that unemployment is negatively related to self-esteem. This finding makes sense, as losing a job can sometimes produce feelings of inadequacy and reduce our ability to achieve life goals. Losing a job also reduces a person's income which may limit our ability to achieve her goals. In many instances, job losses reflect changes in industry that make some jobs obsolete or economic downturns that individuals have no control over. Ultimately, however, these larger events directly impact individuals' lives through the immediate conditions, in this case, their jobs.

The Psychology Principle

Although social structural conditions may affect us either directly or indirectly through proximal forces, there is no guarantee that these effects will lead us to change our behavior. Probably the least studied aspect of social structure and personality research is how we process structural and proximal forces (McLeod and Lively 2003). What makes someone decide to follow a norm? One explanation lies in the feelings we experience when we disobey a social norm or rule. **Social forces** include any way in which other people—or society in general—compels individuals to act in accordance with an external norm, rule, or demand (Simpson 1998). Social forces are often clearly felt when we appear or act inappropriately in a social situation. For example, if you walk into a formal party wearing a T-shirt and jeans, you will likely feel a sense of embarrassment, and your face will become hot and flushed. That awkward feeling will likely prompt you to either change your attire or leave the party. Even if you do not feel embarrassed, you may decide that the clothing is inappropriate and change your behavior accordingly. In either case, social forces create the "feeling" or "decision" that compels you to change your behavior in some way.

We can consciously decide to act against social forces, but if we do, we will likely face some consequence. Most of us generally follow the simple rules in life—obeying traffic laws, for instance—but modify others. The risk of disobeying social rules depends on how important they are to a given group. Formal rules are codified as laws and may be tied to specific penalties, such as fines or jail time. However, rebellions against an existing social order can influence other people and ultimately open the door to social change.

The important issue in this discussion is that people have the ability to internalize social norms in a variety of ways. The psychology principle is about the processes that lead people to follow the rules (or not).

Social norms are more like broad guidelines for behavior than specific prescriptions. Humans have the capacity to decide to break away from traditional expectations or to create new ones. But because breaking with convention requires a lot of emotional work, many people will choose to just "go along to get along." Creating new rules also takes some work but is unlikely to lead to social change unless sufficient resources are involved in leading people to adopt a new way of doing something. Perhaps you break social norms and try a different lifestyle—say, shunning all forms of mass media because you believe dependence on the media promotes dysfunctional neighborhoods where people don't bother to talk with one another. You may find that some people accept this idea, and a few may even follow your example. But you also run the risk that your choice will not be accepted by your friends or acquaintances. Even if their nonacceptance takes the form of good-natured joking, it may be sufficient to break apart relationships due to different values or activities.

Finally, much like the third principle of symbolic interaction, the psychology principle is about how people experience society internally. How do social interactions in a city environment get processed by individuals differently than interactions in a small town? House (1992) argues that we can not fully understand the role of social structure in our lives until we are able to understand how individuals interpret it.

Section Summary

In this section of the chapter, we answered the questions: What is the social structure and personality perspective? How do those in this field of study conceive of the influence of society on the individual? The social structure and personality perspective emphasizes the direct impact of society in our lives using three basic principles. The components principle helps to answer the second question listed earlier, how researchers study the impact of society on the individual. Here we identify important elements of society such as roles and statuses that directly affect the way we interact with other people. The second and third principles in this perspective focus on how individuals are affected by these components. Specifically, the proximity principle states that individuals are affected by society through their immediate social environments while the psychology principle focuses on how individuals internalize proximal experiences.

The Group Processes Perspective

It used to really make me mad. I would sit in my study group and give all of the answers but get none of the credit. My friends thought it was just in my head. They said that people were being fair. Then I started writing down the number of times people contributed to the work group and who got thanked the most. It was just as I thought—I did most of the work, but John got the most compliments by far. He works hard, but I still do more than him! Why does he get all of the credit?

—Jean, freshman Biology major

Group processes refers to the study of how basic social processes operate in group contexts. In this vignette, we see a work group with an unequal distribution of rewards. Jean is trying to understand how she could work so hard yet receive less credit than other people in the group. To see if her perceptions match reality—in social science language, to "test her hypothesis"—she approaches the group interactions systematically, making notes on members' work inputs and the number of compliments received. The data supports her hypothesis: She is getting the short end of the stick.

What is most interesting about this example to scholars in the group processes perspective is that what happened in Jean's group reflects a consistent pattern that occurs when groups form. When people organize in groups to complete tasks, the recognition that people receive for their performances often does not match the quality of their contributions. In other words, the processes that occurred in Jean's group reflect more general social processes.

Group processes theorists and researchers are interested in these general social processes. How do members of groups decide who contributes the most? Who gets the most credit for their contributions? Who talks the most in groups? In our society, work groups tend to organize in a manner similar to Jean's group. For example, when groups form to complete tasks, men tend to get more credit than women do for the same contributions (Troyer 2001). Sociological social psychologists are interested in the processes that lead to these differences.

Many social processes occur in group contexts. By **group,** we simply mean any interaction involving more than one person. The example in Jean's vignette fits what many of us think when we hear the word *group*—people working together to complete some task. But to researchers in the group processes tradition, even an interaction between two people who stop to chat when passing each other on the street would be considered a "group." Other examples of groups are families, sports teams, and even the United States as a whole. In all these examples, the group consists of people who are bound to one another in some way.

The phrase *group processes* implies an interest in two things—*groups* and *processes*. Although it is not a hard and fast rule, sociological social psychologists in the group processes perspective tend to be most interested in the processes that occur in groups, in contrast to psychological social psychologists, who are often more interested in groups themselves. For example, suppose that an organization forms a committee for the purpose of selecting a person to hire for an important job. In the committee's deliberations, a status order would likely form, with some people talking more and others less. *Status* in this instance refers to a basic group process that is of interest to sociological social psychologists. Someone studying this basic process would be less interested in the group's deliberations or their outcomes than in the processes leading to the status order. In contrast, a social psychologist more interested in characteristics of the group itself might seek to determine the factors that affected whether the group was successful at its task, or perhaps how the size of the group influenced its deliberations. In the first case, social psychologists are interested in studying processes that operate in a similar manner across different types of groups. In the second, social psychologists are interested in determining how characteristics of the group affected its deliberations.

A focus on group processes, then, leads to an interest in a broad range of phenomena. In part because of this focus, the group processes perspective does not have a specific set of principles governing its area of expertise. Many group processes scholars, particularly those who are sociologists, study the processes that occur in group contexts. Others study aspects of groups such as their size, purposes, and functions. Next, we discuss these two features of work in the group processes perspective, distinguishing the study of group processes from the study of groups themselves.

Studying Processes

Certain basic social processes tend to play out in group contexts, whether the groups are small (such as family or friends) or large (such as corporations). We experience processes such as power and justice, for example, in relation to other people. That is, they exist only in the context of our relationships with others. If we want to be powerful people, we must have someone to have power over. These examples highlight some of the basic social processes that are of interest to group processes scholars. A few of the main processes studied in the group processes perspective include

- **Power:** The ability to obtain what we desire in a group despite resistance
- **Status:** A position in a group based in esteem or respect
- **Justice:** Getting what is fair from interactions in a group
- **Legitimacy:** The sense that a social arrangement or position is the way that things *should be*

Next we briefly discuss each of these concepts as group processes.

Power

Some people in society have more power than others. We can probably all agree, for example, that the president of the United States has a great deal of power. The president can make decisions that have important consequences for people's lives. As noted earlier, *power* is a group process because people have it only in relation to other people. The types of groups in which power processes operate vary in size but when power differences exist between people, there is always some group context.

What is the source of the president's power? It emanates from his position in a group structure. In other words, nothing about the president himself, as an individual, makes him a powerful person: His power is a result of his position. His personal characteristics likely played an important role in his rise to the position of president, but it is the position that now gives him the power. If you were president of the United States, you would have the same power over other people's lives as does the current president. The source of the president's power is not difficult to identify: Formal rules allow him to make important decisions that affect the lives of many people. In most group contexts, however—such as marriages or groups of friends—the sources of power are more subtle. Group processes scholars seek to determine the characteristics of positions in group structures that lead to power and what the outcomes of those processes are (Bonacich 1998; Burke 1997; Cook and Yamagishi 1992; Markovsky, Willer, and Patton 1988; Willer and Patton 1987).

Status is another group process, defined earlier as a person's standing in a group based on esteem and respect. As with power, people cannot have "status" in and of themselves, but only in relation to other people. As an example, think of the people who work at a restaurant. The restaurant owners probably have higher social status than the cooks who work for them. But the owners may be low in social status compared to some of their customers, who may have other, more prestigious occupations, such as medical doctors or judges. Status involves social comparisons in groups; a consideration of status is meaningless unless we put it into a group context.

In an earlier vignette, Jean talked about her experience of not receiving the credit she deserved in a task group. Task groups are a particularly interesting place to look at how status operates in group contexts. A great deal of research in sociological social psychology indicates that when groups get together to complete tasks, status hierarchies form. People who are higher in the status hierarchy tend to do more of the talking and to get more of the credit for their contributions than do those who have lower status. This finding is consistent in the literature, and social psychologists have developed theoretical accounts of how status processes operate in groups (Berger, Rosenholtz, and Zelditch 1980; Thye 2000; Troyer 2001; Wagner and Berger 1993; Webster and Whitmeyer 2002). The most well-developed of these theories, expectation states and status characteristics theory, is detailed in chapter 4.

Justice

Let's look again at the example we discussed earlier—the power imbalance at the restaurant. In that situation, workers may develop a sense that they are not being treated fairly. Social psychologists refer to such perceptions of fairness as *justice perceptions*. **Justice** is a group process because it involves social comparisons. For example, when people think about whether their wage or salary is fair, they draw conclusions by comparing their salaries to those of other people.

Social psychologists who are interested in justice have come up with many interesting and sometimes surprising findings. For example, when we try to determine whether the amount of money we make is "fair," to whom do we compare ourselves? Research indicates that we tend to compare ourselves to similar others. However, research also shows that this tendency goes only so far: In general, we seek comparisons that will give the highest value to the amount we think we should earn. And at what point do we decide that the distribution of salaries is unfair? We feel more of a sense of injustice about pay distributions that give us less than we think we deserve than we do about distributions that give us more than we think we deserve.

What criteria do most of us think should be used to determine pay distributions? Depending on the context, researchers have found that we apply different criteria to different situations. In some situations, people are likely to think that equal distributions, with everyone receiving the same amount, are the fairest. In other instances, however, people may think that the fairest outcome is an *equitable distribution*—one in which the amount each individual receives reflects how much that person contributes.

These are just a few examples of the many questions confronted by social psychologists interested in justice. Group processes work on justice is varied and addresses multiple aspects of how we determine what is fair (Hegtvedt 1990; Jasso 1980; Jasso and Webster 1999; Markovsky 1985). Important group processes findings on justice comparisons will come up in later chapters throughout the book.

Legitimacy

When disparities exist between our perceptions of competence and actual power differences in the world, we are likely to conclude that some distributions are illegitimate. Like status, power, and justice, legitimacy—the sense that an existing social arrangement is the way that things *should* be—is a social process that occurs in group contexts. When people view social arrangements as illegitimate, a number of outcomes can undermine social order. For example, waiters and dishwashers might not work as hard for the owners of a restaurant if they do not believe that the owner's power over them is legitimate.

Sociological social psychologists who study group processes are especially interested in the legitimacy of persons in positions of authority. Social psychologists, for example, might study how the events of the very close and hotly contested U.S. presidential election in 2000 affected the extent to which Americans and people around the world viewed President George W. Bush as a legitimate occupant of his position. As with justice, various factors affect the views that people have. Republicans, for example, were probably more likely than Democrats to view the election as legitimate.

People can gain legitimacy in a number of ways. In American society, research indicates that some people—men compared to women, for example—tend to be viewed as more legitimate occupants of authority positions. Endorsement, which is the approval of a social arrangement by members of one's peer group, is one source of legitimacy. For example, if one's coworkers at a restaurant believe that the restaurant's owners are exceptionally competent, the worker herself will likely view the owners' power as more legitimate than she otherwise would. Group processes work on legitimacy addresses its sources and outcomes in multiple ways (Thomas, Walker, and Zelditch 1986; Walker, Thomas, and Zelditch 1986; Zelditch 2001).

Power, status, justice, and legitimacy are just a few of the many processes occurring in group contexts that are of interest to sociological social psychologists. As we have noted, scholars in the group processes approach include those who study the processes that occur in groups and those who study characteristics of groups themselves. We now turn to a brief discussion of some of the interests of those who study the "group" in "group processes."

Group Structures

The effect of a group on its members depends, in part, on how the group is configured. Groups can be configured in a number of ways—by size, function (e.g., work or pleasure), or goals, among other things. Each of these configurations can produce different expectations about how to behave in the group.

Group Size

Small groups are defined as groups of two or more individuals—typically between 2 and 20 people—whose members are able to engage in direct, face-to-face interactions. Although there is no official group size at which face-to-face interaction becomes impossible, it is difficult for personal relationships to develop in groups of more than 20. In a five-person group, for example, each person can interact with every other group member. But in a group of 50 people, a leader might direct the entire group (for example, by presenting a lecture) or instead might break the 50-person group into smaller, more intimate groups. An interaction among all 50 group members, however, is unlikely.

Anyone who has been part of a class of 90 students meeting in a large auditorium and has also participated in small classes of about 15 students can understand the impact of group size on interactions. You may enjoy smaller classes more than larger ones. Why? Probably because smaller classes allow for more intimate interactions between students, opening up discussions and giving class members an opportunity to get to know one another. In short, by allowing for more intimacy among their members, smaller classes provide better learning environments.

Dyads and Triads

One of the earliest sociologists to study the effects of group dynamics on individuals was Georg Simmel. Simmel (1950) argued that the size of a group restricts the level of intimacy possible within the group. A two-person group, or **dyad,** is limited to a single relationship. But adding just one more person to that group, to form a **triad,** creates two additional relationships. Thus, simply adding a person to a group increases the number of relationships in the group exponentially while simultaneously decreasing intimacy levels. The effects of group size on group members' thoughts, feelings, and behaviors occur above and beyond the specific individuals involved in the group.

The change from a dyad to a triad is an example of a process that occurs in small groups. The process can be illustrated through considering personal relationships. Suppose you go to a party and meet someone to whom you are attracted. As you start to talk, you become more interested in the other person, perhaps exchanging ideas about different topics. A little later, a friend of yours enters the room and approaches your dyad, transforming it into a triad.

What happens now? Your discussion will very likely change, not only because a new group member brings a different point of view, but also because the group now has two new relationships to balance. As a result, someone will likely talk less, and there will be less opportunity to develop intimacy. Adding still more people to the triad will again create an exponential increase in the number of relationships—for example, a four-person group involves six different relationships—and a corresponding decrease in intimacy (see Figure 2.2).

At the small-group level, group-processes theories in sociology focus on the exchanges—of resources, of information, of emotion—that take place between people and on how our position in a group affects these exchanges. According to many scholars who study small groups, a primary source of motivation for indi-

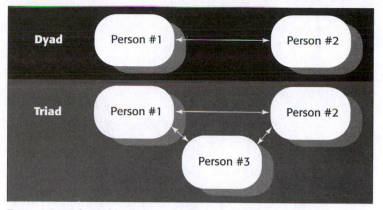

Figure 2.2   Relationships in Dyads and Triads

viduals in groups is to obtain the things they need in life. Those "things" can include physical as well as social objects.

Types of Groups

Social psychologists distinguish between three broad types of groups, which are configured in different ways and serve different purposes:

- **Primary groups:** family members and close friends—the people we are close to and interact with regularly (Cooley 1909).
- **Secondary groups:** people we affiliate with to achieve similar goals or needs— for example, our coworkers or teammates.
- **Reference groups:** people we do not necessarily know personally but look to as a source of standards and identity.

Each type of group holds different expectations of its members. Primary groups serve more emotional needs, whereas secondary groups usually serve instrumental needs. Reference groups, however, can vary considerably. Your membership in the Democratic or Republican Party may serve instrumental needs (e.g., a push for public policy) as well as reference needs (to find support for your ideals). Unlike your relationship to most primary and secondary groups, you may not actually interact with members of your reference groups. Even if you identify with your party's goals and use its ideals as a standard of behavior, for example, you may never actually go to party meetings.

Relationships among Groups

In our previous review of group processes, we looked at behavior within groups, or "intragroup" dynamics. But social psychologists are also interested in intergroup dynamics—that is, relationships between two or more groups. Thus, groups themselves—beyond their individual members—can serve as a unit of analysis. Going along with this, groups can develop an identity that later has an impact on the members of the group.

Intergroup relationships can occur on several levels, ranging from a small group of friends to larger, more formal groups. An important social psychological theory of intergroup relationships, social identity theory, is reviewed in detail later in this book. One area of interest to social psychologists who study intergroup relationships is the causes and consequences of prejudice and discrimination. Sociologists also study the behavior of larger groups through research on such acts as protests and riots.

Both inter- and intragroup behavior can be studied as aspects of **collective behavior**—the action or behavior of people in groups or crowds (Lofland 1992; Miller 2000). Collective behavior has traditionally been associated with riots, protests, and revolutions. But the field can also include the study of popular trends and fads. Theories of collective behavior can vary considerably, with some, such as mass hysteria theory, emphasizing its emotional aspects, whereas others, such as emergent norm theory, focus instead on the rational nature of human behavior in larger groups (Miller 2000). We will focus on collective behavior in Chapter 11.

As you can see from this discussion, a variety of work falls under the broad heading of "group processes." Because the emphasis in this book is on sociological social psychology, we will focus on the aspect of group processes that is of greatest interest to sociological social psychologists—that is, on the processes that occur in groups rather than on features of the groups themselves. In the chapters that follow, our discussions of group processes will generally (but not exclusively) look at social processes such as status, power, justice, and legitimacy.

Section Summary

The last section of this chapter answered the questions: What is the group processes perspective? What are some basic social processes that play out in group contexts? What are the elements of group structure? Group process researchers emphasize the role of status and power in groups. They also study how notions of justice and legitimacy play out in group contexts. Group structures vary by size as well as complexities associated with size. They can also include group types such as primary, secondary, and reference groups. Group size and type can have large impacts on the interaction of members within a group.

Bringing It All Together

Why do we need three perspectives? They only have one theory of relativity in physics!

—Carlos, junior Sociology major

The three perspectives that we have reviewed in this chapter share an underlying interest in how individuals are influenced by their social context. Although we have presented these perspectives as separate, even competing, approaches to the study of social psychology, there is often overlap between them. For example, a researcher conducting a study of gender and work identities might be guided by important principles of both symbolic interaction and social structure and personality. Similarly, work in the group processes tradition focuses on diverse topics—for example, how stereotyping affects scores on standard ability tests such as the SAT (Lovaglia, Lucas, Houser, Thye, and Markovsky 1998) and how gender identities influence interactions between women and men in marriages (Stets and Burke 1996). These are both substantive topics that can also be easily understood through an interactionist lens. Although researchers tend to have a certain "bent," many are flexible enough to approach a research question with the most appropriate conceptual and methodological perspective in the field. This flexibility often makes for creative and boundary-pushing projects on the cutting edge of sociological social psychology.

Some students—such as Carlos in the vignette at the beginning of this section—are skeptical about the need for more than one perspective. But after all, there are many facets to human behavior. It would be difficult to find any one perspective appropriate for studying all aspects of our lives. With multiple perspectives, we are better equipped to study the larger array of people's thoughts, feelings, and behaviors.

Summary

1. There are three broad perspectives in sociological social psychology: symbolic interactionism, social structure and personality, and group processes.

2. Symbolic interactionism is the study of how people negotiate meaning during their interactions with others. Within this approach, two schools of symbolic interactionism exist: the Chicago school and the Indiana and Iowa schools.

3. The social structure and personality perspective emphasizes how social structure affects individuals within a society. Structural forces include status, roles, and social networks.

4. The group processes perspective focuses on interactions that occur in groups, characteristics of groups, and relationships between groups. Processes studied by those in the group processes perspective include power, status, justice, and legitimacy.

5. A group's behavior is influenced by structural conditions, including its size and its function. Group research may focus on structure or on other aspects of group processes, such as the relationship between groups and the behavior of larger groups of people, called collective behavior.

Agency: The ability to act and think independent of the constraints imposed by social conditions.

Chicago school of symbolic interactionism: A perspective within symbolic interactionism that focuses on understanding the social processes involved in a given situation rather than trying to quantify and predict people's thoughts, feelings, and behavior.

Collective behavior: The action or behavior of people in groups or crowds.

Components principle: Within the social structure and personality perspective, the ability to identify the elements or components of society most likely to affect a given attitude or behavior.

Dyad: A two-person group.

Group: Interactions that involve more than one person.

Indiana and Iowa schools of symbolic interactionism: Perspective within symbolic interactionism that focuses on the quantitative study of social interaction processes because of the stable nature of social life.

Justice: Fairness in group interactions.

Language: A series of symbols that can be combined in various ways to create new meanings.

Legitimacy: The perception that a social arrangement or position is the way that things should be.

Power: The ability to obtain what we desire in a group despite resistance.

Primary groups: People we are close to and interact with regularly.

Proximity principle: Element of the social structure and personality perspective referring to how people are affected by social structure through their immediate social environments.

Psychology principle: Element of the social structure and personality perspective referring to how individuals internalize proximal experiences.

Reference groups: People we look to as a source of standards and identity.

Secondary groups: People we affiliate with to achieve common goals or meet common needs.

Small groups: Two or more persons engaged in or capable of face-to-face interaction.

Social construction of reality: The process by which we use symbols and language to give meaning and value to objects and people.

Social forces: Any way in which society compels individuals to act in accordance with an external norm, rule, or demand.

Social networks: A series of relationships between individuals and groups.

Society: In symbolic interactionism, the network of interaction between people.

Symbols: Anything that has a similar meaning for two or more individuals.

Thomas theorem: Theorem stating that when people define situations as real, the consequences of those situations become real.

Triad: A three-person group.

Discussion Questions

1. Which of the three perspectives makes the most sense to you? Why? How does it contribute to your understanding of the social world?

2. Does social psychology really need three perspectives? Why or why not?

3. Which aspects of your life are most affected by society? Apply principles or concepts from one or more of the perspectives to show the effects of social forces in your life.

Studying People

Chapter 3

I have always hated thinking about research methods. Anything to do with collecting or analyzing data was simply not my thing. I got involved in sociology because I was fascinated by research findings. I never thought too much about the methods. But then I had to conduct an observation of a local toy store, analyzing how children reacted to different toys. The research findings didn't surprise me— the boys picked up the guns and the girls always found their way to the dolls—but I began to realize how hard it is to prove anything about my observations. I would look at my notes and ask myself, how do I know that my observations are important? Did I bias my findings? How do I report my findings? Will anybody care? At that point, I went back to my methods book and found ways to improve my research design and analyze the data in a clear way. Being more systematic enabled me to see something I had missed earlier. Younger kids played with what their older siblings were looking at, regardless of their own gender. I feel much more confident reporting my findings to other people, too. I guess methods classes are not all that bad!

—Shelly, senior Sociology major

Shelly's lack of excitement about research methods is not unusual. A lecture or class on methods can seem dry because it entails learning a set of tools rather than exploring a substantive area of research. Students are generally interested in understanding an issue—for example, inequality in society—rather than thinking about the best methods to use for studying the issue. But, as we see, when Shelly is faced with conducting and reporting on a research project herself, she soon changes her mind about research methods. She begins to wonder what it will take to develop a good project, one that people will take seriously.

Learning to use research methods effectively is vital to using social science as a way of understanding the world in which we live. Approaching social science with a critical lens will make you a more informed analyst of information and ideas you read about or hear people discuss. In short, understanding methods can give you a good sense of how to carry out your own research as well as the ability to judge the quality of other people's research and their conclusions about how the world works.

Understanding the effects of social conditions on individuals and groups is challenging. How can you study the effect of culture on individual behaviors if the people you are studying are unaware of its influence? Because of complexities like this, the research methods commonly used by sociologists differ somewhat from those favored by psychologists. Imagine, for example, trying to show that capitalist economies lead people to be more selfish than do other economic systems. You might demonstrate that selfish attitudes are more widespread in nations with capitalist than with socialist economies, but does that actually show that capitalism is the *cause* of selfishness? Having a strong grasp of research methods will help you figure out ways to investigate whether such a connection really does exist.

There are a number of ways to initiate a research project. The goal of this chapter is to provide some background information about the various ways of studying people as well as criteria for deciding which methods are most appropriate for your own research projects. We answer the following questions:

- What is the vocabulary of social science research?
- How is qualitative sociology different from quantitative sociology?
- What are the major forms of qualitative research?
- What are the major forms of quantitative research?
- How do social scientists begin to develop a research project?

Basic Concepts and Issues

Why does my methods professor want me to understand all of these obscure terms? It's so frustrating!

—Samuel, junior Sociology major

Samuel's frustration is understandable. Learning research methods does involve learning a new vocabulary. But this vocabulary is important. Basic concepts help researchers evaluate their projects and ensure that the research they are undertaking will be valuable to—and accepted by—other researchers. In this section, we will first review some important concepts and then discuss the major ways that social psychologists approach the study of people.

Theories and Hypotheses

All research projects in social psychology start with an idea about how some aspect of social life works. Suppose you decide that a friend is being particularly nice to a stranger because she finds the person attractive. That experience may lead you to wonder if people, in general, act more friendly toward attractive people than toward those they see as less attractive. This sort of thinking process can be the starting point for a social theory. You may develop your theory in trying to explain why people show nicer behavior toward attractive individuals than toward less attractive ones. **Social theories** refer to organized sets of propositions about how various elements of social life are related to one another. Social theories focus on people's relationships with one another and with their larger social worlds. A theory typically includes some of the following components:

1. General statements about social relationships.
2. Statements about the causes of those relationships.
3. General predictions, based on these reasons, about how people will react to certain events or experiences or conditions.

Because theories are general, they cannot be tested directly. As an example, consider a theory about how economic systems influence people's selfishness. Selfishness is a difficult concept to measure directly: It is not easy for people to respond accurately to a survey item that asks them how selfish they are. Instead, researchers may try to measure selfishness indirectly, perhaps by seeing how people in a group (in both capitalist and socialist economies) choose to divide up a pay distribution between themselves and other group members. Theories are refined into testable hypotheses before being examined using some form of research method. **Hypotheses** are specific statements about how variables will relate to one another in a research study. **Variables** are theoretical concepts (e.g., selfishness) put into a measurable form (e.g., how much people reward themselves and others when dividing up payment amounts).

Translating a concept into something that can be measured is called **operationalizing** the concept. Simply put, *operationalizing* means "performing operations" on a concept. Thus, hypotheses provide testable statements about theories or parts of a theory. Because hypotheses only indirectly test theories, they only provide evidence for the veracity of a theory.

Operationalizing a concept in the social sciences can be difficult because much social science research investigates concepts that do not exist in the physical world. For example, suppose you want to study the impact of stressors on mental health. How do you measure the concept of stressor? We must first operationalize the concept of stressor—transform it into something that can be measured. You may decide to measure it in terms of stressful life conditions, such as the number of negative life events to which a person is exposed. Alternatively, you may operationalize stressors as a state of being, perhaps asking people to tell you how much strain they are experiencing in work and family relationships on a scale of 1 to 5.

The relationship between theories and hypotheses is not always clear. You cannot necessarily dismiss a theory when research findings do not support a particular hypothesis. In one example, Thoits (1991; 1995) applied identity theory (chapter 5 reviews this theory in detail) to examine the relationship between negative life events and individual well-being. Her research focused on a part of identity theory that claims that people attach meaning to certain roles in their lives and that some of those roles and relationships have more importance or salience than others. Starting with this general premise, Thoits hypothesized that negative events would have a larger effect on psychological symptoms when they threatened highly salient identities compared to events in less salient identities. In fact, her findings generally did not support her hypotheses about the relationship between identity-salient events and distress. But this result did not lead Thoits to conclude that identity theory was wrong or, for that matter, that identity-related stressors do not lead to distress. Rather, she concluded that more details about events would be necessary to make the connection between the general theory and her specific hypotheses. In other words, she argued that the theory may still help us understand the relationship between identity and distress, but that better measures and research techniques would be necessary to connect the two parts, if in fact the relationship exists.

Independent and Dependent Variables

Hypotheses are more specific than theories; they are limited to the variables being studied in a given project. As stated earlier, variables refer to theoretically-relevant measures that have two or more values. For example, the variable "race" is often measured among Americans by the values "African American," "Asian American," "Hispanic," and "White." But the dimensions of a variable may be more complex than a simple list of possible outcomes. Researchers can also allow respondents to provide their own sense of a given concept. For instance, instead of listing a limited set of values for "race," you might ask people to define their race in their own words.

Variables are generally separated into those believed to cause a phenomenon and the phenomenon itself. The variable predicted to lead to a change in another variable is the **independent variable.** The variable that is predicted to change as a result of the independent variable is the **dependent variable.** In the preceding example, Thoits (1991; 1995) was investigating whether the number of negative life events related to important identities (the independent variable) increased psychological distress (the dependent variable) (see Figure 3.1).

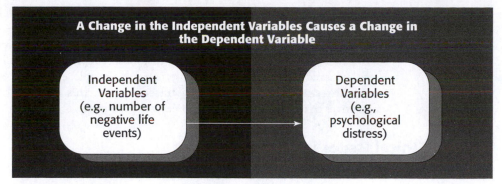

Figure 3.1 *Independent and Dependent Variables*

Sampling Issues

It is almost always impossible to study the thoughts, feelings, and behavior of all the people to whom a theory is intended to apply. As a result, researchers rely on a smaller group of people to represent a larger group. A **population** is the larger group of people about whom a researcher seeks to draw conclusions. A **sample** is a group of people drawn to represent the larger population. **Probability samples** (also called representative samples) are those in which researchers choose participants systematically in an attempt to draw a sample representative of the population. One type of sample, a **random sample,** is one in which participants are randomly picked from a population. The random method is the surest way to obtain a representative sample of the larger population.

Choosing a purely random sample is not possible for many research activities. Imagine that the population of interest to a researcher is all adults in the United States. In this case, obtaining a true random sample is impossible because no complete *sampling frame* is available. A **sampling frame** is a list of all possible elements in the population—and there is no such listing of adults in the United States. If one ever became available, it would immediately be outdated as people immigrated and emigrated or died. Hence, most sampling frames are limited to all elements of a population that are available for sampling (Kalton 1983). For instance, if you wanted to survey all members of a church congregation, you may have to limit your sampling frame to members listed on the church's mailing list, hence missing anyone who neglected to submit her contact information.

When researchers do not know how prevalent a particular phenomenon is in society, they may rely on samples in which probability techniques are not used to draw participants from a population. In a **convenience sample,** any available person is included in the study. In a **snowball sample,** informants provide contact information about other people who share some of the characteristics necessary for a study. Early research on sexual behavior in America, for instance, started with snowball and other nonrandom sampling techniques to develop samples of people willing to be surveyed on such personal, intimate behaviors (Michael, Laumann, Gagnon, and Kolata 1995).

Probability samples are much preferred when trying to apply research findings to an entire group or population. But in cases where representation is less important, nonrandom designs may be appropriate. For example, exploratory and experimental research investigations (discussed later in this chapter) often have objectives that make probability samples less necessary.

Ethical Issues in Studying People

Social psychological research plans must be scrutinized *before* they are conducted to ensure that they follow professional ethical guidelines for conducting research with human subjects. All universities have **Internal Review Boards (IRBs)** made up of academics from diverse fields. IRBs review research projects to make sure that the expected benefits of the research outweigh any potential harm to research participants. If ethical or moral concerns arise, the IRB may recommend changes to a research protocol or, in some cases, may deny the project altogether.

The IRB system was developed after a number of ethically questionable research projects were conducted in the early and mid-20th century. One infamous example was Humphries' (1970) study of the "tearoom trade" involving homosexual sex in public places. He started his research by going to places where homosexuals were known to spend time, such as gay bars. After some time, he developed informants who told him where less-visible homosexual activity occurred, public restrooms in particular. The researcher played a "watchqueen"— a voyeur who served as a lookout so that the men actually engaging in the sexual activity would not be discovered. His research showed that "tearoom" behavior was quite structured, with an organized series of norms and roles. But whatever the value of Humphries' findings, many sociologists questioned the ethics of his research. Humphries did not take any steps to ensure the anonymity of his research subjects; in fact, he even followed them to their homes to find out whether they were married and where they lived. Because he exposed his subjects to emotional and social hardships, Humphries' research methods would almost certainly not be allowed under today's standards.

Section Summary

This section of the chapter answered the question: What is the vocabulary of social science research? Our goal is to give you an understanding of the important concepts social psychologists bring into the study of human populations. First, we noted that theories and hypotheses are used to guide the development of research design and specific measurements of our independent and dependent variables. Second, we discussed the challenges of sampling individuals from the larger population, that is, using a smaller group of people to represent the thoughts, feelings, and behavior of the larger group. Finally, we addressed the unique ethical challenges in the study of human populations.

I had been sitting on the metro for about an hour before I noticed anything peculiar. It was winter, so the warm train was a welcome relief from the cold outside. A woman came in with a huge steamy-hot sandwich from a local vendor. She unwrapped it and started at it. At first, I didn't mind, but the smell started filling up the car. As I watched, I also noticed what she was wearing under her coat and the things she was carrying. Then it hit me: This woman is homeless. Well, given the way she was eating, I think she was at home on the subway! I stayed on the metro another two hours, trying to figure out how other people reacted to those who make a temporary home of the subway. It was a really interesting research project!

—Peter, junior Sociology major

There are many ways to study people. Some approaches are formal and precise; others, such as Peter's study of the homeless, are more fluid in nature. Peter started out with a general goal of studying people on a subway train. Over time, however, he refined his research goals, focusing on people's reactions to homeless people who used the subway for shelter.

In contrast to Peter's rather informal method, some survey research projects begin with precise specification of independent and dependent variables before data collection begins. And many research projects fall somewhere between these two extremes. For example, researchers may decide on the variables they are interested in measuring before they begin a project. Once the project is underway, however, the data they find may take them in new directions and lead them to choose to collect new sorts of information.

The method you choose to study a particular phenomenon depends on several factors:

1. The *orientation of the researcher* will likely influence the methods he or she uses. For instance, some symbolic interactionists are unlikely to carry out large-scale survey research projects because they believe that it is impossible to quantify human thoughts, feelings, and behavior—a point that will be discussed later in this chapter.

2. The population of interest may inhibit the use of certain methods. For instance, a researcher who wants to study the attitudes and beliefs of undocumented immigrants would be unlikely to use a telephone survey, because the respondents would not have listed phone numbers and would most likely be unwilling to talk.

3. Most important, your *research question* and/or the *hypotheses* you are testing should point you to the most appropriate method.

Methods of research fall under two general headings: qualitative and quantitative (see Table 3.1). Although there is overlap in the types of research conducted

Table 3.1	Popular Methods of Conducting Social Science Research
Qualitative Methods	**Quantitative Methods***
Field Research (i.e., Ethnography, Participant Observation)	Survey Research
In-Depth Interviews	Secondary Data Analysis
Focus Groups	Experiments
Content Analysis	Content Analysis**

*Although most of these methods are typically quantitative, they can be qualitative as well.
**This method typically includes both qualitative and quantitative components.

under these headings, we believe that they serve as a good heuristic device for understanding the larger field of social inquiry. As such, we review some of the most popular methods in sociological social psychology under these headings, followed by a discussion of how theory and methods combine to form research projects.

Qualitative Methods

Qualitative research methods focus on in-depth, semistructured modes of observation or interviewing of subjects. Qualitative researchers do not quantify people's thoughts, feelings, or behaviors. Rather, they allow subjects to describe their experiences in their own words or to behave naturally within a research setting.

The major advantage of using a qualitative approach is that it usually does not seek to constrain either people's actions or the conditions to which they respond. A disadvantage is that it is difficult to apply qualitative research findings to new people or groups because phenomena are not usually measured in a consistent way across research studies.

Two popular forms of qualitative research are field research or observation and in-depth interviewing.

Field Research

Field research is the direct observation of people's behavior at a particular site (Cahill, Fine, and Grant 1995) (see Box 3.1). A common type of field research is **ethnography,** a descriptive analysis of a group or organization. A researcher may enter a group (such as Alcoholics Anonymous) or organization (for example, a middle school) and observe how people behave, paying particular attention to patterns of behavior related to a particular theory or perspective.

In some cases, the researcher may actually become part of a group, an approach known as **participant observation.** Participant observers, like a sociologist who is also an Alcoholics Anonymous member, have the advantage of being insiders, so that they can get information from group members as actual participants in the group's activities. But group membership also has its disadvantages (Cahill et al. 1995):

1. Participant observers may develop a bias: They may change their perspectives on the group's behavior because of their affiliation with that group.

2. Participant observers may not know how their participation influences the behaviors of group members.

3. Participant observation projects and field research in general can take a long time to complete.

As an example of the time it takes to conduct this kind of research, Roschelle and Kaufman (2004) spent four years on an ethnographic study of homeless children in San Francisco. One of the authors became a volunteer at several observation sites, where she had the opportunity to take extensive notes based on her observations of social-service agency meetings, residential motels, transitional housing facilities, and homeless shelters. The researchers also made extensive use of qualitative surveys with open-ended responses. Their goal was to understand how these children found ways to "fit in" various environments and the techniques they developed for protecting their senses of self.

Ethical issues are tricky too. MacLeod (1993) began his study of the aspirations of poor teenage African-American "Brothers" and White "Hallway Hangers" when he was basketball director of a youth program, studying how poverty is perpetuated from one generation to the next. He befriended many youths, playing basketball with them frequently. The study had been going on for a few months before MacLeod asked the boys for permission to use them as research subjects. MacLeod's position as a researcher was complex. He talks about times when the "Hallway Hangers" drank and used drugs as difficult ethically, being an "unbiased" researcher watching youth engage in illegal activities.

In-Depth Interviews

There are many ways to interview people, ranging from formal questionnaires to more informal open-ended questions related to a research topic. Many researchers rely on **in-depth interviews,** using an unstructured or semistructured series of questions and probing respondents for more details as appropriate to the goals of the research (Babbie 2002). Such in-depth interviews give researchers more flexibility than traditional questionnaires because they do not limit the types of responses available to respondents and they may also make respondents more comfortable by allowing them to respond in their own words. Another advantage of qualitative interviews is that they allow researchers to probe further in areas that need elaboration. For instance, you might begin by asking a respondent what it is like to grow up in a certain region of the country. As the interview progresses, however, you realize that the individual grew up near a military training camp. As a result, you may decide to ask more specific questions about that camp and its effects on her upbringing. In this way, in-depth interviews allow researchers some flexibility in their research questions.

Qualitative interviews can be used as a part of observational research or as a method of study in themselves. Howard Becker (1953), for example, interviewed

50 marijuana users about their personal experiences with the drug and their attitudes toward it. His interviews gave him insights into the social aspects of the drug experience. For example, he found that many people do not get high the first time they use marijuana. In many cases, more senior users must teach new users the proper technique to induce a high. Thus, the drug's effects on an individual are influenced by the social conditions surrounding that experience.

Other Qualitative Methods

There are many different ways of using qualitative methods to study people. Blumer (1969) argued that researchers should employ a variety of qualitative methods to "explore" and "inspect" social life (see Box 3.2). Other qualitative methods include examinations of newspapers and diaries, analyses of life histories or biographies of subjects, consulting public records, or group interviews (e.g., focus groups). **Content analysis** includes any systematic review of written documents or other media. Although this method often includes categorizing and quantifying texts, it still fits under the qualitative rubric because some level of interpretation is still required (Cahill et al. 1995). Traditionally, researchers will examine a document (e.g., newspaper articles or diaries), trying to assess patterns of thought or speech. Content analysis can also be used to find patterns in television shows, movies, and radio programs. For example, trends in stereotypes of homosexuals might be studied through an examination of how they are portrayed in television shows over time.

Focus groups include semistructured interviews with small groups, usually between 6 and 15 people (Babbie 2002; Neuman 2004). Focus groups allow researchers the flexibility of qualitative interviewing while getting multiple perspectives at the same time. Focus groups are often recorded, allowing researchers to take notes about general response trends during the session, transcribing detailed responses after the session has ended. Researchers may conduct multiple focus groups not only to provide additional data but also to separate groups by some relevant category. A study of student athletes' attitudes toward school programs, for instance, may vary dramatically depending on whether they are interviewing athletes involved in football, track and field, or swimming. Separating these athletes into their respective groups may help participants feel more comfortable sharing their opinions in the focus group session.

In a sense, qualitative researchers are social investigators, seeking out information about a topic or a social phenomenon and developing leads for further investigation. Depending on what a researcher finds in her initial explorations, she might update her research findings as well as the research protocol, or method of inquiry, to fit the new conditions. For instance, as an amateur sociologist interested in countercultural groups, you may start interviewing some friends who are into a particular form of alternative music. As you talk to them, you realize that certain clubs and activities are important in this music scene. You may decide, as a result, to conduct some observations of those clubs and activities. Hence, qualitative research usually requires some degree of flexibility in research design and implementation.

Box 3.1   The Promises and Pitfalls of Going into the Field

Patricia and Peter Adler are two sociological social psychologists well known for their qualitative research projects, including years of observation and qualitative interviewing that are often put under the heading of "ethnography" (see Adler and Adler 1999). Their qualitative research has included diverse topics ranging from participant observations of and interviews with drug dealers (Adler and Adler 1982) to extensive ethnographies of preadolescent children's culture (Adler 1996; Adler and Adler 1994). After more than 20 years of qualitative study, they continue to provide insight into developing and implementing ethnographies. They argue that good ethnographers know how to be "outsiders" in a social setting, being able to analyze individuals' behavior in an unbiased way. This work is very challenging because it is time consuming (often taking years to complete one study) and it is criticized for being unreliable. However, the "promise" of ethnographic research is that it can provide provocative insights into human behaviors that would otherwise go unstudied (Adler and Adler 2003). How else can you study the values and beliefs, for instance, of very young children? Drug dealers? Terrorists?

Quantitative Methods

Quantitative methods include any attempt to quantify—that is, to measure precisely—people's thoughts, feelings, or behavior. After gathering such data, quantitative researchers usually use this information to test hypotheses. Quantitative methods allow researchers to apply statistical analyses to their variables, so that they can test predictions and assess the statistical significance of their findings.

Assessing **statistical significance** means examining the probability that the results found in the sample reflect the true relationships within the population of interest. Suppose, for example, that we find that men and women report very different levels of depression in a probability sample of 4,000 Americans. Statistical analyses allow us to test the likelihood that the gender difference we found in the sample likely reflects differences in the larger U.S. population.

Although quantitative techniques allow us to apply traditional scientific methods to the study of people, they are sometimes criticized as being sterile and unrealistic. In some cases, survey questionnaires cannot capture important aspects of a topic—"friendship," for example. What is more, the subtle exchanges between friends may be difficult to study in a laboratory experiment. Participants might be asked to interact with someone via a computer screen, for instance, to study friendship. Although such conditions may seem a bit strange, this type of research often yields important findings that can inform us about interactions in natural social situations and significance levels can be calculated, indicating the likelihood that the findings exist in the population of interest as opposed to being simply due to chance factors.

Quantitative studies are not designed to capture all the complexities of social behavior. But they are valuable for testing theoretical predictions using precise

Focus groups provide a way of assessing people's attitudes and beliefs in a small-group context.

concepts or under precise conditions. When they are well designed, quantitative studies can provide a rich source of information about social behavior. Two primary forms of inquiry in social psychology include surveys and experiments.

Survey Research

The most commonly used quantitative research method in sociology is survey research. **Survey research** refers to the use of questionnaires to measure independent and dependent variables; the term **secondary data analysis** refers to the analysis of previously collected survey data. Social psychologists use different types of questions to assess individuals' thoughts, feelings, and behaviors. **Categorical** (or nominal) **variables** include questions for which the possible responses have no particular order. Most demographic characteristics are categorical in nature. For instance, the question, "What type of home do you live in?" may include responses of 1 "mobile home," 2 "apartment," and 3 "single-family home," but it makes no difference whether "mobile home" or "single-family home" is listed first. Compare this type of question to a scale question with a response range from 1 "very satisfied" to 5 "very dissatisfied." In this case, the order of the outcome responses is important.

Much of the survey research employed by social psychologists relies on **ordinal variables,** those for which response categories are ordered but the distances between adjacent categories are not necessarily equal. For example, to measure life satisfaction, you might ask respondents the degree to which they are satisfied with their life in general on a response scale ranging from 1 "very dissatisfied" to 5 "very satisfied" with the assumption that higher scores are associated with greater life satisfaction. However, it should be noted that one person's assessment of the meaning of "very satisfied" may be quite different than another person's definition of the words.

Interval variables are those for which the distance between any two adjacent points is the same. **Ratio variables** are interval variables that have zero starting point. Age, measured in years, is a ratio variable because the difference between 12 and 13 years is exactly the same as the difference between 13 and 14 years and

Box 3.2   **Exploration and Inspection**

One symbolic interactionist approach to studying people involves a two-part process of exploration and inspection (Blumer 1969):

1. Exploration involves the development of a comprehensive understanding of the research problem using the following techniques:
   - Seek out well-informed participants.
   - Collect information using direct observation, listening to conversations, reading diaries and letters, and consulting public records.
   - Revise original beliefs and conceptions of the area you are studying.

2. Inspection is the empirical examination of the analytical elements found during the exploration. Analytical elements include processes, organization, relationships, and events. This procedure is achieved in the following ways:
   - Inspect the elements or relationships from a variety of perspectives.
   - Scrutinize the inspection by asking questions about the elements or analyzing perspectives of different subjects.

This method assumes that the best way to study human relationships is to observe and take extensive notes about how people behave and relate to one another in a research situation and then to use those notes and observations as sources of data, applying your theoretical perspective as a guide to your analysis of your information.

---

there is a zero starting point. The same would be true if we decided to measure age in months, weeks, or days.

Indices (also known as scales) include a series of related questions designed to develop one or more dimensions of a given concept. For instance, an index measuring life satisfaction may include respondents' satisfaction with work, family, and school, among other things. Simply asking respondents to indicate satisfaction with "life as a whole" limits the validity of the measure because responses to individual items tend to fluctuate over time, and not always in the same direction. For example, a person's family satisfaction might be high at a point in time when work satisfaction is low. By measuring individual items, indices can provide relatively stable measures of social-psychological concepts.

Although many researchers use the words *scale* and *index* interchangeably, the two terms are conceptually different. Indices simply require researchers to add scores for individual items in a series of questions. Scales require the researcher to weight individual items differently, depending on the type of scale being used. In practice, however, many scales are treated like indices. In Table 3.2, for instance, you can simply add individuals' score to come up with an overall sense of satisfaction with life. In this case, the lowest rating someone can have is 6 and the

Survey researchers employ questionnaires to obtain social psychological information from groups of people.

highest possible score is 30. Hence, scales and indexes produce a higher range of variation than found in single items.

Indices and scales play an important role in social psychology. In addition to giving us insight into complex social-psychological phenomenon, indices allow us to employ advanced analytical techniques, including correlation and linear regression analyses—two techniques that allow researchers to see if a change in one variable is associated with a change in another variable. For instance, we might want to know whether respondents' age correlates with life satisfaction; that is, when age increases, do we see an increase in life satisfaction? Categorical variables, in contrast, only allow researchers to compare responses by category. Hence, using life satisfaction (an ordinal variable) and housing type (a categorical variable), we could compare life satisfaction scores by type of housing unit, assessing if life satisfaction scores are higher for people in single-family homes than for those living in mobile homes for instance.

Experiments

An **experiment** is a type of research procedure in which investigators control participants' exposure to an independent variable. Unlike qualitative research, which can explore social phenomena, or survey research, which seeks to examine relationships between variables in a population, experiments are generally carried out to test theoretical propositions.

Most social psychology experiments are **laboratory experiments,** controlled environments in which different participants are assigned to different levels of an independent variable before a dependent variable is measured. Elements of some theories, however, cannot be studied in a laboratory. In these cases, researchers might conduct **natural** or **field experiments** that take place in people's everyday environments (Meeker and Leik 1995). Modern experimentation has also begun to incorporate computer simulations as part of the process. Computers can be used in experiments to simulate interaction with other people (e.g., a participant exchanging messages with someone she thinks is a real person, but the messages are in fact generated by a computer program) or simply implanting data about

Table 3.2　Example of a Life Satisfaction Scale

How satisfied or dissatisfied are you with each of the following aspects of your life? (*Circle the response that best reflects your opinion.*)

	Very Dissatisfied	Somewhat Dissatisfied	Neutral	Somewhat Satisfied	Very Satisfied
a. Job	1	2	3	4	5
b. Family life	1	2	3	4	5
c. School	1	2	3	4	5
d. Neighborhood	1	2	3	4	5
e. Housing	1	2	3	4	5
f. Life in general	1	2	3	4	5

some human attributes or behaviors and allowing the computer to simulate interactions between virtual people.

The major advantage of experimental designs is their ability to determine causal relationships between independent and dependent variables. Many types of experiments include an **experimental group,** which is exposed to an independent variable before the dependent variable is measured, and a **control group,** which is not exposed to the independent variable. By comparing measures on the dependent variable between experimental and control groups, researchers can determine whether exposure to the independent variable in the experimental group caused changes in the dependent variable.

As a simple example of a study using experimental and control groups, suppose that a researcher is testing a theory that proposes that people perform better after receiving positive feedback. To test this theory, the researcher proceeds as follows:

1. All participants in the experiment are asked to complete some task.
2. The researcher gives positive feedback to participants in the experimental group but gives neutral feedback to those in the control group.
3. Next, the participants are asked to complete another task. If the experimental group performs better than the control group on the second task, the researcher would conclude that the independent variable (positive feedback) produced the differences in the dependent variable (performance on the second task).

How can we know that it was the positive feedback that led to the improved performance? Perhaps the participants in the experimental group were simply

Different Ways to Study People　　69

smarter or better suited to the second task than were participants in the control group. Researchers have two ways of dealing with this issue. First, social psychologists who carry out experiments sometimes use *pretest–posttest designs*. A **pretest** measures the dependent variable before participants are exposed to the independent variable. A **posttest** measures the dependent variable after exposure to the independent variable. Table 3.3 shows results from a study using a pretest–posttest design to measure changes in performance after participants in an experimental group received positive feedback and participants in a control group received neutral feedback. Because the performances of participants in the experimental group improved more than those of participants in the control group, we have some evidence that the independent variable produced changes in the dependent variable.

The most common way to reduce the likelihood that variables other than the independent variable are responsible for changes in the dependent variable is to use random assignment. **Random assignment** involves assigning participants to different levels of an independent variable on a random basis—for example, by tossing a coin. In experimental research, random assignment is the most important feature allowing investigators to determine causal relationships. In the preceding example, researchers would randomly assign each participant to either the experimental group or the control group. This procedure ensures that participants, on average, are equivalent in such areas as motivation and talent across the two groups. In other words, we should expect participants in the experimental group, on average, to have about the same talent with respect to the task as do participants in the control group. With random assignment, experimentalists can be confident that differences in exposure to the independent variable, and nothing else, is producing the changes found in the dependent variable.

Experiments are a powerful tool for determining causal relationships between independent and dependent variables (see Box 3.3). But their usefulness to social psychologists is limited by two factors. First, many phenomena of interest to social psychologists cannot be manipulated in laboratory settings. Suppose, for example, that a researcher is testing a theory about the health consequences of the death of a loved one. This theory would be impossible to test through an experiment because researchers would not be able to randomly assign some participants

Table 3.3	**Example of Pre- and Posttest Interpretation in an Experiment***		
	Pretest	Posttest	Change
Control Group	Score #1: 26	Score #2: 32	6 points
Experimental Group	Score #1: 28	Score #2: 40	12 points

* Note that both groups improved between the pre- and posttest. However, the experimental group's score went up more than the control group's, suggesting that the independent variable—positive feedback—produced an increase in scores.

Box 3.3   **Rats as Experimental Subjects**

Ⓞne of the most influential psychological social psychologists was B. F. Skinner. Skinner developed the field of operant conditioning in which learning is argued to occur by the association of a behavior with the implementation of rewards and punishments. Much of Skinner's work relied on experiments with rats and pigeons. He would "teach" these animals to perform complex behaviors, such as moving in circles, dancing, and playing games, by rewarding them for doing those activities correctly or punishing incorrect behaviors. He also developed the "Skinner box" in which animals learn to press levers to obtain rewards such as food pellets.

Some researchers question whether this type of research can be generalized to humans. Can studies of rats help explain why individuals are prejudiced against others? The complexities of human motives—and social experiences that influences our motives—make it difficult to understand how rats' behavior can explain anything but the very simplest of human thoughts, feelings, and behaviors. What do you think?

to experience the death of a loved one and other participants to not experience the death of a loved one. A survey that asked participants if they have experienced the death of a loved one recently and then measured various health outcomes would be better suited to this type of investigation.

A second limitation in carrying out experiments is that they are usually only appropriate when the researcher is interested in testing a developed theory of some social process. Experiments create conditions in which researchers can measure independent and dependent variables that represent the concepts in some established theory. Because experimentalists create the conditions that participants experience, theories must guide the variables they manipulate and measure. Experiments are not meant to draw direct conclusions about the nature of social reality. Instead, experiments provide evidence for or against theories, which then provide the link between the experiment's findings and natural social interactions.

Mixed-Method Approaches

The line between qualitative and quantitative approaches to studying people is not always clear. For example, we listed content analysis as a qualitative method, but some researchers may define it as quantitative because it often uses numbers to "count" represented items in texts. In addition, each methodological approach has its strengths and its shortcomings. For these reasons, a particularly effective way of studying social psychological phenomena is to bring multiple methods to bear on a research question. Suppose that a team of social psychologists is interested in workplace interaction. In particular, they are curious about the factors that affect the evaluations that people receive at work. The researchers could draw on multiple methods to explore this question.

The researchers might begin their investigation with a qualitative study aimed at exploring workplace interactions. For example, they might conduct an *ethnographic study* in which they observe people interacting in a work organization and record the behaviors they see. The researchers might identify consistent patterns of behavior that they view across different types of interactions.

Suppose the researchers observe that minorities in the organizations consistently receive lower evaluations for their performances than do Whites, even when the quality of their performances seems just as high. The researchers might begin to develop a theory, or draw on existing theories, about the reasons for this discrepancy and decide that they need more data.

As a next step, the researchers could conduct a *large-scale survey project*. They could send questionnaires to a sample of hundreds, or even thousands, of people, asking them about their work experiences. These surveys would include questions about people's personal characteristics, about the workplace structure (for example, the number of employees or the racial composition of the workplace), and about the evaluations they receive at work.

Suppose that the survey indicates that minorities report lower performance evaluations at work than do Whites. Now suppose further that the researchers identify other groups that receive lower evaluations—for example, women. Gender and race are both status markers in our society, so the researchers might develop a general theory that individuals with lower social status get lower evaluations than do others, even when they perform as well as or better than others.

The researchers could then carry out an experiment to test their theory that status influences the evaluations that people receive. For example, the researchers might ask experimental participants to read materials that they believe have been prepared by another person participating in the experiment. All participants would read the same materials, but participants in one group would be told that the person who prepared the materials was a minority, whereas those in another group would be told that the person who prepared the materials was a white. Thus, the race of the partner (i.e., the independent variable) is controlled across conditions. Participants would then evaluate the quality of the materials. If materials thought to be prepared by Whites generally received higher evaluations, then—because participants were randomly assigned to receive Whites or minorities as partners—the researchers would have evidence supporting their theory that status influences performance evaluations.

The researchers also might use mixed-method approaches within their various projects. A survey, for example, might include primarily close-ended (quantitative) questions but also some open-ended (qualitative) questions asking respondents to reflect on their work experiences. By drawing on both qualitative and quantitative approaches and on various types of methods, the researchers would be able to better identify the factors that influence work evaluations.

Section Summary

In this section of the chapter, we answered the following questions: How is qualitative sociology different from quantitative sociology? What are the major forms of qualitative research? What are the major forms of quantitative research? Qualitative and quantitative methods are different approaches to collecting information about people. Qualitative methods include any method of studying people that emphasizes in-depth, semistructured modes of observation or interviewing of subjects. This set of methods is contrasted with quantitative methods based on precise measurement of social psychological variables, typically in the form of surveys or experiments. Quantitative methods are particularly useful when trying to generalize findings to larger populations or test theories of social processes, whereas qualitative methods provide more depth of understanding about a topic, when studying an area of social psychology that has never been studied before, or dealing with difficult populations or topics.

Steps in Developing Research Projects

The biggest problem I have with students is that they don't even know how to begin to do research. I try to describe a research design, but they forget a lot of steps along the way. The texts are good for general outlines, but they don't give students specific pointers for going out and doing their research.

—Morten, Sociology instructor

There is no single set of "rules" appropriate for every type of social research project. The only guidelines that apply to most sociological inquiries are that the research should be driven by some theoretical orientation and that it should have some type of structure that allows other people to assess the quality of the data gathered. The opening vignette shows a sociology instructor trying to find a better way to get students to do their own research projects. However, because social psychology can include any aspect of human life, there are no simple methods for use in all types of research.

The following steps are designed as a general guideline for developing most projects in social psychology. The steps may vary, however, depending on your project or the theoretical perspectives from which you are drawing. The steps explain how a project might proceed when the researcher's goal is to test, rather than to develop, a set of predictions.

Step 1: Assess Theory and Literature

The first step in developing a research project is to examine the theoretical background and literature related to your research topic. If we want to understand causes of depression, we would look to the theories that have been developed on the topic and examine research that has tested those theories. Generally this takes the form of reading books and peer-reviewed research journals. Peer-reviewed journals are composed of research reports that have been reviewed by at least two or three trained professionals or "peers" before the research is allowed to be published. This method of review gives authors feedback on their research report, providing comments about the content and methods of a project, to ensure that it meets standards generally accepted in the field and that the work is of sufficient merit to warrant publication.

This stage of the research project can be laborious and time consuming. If you are studying the relationship between gender and mental health, you will encounter hundreds of citations from books and journals in many fields. Many modern libraries help you narrow your search, if you like, to a specific field such as sociology or psychology using databases called *Psychinfo* or *Sociological Abstracts*. They allow you to refine your search to include multiple **search terms,** words used to find articles on your topic. For instance, ideas related to mental health may also be found under the expressions mental illness, depression, anxiety, or alcoholism. You may also narrow the search for these terms to the article title and its **abstract,** a summary of the research article.

Theoretical and research articles and books provide a background to previous work in the field. They also provide a way to see how other people have studied your topic. You may find that many people study gender and mental health using quantitative methods or that they employ specific theoretical references. Using this information, you may decide to revisit your theory or method, to expand the work found in the literature review or simply to replicate one of those studies. Alternatively, you may decide to keep your approach but to adopt the measures of your variables employed by a particular article or set of articles.

Step 2: Develop Research Questions or Hypotheses

The next step is to develop specific hypotheses about your topic of study. If we want to study the relationship between gender and mental health, for instance, we may predict that women will report higher levels of distress based on the theory and literature on this topic. These hypotheses are important to the development of specific measurements of your independent and dependent variables. In this case, how would you measure gender? Would it simply divide men and women or would it include more complex measures that incorporate modes of sexuality? Similarly, mental health can be manifested in different ways such as depression and alcoholism. Men and women report varying levels of these disorders; hence your measurement may affect the outcomes of your study.

In most cases, the hypotheses of a project follow from the theoretical framework that the researcher is using. The stress process model to be discussed in chapter 8 focuses on how inequality in society affects well-being. Perhaps women "feel" inequality through lower income, poor living conditions, or sexual harassment, and you can measure these variables as well. In this case, you may predict that women will report more mental health problems than men. You may then predict that differences between men and women are a result of inequality. Your literature review should help to develop specific hypotheses.

Step 3: Choose Research Methods

Based on the theories, literature, and hypotheses, you must now choose the precise means with which you plan to test your hypotheses. At this stage, you must decide who you wish to sample, the size of the sample, and how you intend to procure that sample. In addition, you must decide on the kind of method you intend to use to assess your hypotheses. Your decision about the sample and data collection methods depends on your project. In our example, you could conduct in-depth interviews with women about workplace interactions, family processes, and feelings about themselves to determine stresses in those arenas. Alternatively, you could survey a class of students or try to get a random sample of students from your university and use quantitative measures developed in the earlier stages of the project.

The method you choose to employ in a project depends on the nature of the project and your theoretical orientation. An exploratory study means that very few people have investigated the topic; hence, you cannot rely on the work of other people for your theory or measures. As stated earlier in the text, if you are conducting exploratory research, you may want to begin with more qualitative analysis, to "explore" the nature of your variables and how they interact. The theory and research in that area are not complete, they require development and refinement. In our case, there are a number of studies linking gender and mental health that we can use to help develop our project, perhaps replicating others' studies or developing our own project using elements of several different projects.

Step 4: Conduct Data Analysis

After you have collected the data, you must analyze it to determine whether you have support for your hypotheses. If you used a quantitative survey, you can conduct statistical analyses using computer software programs such as Statistical Analysis Software (SAS) or the Statistical Package for the Social Sciences (SPSS), among others. These packages make it easier to compare differences between men and women on mental health outcomes. They can also perform higher-order analysis like regression, a technique that allows you to control for other variables that may affect mental health, such as income. As a result, you can look for "pure" effects of gender on mental health, controlling for other conditions and characteristics associated with the dependent variable. You can also use advanced analysis to see how much of the "gender" effect is related to inequalities in housing conditions or sexual harassment.

If you are conducting qualitative research, analysis will require some additional planning. For instance, you may decide to code the responses to in-depth interviews or try to summarize observational data. Software programs such as HyperRESEARCH and Ethnograph are popular tools for summarizing qualitative text data. You can also simply aggregate the responses to your questions, leaving them in word form but looking for patterns of responses. What are the forms of discrimination reported by your subjects? What are the ways they managed that discrimination? Once you have established a pattern, you can use quotes from your subjects as examples of such patterns.

Step 5: Report Results

Social scientists report their data in two main ways. Initial results are sometimes developed into reports to be presented at conferences. The Society for the Study of Symbolic Interaction (SSSI) is a popular sociological social psychology organization that holds an annual meeting to discuss new research in the field (http://sun.soci.niu.edu/~sssi/). The American Sociological Association (ASA) also holds an annual conference that includes some of the newest research in social psychology (http://www.asanet.org/). Conferences provide researchers feedback on newer projects to help them improve their research. In this case, you may also seek a conference that focuses on the topic of your research. In this case, we are examining mental health. A number of groups devote their research energies to such topics. A thorough search of the Internet will reveal a number of such groups.

Traditionally, authors use conferences to help prepare their research for later publication in peer-reviewed journals (see Box 3.4 for a review of the format of a journal article). Peer-reviewed means that several scholars review a paper without knowledge of the author's name or affiliation. Such reviews ensure that the research meets the standards of the field before it is revealed to the general public. Two of the more popular sociological social psychology journals include *Social Psychology Quarterly* and *Symbolic Interaction*. The study of gender and mental health may also be published in a more topical journal in the field, such as the *Journal of Health and Social Behavior*. Your literature review should help develop a sense of where to send your work for review.

Section Summary

Here we applied five steps in the research process to answer the question: How do social scientists begin to develop a research project? The steps include developing or reviewing appropriate theories and literature related to your research topic, developing hypotheses you plan to test based on that literature and theory, choosing research methods, conducting data analysis, and writing your report of findings. These steps can be applied to almost any social research project.

Bringing It All Together

Symbolic interactionism is not misled by the mythical belief that to be scientific it is necessary to shape one's study to fit a pre-established protocol of empirical inquiry. . . .

—Herbert Blumer (1969, p. 48), *Symbolic Interactionism: Perspective and Method*

There is no rule about whether a particular theory should or should not be examined with quantitative or qualitative methods to study people. In general, the research question should guide the selection of a methodological approach. How-

Box 3.4 **The Research Paper Format**

Every journal has a slightly different set of expectations for formatting a paper for publication. Most of them expect the article or paper to address the following issues:

Theory and Literature Review—The introductory section of a paper gives the reader a sense of the theoretical argument you are making and reviews other research using your dependent and/or independent variables. You must convince the reader that your project is unique from other projects or why it is valuable for you to replicate another research project.

Methods—The methods section discusses how you conducted your research. Specifically, how did you choose your sample (e.g., randomly or snowball)? How many people did you sample and why? You should state how you measured your dependent and independent variables. Finally, you must state how you analyzed your data.

Results—The results section is simply a review of findings. You may start with a simple description of your variables and how they relate to one another. For a quantitative study, you will then likely show how your independent variable(s) affects your dependent variable(s) in some way.

Discussion—The discussion section summarizes your findings from the results section, emphasizing your theory and hypotheses. Did you find support for your hypotheses? If not, why? You should also describe how your findings fit in context of the related literature reviewed earlier in the paper.

References—Your paper should make appropriate citations throughout the text and list those citations at the end of the paper, usually in a separate section. Every field has its own way of citing literature. This textbook, for instance, employs the sociological format for citing work.

Appendix—You will sometimes be asked to include copies of any research instruments (interview schedules or questionnaires) in a section at the end of the document.

---

ever, some perspectives lend themselves to certain techniques. House (1977) argued that the symbolic interactionist paradigm, for instance, focuses more on naturalistic observation than the other faces of social psychology. This idea is echoed by Herbert Blumer, a prominent symbolic interactionist, who questioned the applicability of traditional scientific methods to studying human behavior. He argued that exploration and inspection (refer back to Box 3.2) are the most rigorous ways to study social life. This belief is based on the assumption that social reality is constantly in a state of negotiation, making social life difficult to measure and predict in the same way as the physical sciences.

In reality, researchers often apply multiple methods to studying a particular phenomenon. For instance, a researcher may use qualitative methods to determine the dimensions of a concept, such as romantic love, and then use this knowledge to develop questions for a quantitative survey. It is important to note that some methods are more applicable to some areas of research than to other areas. For instance, quantitative methods may not be appropriate for the study of the modern illegal drug trade. Imagine trying to survey a group of drug dealers using random sampling techniques! How would you get such a sample? Even if you could get a good sample of drug dealers, do you think that many of them would be willing to fill out a questionnaire with questions about their illicit dealings? Probably not. As a result, researchers may be limited to in-depth interviews with available dealers and/or observations of the trade itself.

This chapter is designed to give you the basic tools necessary to initiate a research project as well as critique social science research. Be aware that most projects lack some of the ideals described in this chapter. Some projects may suffer from a poor sample, whereas other projects are limited by how variables are operationalized. You must review each project in its totality, using your knowledge of methods to guide your assessment of the validity of its findings.

Summary

1. Several concepts apply to almost any research project. Researchers regularly use terms like *theory, research questions* or *hypotheses,* and *variables* to describe ways of studying people.

2. Researchers employ qualitative and quantitative techniques to study human subjects. Qualitative research methods include field research and in-depth interviews. Quantitative methods include survey research and experiments.

3. The steps in completing most research projects include assessing the theory and literature on the research topic, developing research questions or specific hypotheses, choosing the appropriate research methods, conducting data analysis, and reporting your results.

4. Although there is no rule about whether a particular theory should or should not use quantitative or qualitative methods to study people, symbolic interactionists have traditionally relied more on qualitative methods. Many researchers try to employ multiple methods of studying a particular phenomenon.

Key Terms and Concepts

Abstract: The summary of a research article.

Categorical variables: Measures for which the possible responses have no particular order.

Content analysis: Any systematic review of documents or other media.

Control group: Participants of an experiment that are not exposed to the independent variable.

Convenience sample: A sample in which any available person is included in the study.

Dependent variable: The variable that is predicted to lead to a change as a result of the independent variable.

Ethnography: A form of field research that includes a descriptive analysis of a group or organization.

Experiment: A type of quantitative research procedure in which investigators control participants' exposure to an independent variable.

Experimental group: Participants of an experiment that are exposed to an independent variable.

Field research: A form of qualitative study in which researchers directly observe people's behavior.

Focus groups: Semistructured interviews with small groups of people.

Hypotheses: Specific statements about how variables will relate to one another in a research study.

Independent variable: The variable predicted to lead to a change in the dependent variable.

In-depth interviews: A qualitative research method employing an unstructured or semistructured series of questions.

Indices: A series of related questions.

Internal Review Boards (IRBs): Groups that ensure that the benefits of a research project outweigh any potential harm to research participants.

Interval variables: A type of variable in which the difference between any two adjacent values is the same.

Laboratory experiments: Those in which the experiences and behaviors of participants are monitored in a controlled laboratory setting.

Natural or field experiments: Those that take place in people's everyday environments.

Operationalize: Translating a concept into something that can be measured.

Ordinal variables: Variables for which response categories are ordered but the distances between adjacent categories are not necessarily equal.

Participant observation: A form of qualitative research in which a researcher becomes a member of the group being studied.

Population: The larger group of people about whom a researcher seeks to draw conclusions.

Posttest: A measure of the dependent variable after exposure to the independent variable in an experiment.

Pretest: A measure of the dependent variable before participants are exposed to the independent variable in an experiment.

Probability samples: Samples in which researchers choose participants systematically in an attempt to ensure that they are representative of the population.

Qualitative research methods: In-depth, semistructured modes of observation or interviewing of subjects.

Quantitative methods: Any research method that attempts to precisely measure people's thoughts, feelings, or behavior.

Random assignment: Assigning participants of an experiment to different levels of an independent variable on a random basis.

Random sample: A sample in which participants are randomly picked from a population.

Ratio variables: Interval variables that have a zero starting point.

Sample: A group of people drawn for use in a study.

Sampling frame: A list of all possible elements in the population.

Search terms: Words used to find articles on a topic during a literature review.

Secondary data analysis: The analysis of previously collected survey data.

Snowball sample: Samples in which informants provide contact information about other people who share some of the characteristics necessary for a study.

Social theories: Organized sets of propositions about how various elements of social life are related to one another.

Statistical significance: The probability that the results found in the sample reflect the true relationships within the population of interest.

Survey research: The use of questionnaires to measure independent and dependent variables.

Variables: Concepts that are put into a measurable form.

Discussion Questions

1. Which method or methods of inquiry do you find most useful in studying human behavior? How would you employ this method to study a specific social phenomenon?

2. What are the strengths and limitations of qualitative and quantitative methods? Can you think of a way to employ the best of both approaches to studying people? That is, how could you incorporate qualitative and quantitative methods in one study?

3. Why is the development of a literature review critical for a research project? What specific social psychological literature excites you and why?

PART 2

The Individual in Society

We are now entering into the study of the some of the core areas of social psychological research: Stratification, self and identity, and socialization. They are considered foundational because they are essential aspects of human organization and interaction, through which people develop a sense of who they are. These dynamics affect other aspects of social life. Stratification, for instance, across race and gender and social class lines help us to understand the mental health process more fully, an area of research that will be reviewed in the next section of the book.

Each chapter in this section divides research and theories under headings representing each of the three major perspectives in the field: symbolic interaction (SI), social structure and personality (SSP), and group processes (GP). Although there is a great deal of overlap across these fields, we find that these distinctions serve as a good heuristic device for analyzing many social psychological processes. As with previous chapters, we start each one with a series of questions. We end each chapter with a section that brings together the three perspectives, summarizing how each paradigm contributes to understanding the chapter topic. In the end, we believe that using multiple perspectives will help us develop a better understanding of social life.

The Social Psychology of Stratification

I really did not think much about my position in society until I got to this university. Once I looked around here and saw lots of kids from good high schools like mine, I realized that I would not be going here if my parents didn't have the money. I probably would have taken courses at our local community college while working full-time. It might have taken a very long time to finish a B.A., if I ever did. Now I have time to go to club meetings, do some internships, and learn about different fields of research. And I will probably finish in four years. I wouldn't say I am lucky, but may be just using what's been given to me.

—Daniel, freshman Undeclared

In the opening vignette, we see a student realize that his attending a four-year university was due, in part, to factors beyond his control. Although he may have obtained a good college education without his parents' help, he knows that the experience would have been quite different without it—he would have struggled and probably would have had to work harder. A key factor in getting Daniel where he is today is his social class status. His parents' high income and social resources gave him the opportunity to choose a more prestigious university, where he has more options and will receive a degree that carries more status. The fact that he does not need to struggle with financing his education means he has more time to focus on other pursuits, including studying. So he expects he can graduate on time with a degree he enjoys.

Daniel's vignette highlights the relationship between society and the individual, but it also shows the significance of social standing. **Social stratification** refers to ways in which individuals or groups are ranked in society, according them different amounts of power, status, and prestige. Important statuses include our social class, race or ethnicity, gender, age, and sexuality. In Daniel's case, his parents' (and his own) social class status served as a basis for him to have many "good" choices about which university to attend. Without having access to certain upper-middle class resources (e.g., money and educated parents who know the ropes about college applications and how to specifically prepare for college from a young age), he would have had fewer options. Daniel's choice is not available to everyone. And it leads to many positive consequences in his early adult life course that many working-class or poor high school students may not experience.

One of the major ways that sociological social psychology is different from its counterpart in psychology is its greater emphasis on the role of stratification in social psychological processes. There are several ways in which stratification affects our lives and relationships. As noted earlier, symbolic interactionists sometimes address how we create and maintain definitions of different classes of people. Social structure and personality scholars emphasize how structural conditions, often related to work, education or family settings, affect people. Those in the group processes perspective examine how stratification systems from the larger society become reproduced in groups. We will use each of these perspectives to examine how stratification processes occur in our day-to-day lives. We will address these perspectives with the following questions:

- How do people construct inequality in society?
- How does social structure contribute to the development of inequalities in people's experience?
- How does stratification develop in group interaction?
- How do inequalities from society-at-large get reproduced in groups?

SI   Constructing Inequalities

I really think that you have to be a woman to know what I am talking about. It is very subtle. You will be in class sometimes, or at a party, or meeting and it is almost like you are not even there. The guys don't try to discriminate, they just do it. I mean, they go on talking and making decisions without ever considering you. Sometimes they may ask your opinion—not often really—but then they don't act on it. It is as if they were being polite but they never intend to include your ideas in the decision. How am I ever going to make it in business?

—Clara, senior Business major

How does symbolic interactionism—a perspective focused on meaning—take account of and address social stratification and inequalities? The way in which these status-making processes operate can be very subtle. In the opening vignette, Clara is discussing ways in which the men she interacts with keep her from making major contributions to discussions. She does not fault them for being sexist but still feels that "something" is not right in their interaction. There is "something" that is keeping her from contributing fully to the group. Symbolic interactionists try to uncover the subtle and not so subtle ways that social hierarchies develop and are maintained in social settings. Although symbolic interactionists have sometimes been criticized for not emphasizing social stratification enough in meaning-making processes, some important research is being conducted using this perspective (Hollander and Howard 2000).

Basic Stratification Processes

Scholars who employ the interactionist perspective to study stratification focus on the processes of developing and maintaining differences within and between groups of people (Sauder 2005). There are three important ways interactionists speak to stratification processes and take account of inequalities. First, social structure shapes who we interact with, and "how" we interact with other people (Sauder 2005; Stryker 2002). In fact, this is an important way that social structure enters into daily life—by constraining the kinds of people with whom we come into contact. Shirley Brice Heath (1983), for instance, conducted an ethnography of two separate communities—White and Black working-class towns in the rural Piedmont Carolinas. She detailed the different ways the two groups used language and storytelling with young children. White working-class babies and toddlers were spoken to in factual ways, with questions directed to children but little in the way of manipulating language in ways that middle-class children do. Black working-class youngsters were not directly spoken to, but instead were interacted with in a challenging, conflict-oriented style. When they were toddlers, these children were challenged to come up with creative responses to adults' words, a skill that community members valued highly.

Heath (1983) proposed that the ways parents and other community members interacted with children were not random, but derived from historical circumstance; Whites from their experiences working in factories, where they had to conform to authority of supervisors; Blacks from days where they overcame obstacles related to slavery or sharecropping. In any case, when the working-class children entered the middle-class elementary schools in a nearby town, they had trouble interacting in the "right" ways with middle-class teachers. Middle-class children, both Black and White, achieved success, but working-class Black children were frustrated by time and space limitations imposed on them, and teachers said that these students could not answer questions in a direct manner. The White working-class kids had trouble with fiction and refused to contradict authority. Working-class children, although as intelligent as middle-class children, had styles of interaction that conflicted with those of middle-class institutions and teachers and failed more often than middle-class kids. Thus, the types of interactions that children experienced early on with significant others were stratified by social class and helped to perpetuate a system that sustained societal inequalities.

A second way that interactionists focus on stratification processes is through explicitly accounting for inequalities in the content of interactions. Symbolic interactionists have argued that interacting partners usually have different levels of power. Ferguson (1980) argued that people in lower-status positions—women, those with lower education levels, ethnic minorities, younger people, homosexuals, and so on—have to take the role of the other *more often* than their more powerful counterparts who hold more prestige and status. Why would this be? More powerful people do not need to understand their partners' thoughts and emotions in much detail, nor do they need to view their own behavior through the eyes of others. But lower-status interactants do. For example, does a secretary need to be concerned with how a boss sees her? Yes! She must anticipate her boss's moods and whims and prioritize tasks so she can quickly get to the things that she imagines the boss wants her to be doing. She sometimes must tolerate his boring stories or unreasonable requests (things he defines as reasonable, of course). Note that there is nothing inherent in a person that makes her unequal—it lies in the interaction between two people with two different statuses. Thus, the secretary is likely to be more powerful in interactions with her daughter. But with her boss, she must be sure he sees her as a "good worker" or potentially get fired.

Does a boss need to take the role of his secretary—that is, imagine what she is thinking and assess how she views him during interaction? Not as much. He can make decisions, act nasty or nice, and generally carry on with little concern about how she views him (a reflected appraisal, discussed more in chapter 5) and his behavior. Thus, those with more power do not have to be as concerned about the other's perceptions and views as they interact with others.

A third way that interactionists contribute to our understanding of social stratification and inequality is through showing how individuals with certain statuses have more power to define situations and to define themselves. Thus, meaning-making itself is stratified! Brent Staples (1995) wrote about being a tall and imposing, but very gentle, African-American graduate student at the prestigious University of Chicago. As he walked around at night in Hyde Park, where the university is located, he found that he was altering public spaces in unintentional and ominous ways. People, especially women, would cross the street and increase their pace. Those people defined the situation as threatening, and him as dangerous, though he was not. But for Staples, being *perceived* as a threat was hazardous in itself because of the embarrassment, dismay, and alienation that it created for him. Not to mention that fear—even when evoked falsely—sometimes leads to the use of weapons, especially in urban America, and Staples could have become the victim of an interaction gone bad by an armed pedestrian or even a police officer. In addition to learning to "smother the rage" that comes with being mistaken for a criminal so often, a step important for his own mental well-being, Staples "works" at staying "safe" in public spaces. He wears professional business attire even when he does not need to (whereas other groups are more free to dress as they want), gives people extra wide spaces, adopts a polite, deferential manner, particularly when dealing with police officers, and on dark city streets whistles melodies from Beethoven and Vivaldi in an attempt to be viewed as nonthreatening. Black men must often take extraordinary measures to present themselves as normal or safe, self-presentations that others can take for granted.

An important part of the stratification process, then, is that certain groups are not able to execute their own definitions of the situation as easily as others. Related to this, some cannot define themselves in as free, varied, or positive ways as easily as others. Milkie (1999) showed how adolescent girls had difficulty resisting the societal definitions of female beauty that showed artificially thin, perfect, and "whitened" images. Even though they often did not believe the images were realistic, these images still dampened girls' own evaluations of themselves (i.e., their self-esteem). This is because girls, especially Whites, believed that others—their interacting partners, like adolescent boys—would judge them based on these media standards. Even if this wasn't true, how we *think* others think of us is very powerful. Although males also have ideal societal images to contend with, there are often wider and more varied images of ideal males on television, in magazines, and on the Internet. An older, bald male can be considered attractive and "normal," whereas women are often not afforded the luxury of feeling good while being themselves. Milkie's study showed that although boys and girls both agreed that being good-looking was important to them, boys, on average, actually felt they were good-looking, whereas girls were more neutral about this—the narrow societal definitions probably made it harder for them to see themselves as positively.

In sum, symbolic interactionists' focus on meaning is an important part of understanding social stratification and inequalities, although interactionists need to attend to these processes more (Hollander and Howard 2000; Sauder 2005). Specifically, interactionist research tends to focus on the following stratification processes:

1. Social statuses shape who we interact with, often people from our own social class and racial backgrounds.

2. Social status affects how we interact with other people (e.g., those with lower status must "take the role of the other" more than those with higher status).

3. People with lower social statuses have less power to define situations and to define themselves than those with more power.

These processes are essential to advancing our understanding of social inequalities. Only through these processes do we see how inequalities are maintained in our everyday life.

It is also important to understand the subtle ways that people manage inequalities—people do not necessarily sit down and "take it" but actively work to secure their senses of self. Greta Paules (1991), for instance, showed how waitresses in a chain restaurant resisted management's attempts to label them as "servants" and worked informally to change their role in the group. They developed informal norms about relating to customers and management. Although management, technically, makes rules of conduct in service, waitresses used their job skills as leverage for negotiating what is expected of them by threatening to leave the job. The result is a constant struggle redefining the norms expected in the organization. These dynamics reflect the importance of agency in symbolic interactionism, that humans do not necessarily just "take it" when they are faced with inequality. In these ways, individuals "manage" or attempt to change inequalities in their day-to-day lives.

Doing Gender

West and Zimmerman (1987) argued that one of the foundational guidelines for social interaction is our gender. The authors distinguished between our biological sex and gender, the cultural definitions of masculinity and femininity usually associated with individuals' biological sex. **Doing gender** is a social process in which individuals act according to the social rules or norms associated with being a man or a woman in society. Gendered norms become associated with every aspect of a person's interactions with others. Unlike some other elements of our identity that are limited to certain social arenas (e.g., school or work), gender crosses many social boundaries. Thus, men are expected to act masculine in leisure settings, such as when they play team sports or even chess. They must "be men"—accountable to standards, which include being unemotional, cool or sturdy, and competitive, strong, or aggressive—in play, at work, and even at home.

Barrie Thorne (1993) showed how gender processes occur at very early ages and involve elaborate rituals. Her study of elementary school children demonstrates that boys and girls act in ways that separate themselves from the others. **Borderwork** refers to the creation of social and physical boundaries between boys and girls. Both groups perform a number of acts to help strengthen differentiation. For instance, a game of chase-and-kiss or the concern over "cooties" provides these groups a sense of difference. Differentiating genders provides individuals one of the most basic elements of their identities (boy versus girl).

Psychologist Madeline Heilman and her colleagues (2004) conducted a series of experiments to help elaborate gender processes in the work setting. Their research generally found that being disliked affects our work evaluations—people who are disliked generally receive lower evaluations than people who are liked. The researchers also found that women who achieve in work groups tend to be less liked than their male counterparts. Moreover, this attitude only occurs when women achieve success in traditionally male work arenas. This research is important to understanding the subtle ways in which we "do gender" in the work environment. It also shows that discrimination can occur on many levels (e.g., liking and evaluations) and in very specific contexts (i.e., male-dominated work arenas).

Race and Poverty

Several notable studies have applied the interactionist perspective to understanding the complexities of race and poverty on a day-to-day basis. We briefly discussed *Tally's Corner* in chapter 1. In that work, author Elliot Liebow (1967) observed a

Gender inequalities exist both in the position we have in society and in the ways we interact with other people.

group of poor African-American men living in Washington, D.C. during the 1960s. In more recent research, Elijah Anderson (1999) studied poor African Americans in Philadelphia. Many of the same attitudes from Liebow's research were present but the rules of life in modern inner cities include the influence of drugs and crime less prevalent in the older study. Inner-city life reflects both the drug economy as well as some traditional middle-class values, reflecting two sets of apparently divergent norms. Children are taught to act tough in the face of drugs and violence but also to accept societal expectations of being good children, which is supposed to lead to a better life in the future. Thus, children in the inner city are

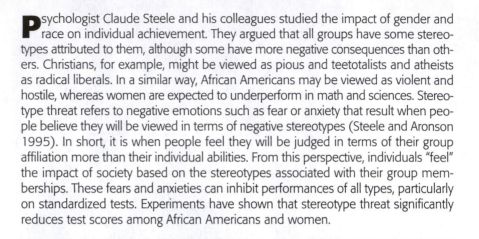

Box 4.1   Stereotype Threat

Psychologist Claude Steele and his colleagues studied the impact of gender and race on individual achievement. They argued that all groups have some stereotypes attributed to them, although some have more negative consequences than others. Christians, for example, might be viewed as pious and teetotalists and atheists as radical liberals. In a similar way, African Americans may be viewed as violent and hostile, whereas women are expected to underperform in math and sciences. Stereotype threat refers to negative emotions such as fear or anxiety that result when people believe they will be viewed in terms of negative stereotypes (Steele and Aronson 1995). In short, it is when people feel they will be judged in terms of their group affiliation more than their individual abilities. From this perspective, individuals "feel" the impact of society based on the stereotypes associated with their group memberships. These fears and anxieties can inhibit performances of all types, particularly on standardized tests. Experiments have shown that stereotype threat significantly reduces test scores among African Americans and women.

caught between norms to protect them in their current conditions and those norms that are designed to provide a better future. Anderson showed that traditional norms are present in the inner city, but additional norms are necessary to help individuals survive in their harsh social environments.

Anderson also argued that these two sets of norms are not necessarily exclusive. The life of drugs and violence relates to the desire to achieve success in the world, much like middle-class families in the suburbs. Many inner-city residents are left to choose between traditional norms of getting an education and finding work or the drug culture. However, traditional norms are less likely to produce financial success in the inner-city environment, whereas the latter set of norms uses alternative means to achieve traditional goals.

Understanding life in the inner cities may help to elaborate day-to-day processes that recreate poverty. Although structural conditions may influence lives directly, there are multiple ways that people manage these challenges. In many cases, as Anderson pointed out, people adopt traditional norms, hoping that choice will help them out of their poverty. In other cases, they adopt new norms, trying to end their poverty by other means.

Section Summary

The first section of this chapter applies symbolic interactionist principles to answer the question: How do people construct their lives in a stratified society? Here we examined interactionist research on how individuals construct differences between people based on their positions in society, especially related to social class gender, and race. Patterned inequalities shape who we interact with and what choices we have.

I never really planned to go to college. I mean, I had a 1.76 average coming out of high school and spent more time partying than studying. But I was with my buddy when he went to get into a law enforcement program at the local community college. He just filled out a form, some guy took it into another office, came out and said to my friend, "Congratulations! You have been accepted into college . . ." Now, my friend only had about a 2.0 grade-point average, so I thought, "Maybe I can do this thing too." The next thing I know, I filled out the form and got accepted to college. Two years later, I improved my GPA to about a 3.0 and got into a four-year school. The rest is history.

—Paul, senior Law-Enforcement major

The symbolic interaction perspective on stratification and inequalities represents one approach to social stratification processes in social psychology. A more structural perspective takes hierarchy as a "given" and "seeks to understand the processes by which individuals become distributed in that hierarchy" (Kerchoff 1995: 476). In industrialized nations, our status derives from our social class position, among other things. **Social class** refers to a group of people who share the same relative status in a given society. Class position is not distributed evenly because some ethnic and racial groups, especially African Americans and Latinos, are disproportionately living in poverty (see Figure 4.1).

Stratification processes in society can be complex to study at the individual level. In Paul's example, he had no intention of going to college. In fact, his only reason for going to college was his relationship to a friend who had some intention of going on to college after high school. Both of these men were not the greatest

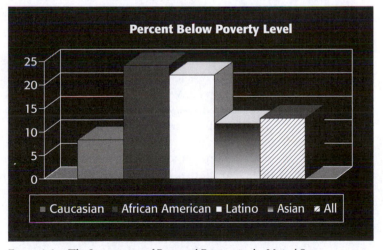

Figure 4.1   The Intersection of Race and Poverty in the United States

Source: 2003 and 2004 Current Population Survey

students, probably sharing similar backgrounds and lifestyles. But Paul's friend knew enough to enter community college as a means of maintaining or developing his life chances. That is, his friend believed that college was a means of keeping his class position or improving it. Paul's decision results from his relationship with his friend; Paul goes on to college, thus improving his chances of doing well in the world. In short, his friend's knowledge helped change the life course he had originally set (or not set) for himself.

The effects of relationships on our life trajectories are enormous. Our relationships with family members provide information about available careers and lifestyles, as do our friends. These relationships also provide tangible resources, such as money to pay for education. They also provide less tangible resources, such as knowledge about different career choices as well as connections with people who may be able to provide that knowledge, perhaps even access to specific jobs. The expression, "It's not what you know, but who you know" applies here. A structuralist perspective on mobility processes tries to explain how inequality is passed from generation to generation and how it is maintained within the same generation. Ultimately, we interact with people who share similar class positions during youth, usually leading to similar economic statuses as adults.

The Wisconsin Model and Education

Social mobility refers to upward or downward change in social class over time. Most research in social mobility examines the relative income and prestige associated with different occupations. People in more prestigious jobs tend to make more money. Because many people are motivated to obtain these prestigious positions (for the money or the prestige) a reasonable question is: Why do some people achieve these positions while others do not? Sociologists look to family status and experience as primary sources of status development and maintenance. That is, our parents represent the primary means of status development. In fact, research in the 1960s showed a considerable overlap in fathers' and sons' occupations (Blau and Duncan 1967).

The Wisconsin Model of Status Attainment (see Figure 4.2) is based on a study that began in 1957 among a group of researchers from the University of Wisconsin, primarily led by Dr. William Sewell (Sewell, Hauser, Springer, and Hauser 2004). They conducted a survey of all high-school seniors in Wisconsin to assess students' educational plans and their future aspirations. A third of these students were selected to participate in a follow-up study. In addition, parents of students were surveyed on a range of topics including youth aspirations, social influences, and schooling, among other things. Sewell and his colleagues were also able to obtain cognitive test scores for a significant portion of the respondents. Hence, the researchers were able to assess the relative effects of social experiences and cognitive abilities on long-term life goals. Additional surveys and other forms of data were compiled through the 1990s and beyond.

The Wisconsin Model ties together the relative impact of social background characteristics and ability on long-term status attainment. The model shows that

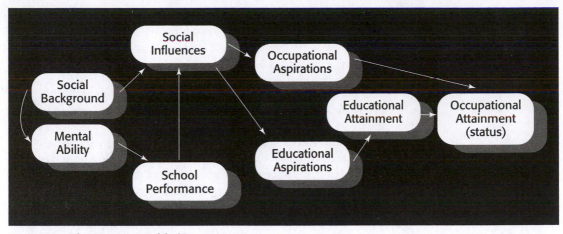

Figure 4.2   The Wisconsin Model of Status Attainment

Source: Adapted from Sewell and colleagues (2004)

our parents' social class background influences our expectations and aspirations about the future—both our educational and occupational goals—as well as affecting our performance in school. Our class background can be understood as having a snowball effect. Children who do better in school are tracked into groups of achievers who are encouraged to develop their educational skills. Hence, early resources develop better school performance, leading to more support. In the end, students develop different levels and types of educational aspirations. The effects of educational goals and attainment cannot be understated because education and occupational attainment are highly correlated.

The Wisconsin Model of Status Attainment displayed in Figure 4.2 may appear quite complex, but think about all the things you must consider when you are developing goals and plans for life. You must decide what you want to do in your life in context of what you think you are able to do. Friends and family are primary sources of information about our abilities. If you believe that you are not good at math, this limits the number of prestigious and well-paying occupations available to you, such as engineering and accounting. Shelley Correll (2004), for instance, found that at similar math ability levels, boys overestimated their capabilities and girls underestimated their abilities when exposed to a belief that men are better at this task.

Recent research using the Wisconsin model has focused on the role of cognitive ability in this process (Warren, Hauser, and Sheridan 2002). Researchers found that the effects of family social class on long-term status operates almost entirely through education and cognitive ability: Occupational attainment is a result of educational attainment and cognitive ability. However, the impact of education on occupational attainment attenuates over time, meaning that education is most important at younger ages. The effects of cognitive ability remain relatively steady over someone's life. Hence, education seems to be an important starting point of status attainment, but it diminishes in strength over time. However, cognitive ability continues to affect status attainment throughout our lives.

Networks and Social Capital

Stratification processes begin with families' economic background, but they also exist in our relationships with other people. Friends, family, and organizations of which we are a part provide access to a wide variety of social networks. Our friends link us to their friends and to organizations and groups with which they associate. Social networks act as a conduit between different people, providing resources and information that may not be readily available from the people with whom we have direct contact. Organizations provide a bridge between strangers, a way of giving someone a sense that the other can be trusted in some way.

We often think of collateral in economic terms. However, collateral can exist in relationships. We trust people because we know them well enough to share important things with them, perhaps even money. Social networks (see chapter 2) serve as the basis for the exchange of both fiscal and **social capital,** the trust and social support found in relationships with other people (Coleman 1988; Putnam 2000). The number and types of people we have access to determine the availability of social capital. Not only do we turn to people for emotional support, something that will be discussed in more detail in chapter 8, but we also turn to others for advice and help in pursuing our goals. Our networks determine the amount and types of social capital available to us.

The effects of networking between individuals from different groups create a variety of outcomes for individuals, depending on the status of the individuals in a group as well as the status of the group itself. A group of neighbors at a local pub likely have less clout in the larger world than a group of senior business executives. Hence, having access to the relationships in the latter group will likely provide different resources, including things such as money, useful knowledge about how to find good jobs, investments, and access to better medical and mental health services.

The Strength of Weak Ties

A typical way that relationships are important to us is found in research assessing how people find work. A Harvard accounting student probably has access to people with more powerful positions than a student at a community college. The job outcomes of these students are going to be related to the information available within their respective networks. The Harvard network is likely to provide information about and access to higher-level accounting jobs than the community-college network. Hence, our social class position is intimately tied to social networks, affecting our ability to succeed in society.

Two ways we are connected to other people are by strong and weak ties. **Strong ties** refer to people with whom we are close, such as friends and family. **Weak ties** refer to people we do not know as well, such as acquaintances or more distant friends. We can further contrast both of these types of ties with more formal relationships in which people are connected via structured positions in organizations.

Granovetter (1973), in the original theoretical discussion of weak ties, said that "those to whom we are weakly tied are more likely to move in circles different from our own and will thus have access to information different from that which we receive" (1371). Thus, for job seekers, the quantity of ties is argued to be more important to finding work than the quality of those ties. His research supported the contention that weak ties are more important than strong ties for finding work. He reports that of people who find work through contacts, 84% reported seeing those contacts rarely or occasionally; the rest reported seeing their contacts often.

Granovetter's (1995) more recent work combines ideas about both strong and weak ties in assessing job-searching strategies. He found that 56% of the professional, technical, and managerial workers experiencing job transitions in New England reported finding work via **personal ties** (both strong and weak), followed by another 19% who found jobs through formal means (e.g., ads or employment agencies), 19% through direct application, and the rest via miscellaneous other methods. Personal ties not only produce jobs but are also associated with finding better jobs: workers who found jobs via networks (personal ties) were more satisfied with their work and reported higher incomes than those who found work through other means.

Gender, Race, and Stratification Processes

The research on status attainment discussed earlier in this section varies significantly for men and women. Although the impact of education and ability is similar for men and women, women tend to start their careers in occupations that pay significantly less than men (Warren, Hauser, and Sheridan 2002). Similar patterns exist for minority group members in the United States (see Table 4.1).

Men and Whites are more likely to be in managerial and professional positions than are women or minorities. They are also more likely to be in skilled blue-collar jobs. Conversely, men and Whites are less likely to be in clerical or less-skilled blue-collar jobs than women and minorities. These status differences can have a lasting effect on access to networks to find similar work. If you are in a clerical position seeking a more skilled job, like an accountant, you will not likely have the social capital necessary to obtain such positions because you do not have access to the types of people who can give you the resources to help you find that kind of work. Accountants at a particular firm, for instance, may be able to inform you of an opening or help you submit a more marketable application. This situation assumes that you have friends who are accountants or have access to an accountant through a contact. Getting contacts from friends and family is often referred to as "networking."

Education, Occupations, and Aspirations

We defined values in chapter 1 as deeply held ideals and beliefs. Values serve as a guide for making decisions about the future. Melvin Kohn and Carmi Schooler (1983) carried out a research project to study the long-term consequences of our social class position on values. The researchers wanted to know how our class

Table 4.1	Occupations by Sex, Race, and Ethnicity						
	Married Men	Married Women	White	Black	Hispanic	Other	Total
Managers, doctors, and lawyers	11.5%	5.7%	8.8%	3.9%	4.2%	7.2%	7.8%
Other professionals	15.1	15.2	15.7	10.5	7.4	16.1	14.5
Clerical and sales	4.9	16.7	10.7	14.5	10.4	11.6	11.1
Skilled blue-collar and supervisors	25.8	9.3	16.6	12.2	15.4	17.4	16.1
Less-skilled blue-collar and service	16.6	11.0	11.6	23.3	25.6	16.1	14.2
Farmers and farm laborers	1.7	.4	1.0	.1	1.7	.5	.9
Unemployed	2.4	2.1	2.0	4.8	4.0	3.3	2.5
Not in labor force	21.9	39.3	33.6	30.7	31.2	28.0	32.9
Total	100.0	100.0	100.0	100.0	100.0	100.0	100.0

Source: Adapted from Rose (2000).

position interacts with our cognitive abilities in maintaining our class positions in the form of our "ultimate" occupation. They argued that there is an ongoing **feedback loop** in which our class position influences the development of values that, in turn, influences the type of job we look for (Schooler, Mulato, and Oates 2004). The type of job we get then influences the type of people we are—our personality. We then continue to seek jobs over our life course that match the kind of values we have.

Consider a situation in which a person is working at a factory every day, putting furniture hardware into bags, counting the pieces before sealing the bag. She is required to seal a certain number of bags with some accuracy for at least eight hours a day. The job is repetitive and requires very little creativity or cognitive ability. This type of job does not provide the skills necessary to find more complex work. She will not easily be able to use the job on a resume designed to find work in the marketing industry, for instance. Kohn and Schooler (1983) argued that the type of jobs we get also influences the development of our values; repetitive work leads people to believe that there is something good about conformity. In short, if you are working in a repetitive job, you come to believe that there is something good in that job in the first place.

Kohn and Schooler's project started in 1964 with a survey of 3,101 men from around the United States. The men were all at least 16 years old, the age of legal employment in the United States. The study also focused only on those men who were employed at the time of the survey. Another survey of these men was conducted in 1974 with a sample of the original men, producing 687 respondents for the second wave of interviews. Wives of the initial respondents were also interviewed, producing an additional 269 respondents. Finally, between 1994 and 1995, the researchers interviewed as many of the men and women from the 1974 sample as possible, focusing on those people who were still employed. The final sample included 166 men and 78 women (244) (Schooler et al. 2004).

The initial study of occupational attitudes and values focused on three elements of a job predicted to influence the development of personal values. Kohn and Schooler (1983) showed that the following aspects of our jobs can have long-term effects on the development of our values:

1. The closeness of the supervision
2. The routinization of the work
3. Substantive complexity of the work

Closeness of supervision refers to the level of control supervisors have over workers. It is measured simply by asking respondents how much freedom they have to disagree with their boss, their supervisor's style of assigning tasks, and the importance of doing what they are told. **Routinization** of work refers to the level of repetitiveness found on the job, generally measured in terms of workers' ratings of how predictable their work tasks are. Finally, **substantive complexity** refers to how complicated the actual work is. Complexity is measured in terms of how often people work with people or data/information as well as the complexity of work required when working with people or data.

Kohn and his colleagues wanted to know how these work conditions influenced individuals' personalities and vice versa. They studied personality in terms of **intellectual flexibility,** how flexible people are in handling complex situations, and **self-directed orientation,** measured in terms of individuals' level of conservatism, fatalism (the belief that life is controlled by fate), and personally responsible morality, how much we hold ourselves accountable for the things we do. The researchers examined these personality characteristics in the context of socioeconomic characteristics including sex, race, and education levels.

Take a moment to think about the long-term effects of valuing obedience to authority and routinization. What kinds of jobs are characterized by routinization? They are not likely to be management jobs that are based on *making* decisions rather than following orders. Supervisors at a fast-food restaurant, for example, must be ready to be flexible on the job as they manage disputes among and between employees and customers. Routinized jobs are those that require consistent service or manufacturing products where each step is calculated in advance. These jobs are often some of the lowest-paying jobs. Hence, our personality (i.e., flexibility and self-directedness) may lead us to jobs with lower status; if we value obedience, we are more likely to prefer lower-status jobs. Alternatively, if we engage in this kind of work, we may develop personality characteristics that suit these conditions.

The relationships between socioeconomic background and long-term occupational and personality outcomes are illustrated in Figure 4.3. The research assessed three interrelated issues:

1. How social-structurally determined environmental factors affect important psychological characteristics such as intellectual functioning and self-directedness of orientations.

2. How changes in such psychological characteristics reciprocally affect individuals' positions in the social structure of their societies.

3. How psychological changes may affect the very nature of societies' social structures and cultures (Schooler et al. 2004: 189).

Schooler and his colleagues (2004) found that our social and economic backgrounds determine the types of jobs we get early on in our lives. People with fewer resources early in life tend to find jobs with low levels of substantive complexity and high levels of supervision. These jobs, in turn, affect our personalities in ways that conform to the types of jobs we are in. People in low-end jobs tend to develop

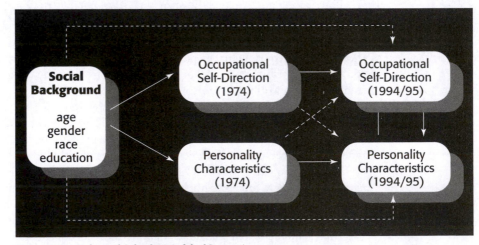

Figure 4.3   Kohn and Schooler Model of Status Attainment

Source: Adapted from Schooler and colleagues (2004).

personalities with lower amounts of intellectual flexibility and have a less self-directed orientation. In turn, people with lower levels of flexibility and self-direction go on to other jobs with less complexity and more supervision. The researchers also found that this feedback loop continues into late in our lives.

The implications of the Kohn–Schooler studies are enormous. Their research shows that society can structure our development in a way that maintains our class position. In other research, for instance, Schooler (1976) used survey data of European immigrants to America, assessing personality characteristics and occupational outcomes. He found that men from ethnic groups with a history of serfdom showed personality characteristics associated with the working class in America: intellectual inflexibility, authoritarianism, and pragmatic legalistic morality. Hence, the system of serfdom prevalent in Europe was transferred to America through immigration. This work also implies that economic conditions can affect the development of individuals, above and beyond abilities, and that the effects of class may exist in different cultural environments.

Section Summary

This section of the chapter addressed the question: How does social structure contribute to the development of inequalities in people's experience? Here we reviewed two models connecting our class background with future life goals and outcomes. The Wisconsin, Kohn and Schooler models of status attainment examine the direct and interactive ways that our position in society in youth affect long-term educational and occupational aspirations and outcomes. We also examined the importance of networks in our lives, ultimately leading to specific employment opportunities.

GP | Stratification Processes in Groups

I really don't mind being one of the only people in my class to raise my hand and talk. I know that other students may think that I am a "suck up" but I don't care. I am here to learn and class goes by really slowly if you do not say anything. But even though they might mock me, other students always turn to me for notes and help in the class. I guess you could say that I am a class leader of sorts.

—Sandy, freshman Business major

Sandy's story is typical for many college classrooms. She participates in class by asking questions and engaging in discussions. The results are both positive and negative. Her participation increases her enjoyment of and learning in the class. However, it may also cause some friction with students who participate less. In the end, she believes that she is seen as a leader because of what she is able to contribute to the rest of class.

According to symbolic-interactionists, social structure is manifested in relationships between people. Individuals in groups clearly share thoughts and feelings with one another during their interactions. However, group members do not necessarily enter the group with equal access to the rest of the members. Some people bring more to the table—or the classroom—than others.

The group processes tradition contributes to our understanding of structural developments by studying the exchanges between individuals in groups (Smith-Lovin and Molm 2000). Social exchange theory is based in the group processes perspective. It provides a template for understanding individual motivations to participate in and contribute to group interactions, whereas status characteristics theory shows how social expectations can influence those dynamics. First we will review some basic theory and research on group processes, followed by a review of theories of status processes in groups.

Status and Power in Social Exchange Processes

Social exchange theory is based on the premise that individuals enter into relationships that provide some benefit to them and end or leave relationships that do not provide some sort of reward. Molm and Cook (1995) argued that exchange theory has four core assumptions:

1. Exchange relationships develop within groups in which members have some degree of dependence among them.

2. Group members will act in groups in a way that maximizes personal benefit.

3. Interaction in groups will continue as long as reciprocity between individuals continues.

4. Groups operate on the satiation principle, that the value of what is exchanged will diminish after a period of exchange.

If you think about some groups to which you belong, this theory probably makes some sense. Essentially, it argues that we enter and maintain relationships that give us something. We exchange our labor for money, for example. Many of our relationships fit this simple kind of exchange found in secondary groups, people with whom we share less-intimate relationships than with close friends or family.

Applying exchange theory to primary groups, those people with whom we have an emotional connection, is more challenging. What do you exchange with friends and family? Although people exchange tangible objects such as money or goods, they can also exchange things such as emotional and instrumental support (Liebler and Sandefur 2002; Shornack 1986). You help your friend or neighbor paint her house, assuming that she will help you with some other project in the future. You may also engage in a relationship with someone because that person "makes you feel good." These thoughts and feelings may not be tangible, but they provide some basis for staying in the relationship. You may end your relationship with a friend if she continually refuses to help you when you need it. Similarly, you will likely end your relationship with your friend if your feelings of interest, warmth, and intimacy toward her begin to fade.

Box 4.2   **Homans' Experience on a Small Warship**

George Homans (1910–1989) was one of the first sociologists to extensively develop and test exchange theory. During World War II, Homans captained small ships designed to destroy enemy submarines. Homans applied his sociological knowledge to understand social relations on ships in the article, "The Small Warship." He argued that his influence as captain depended in part on reciprocity, a series of exchanges with the crew. Although the captain had legitimate authority on the ship, he could not maintain that authority if he did not give something back to his men. There needed to be some form of reciprocity between and within ranks. In exchange for their support, he had to show his men that he cared for them by listening to them without interruption, helping them receive citations and promotions, and protecting them from unnecessary irritations, "even if it meant protecting them from the Navy itself" (Homans 1946: 297). Hence, the ship served as a microcosm of the larger society in which a series of informal reciprocal exchanges served to maintain roles inside the ship.

Most of our discussion has focused on **direct exchanges,** exchanges between two people. But exchanges can occur with multiple people, as well as between groups (see Box 4.2). **Indirect** or **generalized exchanges** occur when people do not receive benefits directly from those to whom they give benefits (Emerson 1992; Molm and Cook 1995) (see Figure 4.4). Indirect exchanges may explain situations in which people enter relationships that are not directly rewarding to them. Suppose, for example, that you are driving on a highway and see a disabled car on the side of the road. Further suppose that you stop to help the person who has broken down. You might enter the situation as one of direct exchange—in other words, you help the person in expectation of some reward, perhaps gratitude. However, you more likely view the situation (although perhaps not consciously) as one of generalized exchange. According to exchange theory, you might stop to help someone whose car has broken down because you hope that someone else would do the same thing for you. Similarly, exchanges in families may include a series of direct and indirect exchanges of love, help, and fiscal exchanges with extended family over time (Peterson 1993).

Status in Groups

Early work in social exchange theory focused on the direct exchanges between individuals and groups but generally did not account for social structure. Later work by Peter

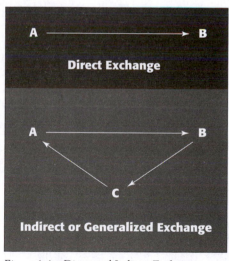

Figure 4.4 Direct and Indirect Exchanges

Blau (1964) and other sociologists began to examine exchange processes in the context of larger structural conditions. The development of status in groups provides a venue for understanding how macrostructural conditions can influence micro-level interactions. Exchange processes lend themselves to the development of status structures simply because people bring different types and quantities of resources into the process. In addition, some individuals contribute more to interactions than others. People who are expected to contribute more to a group or have more resources achieve higher status in groups. In a classic series of group studies, Robert Bales and his colleagues (Bales 1965; Borgatta and Bales 1953; Borgatta, Bales, and Couch 1954) analyzed interactions between groups of strangers brought together to perform a task. They found that leadership status was attributed to those individuals perceived to contribute the most to group discussions. This finding makes sense in light of exchange theory: Those perceived as contributing most to the group good were given leadership status.

The development of status in groups may simply reflect what people bring into a group. A gifted leader may take control because she has more ability than other people. Because gifted leaders give more to the group, we concede higher positions to them. However, individuals' social positions (from the larger society) can influence these exchange and status-building processes, suggesting that larger structural forces influence micro-level interactions. Status characteristics theory accounts for our larger social position in exchange processes.

Status Characteristics Theory

Status characteristics theory links social roles and expectations from a larger society to stratification processes in groups. The theory was developed by Joseph Berger and a group of colleagues at Stanford University (e.g., Berger, Cohen, and Zelditch 1966, 1972; Berger, Webster, Ridgeway, and Rosenholtz 1993; Fisek, Berger, and Norman 2005) and is perhaps the most widely studied and well-supported theory in the group processes tradition. Status characteristics theory is concerned with stratification processes in certain types of groups—groups collectively oriented toward some task outcome. If a group is formed to complete some task and the members of the group work together toward the task's completion, then status characteristics theory makes predictions about how members of the group will become stratified. Groups in all sorts of settings meet these basic conditions. A jury is one example of a collectively oriented task group: Members come together to solve a task (i.e., reach a verdict or other decision), and everyone contributes to completing the task. Another example could be a committee of citizens from a community getting together to decide how to deal with a civic problem. A collectively oriented task group could also be a group in an organization formed to decide who to hire for a particular job. For all groups that meet the theory's basic conditions (that the group is working together toward a goal and that everyone in the group is expected to contribute), status characteristics theory has proven to be remarkably capable of explaining the methods that group members will use to stratify themselves.

A common finding in research on task groups is that these groups tend to organize themselves into hierarchies (Berger, Wagner, and Zelditch 1985). Some people in the groups talk more, get more positive feedback for their performances, and have more influence over the group than do other members. This has been a consistent research finding dating back to the 1950s. Even when it does not appear as though some group members are more competent than others, hierarchies form when groups complete a task. Researchers call these **status hierarchies.** In the group processes perspective, status refers to a position in a group based on the esteem or respect in which a person is held. People higher in the status hierarchy of the group talk more, get asked for their opinions more often, have their contributions evaluated more highly even when the contributions are no better than those of other group members, and have more influence over group decisions.

One interesting thing about status hierarchies is that group members generally agree (through their behaviors if not through spoken agreement) about the status order of the group (Wagner and Berger 1993). From this discussion, it is clear that high-status group members get benefits that low-status group members do not. However, status hierarchies in groups usually form almost instantaneously; it is not as though members openly compete for positions in the hierarchy. How do group members decide who gets to be high status in the group and who is low status? Why do group members, even those in low-status positions, tend to go along with the inequalities that come from the status hierarchy? Status characteristics theory provides answers to these questions.

According to status characteristics theory, cultural expectations are associated with characteristics that people bring with them to group interactions. The theory specifies two types of status characteristics. **Diffuse status characteristics** are characteristics that carry with them social expectations for performances in diverse situations. Gender, race, and education level are examples of diffuse status characteristics. Western culture expects men, for example, to be better than women at a number of tasks, from leading groups to fixing cars to solving complex problems. It doesn't matter that there is no evidence that men are better at these tasks than women (evidence, in fact, overwhelmingly indicates that there are very few tasks at which we should expect either men or women to be inherently better)—we operate in a cultural context that gives higher status to men than to women. A similar process operates for race. The contributions of Whites in the United States, even when they are no better than those of members of other racial and ethnic groups, are more highly valued than those of others (Lovaglia, Lucas, Houser, Thye, and Markovsky, 1998; Webster and Driskell 1978).

Specific status characteristics are characteristics that create expectations for performance in limited settings. Skill at basketball is an example of a specific status characteristic. If we know that someone is an excellent basketball player, we would likely draw few conclusions about her ability to lead groups, fix cars, or solve complex problems.

According to status characteristics theory, and supported by voluminous research, status hierarchies in task groups form based on the status characteristics of the members of the group (Carli 1991; Lucas 2003; Pugh and Warhmer 1983;

Sociological social psychologists study the ways that social statuses such as race and class intersect with group processes to produce differing levels of power and prestige among members.

Ridgeway and Diekema 1989; Webster and Driskell 1978). The theory proposes that when groups form, members look to the status characteristics of themselves and other group members to develop expectations for performance. The expectations they develop are consistent with those of the larger society. This finding explains why there is little conflict about status orders in task groups: Because everyone in the group operates within the same larger society, everyone brings with them the same cultural expectations to the group. So, for example, if an engineer and a janitor are working together in a group to solve some task, both members would share the expectations that give engineers higher status than janitors. Thus, both members would agree that the engineer should have a higher position in the group's status order than should the janitor.

You might be recalling task groups you have worked in and thinking, "Wait a second. I have never talked with people in a group about who should have the highest position in the group's status hierarchy. And, I have never thought, 'That person should be high status because he is a White man.'" It is true that people usually don't come to verbal agreements about the status orders of groups. It is also true that people don't consciously give higher status or accept lower status based on things like race, gender, education, and occupation (Webster and Foschi 1988). These processes occur in large part outside the conscious awareness of people.

That fact makes these status hierarchies even more stable and difficult to change. If you ask people in a group why the White man in the group talked more than anyone else and had the most influence, the answer you get will usually not be "because he is a White man." Instead, group members will say it was because he seemed the most competent person for the task. But, research shows that cultural expectations significantly affect our decisions about who seems the most competent, with people who possess certain, more highly valued status characteristics seeming more competent, even when they are not (Berger, Rosenholtz, and Zelditch 1980).

You also might recall groups you have been in that did not follow these conventions. For example, you may have been in a group in which a woman was the most active member of the group. There are three things that you should keep in mind. First, remember that the theory applies to particular types of groups—groups formed to complete a task with everyone in the group contributing to the task outcome. Social groups can often form without developing the types of status hierarchies that are found when groups are working to complete a task.

Second, we noted that status hierarchies in task groups, once they form, are resistant to change. They can, however, change over time. If a woman or minority group member is the most competent person in a task group, that person very well may become the highest-status person in the group. However, the person will likely have to work harder than majority group members to attain a high-status position. In the case of gender, a great deal of evidence indicates that women are held to higher performance standards than are men. Research in double-standards theory (e.g., Foschi 1996, 2000) has found that people evaluate contributions from women and men differently, with women having to perform better to get the same evaluations as men. Thus, members of disadvantaged groups have to work harder and perform better to get the same status in groups as members of advantaged groups.

Third, we form impressions of other people based on multiple characteristics. So, if a woman is higher status than a man on characteristics other than gender (e.g., age, race, education, task expertise), we would expect her to have a higher position than him in the group's status hierarchy. In general, status-characteristics theory proposes that we act as though (remember, these processes often happen outside people's conscious awareness) we combine the expectations associated with all of a group member's characteristics. You can think of it as group members developing overall expectation scores for themselves and others. Because all group members draw their expectations from the same larger culture, the theory expects everyone in the group to produce the same overall expectation score for each member. Members with higher overall expectation scores will then have higher positions in the group's status hierarchy. We would expect these members to talk more in the group, be evaluated more highly, and have more influence in the group.

This theory might seem to you to present an unrealistic picture of interaction in groups. Do people really consistently develop expectations about people based on things such as their race and gender? There is no doubt that we do. Status characteristics theory has been supported by hundreds of studies over the past 30 years, studies showing that status hierarchies form in task groups based on the characteristics of group members. The theory, for example, can predict with a great deal of accuracy who jurors will select as their foreperson.

How to Get Status in Groups

The processes laid out by status characteristics theory, and overwhelmingly supported by research on the theory, probably seem to you to be less than fair. Some people get higher evaluations and have more influence in groups than other people, even when their contributions are no better. The process is unfair: The contributions of majority group members (such as men and Whites in U.S. society) are overvalued in groups, and the contributions of minority group members are undervalued or ignored.

Almost all of us will at some point in our lives work in groups in which we are low in status. When you graduate from college, for example, you may work in an organizational group in which you are younger and have less experience than other group members. You also might face situations in which your contributions are devalued because of your race or gender. What can be done to improve things in these situations? How can we create a situation in which the contributions of all group members are given their proper recognition? What can you do to increase your status in a group?

Research in the group processes perspective has identified two primary ways that people with status characteristics that carry low cultural evaluations can effectively hold high-status positions in groups. First, one problem that people encounter in groups when they have characteristics with low status in the larger culture is that others do not think it is legitimate for them to hold high-status positions. A great deal of research, for example, has found that people in Western culture often view it as illegitimate for women to hold leadership positions in groups (e.g., Ridgeway and Berger 1986). This situation has improved in recent decades, but Western culture is still one that tends to associate men with leadership. Research has found that it helps to lead group members to believe that it is legitimate for women to occupy high-status positions. Lucas (2003), for example, carried out a study in which women or men acted as leaders of groups. He found, as research typically does, that men were more influential as leaders than were women. He then legitimately appointed women to leadership positions by leading group members to believe that it was proper for women to hold such positions. In these cases, women in leadership positions were just as influential as men in leadership positions.

Thus, legitimacy can help people with status characteristics that carry a low cultural evaluation receive proper recognition for their performances. Legitimacy, however, typically comes from some higher authority, and if you try to convince fellow group members that you should legitimately have high status in a group, you probably will not be successful. When you have low status in a group based on things like race and gender, what can you personally do to improve the situation? Research has identified a method that appears to be particularly effective.

One reason that people with higher status have more influence in groups is that group members expect these people to make contributions with the interests of the group in mind. This is a common research observation: People assume that high-status people will be oriented toward the success of the group, whereas low-status people will be more selfishly oriented. This is one reason why women and minority group members meet so much resistance when they are in leadership positions in groups. In the case of gender, for example, people will assume that the behavior of a man was carried out to promote the interests of the group, while assuming that the same behavior by a woman was carried out for personal benefit.

Cecilia Ridgeway (1982), a researcher who uses status characteristics theory, noted this pattern and identified a possible solution to the contributions of low-status individuals being devalued in groups. She theorized that if individuals with low social status make it clear that they are carrying out behaviors with the interests of the group in mind, then they can increase their status.

This strategy turns out to be very effective. Ridgeway (1982) conducted an experiment in which group members worked with a partner who presented himself or herself as either group motivated or selfishly motivated. Half of the people in the study had a male partner and half had a female partner. Group-motivated partners stressed the importance of cooperating and working together as a group. Selfishly motivated partners made it clear that they were looking out for themselves. When partners presented themselves as selfishly motivated, Ridgeway found the typical result: Male partners were more influential than female partners. When partners presented themselves as group motivated, however, the effect disappeared: Male partners were no more influential than female partners.

Shackelford, Wood, and Worchel (1996) replicated Ridgeway's study and found the same results. They also studied whether women could increase their status by acting assertively in a group. They found that women who acted assertively did increase their influence, but they also met resistance and encountered problems in the group. Presenting themselves as group motivated did not lead to these problems. Presenting yourself as group motivated is an effective strategy to increase your status in a group. The strategy is particularly effective for people with status characteristics that carry a low social evaluation. The influence of men, for example, increased very little in the Ridgeway study when they presented themselves as group motivated, perhaps because people already assumed that they were acting with the interests of the group in mind. The influence of women, in contrast, increased dramatically when they presented group motivations. So, if you want to increase your influence in a group, especially when you think you are in a low-status position, present your behaviors as motivated by group goals. When you make suggestions, note how they will benefit the group and stress that you have the interests of the group in mind. With these behaviors, you can overcome the tendency that people have to devalue the contributions of some people based on the characteristics they possess.

Power in Networks

Status is one important process that leads to inequality in groups. Power is another. In chapter 2 we defined power as the ability to get what you want despite resistance. Imagine, for example, a professor telling you one Friday afternoon that a major course paper will be due the following Monday. If you do not turn in the paper, you will fail the class. You do not want to write the paper, and you think that the assignment is unfair, but you write it nonetheless. In this situation, the professor has power. She gets what she wants despite your resistance.

Those in the group processes tradition are interested in a particular type of power—structural power, or power in networks. In the preceding example, it is clear that the professor's power rests in her ability to determine your grade. She has control over an outcome that is valuable to you and as a result, can get you to do things that you do not want to do. Power in networks can be more subtle than this. In chapter 2 we defined social networks as a series of relationships between people and groups. In the group processes perspective, a network emphasizes the idea that these people or groups are bound together through connections.

As an example of a network, imagine three people who all work side jobs as furniture movers in some small town. These people—Alice, Bob, and Charles—all work for themselves, but two people are needed to perform any individual job. Let's suppose that Bob knows Alice and Charles, but Alice and Charles don't know each other. We could graphically represent the network to look like this:

Alice—Bob—Charles

Every moving job pays two people $400. Alice, Bob, and Charles would each be willing to do a job for about $50. Anything less than that and it would not be worth their time. So, each time a job becomes available, a two-person team must be put together to do the job, and they must decide how to distribute the money.

What do you think would happen if a furniture moving job became available in this small town? Alice, Bob, and Charles would all want the job. Moreover, Alice and Charles would both ask Bob to do the job with themselves. How do you think Bob would decide between Alice and Charles? He would probably demand more than half the money and go with whoever gave him a bigger share of the $400.

Suppose that Alice proposes to Bob that they do the job together, with her collecting $150 of the $400 and Bob netting $250. Charles gets left out. What do you think will happen the next time a job becomes available? Charles will probably propose giving Bob more money so that he can be included. Charles might offer Bob $300 of the $400 if they do the job together.

Bob clearly has power in the network. As long as Alice and Charles do not know about each other, Bob will be able to set the terms of their exchanges. Over time, we would expect things to get to a situation where Alice and Charles would take the minimum amount necessary to make a job worth their while. In other words, we would expect Bob to collect $350 from each job, with either Alice or Charles (whoever Bob completes the job with) collecting $50.

The primary question of interest to group processes scholars that comes out of this network and others like it is this: What is the source of power in networks? What gives Bob power over Alice and Charles? If you look at the furniture movers' network, two things become apparent about Bob's position. First, Bob has the ability to *exclude* Alice and Charles from what they want. In other words, by working with Alice, Bob can deny Charles the opportunity to make money. Second, Bob has a *central* position in the network. If you look at the picture, you will see that Bob is centrally located.

Centrality and exclusion represent two possible sources of power in networks, and there was once some debate in the group processes perspective about which is the primary source of power. We can resolve the question by looking at networks that are just a little more complex. Although networks can involve numerous connections among participants, we will focus our discussion on line networks like the preceding one for simplicity.

What do you think is the primary source of power in networks—centrality or exclusion? Let's expand the example by imagining that Charles has brought a friend, Denise, into the furniture moving business. Alice and Bob don't know Denise, and the new network would look like this:

Alice—Bob—Charles—Denise

Who do you think would have power in this network? It is harder to tell than for the earlier network. However, we can guess how things might work. At first, Alice and Bob would probably complete jobs together, while Charles and Denise worked together. They would likely all collect $200 from each job. If Alice or Denise demanded too much from any job, however, we might expect Bob and Charles to complete a job together. After being left out, Alice and Denise would probably offer a little more on the next job. Over time, Bob and Charles would probably make a little more than Alice and Denise, but things would not get to the extreme differences we would have expected before Denise came along.

Bob and Charles, then, have power in this network, but not as much power as the middle position in a three-person network. Does this network help to resolve whether centrality or exclusion leads to power? Not really. Bob and Charles are centrally located, but not as central as Bob was when there were only three people—the center of the network here falls between the positions. Bob and Charles also have the ability to exclude Alice and Denise, but not as easily as Bob could have excluded Alice or Charles in the original network. Bob and Charles can only exclude others here by working together and probably taking less profit than they would get by trading with the outside positions. So, both the centrality and exclusion views would probably say that Bob and Charles will have power in this network, but not as much power as Bob in the three-person network. That is in fact what happens in controlled research on network power, and the four-person network does not allow us to determine the source of power.

We can resolve the issue by adding one more person to the network. Imagine that Denise brings a friend, Erik, into the furniture moving network. The new network looks like this:

Alice—Bob—Charles—Denise—Erik

Who is the most central position in this network? Charles. He is right in the middle of the network. Which positions have the ability to exclude others from what they want? That is more difficult to determine. We can figure it out, however, by imagining what might happen as jobs become available.

Suppose that two furniture moving jobs become available in the preceding network. Bob and Charles decide to do one job together. Because Alice does not know either Denise or Erik, she cannot do the other job with one of them. As a result, Denise and Erik do the other job together. Alice gets left out. The next time a job becomes available, Alice would likely offer Bob a little more to be included. Suppose she does. Bob and Alice complete a job together, and Denise again works with Erik. This time, Charles was left out. He would probably offer more to Bob and Denise to be included in one of the next jobs.

In this network, Bob and Denise will always be included whenever two jobs become available. Either Alice, Charles, or Erik is always left out. We would expect big power differences to develop in this network. The people that are subject to being left out will probably eventually take $50 just to be included in jobs, with Bob and Denise typically earning $350 each job.

We can now draw some conclusions about the roles of centrality and exclusion in determining power. Although Charles has the most central position in the five-person network, he has very little power; as little, in fact, as the positions on the ends. The positions with the ability to exclude, on the other hand, have a great deal of power. Bob and Denise can exclude the other people from exchanges, and they can use this ability to get more money. Power in networks, then, rests in the ability to exclude others from things they want. Cook, Emerson, Gillmore, and Yamagishi (1983) were the first group processes scholars to identify flaws in the logic behind centrality as a major source of power. The ability to exclude others from exchange is the driving element behind power in network exchange theory, a prominent group processes perspective on power in networks (Markovsky, Willer, and Patton 1988; Willer and Patton 1987).

There is a helpful lesson to take from the knowledge that exclusion rather than centrality is the primary source of power in networks. One common piece of advice for people starting new jobs is to get an office or cubicle located near the center of the action. The idea is that a central location will allow one to develop a strong base of power. Although this may be true, evidence from group processes theory and research indicates that other strategies may be more effective. In particular, if you want power in a network, put yourself in a position from which you can exclude other people from the things they desire. Pfeffer (1993) noted that the very best way to do this is to *create* something that people want. You can also, however, position yourself to control resources that people value. Controlling pay distributions, for example, is an important source of power in organizations.

The Differences between Power and Status

Power and status share some common elements. Both are group processes, and both involve inequalities in rewards. People follow the directives of people with high status, just as they do the directives of people high in power. The difference between status and power lies in the reasons why people comply.

We usually do what people with power want us to do because we are afraid of the consequences if we do not. We gave an example earlier of a professor having power over you because she controls your grade. You might do an assignment you saw as unfair because you are afraid your professor will punish you if do not do it. We do what people with high status want us to do because we hold those people in esteem or respect. You might follow the leader of a voluntary organization, for example, because you respect the person's integrity and views. Although you do what the person wants, she has no power over you—she cannot fire you from the organization.

Power is structural. It rests in the positions that people have in relation to others, not in the people themselves. In the original furniture mover example given earlier, nothing about Bob gave him power over Alice and Charles—his power came from his position in the network. Status arises from the features of people. The status people get may be deserved (e.g., people who have high status because they are experts at some activity) or undeserved (e.g., men having higher status than women at activities that men perform no better than women), but status in either case rests in individual characteristics.

Although power and status arise from different sources, they are often related. Being high in status can significantly affect access to powerful positions (Ridgeway 2001). As we noted in the first chapter, the president of the United States has a great deal of power. His power is rooted in his position, and when he leaves office, his power is much lessened. It is difficult to imagine, however, someone gaining the power that comes with being president without first being high in social status.

One way that status helps people get power is that people value the resources held by higher-status people more than the resources held by lower-status people. At the time of this writing, a letter signed by Martin Luther King Jr. was for sale on eBay at a price of over $4,000. We value things that are possessed (or were once possessed) by people we hold in high esteem. Thye (2000) carried out a study in which participants in an experiment traded resources with each other. Although the resources that people traded were equal in monetary value, participants in the study valued the resources held by high-status people more than resources held by low-status people. High-status people, then, can gain power by controlling access to things that other people desire.

Power can also be used to gain status. For one thing, people tend to assume that powerful people are competent, even when their power rests in structural positions they hold through no effort or ability of their own (Lovaglia 1995). Think of the furniture moving network in which Bob knew Alice and Charles, but Alice and Charles did not know each other. Bob had power in the network, and we said that he would probably eventually earn about $350 of a team's $400 per move. Distributions would end up this way whether or not Bob was particularly competent because Bob is in a powerful position. People who knew that Bob earned the most, however, would probably assume that Bob was more competent than Alice or Charles.

Another way that power can be used to gain status is by using power to "purchase" status. In the movie *The Godfather*, Marlon Brando played a mafia boss with a great deal of power. He turned that power into status in his community by using his power to do favors for people. Pablo Escobar, a ruthless Columbian drug lord who killed or had killed countless Columbian citizens and officials, gained status in his community by hosting events and building parks and fields for children.

Power and status, then, are distinct but related. There are some jobs, for example, that are not high in both status and power but that are high in either power (e.g., prison guards) or status (e.g., ministers). It is much more common, however, for occupations to be similarly matched in both power and status. A large company's Chief Executive Officer (CEO) will probably have a great deal of power and status. That same company's mailroom workers will likely be low in both status and power.

Section Summary

The last section of this chapter applies research and theories from the group processes perspective to answer the questions: How does stratification develop in group interaction? How do inequalities from society at-large get reproduced in groups? Research from this perspective shows that hierarchies naturally develop in most groups. According to exchange theory, those perceived as contributing more to a group often receive more status or power in a group. Status characteristics theory shows that status characteristics such as gender influence these perceptions about who contributes the most to a group. In contrast to status, which rests in individual characteristics, power is conferred by structural position. The ability to control resources also influences your power level in a group.

Bringing It All Together

I don't think anyone likes inequality. I mean, who thinks some people deserve more money than others, if they do the same work, right? Anyway, if inequality occurs at every level, how do we fix the problem? It seems to me that there are too many things to tackle at the same time.

—Dave, junior English major

We started this chapter asking how people construct inequalities. The symbolic interaction perspective emphasizes how we construct the meaning of difference— in terms of gender, race, and other types of differences. Different cultural meanings about our status in society (i.e., race, class, and gender) have significant impacts on our lives, the way people treat us, and how we treat other people. The social structure and personality perspective focuses on how inequalities influence specific outcomes for people. For example, the role of social class on educational outcomes and how our position in society gives us access to different networks of people—helping us find work, among other things. Finally, the group processes perspective helps us answer the questions related to how power and status develop in groups. First, our status from the larger society is a major factor in gaining status in groups. Second, our ability to control resources in a group helps us to gain power and status in that group.

Dave's concern about "fixing the problem" of inequality seems justified—there are a lot of different ways to study it. Together, these perspectives incorporate microprocesses in constructing inequalities between people and understanding the impact of social inequalities once they are formed. The answer to Dave's problem is to say that we need to look at inequality at every level—the stereotypes we employ when we are hiring someone or just interacting with them in a group. Do we judge somebody as less competent than another based solely on their contributions to a group, or do we rely on preconceived understandings based on the larger society? Some social scientists focus on managing inequalities in our day-to-day interactions, whereas others emphasize the need to change laws, making them less discriminatory or giving people who have been discriminated against the same opportunities to succeed as the rest of society. In the end, we need to address all the ways that inequalities exist if we want to change society.

Summary

1. Three ways that interactionist researchers focus on stratification processes include examining how social structure shapes who we interact with, accounting for inequalities in the content of interactions, and acknowledging how people with certain status characteristics have more power in terms of role taking, and examining people's power to define situations and define themselves.

2. The Wisconsin Model of Status Attainment traces the relationships between individuals' class position, their actual abilities, and their long-term occupational outcomes in society.

3. The effect of networking between individuals from different groups creates a variety of outcomes for the individuals, depending on the status of the individuals in a group as well as the status of the group itself.

4. Values serve as a guide for making decisions about the future, ultimately affecting the types of jobs we attain and class position we have in life, producing a feedback loop between our personality and social positions.

5. Group processes contribute to our understanding of structural developments by studying the exchanges between individuals in groups. Exchange processes lend themselves to the development of status structures because people bring different types and quantities of resources into the process. People who contribute more to a group or have more resources generally achieve higher status in groups.

6. According to status characteristics theory, status hierarchies in task groups form based on the status characteristics of the members of the group; members

look to the status characteristics of themselves and other group members to develop expectations for performance.

7. Power in networks is a structural capacity that results from the ability to exclude other persons from resources that they desire.

Key Terms and Concepts

Borderwork: The creation of social and physical boundaries between boys and girls.

Closeness of supervision: Part of Kohn and Schooler's model of status attainment referring to the level of control supervisors have over workers.

Diffuse status characteristics: Characteristics individuals carry with them for performances in diverse situations.

Direct exchanges: Exchanges between two people.

Doing gender: A social process in which individuals act according to the social rules or norms associated with being a man or a woman in society.

Feedback loop: A process in which our class position influences the development of values that, in turn, influences the type of job we seek.

Indirect or generalized exchanges: When people do not receive benefits directly from those to whom they give benefits.

Intellectual flexibility: Part of Kohn and Schooler's model of status attainment referring to how flexible people are in handling complex situations on the job.

Personal ties: Combination of strong and weak ties.

Routinization: Part of Kohn and Schooler's model of status attainment referring to the level of repetitiveness found on the job.

Self-directed orientation: Part of Kohn and Schooler's model of status attainment referring to an individual's level of conservatism, fatalism, and personally responsible morality.

Social capital: Trust and support found in relationships with other people.

Social class: A group of people who share the same relative status in a given society.

Social exchange theory: Theory based on the premise that individuals enter into relationships that provide some benefit to us and end or leave relationships that do not provide some sort of reward.

Social mobility: The upward or downward change in social class over time.

Social stratification: Ways in which individuals or groups are ranked in society.

Specific status characteristics: Characteristics that create expectations for performance in limited settings.

Status characteristics theory: Theory that links social roles and expectations from a larger society to stratification processes in groups.

Status hierarchies: Hierarchies that develop in task groups.

Strong ties: People with whom we are close like friends and family.

Substantive complexity: Part of Kohn and Schooler's model of status attainment referring to how complicated the actual work is on the job.

Weak ties: Acquaintances or people we know through association with a third party.

Discussion Questions

1. Can you see how status plays a role in your interactions with other people? Can you see the subtle—and not so subtle—ways that race or gender play a role in interactions?

2. How do you relate to your professors differently than to your friends or family? Think about the role of status and power in explaining how and why you might act differently with people from each of these groups.

3. How might your understanding of the role of networks in society help you find a particular type of job?

4. Think about a recent group activity in which you had to make decisions about getting things done. How might group processes research inform your analysis of the group's behavior?

Self and Identity

Chapter 5

*I am a mother, first and foremost. So if my baby gets sick, I just
can't study as much as I want to. Sometimes my grades suffer.
And sometimes I am frustrated by all the things I can't do. The
other day, some of the people in my class were talking about a big
party that they went to. That kind of "fun" stuff is almost always
out of the question now. But, you know, people tell me I am a
really good mom to my baby, and I feel like I am working for something—I am making a good life for her.*

—Marsha, junior Sociology major

Marsha has a lot of roles to juggle in her life. But for her,
being a mother is her most salient, important identity.
As a result, when she has to choose how to use her time,
she will often spend it with her child. And, she explains her
behavior to herself and others based on her identities. Her story
also reveals that she feels good about who she is and what she is
capable of doing as a mom.

Most of us have some familiarity with the concepts of self,
identity, and personality. We may explain our behaviors by saying we did something because "that's the way I am." Sociologists
believe that a significant part of what people might call personality is socially constructed. If objects, social relationships, and
society are constructed via social interactions, then our selves
and identities must also reflect social conditions.

Sociologists do not study personality per se but rather the
self, a process in which we construct a sense of who we are

through interaction with others. Because the self is a process, it changes over time. We can take snapshots of our sense of self at a given time, but it regularly gets updated as we interact with people and adapt to new events and transitions in our lives. That snapshot, or the outcome of the self process at a given point in time, is the **self-concept.** Rosenberg (1986) defined the self-concept as the sum total of thoughts and feelings we have about ourselves as an object. Essentially, the "self process" creates the "self-concept," or an understanding we have about ourselves. The self-concept is an "object" or thing, and just like other things—such as a baseball, a hat, or any other physical object—we can talk about and reflect on our self-concept. Scholars examining the self-concept focus on **self-identities** (the kind of person we see ourselves as) and on **self-evaluations** (judgments we make of ourselves). Three self-evaluations we will discuss in this chapter are self-esteem, mastery, and mattering.

Social psychologists approach the study of the self in diverse ways, often dependent on the broad theoretical traditions of which they are a part. Some symbolic interactionists focus on the self as a process, examining how we present ourselves to others in interaction, and how we make meaning of who we are, in concert with significant others. Other, more structural, symbolic interactionists focus on how, through interaction, our self comes to reflect the structure of society in a stable understanding of who we are. Because society is highly differentiated, the self is composed of multiple, complex parts. Social structure and personality scholars explicitly consider how social structural conditions, notably our positions and statuses in society, affect the self-concept. ("Social structure and the 'self-concept' may in fact be a better title for this field of study than 'social structure and personality.' ") Finally, group processes scholars emphasize the role of group processes in affecting identities. We will address the following questions in this chapter:

- What are the components of the self?
- What are interactionist theories of the self and identity?
- What are three dimensions of the self-concept? What do we know from research on the self-concept?
- How do group processes affect identity?

SI | The Self as a Process

When I first came to college, I was such a party animal. I would miss most of my classes and just get drunk or high. There was always a party to go to. I am not sure why I became that way. I did well in high school and was always a "good girl" growing up. I guess going to school just changed me. Maybe I took advantage of the freedom of being away from home. It was so funny to be called a "party girl" in college! Well, when my parents heard about my grades, the funding stopped and I had to drop out. I started taking classes at a local college. I didn't go back to being a "good girl" but I was certainly not the party girl anymore. I guess place and time can change you.

—Quinn, junior Journalism major

According to the symbolic interactionist perspective, the self is a process, just like the construction of any social reality. We give meaning to our self in many different ways. Are we good or bad people? How well do we do the tasks we set out to do? We continually take information from the world around us to answer these types of questions. The subtle feedback that we get over many, many experiences with significant others shape us. It's not that we fail an exam and simply think that we are bad students. An exam is only one experience in our role as students, and we will assess many other aspects of the environment, such as how many students failed, how difficult the class is, and so on. We do sometimes make conscious choices to become a certain kind of person; we may try to lose weight, to become an accountant, or to appear more intelligent. The process involves grafting on thoughts and behaviors necessary to achieve the best outcomes for ourselves in an interaction. For instance, if a graduate student concerned about her status in an intellectual community enters a room full of older professors, she may start acting more mature, using formal language, and trying to make clear, cogent statements to the people around her. This process may only last the duration of the meeting, with her goal being to look intelligent in front of the professors. However, the "act" of being more mature and intelligent may become a more permanent part of her sense of self as she interacts more with professors and students similar to her. How could her behavior become a permanent part of her sense of self? Over time she may begin to think of herself as "smart," and her "student" identity may become more salient in future interactions with people.

In Quinn's example, going away to college changed the ways she thought, felt, and behaved. Instead of being the "good girl" she was at home, she started missing classes and going to more parties. Her networks and her priorities changed in her new social environment. The changes had some long-term consequences for her sense of self. Even when she was forced to go home, she never totally relinquished her party identity. Quinn was able to dialogue about herself as an object. She can see how she is now and compare it to the past. Furthermore, she was able to negotiate her sense of self using the alternatives available to her. When she was faced with returning home, she recognized that it limited her ability to "party," but she did not completely submit to her previous sense of self.

In this section of the chapter, we examine the way that the self is constructed and how we incorporate societal roles and expectations into our sense of self.

The I and the Me

We use symbols and language to communicate with other people, but we also use language to think internally, a process that Blumer (1969) calls **self-indication.** We can have a conversation with our selves just as we can with other people. Further,

Box 5.1   Freud's Approach to Personality

The psychoanalytic approach to personality assumes that people are largely irrational, trying to manage passions and inner conflicts from the past. The approach is largely associated with Sigmund Freud (1859–1939), an Austrian psychologist. Freud was one of the first to popularize the idea that we have an "unconscious" mind—that there are things going on in the brain that affect our thoughts, feelings, and behavior of which we are unaware. According to Freud, only through psychotherapy can we tap this inner room. Freud argued that personalities are made of three components: the Id that houses our basic instincts, seeking only pleasure or carnal fulfillment; the Ego, which helps to restrain the Id until it can achieve its wants in a reasonable way given different physical and social conditions; and the Superego, which houses an individual's ideals, larger social and cultural norms, and standards. In some sense, the Ego and Superego contain elements of society, where we learn specific ways to constrain the Id. These internal processes share some things in common with the relationship between the "I" and the "Me" outlined by Mead, with one dimension of our selves interacting with other aspects of the self on a day-to-day basis.

we can internally negotiate the meanings of objects, including our "self." In fact, there are several situations in which internal dialogues are the only appropriate ways to assess meaning.

According to Mead (1934), a large part of our internal dialogue occurs as interplay between two characters within ourselves: the I and the Me. The **Me** is the organized set of attitudes toward the self, based on the views of significant others, such as friends and family, as well as society as a whole. The **I** refers to our active self; the I is the one on stage, in the moment, talking to other people. The "I" and the "Me" form a constant dialectic regarding our thoughts, feelings, and behaviors (see Box 5.1).

This internal dialogue reflects the importance we give to social conditions when deciding how to think, feel or behave. In some sense, society resides in the Me. Because we have human agency, the ability to make choices about our actions, the "I" is able to act based on the "Me" in a number of different ways. Hence, the self is fluid, changing to meet social conditions.

Identity Theory

Identity theory (which derives from the symbol interaction perspective) emphasizes the enduring nature of one's thoughts about who she is. **Identity** refers to our internalized, stable sense of who we are, including role identities, social categories, and personal characteristics (Burke 2003). Hence, identity includes our understanding of our unique nature (personality) *as well as* our social roles. **Role identities** are the internalized expectations associated with different positions. Some examples of role identities are college student, politician, or brother. For adults, the most important role identities typically stem from work and family positions. **Social categories** include identities related to social groups to which we belong, such as Canadian, woman, or Latino. Last, **personal characteristics** include anything we use to describe our individual nature, such as being kind or generous or athletic.

Identity theory examines the ways society shapes how we view ourselves, and how those views, or identities, affect our behavior.

Stryker (2002) offered five principles that are at the root of identity theory:

1. Behavior is based on an already defined and classified world.
2. Positions in society are among the things classified in the world.
3. People develop their identities based on their positions in society.
4. We incorporate our social positions into our sense of identity; our positions become a part of our sense of self.
5. Social behavior is derived from the shaping and modifying of the expectations of our positions.

The theory is rather simple and eloquent and tries to predict behavior when people have choices. The premise is that society affects self, which affects behavior. By society, identity theory refers to patterns of commitments to other people. Commitment includes the number of significant others tied to a given identity or to being a certain kind of person and the intensity of those bonds. Commitment shapes the salience of an identity, which in turn shapes how we will behave. For instance, living with many close friends in a sorority house makes a "Greek" identity very salient and, according to identity theory, would make us act in ways to express the meaning of being Greek or, more specifically, say, a Gamma Phi Beta (wearing symbols, talking like others, doing the philanthropy of that organization) when we have the opportunity to do so.

Identity theory extends symbolic interactionist principles by focusing on the social construction of the self (principles #3 and #4) and the belief that there is an existing social reality that we use as the basis for self-identification processes (principles #1 and #2). Thereafter, identities generate behavior (#5), but we are able to "make" or play out roles in somewhat unique ways. That is, how we act in a given situation is contingent on the *meaning* we give our identity. According to identity theory, then, we use identities to guide our own behavior, but that behavior depends on the meaning of the identity.

Consider two fathers. How they act out their father roles (or behave as fathers) can be quite different. Their behavior will depend on both the salience and the meaning of the father identity. In one study, Rane and McBride (2000) found that fathers who considered the nurturing aspect of the father role more meaningful to their sense of identity interacted with their children more often than those who did not. If being a good father means being more attentive to children's needs, then how should the father act? He should probably spend more time with them.

There is often some latitude in acting out identities; for example, it is generally viewed as important for fathers to provide for children, but emphasis on the nuturing aspect is fine, too. We also assess our identities when we are with other people, making sure that they correspond with our sense of self. We make small adjustments to our behavior to maintain our identity (Cast 2003a). We may do the same for other people, too, helping them maintain their sense of identity through our interactions with them (Cast 2003b). Ultimately, these identity processes are designed to make the world controllable; self-confirmation can provide us a guide in awkward social situations and an emotional anchor in otherwise changing world (Stets and Burke 2005).

Identity, Emotions, and Behavior

When most of us think of the "self," we think of our cognitions, or thoughts, about who we are. The self also includes our emotions and behavior. Emotions and behavior help to represent who we are and provide information to be evaluated. We tend to believe that our thoughts cause certain behaviors. But behaviors can also change our way of thinking in the world. For instance, you may not consider yourself very athletic until you find yourself obligated to play on the fraternity or sorority softball team. If you find that your performance is good after a few games, you may start to reevaluate your sense of your athleticism, incorporating this new information into your self-concept.

Thoughts, feelings, and behavior are all part of the self process. We use information from one or more dimensions of the self to develop the other parts. We also shape feelings and behavior in a similar manner as for the cognitive processes reviewed in the last section. **Affect-control theory** incorporates elements of symbolic interactionism and identity theory to explain the role of emotion in identity processes (Smith-Lovin 1995). The theory states that emotions serve as signals about how well we are producing our identities and reproducing others' identities (Heise 1985). Negative emotions often signal that something is not right about a situation. If you see yourself as a good athlete and then fumble the ball, the bad feelings serve as a sign that you are failing at your identity. You may later use the exchange between the "I" and the "Me" to contemplate the feeling that your are experiencing. Perhaps you will decide to act on that feeling or decide that it is not that important to you. Regardless, the initial signal initiates this thinking process. In another example, if you make a mistake on the job, the bad feeling may lead you to question your ability to do the job. The feeling of shame or doubt suggests that you cannot live up to expectations of the job. To restore a positive feeling about yourself (i.e., self-esteem), you begin to use an internal dialogue in defense of your position. You may explain your poor performance as an anomaly or blame someone else for the problem. If the explanation reestablishes your identity on the job, the negative emotion will subside.

Emotions are also part of the identity-verification process discussed earlier. Emotions serve as a guide to when we are acting according to our identity in a given situation. We expect a similarity between how we perceive our own identity and the information we are receiving about ourselves from the world around us. Congruence between our self-perceived identity and the information we receive about ourselves generally produces positive emotions, whereas a lack of congruence produces negative feelings, motivating people to restore their identity or to reduce commitment to it (Burke 2004; Burke and Stets 1999; Stryker and Burke 2000). If we view ourselves as a caring friend but continue to get negative feedback from our friends, we can choose to find ways to show our affection or simply end the friendship. However, in an experiment designed to simulate workers receiving feedback on the job, Stets (2005) found that when people got feedback about their identity that is *better* than expected (i.e., nonverified identity), it produces *positive* emotions. Hence, the emotional response to identity verification depends on the nature of the situation, suggesting that negative emotions only occur when disconfirming a positive identity.

Dramaturgical Sociology and the Presentation of Self

Symbolic interaction emphasizes the fact that humans have agency, the power to act independently of constraints. Thus, individuals can act apart from their sense of self. You may consider yourself to be a bad student but decide to "act" like a good one in front of a professor. The study of how we present ourselves, playing roles and managing impressions during interactions with other people, is called **dramaturgical sociology.** Dramaturgical sociology is most closely associated with Erving Goffman (1922–1982). It includes the study of impression formation and the management of impressions. It is also associated with short-term changes in the self through the impression processes.

In a sense, identity and affect control theories incorporate elements of dramaturgical sociology. These theories posit that when our identity does not match the environment, we change in some way to ensure that the two are commensurate. The theories assume that we have some control over what others think about us in a given interaction, a basic premise of dramaturgical sociology. Dramaturgical sociology also incorporates that idea that we can choose to act different than our identity during a social exchange and that we have to practice identities before fully incorporating them into our sense of self. Our personal sense of identity and our perceptions of the conceptions people have of us form a constant dialectic under the heading of impression management.

Impression Management

Erving Goffman (1959) believed that we naturally seek information from people when we come in contact with them. We use such information to help establish expectations of our behavior and that of the people around us. Information comes from the physical attributes of the other people—their race or gender, for instance—as well as our histories with those people. We also have some control over the information we give to other people. For instance, we can dress formally to give people the impression that we are mature and serious. Similarly, we can wear jeans and a T-shirt if we want to look relaxed. The former dress may help get a job, whereas the latter is more appropriate among friends and family.

Impression management refers to the ways individuals seek to control the impressions they convey to other people. Impression management is a social process, involving more than just our own behavior. For instance, you can try to impress a potential employer by wearing nice clothing but cannot ensure that the employer finds the dress appropriate. Hence, there are **impressions given** and **impressions given off**—the impression you believe that you are giving and the impression the other person has of you.

Goffman argued that we are driven to maintain positive impressions, probably because outcomes of interactions serve as a source of self-esteem. You would feel embarrassed if you tried to present yourself as a serious job candidate but lost your keys and spilled coffee. However, Goffman also observed that other people are driven to help support our impressions. For instance, the employer may make a joke about your clumsiness or give you an opportunity to explain why you are especially clumsy that day. You might respond in agreement, finding an excuse like the wobbly new shoes you are wearing. Thus, both of you have found a way to make the impression as favorable as possible under those conditions.

The motivation to support others' impressions is somewhat self-serving. First, helping other people maintain their impressions helps maintain the interaction, helping us predict future behavior and making it easier for us to know what to do. Second, we may need support in our own impression management efforts later in the interaction. Helping the other person makes it more likely that the other person will reciprocate support for us.

Goffman described two regions of impression formation and management. Goffman's **front stage** is the place where we present ourselves to others. The **backstage** is the region where we relax our impression management efforts and we may practice our performances (Goffman 1959). We think of the job interview as the front stage, trying to look and act in a way that will make a certain impression and allow us to reach a goal—employment. When you see your friends (your back stage), you may express a very different attitude toward the job and the employer. Similarly, you may want to sound serious and polite when you approach a professor about a test grade, then report your anger and disgust about the grade and the professor with your friends in the campus dining hall after the meeting. This usually works fine, unless your "backstage" is revealed. That is, if your friends point out to you that your professor is eating her lunch right behind you.

Spencer Cahill and his colleagues (1985) studied behavior in public bathrooms, assessing the role social structure plays in the most "private" or "backstage" areas of our lives. He and his colleagues observed and took notes of behavior for hundreds of hours in the bathrooms of malls, student unions, restaurants, and other places over a nine-month period. Among other things, they found that bathrooms serve as a place to "retire" from front-stage performances. The researchers showed that bathrooms serve as "self-service" repair shops, where individuals can take off their "fronts." Mirrors allow us to check our front (makeup, clothing, etc. . . .) before entering public again. Bathrooms also serve as a retreat from embarrassment, a place to prepare for publicly awkward situations—giving people a "staging area" for their public performances.

The Situated or Postmodern Self

Some symbolic interaction theorists view the self as constantly changing. They claim that it is therefore difficult to study the self using quantitative techniques (see chapter 3). These scholars tend to study the self qualitatively and through "narratives" regarding how we discuss who we are. One of the main questions of interest for these researchers is the question of authenticity. Authenticity is how well the self we portray to others fits with the self we really feel like inside.

One of the reasons people change is that their social environments change. The **situated self** is a temporally based sense of who we are. For the brief time we are interviewing for the job, we may really believe that we are good, trustworthy employees who would take the job and employer seriously. That perspective may change after leaving the office and discussing the interview with friends and family. Thus, impression management is an integral part of the situated self. Postmodern theorists argue that the self has become "saturated" in recent years because we have so many "others" with whom we interact. Because of social forces like globalization and technological advances such as the Internet, we can interact with many different others from around the country or world within a very short time span (or even at the same time). This creates a "multiphrenia," or inability to know who we really are, because we are playing so many roles at once and we have so many others with whom we receive different, sometimes conflicting, feedback. Gergen discussed how technological advances in transportation, computers, television, and so on are replacing our small number of significant others with an "ever-expanding array of relationships" (2000, xi). To Gergen, these changes in society fragment and erase a core or true self.

Section Summary

This section applied the interactionist perspective to answer the questions: What are components of the self? What are interactionist theories of the self and identity? According to symbolic interaction, the self is comprised of the Me, the organized set of attitudes toward the self, and the I, the part that is on stage, actively engaging with others. Identity theory examines how our roles and statuses help develop a sense of who we are. In addition, affect control theory helps to show the role of emotions in the identity process. Finally, impression management shows individuals' ability to actively manipulate others' perception of their selves in a social context.

SSP | The Self and Social Structure

I was only in school for a month before dropping out. I just couldn't handle the deadlines or the homework. It just seemed like too much. I took a job at a local fast-food restaurant. They gave me a promotion to assistant manager after awhile. It kind of made me rethink going back to school. I thought, "If I can manage all these people,

I can manage a little homework too." So, I signed up for classes again the following year. And here I am!

—John, freshman Business major

Scholars from the social structure and personality perspective focus on how our social positions and relationships affect our self and identity. As mentioned earlier, the self-concept refers to all our thoughts and feelings about ourselves as objects (Rosenberg 1986). Thus, social structure and personality theorists carefully examine how social structure and culture affect identity, esteem, and other evaluative components of the self. In the story by John, we see a student who initially does not believe that he is capable of finishing college. As a result, he decides to drop out and starts working at a local fast-food restaurant. He slowly rises to an assistant manager position. After several months at this position, he starts rethinking his abilities, wondering if he is in fact capable of finishing the degree. John's thinking process may be related to the fact that he was in a position that required him to be responsible for other people. After experiencing some of the challenges associated with management, he began to rethink his decision about school. Taking the management position helped him both develop his skills as well as provide alternative ways of seeing himself.

The focus in this section is on the role that larger social conditions play in everyday interactions. In this case, John's "position" is not constructed through interaction, but something developed long before he arrived at the situation. As such, the position has meanings and expectations already attached to it from the larger society. Although John may be able to change them, he must negotiate these meanings from an established point. That is, he must take into account what other people expect of him based on an already established position and decide how much to change the nature of the position or change himself to live up to the expectations of that position. Researchers from this tradition often study the relationship between social positions and the self-concept in the form of self-esteem, mastery, and mattering. We will review these dimensions of the self-concept, followed by a discussion of how they are measured and how our social positions affect them.

Evaluative Dimensions of the Self-Concept

As we discussed in the beginning of the chapter, in addition to self-identities, self-evaluations are central to self-concept research. There are three evaluative elements or dimensions of the self that are seen as foundational to the self processes described earlier. We evaluate ourselves in key ways by asking "How worthy am I?" "How powerful are my actions?" and "How much do I matter to other people?" Self-esteem and mastery, represented by the first two questions, both motivate the self-process and filter interactions with our social worlds. Mattering, addressed by the third question, is a dimension of the self that is less studied but also serves as a foundational dimension of the self (Elliott, Kao, and Grant 2004; Rosenberg and McCullough 1981).

Self-Esteem

If you enter the expression, "self-esteem" into an Internet search engine, you will find dozens of Web sites designed to sell products guaranteed to boost your self-esteem. Self-esteem has become a common expression in the Western world; parents try to build their children's self-esteem, and a few adults participate in self-esteem-boosting programs. Much of the early research in self-esteem suggested that it is at the core of psychological development (see Elliott 1986; Owens and Stryker 2001; Rosenberg 1986); that is, all other aspects of our life will fail without positive self-esteem. For instance, a person with low self-esteem may find it more difficult to finish a college program, believing that she does not "have what it takes." Therefore, the logic goes, we must first build strong self-esteem and then worry about the other details of life. But this is not quite true. Instead, successful social experiences and a lifetime of supportive interactions with significant others are primary in *creating* self-esteem; it cannot be quickly "built" and then used as a tool for success (Rosenberg, Schooler, and Schoenbach 1989).

Self-esteem is the positive or negative evaluation of our self as an object (Rosenberg 1986). It answers the question: How good am I? In addition to thoughts about how worthy we are, social psychologists also understand self-esteem to be the emotional reactions to the self (Hewitt 2003a). Self-esteem has at least two dimensions; we can both cognitively and affectively react to the self. For instance, we may think very highly of our selves and concurrently feel good about our selves. Alternatively, we can think poorly of our selves and feel bad too. We can also think about self-esteem in terms of global or specific, that is, an overall sense of worth and a sense of worth based on specific roles or spheres of life. Academic self-esteem is our worth as a student (Rosenberg, Schooler, and Schoenbach 1989).

Self-concept theorists often study the effects of social structure and culture on self-esteem. For instance, people who work in jobs that require little supervision from others and who engage in intellectually complex tasks have higher self-esteem years later than others who perform more mundane work (Schooler and Oates 2001). Another study examined how girls were affected by unrealistic images of female beauty prominent in the media (Milkie 1999). For White girls, even when they were critical of the "perfect" images, the images depressed self-esteem, because girls still made social comparisons with these models and assumed that boys bought into the images and viewed the real girls more negatively. But Black girls' self-esteem was not affected by these comparisons—they understood that significant others did not believe the images were a standard for African-American beauty. Hence, our status and social relationships help us to interpret information from the media and other sources in assessing our self-worth.

The importance of self-esteem, according to some scholars, is profound. Many social psychologists believe that self-esteem serves as a basis for motivation of the self process. Gecas (2001) argued that self-esteem may be a more important motivational force for us than other self processes. He says that individuals are motivated by the **self-consistency motive** to maintain a consistent sense of self and the **self-esteem motive,** the desire to maintain positive self-images. The latter force

Children learn positive self-esteem and mastery at the earliest ages through their accomplishments and positive interactions with friends and family.

is probably more prominent than the former. That is, maintaining adequate self-esteem affects our everyday behaviors and future goals. For example, the threat of bad grades (which could produce lower academic self-esteem) may motivate us to study harder for class. Alternatively, it may motivate us to leave school and find an alternative source of esteem.

The set of research discussed earlier shows that self-esteem is, in part, derived from social interaction. In fact, there are four sources of the self-concept, including self-esteem: social comparisons, reflected appraisals, psychological centrality, and self-attributions (Gecas 1982; Rosenberg 1986). **Social comparisons** refer to using other people and groups as a point of reference for our thoughts, feelings, and behaviors. **Reflected appraisals** are the ways that we believe others view us. **Psychological centrality** is our ability to shift aspects of the self to become more or less important to our overall self-concept. Finally, **self-perceptions** are observations of our behavior and its consequences.

An internal dialogue forms the self. Positive or negative evaluations of your self (self-esteem) are the result of your internal dialogue, compiling self-perceptions, social comparisons, and reflected appraisals. Marsha, in the vignette at the start of the chapter, indicated that she felt good about herself as a mother. Her mothering self-esteem was built through all the processes described. She probably made social comparisons with other student mothers and believed that, compared to them, she was doing quite well taking care of her baby. Through interacting with others, her parents, her partner, her friends, and her baby, she is able to form a view of how *they* viewed her mothering (or reflected appraisals). In terms of psychological centrality, her mothering identity is very important and thus provides a positive global sense of worth as well. And finally, by observing her own behaviors, sacrificing time at parties and for studying when necessary she sees evidence that she is a good mother.

Research generally supports the self-esteem dynamics reviewed. Levels and sources of self-esteem are theorized to be different for people in various social categories. For instance, of the four sources of the self-concept, reflected appraisals, or our sense of how others view us, have the strongest effect on self-esteem for both men and women, although the effects on women are somewhat stronger than men (Schwalbe and Staples 1991). Research also shows that self-esteem is relatively high for most people (Rosenberg 1986). This finding supports that idea that self-esteem serves as primary element of the self-concept.

Mastery

Another important dimension of the self is mastery. **Mastery** refers to our perceptions of our ability to control our environments. It addresses the question: How powerful am I to do the things I would like to do? Mastery is similar to the concepts of self-efficacy and locus of control (see Box 5.2). Much like self-esteem, sociologists believe that our desire for control serves as a motivational aspect of our self-image (Gecas 1989). There may be a **self-fulfilling prophecy,** a case of expectations producing a reality consistent with the assumptions at work: If we do not believe that we can do something, we may not even try. If you or others do not believe that you are capable of doing a job, you will likely find ways to avoid the job or fail at it. By failing at the job, you continue to believe that you are not capable of doing it.

Mastery is associated with both physical and mental health outcomes. Several studies show the effects of these concepts in our lives. People with a higher sense of efficacy report fewer mental and physical health problems than those with a lower sense of efficacy (Caputo 2003; Cheung and Sun 2000). Mastery is also highly related to self-esteem: people with a high sense of mastery report higher levels of esteem (Turner and Roszell 1994). Mastery also serves as a personal resource to cope with life's problems. For instance, Pearlin and colleagues (1981) found that people with a higher sense of mastery react less severely to job loss than do those with a lower sense of mastery, probably because they believed that they would be able to overcome their problems.

Development of one's sense of efficacy starts in infancy as children begin to understand causality in their environments (Gecas 1989). As children try to change their worlds, they assess whether such attempts have an effect. If so, children learn that they have ability to make such changes. Hence, a sense of efficacy begins through **personal accomplishments,** being able to achieve what we start out to do. Personal accomplishments continue to be a most important source of efficacy in adulthood, but there are other sources of efficacy. **Vicarious experience** occurs

Box 5.2   Mastery, Self-Efficacy, and Locus of Control

Mastery, self-efficacy, and locus of control are measures of the self-concept assessing our sense of control (or lack of control) over the world around us (Turner, Lloyd, and Roszell 1999). Locus of control measures our "internal" and "external" sense of control (Gecas 1989). Do you think that people get promoted because of hard work or simply as a matter of chance? If you believe that promotions are a result of hard work, you probably have a stronger "internal" sense of control. Self-efficacy refers to our beliefs about our ability to produce results from our actions (Bandura 1997). Mastery focuses on more general perceptions of our ability to achieve our goals. Mastery is often assessed by asking respondents how much they agree with statements such as, "I have little control over the things that happen to me" and "There is really no way I can solve some of the problems I have" (Pearlin and Schooler 1978). If you strongly agree with these items, you probably have a low sense of mastery. The three concepts are similar but have developed within different research traditions.

by seeing other people perform tasks, showing us that the task can be accomplishabled. **Verbal persuasion** is information from others about our abilities. Finally, **emotional arousal** refers to inferences about our abilities based on our emotional states (Bandura 1977). For instance, we hesitate to give a speech to a club or group to which we belong. However, our friends try to boost our confidence by using verbal persuasion, arguing that we are capable of making a great speech, increasing our sense of mastery. We then start observing other people's speeches, making the task seem more reasonable for us to accomplish. We may then reflect on the large amount of fear provoked when we consider making the speech. This series of internal and social negotiations influences our decision to make the speech, how well we perform if we do make the speech, and the likelihood of making future speeches.

Mattering

Mattering refers to our sense that we are important to other people in the world (Elliott Kao, and Grant 2004; Rosenberg and McCullough 1981). It answers the question: How much do I matter to others? According to Rosenberg and McCullough (1981), we have an intrinsic need to feel that we are needed by the people around us. The link between mattering and well-being is related to the work of the classic sociologist Emile Durkheim. Durkheim (1951, originally 1897) studied the social conditions that influence individuals' decisions to commit suicide. He argued that people who are more integrated in society fare better and are less likely to commit suicide than those who are less integrated in society. Because mattering measures, in part, how much people feel needed by others, those needs may represent the sense of one's integration into a group. Rosenberg's (Rosenberg and

McCullough 1981) early findings showed mattering to be positively related to self-esteem and negatively related to depression and anxiety, independent of self-esteem. People with a greater sense of mattering tend to have higher levels of self-esteem and lower levels of depression and anxiety.

Recent research supports Rosenberg's original findings. Pearlin and LeBlanc (2001) found a direct relationship between loss of mattering and depression among older adults, such that those who recently reported a loss of mattering due to the death of a loved one had higher levels of depression than those who did not. Adolescents who believe they matter more to others are also significantly less likely to consider suicide than those who believe that they matter less (Elliott, Colangelo, and Gelles 2005). The authors argued that mattering ultimately affects our lives through self-esteem: Levels of mattering affect our sense of worth, leading us to positive behaviors and attitudes.

Some research shows that levels and effects of mattering vary by gender, with women reporting higher levels of mattering than men (Schieman and Taylor 2001; Taylor and Turner 2001). This is different from what we find with other social resources such as mastery (with men higher) or self-esteem (where women and men tend to have similar levels), perhaps because mattering may represent social connections, typically more central for women than men (Liebler and Sandefur 2002; Pugliesi and Shook 1998). It also appears that the relationship between mattering and mental health is stronger among women compared to men (Schieman and Taylor 2001; Taylor and Turner 2001).

Measuring the Self-Concept

Psychologists regularly conduct personality tests using instruments designed to place people within a limited set of personality dimensions. For instance, the Myers-Briggs personality inventory includes a battery of questions that divides personality into four different dimensions. In contrast to most psychologists, social psychologists—in psychology and sociology—tend to focus on the self-concept rather than personality per se. Measures of the self-concept include more qualitative assessments of who we are as well as quantitative measures similar to the type found in personality tests.

The Twenty-Statements Test

One of the ways that you can assess your own identity is by taking the *Twenty-Statements Test* or *TST* (see Figure 5.1). Go try it now! The TST was developed by Kuhn and McPartland (1954) as a way of assessing individuals' self-concepts. The test simply asks respondents to answer the question, "Who am I?" 20 times. Responses to the TST are generally divided into four categories or "modes": the physical self, the social self, the reflective self and the oceanic self, (Zurcher 1977). The **physical self** refers to physical characteristics such as hair color or height. The **social self** refers to roles and statuses, such as student, daughter or son, and gender. The **reflective self** refers to our feelings and traits such as being shy or

On each line below, write a different answer to the question "Who am I?" As you write these answers, respond as if you are giving these answers to yourself and not to somebody else. Also, write your responses quickly and in the order they occur to you. When you have completed 20 lines, you have finished taking the TST.

Who Am I?

1. _____
2. _____
3. _____
4. _____
5. _____
6. _____
7. _____
8. _____
9. _____
10. _____
11. _____
12. _____
13. _____
14. _____
15. _____
16. _____
17. _____
18. _____
19. _____
20. _____

Interpreting Findings: Review each of your responses and try to code them into one of four categories: physical characteristics, social roles or group membership (social self), personal traits (reflective self), or some holistic sense of self (oceanic self) (e.g., "I am one with the universe"). What do your results say about who you are? Do you see yourself more in terms of in the context of groups and society (social self) or your personal traits (reflective self)? Most modern American students focus on their reflective or social selves. How about you?

Figure 5.1   The Twenty-Statements Test

Source: Adapted from Kuhn and McPartland (1954).

kindhearted. An additional category, the **oceanic self,** includes those dimensions of the self that do not easily fit into the first three categories, usually referring to some holistic sense of self.

TST results can be influenced by context. If you took it in the classroom, for example, the "student" identity might be highly salient and listed among the first few responses. You can try to match your responses to your peers, comparing self-ratings with people around you using the categories listed. Early research in the TST from the 1950s found that most students characterized themselves primarily in terms of the social self, identifying themselves in terms of the social roles and groups to which they belonged. More recent work shows a move to the reflective self, focusing on feelings and personal traits (Grace and Cramer 2002; Snow and Phillips 1982). Further, although women are somewhat more likely to report family roles than men, there is little difference in test outcomes among men and women, related to issues of gender (Mackie 1983).

Responses to the TST tend to be positive. Very few people report things such as, "I am a bad person." Recent research using the TST has attempted to explore this issue with the development of the "What Am I Not" (WAIN) test (McCall 2003). Instead of asking who I am, the WAIN asks respondents to answer the question, "Who am I NOT?" Results from the WAIN showed that people are more likely to put positive statements about themselves in the TST (90% of the self-descriptions were positive) compared to the WAIN, where only 63% of the statements were positive. These findings suggest that the wording of the test can have a substantial impact on the outcomes and that there may be two poles of our identity, one positive (the "Me") and one negative (the "Not-Me").

The Rosenberg Self-Esteem Scale

Self-esteem, mastery, and mattering can be measured quantitatively. One of the most popular measures is the Rosenberg Self-Esteem Scale (see Table 5.1). These measures assume that responses to a series of questions about our thoughts and feelings accurately portray a dimension of the self-concept. If this is true, we can use such measures to test empirical relationships between social processes and our self-concept using experiments and surveys (see chapter 2).

Social Class, Race, and the Self-Concept

Our positions in society have important effects on our thoughts, feelings, and behaviors. Two of the most profound ways that our position in a social structure can affect us is via our class position or status. Social class was defined in chapter 4 as a group who shares the same status in society. Our class position affects the number of resources we have available to manage problems as well as to develop talents and abilities. Class also influences the activities we engage in, the types of people with whom we spend time, and how we spend our time (Lareau 2003). These factors, in turn, affect what we value in life and who we believe we are.

Table 5.1   Rosenberg Self-Esteem Scale

	1. Strongly Agree	2 Agree	3. Disagree	4. Strongly Disagree
I feel that I'm a person of worth, at least on an equal plane with others.	SA	A	D	SD
I feel that I have a number of good qualities.	SA	A	D	SD
All in all, I am inclined to feel that I am a failure.*	SA	A	D	SD
I am able to do things as well as most other people.	SA	A	D	SD
I feel I do not have much to be proud of.*	SA	A	D	SD
I take a positive attitude toward myself.	SA	A	D	SD
On the whole, I am satisfied with myself.	SA	A	D	SD
I wish I could have more respect for myself.*	SA	A	D	SD
I certainly feel useless at times.*	SA	A	D	SD
At times I think I am no good at all.*	SA	A	D	SD

————————————

*Items to be reverse-coded.

Source: Adapted from Rosenberg (1986).

Class and Self-Esteem

Some early work on social class and the self explored the relationship between class position and the self-concept. Morris Rosenberg and other researchers in the 1960s and 1970s believed that poor economic environments would lead to lower self-esteem among children (Rosenberg and Pearlin 1978; Rosenberg 1986). They hypothesized that self-esteem would be linked to social status, that economic conditions would reflect people's sense of worth in society. Class would serve as an indicator to people of where they stood in the world. In this view, children at the lower end of the social system should report the lowest sense of self-worth because they are on the bottom of the social system relative to their middle- and upper-class peers.

Rosenberg and Pearlin (1978) used data from surveys of children, adolescents, and adults from Baltimore and Chicago to compare levels of self-esteem at different class levels. Findings showed that the relationship between class and self-esteem is somewhat complicated. The researchers found that social class position affects self-esteem as predicted, at least among adolescents and adults. However, findings from children showed no effect of class on self-esteem. Additional analyses suggested that the effects of class are only felt as children enter adolescence, when occupation, income, and education become more important to one's identity. These characteristics provide a sense of relative position that only becomes salient to children as they enter the adult world. Thus, class position starts to affect the self-concept only when an individual becomes aware of her position in society. Social comparisons and reflected appraisals matter.

Young children have little awareness of their positions in society, limiting their social comparisons to their immediate surroundings. If we and all our friends have lots of expensive toys and games, then we may believe that the rest of the world is the same. Moreover, because others do not judge them (i.e., they do not get reflected appraisals) based on social class, children have had little chance to advance into a higher social class yet. However, as children enter adolescence, they obtain more information about the larger society from more sources. Through images in the media and through interactions with their adult family members, children begin to see that there are great variations in the ways people live. These images and interactions show them what other people have—or do not have—relative to the rest of the world. This information also gives them a sense of what they can expect of their own lives. As youth process this information over time, they may question why they have more or less than other people in society and adjust their senses of self accordingly, lowering the sense of self-esteem to reflect their status in society.

Identity and Ethnicity

Ethnicity is another important social status, and one that has connections to individual identity. How people understand themselves as having a certain ethnicity is in no small part connected to the beliefs and practices of the larger society. One interesting study by Joanne Nagel (1995) examined the following puzzle: U.S. census data from the 1970s and 1980s showed a very large increase in the number of residents identifying themselves as "American Indian." Yet there had been no increase in birthrates, no decrease in death rates, nor any immigration from other parts of North America that could account for the shift.

Nagel (1995) found that large numbers of people who had some American Indian ancestry identified themselves as "White" on their census forms at one point and later switched ethnicities, claiming American Indian identity. She argued that three social factors affected the likelihood of "feeling" and "being"

Indian. First, legal changes made government resources, such as scholarships and programs, available to Indians. Second, the "Red Power" movement, in some ways similar to the Civil Rights movement, shifted negative stereotypes of Indians to become more positive. Each of these made claiming an Indian identity more appealing. Third, urbanization created larger groupings of individuals with some Indian background, allowing them to form collectivities that helped people understand themselves as part of this "Supertribal" ethnic group.

Some groups, those with more status and power than others, such as Whites, have more options to define their ethnic identity. For example, Mary Waters (1999) found that for Whites, ethnicity was a fun part of their background, where they could pick and choose whether and when to call themselves "Irish" or "Greek," for example. For others, those with dark skin and certain other characteristics or physical features that U.S. society terms "Black," it is much more difficult to "decide" or project an ethnic identity, such as Jamaican, for example, in that others often assume that they are African Americans and treat them this way. These studies show the importance of social structural conditions in our attempts to construct or take on ethnic identities.

Section Summary

In this section, we used the social structure and personality perspective to answer the questions: What are the three dimensions of the self-concept? What do we know from research on the self-concept? Although there are many dimensions to the self-concept, a considerable amount of research has been done on self-esteem, our sense of self-worth; mastery, our sense that we have control over what happens to us; and mattering, our sense of importance in the world. Social structure and personality researchers attempt to study the impact of our social position on our self-concept. For instance, we examined research showing that class position affects our global sense of self-worth, though only as we reach adulthood, when we begin to see our relative position in the social structure.

GP | Identity and Group Processes

Joining the local Veteran's Club changed the way I felt about being in the Army. I pretty much did my service like anyone else. I joined for the benefits. After coming back from the Persian Gulf, I felt like I should do something more. I left the service and joined the Vet's Club. I pretty much stick with the others in the club, they understand what it was like over there. Maybe I am just comfortable with these guys. People outside the club just don't get it.

—Sam, senior Philosophy major

Many of the self and identity processes we have discussed thus far occur in the contexts of groups. Groups serve as a way to establish and maintain our sense of self. Groups can also serve to give you an identity that is a collective one. A group identity may become part of how you describe yourself. In Sam's case, he began to think of himself as a veteran *after* he joined the Veteran's Club. Thus, in an objective sense, he was a veteran but did not take on that identity until he joined the group. In addition, this identity changed his view of himself and the people around him—other people "just don't get it."

Social Identity Theory

If you filled in the Twenty Statements Test in Figure 5.1, you noticed that your self-concept is comprised of various components. You may see yourself in terms of your gender, your nationality, your race or ethnicity, the college or university you attend, and any other number of factors. According to **social identity theory,** we carry self-definitions that match all the categories to which we belong. In the theory, these self-definitions are called **social identities.** The theory argues that people define themselves, in part, by their group memberships (Hogg and Ridgeway 2003, Tajfel 1982).

Group events give us an opportunity to reinforce our sense of identity with people from similar backgrounds.

Originally developed in psychology, social identity theory proposes that our social identities describe to us who we are, provide us with information about how to behave, and tell us how we should evaluate other people (Hogg, Terry, and White 1995). The theory argues that we view ourselves and others according to our group memberships. Also, in any given social context, some of our social identities will be more salient to us than others. Imagine, for example, being a staunch Democrat in a meeting of your university's Young Republicans Club (or vice versa). In that case, your social identity tied to your political views would probably be very salient.

When a social identity is salient, social identity theory says that we will perceive ourselves according to that identity. Further, we will tend to behave in ways that are stereotypical of that identity. If you are a woman in a situation in which your gender identity is highly salient, for example, social identity theory says that you will tend to act in ways that are gender-stereotypical for women in our society. Perhaps most important, social identity theory argues that when identities are salient, we will view members

by making school more important
we risk damage to us

of other groups in ways that are stereotypical for their group. Thus, when social identities become salient, our relationships with and perceptions of people in different categories of the identity will be competitive and discriminatory (Hogg and Ridgeway 2003).

As discussed earlier, we tend to carry out actions that will promote our own sense of self, or our self-esteem. Because of this, and because we view ourselves in terms of our group memberships, we are motivated to adopt strategies in interactions that make our own groups look better (to both ourselves and others) than other groups. Social identity theory argues that we engage in two processes that allow us to draw favorable comparisons between our own groups and other groups—categorization and self-enhancement.

According to social identity theory, we do not only see ourselves in terms of our category memberships but also seek to assign other people to social categories. **Categorization** is the process through which we draw sharp dividing lines between group membership categories and assign people (including ourselves) to relevant categories. You might, for example, see stark differences between Democrats and Republicans and seek to assign people to one category or another. When we do this, we accentuate similarities we perceive between people in the same categories (Deaux and Martin 2003). For example, we might tend to see all Democrats as highly homogeneous in their views. We also accentuate perceived differences across categories. You might, for example, see Democrats and Republicans as fundamentally different in how they view the world when there are many similarities. When these processes happen, people (including ourselves) are depersonalized and seen only in terms of their category memberships.

Self-enhancement refers to the process through which we make comparisons that favor our own groups. This can be done in multiple ways. One way we draw comparisons that favor our own groups can be to essentially delude ourselves into seeing our group as better than it really is. Another way is to focus specifically on differences that favor our own group while ignoring differences that do not. For example, when students at a state university and students at a community college compare themselves on their identities associated with their colleges, social identity theory would expect each to make comparisons most favorable to their own groups. The university students, for example, might focus on the diverse opportunities available to them, whereas the community college students might focus on their small class sizes and access to professors.

The ramifications of social identity processes can be quite large. Sunshine and Tyler (2003) showed that people are more likely to cooperate with police, for instance, if they think that the police represent the moral values of a society, that they represent "one of us." Thus, we may use our group affiliations to bias our understanding of other people's motives. We may also use social identities to judge the competency of other people, showing favoritism toward people in our own social category over others (Oldmeadow, Platow, Foddy, and Anderson 2003). Social identity theory shows how group processes affect our identities. Our sense of self derives in large part from the groups to which we belong, and we tend to view both ourselves and others in terms of group memberships.

Section Summary

The last section of this chapter addressed the question: How do group processes affect identity? Here we reviewed social identity theory. Social identity theory proposes that our social identities describe to us who we are, provide us with information about how to behave, and tell us how we should evaluate other people. Group memberships include racial and ethnic groups, among others. Once accepted, we employ group identities into interactions with other people, using them to differentially evaluate the attitudes and behavior of people inside and outside of the group.

Bringing it All Together

In the end, I think it is all about our genes. I mean, you can't change the way people are.

—Josh, senior Marketing major

Josh's philosophy of human personality is pretty deterministic. He views our sense of identity as formed by a genetic code that is not likely to change over a lifetime—bad people are born bad and they stay that way. Most of us would give some credit to the influences of parents, teachers, and role-models in our lives. Symbolic interactionists would extend these influences to our own agency too, that we can make decisions that affect our sense of self over our lifetime. Here, too, scholars would disagree with Josh. Interactionists would question Josh's deterministic attitude because humans have the capacity to manipulate the meaning of different identities both internally, through self indication, and externally via relationships with other people. What is more, we can manipulate our impressions regardless of who we really are.

The social structure and personality perspective emphasizes the evaluative dimensions of the self-concept like self-esteem, mastery, and mattering. Research shows both social and social-structural conditions impact our self-concept. Our social position, notably in the form of social class, race and gender influences our sense of self worth. Social identity theory, from the group-processes perspective, extends this work to include the role of our group memberships in our sense of self.

Together, these perspectives show the role that society plays in the development and maintenance of our senses of self. Genetics may play a role in our dispositions but society provides the context for evaluating and acting on those dispositions, and structures the kind of positions we will take part in.

Summary

1. From a symbolic interactionist perspective, the self is a process in which we construct a sense of who we are. We use symbols and language to communicate with other people but we also use language to think internally. The self includes a dialogue between the I and the Me.

2. Identity includes our social categories and personal characteristics. Identity theory examines how social conditions affect the salience of identities and thus our behavior. Affect-control theory incorporates emotions in identity processes.

3. Dramaturgical sociology is a branch of symbolic interactionism that studies impression formation and management.

4. The self-concept refers to all our thoughts and feelings about ourselves as an object, often studied in the form of identities, self-esteem, mattering, and mastery.

5. Class, race, and gender are important social statuses that influence our self-development over time.

6. Social identity theory argues that people define and evaluate themselves in terms of the groups they belong to, including one's race and gender.

Key Terms and Concepts

Affect-control theory: The theory that incorporates elements of symbolic interactionism and identity theory to explain the role of emotion in identity processes.

Backstage: Part of dramaturgical sociology referring to the region where we relax our impression management efforts.

Categorization: In social identity theory, the process through which we draw sharp dividing lines between group membership categories and assign people (including ourselves) to relevant categories.

Dramaturgical sociology: The study of how we present ourselves, playing roles and managing impressions during interactions with other people.

Emotional arousal: Inferences about our abilities based on our emotional states that we use to build our sense of mastery.

Front stage: Part of dramaturgical sociology referring to the place where we present ourselves to others.

I: The part of the self that is active, engaging in interactions with others.

Identity: Our internalized, stable sense of who we are.

Identity theory: Interactionist theory that describes how society shapes our sense of self and how those views affect our behavior.

Impression management: The ways individuals seek to control the impressions they convey to other people.

Impressions given: The impression you believe that you are giving.

Impressions given off: The actual impression the other person has of you.

Mastery: Our perceptions of our ability to control things important to us.

Mattering: Our sense that we are important to other people in the world.

Me: The part of the self that includes an organized set of attitudes toward the self.

Oceanic self: Dimension of the Twenty Statements Test referring to a holistic description of the self.

Personal accomplishments: Being able to achieve what we start out to do; used in the development of mastery.

Personal characteristics: Anything we use to describe our individual nature.

Physical self: Dimension of the Twenty Statements Test referring to our physical characteristics like hair color or height.

Psychological centrality: Our ability to shift aspects of the self to become more or less important to our overall self-concept.

Reflected appraisals: The ways that we believe others view us.

Reflective self: Dimension of the Twenty Statements Test referring to our feelings and traits like being shy or nice.

Role identities: The internalized expectations associated with different positions.

Self: A process in which we construct a sense of who we are through interaction with others.

Self-concept: The outcome of the self-process at a given point in time; the sum total of our thoughts and feelings about ourselves as an object.

Self-consistency motive: A drive to maintain a consistent sense of self.

Self-enhancement: In social identity theory, the process through which we make comparisons that favor our own groups.

Self-esteem: The positive or negative evaluation of our self as an object.

Self-esteem motive: The desire to maintain positive self images.

Self-evaluations: Judgments we make of ourselves.

Self-fulfilling prophecy: A process in which expectations produce a reality consistent with the assumptions.

Self-identities: The kind of person we see ourselves as.

Self-indication: The use of symbols and language to communicate internally.

Self-perceptions: Observations of our behavior and its consequences.

Situated self: A temporally based sense of who we are.

Social categories: Identities related to social groups to which we belong.

Social comparisons: Using other people as a point of reference for our thoughts, feelings, and behaviors.

Social identities: A form of self-definition used in social identity theory based on our group affiliations.

Social identity theory: The theory based on the principle that we carry self-definitions that match all the categories to which we belong.

Social self: Dimension of the Twenty Statements Test referring to our roles and statuses, such as student, daughter or son, or gender.

Verbal persuasion: Information from others about our abilities used to derive mastery.

Vicarious experience: A way of building mastery by seeing other people perform tasks; it shows us that the task is accomplishable.

Discussion Questions

1. Think about your sense of self. What role do you think that your race, ethnicity, gender, or age plays in your day-to-day interactions?

2. Would it be possible to change your sense of self? Apply some of the information from this chapter to figure out how you could negotiate social forces to help you "construct" a new self.

3. Take the Twenty Statements Test. Did anything surprise you about the findings? How do you think the order of your responses would be different if you took it at school? Work? Home?

Socialization over the Life Course

I was just 14, and my friend and I became a volunteer at a local hospital. Because we had these uniforms, patients, their families, nurses and other staff were treating us like we knew what we were doing. But it was just a summer job and I was sure I would mess it up! It was strange, but after about a month, I really felt competent at getting the patients where they had to be. I was proud when people asked me questions and I had learned the answers. The hospital setting was routine, but there was some real drama in the hallways and being a part of that place was something I really liked.

—Maya, senior Biology major

The ways in which individuals attempt to align their own thoughts, feelings, and behavior to fit into society or groups is called **socialization** (Corsaro and Fingerson 2003; Stryker 2002). As with Maya's story, socialization can occur informally through observation and interaction. Socialization can also be more formal as children enter educational institutions to learn the appropriate skills necessary to successfully enter the economy of a given society. Although most people associate socialization with children's development, adults continue to be socialized over the course of their lives, learning norms and values in new social contexts as well as age-appropriate ways to think, feel, and behave (Crosnoe and Elder 2004; Elder 1994; Mortimer and Simmons 1978). In the preceding example, Maya is socialized a hospital worker—she learns what it means to be that kind of person, interacts with others on the basis of that role, and finally comes to feel that the role is central to who she is.

Sociologists study socialization processes at every stage of development. We will review symbolic interactionist perspectives on childhood development of the self and self-concept, followed by a review of the life-course perspective in sociology, which derives from the social structure and personality perspective. Group processes work does not tend to focus on socialization, but can be related to it. This chapter addresses the following questions regarding socialization and life-course sociology:

- How does society influence the social construction of the self? What are the stages involved in developing the self?
- What are the four elements of life-course sociology? What are agents of socialization, and how do they affect our lives?
- How do group processes researchers study socialization?

SI   Developing the Self

I never really played "house" growing up. Then a friend brought a couple of Barbie dolls over and asked me to play. I kind of felt obligated to participate. She had a Ken doll and we tried to get a boy to play with us. It did not work. So, we just asked a girl down the street to play Ken, the boyfriend. It worked fine. She was the best Ken I ever met.

—Betty, *Physics major*

As discussed in chapter 5, interactionists view the self as a process. We pick up and drop aspects of our characters in different circumstances and social contexts. We learn these new aspects of the self by observing how other people act under certain conditions and decide which of them to adapt as our own. In Betty's case, she did not necessarily desire to play dolls when she was young, but instead found herself pulled into the experience by a friend. Social psychologists generally believe that such experiences are important to socialization because they provide opportunities to learn how people behave in society. In Betty's story, gender is being taught in many ways. Betty learns that little girls play with dolls in our society. In addition, while playing dolls, she instills gender-role behavior to the dolls. The girls try to find a boy to play Ken, the man's role. They only turn to a girl out of need. It turns out that the girl can play the role of Ken as well as any boy.

The key point to this interaction is the importance of playing a part in society. The interactionist perspective sees this process occurring as a progression of role changes over time (Holstein and Gubrium 2003; Stryker 2002). It starts by practicing roles in society or simply acting out a part, something akin to dramaturgical sociology discussed in chapter 5. We take on roles in our lives and then get shaped by them. We also sympathize with other people's roles, giving us the ability to predict what other people will do in a given situation and how to react accordingly. Over time, we develop the ability to coordinate multiple roles while incorporating other people's points of view. We will review some of the basic stages associated with childhood development of these processes and then examine how these dynamics are demonstrated in children's lives.

Stages of Development

The exchange of language and symbols is essential to the symbolic interactionist perspective of human interaction. If the self is a symbolic process, then children need to learn language skills before they can fully develop their senses of self. Although children pick up symbolic acts within the first few months of life (e.g., smiling at others), they do not fully develop their language skills until at least five or six years of age (Hurh 2003). Thereafter, children's development of the self occurs in stages as children acquire symbols and language over time.

Our ability to take the role of other—seeing social interaction from other people's perspectives—takes time and practice. At first, children simply mimic the attitudes and behaviors of their parents and caretakers. This is called the **preparatory stage** (Mead 1934). The preparatory stage provides the cognitive information necessary for children to act out other people's roles. Anyone who has seen a two-year-old around a group of adults can understand the preparatory stage. Children will often repeat words or short phrases without knowing what they mean. Imagine a father dropping something on his foot and screaming a profanity in reaction to the event. Thereafter, the child might find herself yelling profanities any time something bad happens to her. The parent realizes that the child is mimicking his own behavior and prepares to "resocialize" the child to a new vocabulary.

As children begin to develop more language skills, they can start using these skills to think symbolically. At the **play stage,** children begin to use language to make-believe as they play others' roles. A child may start pretending that she is a firefighter or a teacher. In this stage, children generally take on one role at a time. For instance the three-year-old son of one of this book's authors recently got in trouble while pretending to be Batman. When his father sent him to time out, the child angrily cried, "Batman doesn't go in time out!"

Finally, children learn to integrate their knowledge into a cohesive picture of their social world. The **game stage** occurs when children are capable of managing several different roles at the same time. This power allows the individual to participate in organized role relationships. For instance, we must understand the role of the other team players in a baseball or football game, knowing how other people are likely to respond to our actions in a competition. This ability requires that we can situate ourselves amidst several different people, and thus roles, at the same time.

There are no specific rules about when these abilities will develop in children because they vary across individuals. Some children learn these processes readily, whereas others take longer, depending on their own abilities to acquire and manipulate symbols and their social environments. The ability to adapt and integrate

| Box 6.1 | Piaget's Stages of Cognitive Development |

Jean Piaget (1896–1980) was a famous psychologist who studied individuals' cognitive development. He argued that all people develop their mental and physical abilities in the following stages:

1. *Sensorimotor Stage (birth to 2)*—Children develop a sense of cause and effect of their behaviors by physically investigating their worlds and by imitation of other people's behavior.

2. *Preoperational Stage (2 to 7)*—Children learn to use symbols and language to communicate but are not able to think in complex ways.

3. *Concrete Operational Stage (7 to 11)*—Children start developing reasoning skills by classifying, ranking, and separating physical objects.

4. *Formal Operational Stage (11+)*—Children develop their abstract reasoning skills, working out problems and issues in their minds.

Sociological social psychologists generally agree with psychological perspectives on development but view the process as much more fluid. That is, our development is partly related to biological development but also influenced by our social surroundings as well as our ability to make decisions in the development process. For instance, a lower SES child interacts within a less rich symbolic environment, thus, affecting developmental processes described. Interactionist approaches to development incorporate these sorts of variations.

---

symbols is essential to these dynamics; hence, some basic cognitive development is required to move into the play and game stages (see Box 6.1).

The Role of the Other

An essential aspect of self-development is the ability to take the role of the other. We must be able to understand the perspectives of other people before we can understand ourselves. We cannot "play doctor" unless we have the ability to understand what a doctor does relative to other people. This understanding helps us know the appropriate ways to behave in a given context. Charles Horton Cooley (1922) argued that the self relies on other people's responses. This idea has been deemed the **looking-glass self.** In other words, our sense of self is partly a reflection of the sentiments of other people. For instance, if you give a speech and find that the audience is frowning, yawning, and making comments as you talk, you will likely interpret this reaction to mean that you are not a good speaker, and you may feel embarrassed or ashamed.

We also have the ability to understand how the larger society may view us. The **generalized other** refers to our perceptions of the attitudes of the whole community (Cooley 1922; Mead 1934). Hence, we can imagine how other people in general would react to a thought or behavior. Think about a situation in which you go to an event where you know almost no one. You may want to light up a cigarette but will probably consider what other people may think of you. Because you do not know anyone very well, you must rely on your knowledge of your culture's (or subculture's) attitude toward tobacco use. Because smoking indoors, legally or otherwise, is unacceptable in many places in the United States, you know not to "light up" at many social activities. You may even consider asking permission before smoking at an outdoor event; in Europe, smoking is probably more accepted in a variety of places.

Because we continue to adopt and drop roles in our lifetime, symbolic interactionists view socialization as an ongoing dynamic that occurs internally (what we are thinking about ourselves, others, and the generalized other) and externally (through the words, mannerisms, and other symbolic exchanges with other people). The self also changes given different cultural and societal conditions because the generalized other can also change over time. Under this paradigm, the self can change as quickly as our environments and our ability to process the information from those environments.

The Sociology of Childhood

A significant amount of the literature on socialization focuses on children. However, the concept of "childhood" has changed dramatically over the last few centuries (Jencks 1996). Being a child has generally been conceived of as a temporary stage, at best, or as a state that must be transformed or "civilized" in some way. Recent research in sociology has started to view childhood as a state in life in which competent actors negotiate their social realities in a similar fashion as adults (Cahill 2003).

Children's Culture

Norman Denzin (1971, 1977) studied the subtle ways that children interact with one another. He found that even very young children, 8 to 24 months, can participate in a "conversation of gestures,"[1] nonverbal and preverbal ways of indicating meaning to other people. They use these gestures to designate particular objects or ownership of objects. Denzin argued that these "conversations" evolve into verbal exchanges over time. Hence, even at very young ages children begin the same interactional and negotiation processes as their parents. Indeed, they negotiate *with* their parents.

Because children are capable of the same interaction processes as adults, they can also develop their own cultures. Corsaro (2005) defined **children's cultural routines** as stable sets of activities, objects, and values that children produce and share in interaction with each other. However, since children have meaning-making

---

[1]The basic concept of a conversation of gestures comes from Mead's description of the general interaction process.

School contexts provide children a means of formally learning their culture through teaching as well as place for the development of peer cultures.

capacities similar to adults, they engage in an **interpretive reproduction** of adult culture creatively taking on elements of adult culture to meet the needs of their peer group (Corsaro 1992; 2005).

Children mold specific roles to meet the needs of the peer groups in three ways:

1. Children take information from the adult world to create stable routines.
2. Children use language to manipulate adult models to address specific needs of their peer culture.
3. Children improvise "sociodramatic" play to acquire the dispositions necessary to manage their daily lives.

In summary, children use the patterns of behavior learned from their parents and siblings and others to help them get through interactions with other people. Children know what to do and say at the dinner table because they have practiced it at home so many times. However, children have human agency, the ability to make decisions above and beyond their training at home. In a group of peers, formal exchanges like "please" and "thank you" may be replaced with jokes and play, depending on the composition of the group. Children can improvise the behaviors and roles learned from their parents to meet the needs of a particular group or social setting.

As active participants in the socialization process, children's routines serve as a basis for developing and maintaining larger cultures. Gary Alan Fine (1979) studied a group of youth baseball teams over time by observing the culture of each group and the changes in those cultures over time. He found that the culture of the group changed as new people entered and left the groups, but some consistency was maintained as new members learned ways of the group from older, senior members of the team. Fine (1979) referred to the culture of these small groups of boys as **idiocultures,** "a system of knowledge, beliefs, behaviors, and customs shared by an interacting group to which members refer and employ as a basis of further interaction" (734). These cultures are a hybrid culture comprised of elements of the larger culture of baseball mixed with elements of the local cultures surrounding those teams and the personalities of the children playing on them. The merging of these worlds (individual and community) allows individuals to participate in culture construction without abandoning the culture of the larger community, in this case, the culture of baseball.

Learning Racism

The subtle nature of children's play can help us understand the roots of the replication of racist attitudes and behaviors. Children find creative ways to develop independence from adults as well as ways of excluding others from their play (Corsaro 2005). Race and ethnicity can be one of the ways children distinguish themselves or their group from others (Ausdale and Feagin 2002). Thus, race can serve as one of many markers between groups of people, especially if racial differences are readily apparent (e.g., skin color). However, children are capable of finding ways to differentiate between groups based on things other than the color of skin. If language is the building block of symbolic interaction, then language differences can be one of the first methods of differentiation. Language can serve as a way to exclude children from play. For example, children may interact such that only Spanish or English is allowed, excluding those who do not speak a particular language.

Ausdale and Feagin's (2002) research shows that racist thoughts and beliefs can be brought into children's interaction at a very young age, even before they have the ability to fully understand its ramifications. Some racist epithets may simply be heard and repeated among peers. Racist thoughts and feelings may start with simple imitation, but children can use those memories to create more extensive conceptualizations of race and ethnicity. From an interactionist perspective, children can actively develop and manipulate simple racism into complex sets of meaning about categories of people. The process involves intellectual and social components, some related to race and some not. For instance, a child may hear a racial epithet but do nothing with the thought until social conditions require some means of differentiation between peers. The child may then use and elaborate on a simple epithet as a means of defining oneself and others in an interaction. Hence, some of the same basic interactionist principles of socialization are used to negotiate racist and ethnocentric attitudes and behaviors.

Section Summary

The first section of this chapter addressed the questions: How does society influence the social construction of the self? What are the stages involved in developing the self? Symbolic interactionists focus on how children develop the ability to construct their senses of self over time, starting with simple imitations of attitudes and behaviors and then actively manipulated their sense of self with other people. Interactionists also study children's culture and the ways that they take information from adult society, such as race, and use it in their own culture.

SSP | Structural and Time Dimensions of Socialization

I still vividly remember the feeling that I had as the bomb went off. For a split second, I thought that I was dead. I had only been in Iraq for two months, I thought, and I was dead. The bomb went off . . . everything went black for a second, then I woke up in a kind-of white daze. Then I heard my buddy screaming, "MEDIC! MEDIC!" at the top of his lungs as I lay bleeding on the ground. It was then that it really hit me. I mean, why I was there. I began to cry as I realized how important our mission was . . . and that I was helping in that mission. I guess you could say that it was a life-changing event.

—Robert, senior History major

The word *socialization* is often applied to childhood development. This application seems natural because children are not born with any knowledge of their society or its culture. But people change even after they learn the rules of a society. In fact, they can participate in changing those rules after they have learned them. In addition, our bodies change over time. Just as children change socially and psychologically with their biological growth, there are social and psychological shifts associated with the changes that accompany adolescence, middle age, and the deterioration of adults' bodies as they enter later stages in life.

There are other ways that society can affect socialization processes. **Life events** are any experiences that cause significant changes in the course of our lives. In Robert's case, his experience in Iraq changed the way he viewed his mission overseas. Before being wounded, he saw his role in the military as simply part of his job. He came to accept his role in the conflict as something more substantial when he viewed it through the lens of a wounded veteran. The event caused him to rethink his place in the world.

These events do not occur in a vacuum; we experience them with other people, and we learn about the world through important social institutions such as the family and education. In Robert's case, his role in the military institution affected his life in a dramatic way. Research and theories from the social structure and personality perspective also examine the impacts of primary **agents of socialization,** groups most influential in the process of teaching children the norms and values of a particular culture. First, we will review the life-course perspective and then examine the role that institutions such as family and education play in the socialization process.

The Life Course

We do not know what long-term effects military service will have on Robert, but a significant amount of research in life-course sociology suggests that it will have some effect on his life. The study of the **life course** is assessing the process of personal change from infancy to late adulthood resulting from personal and societal events and from transitions into and out of social roles (Elder 1994). The life course incorporates the larger social world into how individuals develop and change over time, usually in the form of large-scale life events such as war or famine. In

Socialization experiences can be different for each generation as cultures change. Many women in modern, Western nations juggle multiple roles when raising their children.

Robert's example, he is clearly affected by the wounds he received in service. However, the war itself is the result of societal-level events. One nation started fighting another nation (and later, insurgents), placing Robert in a unique position in history. In this case, the historical condition of war places Robert in a life-changing situation.

Life-course sociology is more than just the study of life events. It is also about life transitions, ways in which people move from one role to the next and the factors that affect those changes. According to Elder (1994), there are four major themes in life-course sociology:

1. **Historical context**—how historic events affect development for different birth cohorts.
2. **Timing**—incidence, duration, and sequence of roles, and relevant expectations and beliefs based on age.
3. **Linked lives**—our relationships with other people.
4. **Agency**—our ability to make decisions and control our destinies.

These factors interact to produce different outcomes for people experiencing them. We will review each of these factors in more detail next.

Historical Times

A **birth cohort** refers to a group of people born within the same time period. People sometime use the word *generation* to refer to a birth cohort. Popular discussions of the influence of birth cohorts have focused on the influence of the birth cohort or generation known as the baby boomers. Boomers are people born after the end of World War II (1944) until 1964. The baby boomer generation is one of the largest birth cohorts in American history. This generation was exposed to some of the greatest cultural and technological changes in American society: the space race and the sexual revolution, for example. They also witnessed moments of horror such as the assassinations of John F. Kennedy and Martin Luther King, Jr. The subsequent generations "X" and "Y" also experienced a number of historic events in their formative years of development (see Table 6.1).

Differences in exposure to historical events, especially those occurring at "critical times" in the life course, may have long-lasting effects on our personal growth and development. The effects are likely to be much greater for those experiencing the culture and events of the time, such as the sexual revolution, as adolescents and young adults than those who are already adults or who are born later. Historical contexts also present constraints and options from which to make decisions in our lives. In this sense, our birth cohorts merely represent a proxy for exposure to specific historical events and changes (Elder 1994).

In a classic life-course study, *Children of the Great Depression*, Elder (1999, originally 1974) studied the long-term effects of the Great Depression on children's development. He followed a group of 167 children from California born in 1920

Table 6.1   Generations and Historical Influences

Generation Title	Birth Years	Historical Events during Youth
Baby Boom	1944–1964	• Vietnam War • Cold War, arms race • Sexual revolution • Move from industrial to service economy • Space race • Assassination of John F. Kennedy • Civil rights and feminist movements
Baby Bust; Generation X	1965–1979	• Fall of Berlin Wall, end of Cold War • Shooting of Ronald Reagan • Persian Gulf War • Newt Gingrich and the "Contract with America"; the subsequent government shutdown • The space shuttle Columbia explodes, killing a civilian teacher
Generation Y	1980s–1990s	• 9/11 attacks on World Trade Center and Pentagon • Global war on terror • Iraq War

and 1921. They were about 10 years old when the Great Depression started and in their 30s and 40s at the end of the study period. Elder wanted to know if children developed differently over their life courses based on their economic positions (middle or upper class) and the amount of deprivation they experienced as a result of the failing economy of the 1930s, in which stock prices fell some 89% and unemployment rates went over 20%. Elder divided the sample into four groups of children: (1) middle-class nondeprived children, (2) middle-class deprived children, (3) working-class nondeprived children, and (4) working-class deprived children. Being deprived was defined as having a substantial loss of family income (over 50%) during the Depression period.

Elder found that the Great Depression did have ramifications for the people's long-term development, depending primarily on whether the children actually experienced deprivation during that time period. This finding may seem obvious, but folk wisdom suggested that everyone in the Great Depression cohort experienced the Depression equally, that all of them felt its effects one way or another. Elder also found that the effects of deprivation were primarily felt by changing roles within the family. As income and savings began to disappear, family members would turn toward alternative means of maintenance, with girls specializing in domestic tasks and boys on economic roles. In particular, boys obtained more freedom from parental control because they were forced to work more outside the home. Meanwhile, girls were expected to help more with household activities because the boys were away making money for the family.

The long-term effects of economic deprivation associated with the Great Depression included the loss of occupational status among some parents of the children in the study, though most recovered from these losses over time (Elder 1999). He also found long-term consequences for the children's self-concepts, with an increase in emotional sensitivity and emotionality, especially for the girls in the study. Deprived children tended to leave the Depression valuing job security, family responsibility, and family satisfaction over a focus on leisure and taking chances with job opportunities. Hence, the Great Depression did have long-term consequences on the behavior and personality of those growing up at that time period, but much more so for those who experienced some form of deprivation, supporting the premise of the proximity principle reviewed in chapter 2, that we feel the impacts of social forces through our immediate environments.

Social Timing

Another important aspect of life-course development is social timing. Social timing refers to the "incidence, duration, and sequence of roles, and to the relevant expectations and beliefs based on age" (Elder 1994: 6) (see Box 6.2). Social timing can affect reactions to life-course events in a number of ways. First, every society has age-linked patterns of behavior. For example, the median age for first marriage in the U.S. is 27 for males. Life-course events that interrupt marital possibilities will likely produce a greater impact on life outcomes than those events that do not interrupt that life stage. Further, the age at which an event occurs can also determine the resources with which we are able to manage those events. Younger people, for instance, typically have less income than their middle-aged counter-parts.

In the case of the Great Depression, Elder (1999) commented that the children in his sample experienced the Depression at an interesting point in their lives. Had they been just a few years older during the study, he believed, they may have had very different outcomes. In his study, they were old enough to understand the Depression without being old enough to feel its full brunt. If the children had been studied when they were teenagers, they might have taken an even larger role in the economy, losing opportunities associated with more typical childhood development. Ten-year-olds were given a comparatively limited set of responsibilities.

When our "normal trajectory" in our lives is interrupted, it is referred to as a **turning point** (Ivie, Gimbel, and Elder 1991). Turning points can be very difficult to study because individuals may have different subjective understandings of those events. Two people experiencing war, for instance, may have very different perspectives of the same events. The Great Depression served as a turning point for some of the children in Elder's study discussed earlier, but perhaps not all. Other events that can act as turning points in our lives include large storms that destroy towns, famines, and war. For example, in 2005, Hurricane Katrina left New Orleans and other areas devastated; however, a few individuals may have experienced a positive turning point, if they moved to a more economically viable area and obtained a new job, for example. The degree to which these turning points influence individuals' lives depends in part on when they occur. For instance, Elder's (1987) study of World War II found that entering the war at a later age produced greater disruption in family and career patterns than for those who entered the war at an earlier age.

In a series of studies, Sampson and Laub (1990, 1996; Laub, Nagen, and Sampson 1998; Laub and Sampson 1993) demonstrated the role of large-scale events such as WWII as a turning point in people's lives. Their research followed a group of 1,000 men from poor areas of Boston, initially assessing things such as IQ and antisocial behavior. These men were then tracked and periodically surveyed about their lives. Longitudinal research showed the powerful effects WWII had on these men's lives, creating long-term socioeconomic outcomes. They found that much of the effects of the war were felt through things such as overseas duty, in-service schooling, and the GI Bill. Through these experiences, these men were able to obtain better, more stable jobs and social lives after the war than they would have otherwise. Such research shows how macrosocial, structural conditions can influence our lives long after they occur, above and beyond our personal background and abilities.

Linked Lives

The third theme of life-course sociology is that people lead interdependent lives: Events occurring for individuals affect the other people in their lives and vice versa. Friends, family, and coworkers are affected by the things that happen in our lives. For example, job loss not only affects the person losing the job but her family as well. The effects can be monetary (e.g., loss of income) but can also be emotional (e.g., depression), as family members must relate to a person going through such an event.

Linked lives also have implications for access to varying amounts of resources with which to cope with life events. For instance, Elder's (1999) study of the Depression showed that middle-class children had the advantage of more social support during periods of deprivation than working-class children. In a more recent study, Elder and Conger (2000) studied a group of 451 rural families in Iowa to determine the effects of social integration in the life course of children over time. They found that rural children "tied to the land" (e.g., in families with farming-related businesses) had more involved parents, had stronger ties to parents, and were generally better integrated into the community than those who had no ties to the land. As a result, children tied to the land did better in school and had fewer behavioral problems as they got older.

Human Agency

Life-course sociology also recognizes that individuals have the ability to make decisions, albeit within a limited set of options. We introduced the idea of agency in chapter 2, emphasizing individuals' abilities to act and think independently. This concept is important to life-course sociology because individuals are able to act within the constraints imposed by social and historical conditions, leading to myriad possible outcomes. For instance, many children of the Great Depression found ways to overcome the economic adversities of the time. They may have

Box 6.2   **Erikson's Stages of Social Development**

Erik Erikson (1902–1994) was a psychologist who argued that people go through certain stages of social development from birth until later life. The earlier stages are more distinct and linked to biological development compared to the later stages. Erikson argued that our decisions about how to proceed at any given stage can have long-lasting effects on our future development. The following are Erikson's eight stages:

1. ***Trust vs. mistrust (birth to 1.5 years)***—This developmental period is when a basic sense of trust develops as children come to rely on their caregivers for feeding and basic nurturance; if trust is not established, children will believe that people are unreliable.

2. ***Autonomy vs. shame/doubt (1.5 to 3 years)***—This stage is when a child's muscular activities (walking, climbing, etc.) rapidly develop; when these activities are learned well and supported by others, the child learns a sense of control and pride; otherwise the child will develop feelings of shame or doubt regarding their abilities.

3. ***Initiative vs. guilt (3 to 6 years)***—Children learn to explore their worlds (social and physical), initiating ideas and activities and reflecting on their effects. If these attempts are not met with approval, the child will develop a sense of guilt.

4. ***Industry vs. inferiority (6 to 12)***—At this stage, children are being taught certain skills (using tools and utensils, education), developing a sense of industry. If children are not given the ability to complete the things they start, they may feel inferior to peers.

5. ***Identity vs. Role Confusion (12 to 18)***—At this stage, children are somewhere between youth and adulthood. It is here that they must learn their own sense of where they stand in the world, a sense of identity. Alternatively, a sense of role confusion ensues, leading to problems such as authoritarianism, sexual promiscuity, or racial bigotry.

6. ***Intimacy vs. Isolation (18 to 40)***—Individuals must develop intimate relationships (e.g., family and friendships) or suffer feelings of isolation.

7. ***Generativity vs. Stagnation (40 to 65)***—Individuals must feel as though they are contributing to the development of future generations (e.g., raising children) or develop a sense of stagnation ceasing to be a productive member of society.

8. ***Ego Integrity vs. Despair (65 to death)***—Individuals begin to reflect on their lives and must determine whether they have led a good life or they may fall into despair.

Erikson's work shares much in common with sociological perspectives on aging and development. His model takes into account the importance of other people in our lives as well as our personal decisions in development processes.

had to change their educational plans, for instance, but coped with economic hardship by taking on additional work.

Deluca and Rosenbaum (2001) studied the complex relationship between social status and individual agency in later educational attainment. Deluca and Rosenbaum found that students' high-school efforts are important to later educational attainment, regardless of their economic standing. Hence, individuals do have some control of their outcomes in life. However, they also found that socioeconomic status was associated with higher levels of student effort (higher-status students worked harder) and higher-status students benefited more from their effort than those from lower socioeconomic backgrounds; hence, agency does have an effect on life outcomes, but it also interacts with our social positions and conditions surrounding our efforts.

Agents of Socialization

Earlier we defined agents of socialization as groups most influential in the process of teaching children the norms and values of a particular culture. It is important to understand that sociologists generally view agents of socialization as mediators of the larger society, rather than direct causes of socialization (Corsaro and Eder 1995). That is, families may affect child development directly through their parenting techniques, but those techniques reflect larger cultural patterns. The famous pediatrician, Dr. Spock, wrote *The Common Sense Book of Baby and Child Care* in 1946 with several follow-up versions printed over the last several decades. His ideas helped to change the way parents thought about parenting, emphasizing more flexible parenting techniques. Spock encouraged parents to be more emotionally attached to children and less strict in their discipline. Children were to be thought of as individuals rather than subjects of training and development. Through the middle of the 20th century, Spock and other child specialists moved families away from traditional parenting styles. In a sense, parents implemented larger societal changes in attitudes toward children (as individuals) and parenting styles more generally (loving and affectionate and independent) displayed in Spock's books.

There are many agents of socialization. Here, we emphasize only some of the most important ones: families, school, and peers. We also discuss the media as another source of socialization in Western societies.

Families

Families are considered the first or primary agent of socialization because most children are raised from infancy with parents and siblings. However, the family has changed dramatically over the last century. For example, people in Western countries are having fewer children—almost half the world's population in 2000 lived in a country that was at or below replacement level (the point at which populations stabilize), primarily in richer, Western nations like Italy and Germany (Morgan 2003). Since 1970, the number of individuals living alone in the U.S. has increased from 16% of households to 25% (see Figure 6.1). The nuclear family, married couples with children, has declined from 40% of households to just 24%, with a corresponding increase in the number of nontraditional households (e.g., single parents).

Family Structure and Children. Structural changes in the family are important to track because they can have ramifications for child socialization. Only about one in three children

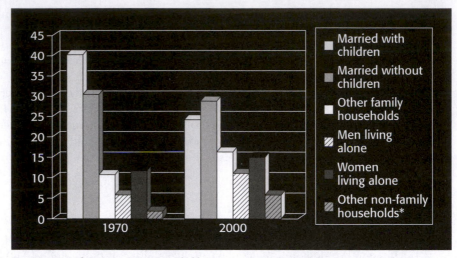

Figure 6.1   Changes in U.S. Household Composition, 1970 and 2000

*Mostly single men and women.

Source: U.S. Census Bureau, Current Population Survey, March Supplements: 1970 to 2000.

lives in a family with a stay-at-home parent; the rest are in dual-earner, single-parent, or other types of families (Waite and Gallaher 2000). Children from single-parent families often struggle for at least two reasons (Gecas 1992; Waite and Gallaher 2000). First, single-parent families earn less money than their married counterparts, partly because there is one less person to contribute to the household income and partly because women are more likely to be single parents than men (Demo 1992). (In 2002, the gender-wage gap in the United States was 23 cents; women earned about 77 cents for every dollar earned by men.) Hence, single parents typically lack the fiscal resources found in more conventional families.

Second, single-parent families may lack the same social resources available to two-parent families. Children in single-parent households must rely on one person to provide the love and intimacy found in families with two caregivers (Gecas 1992; Waite and Gallaher 2000). Single parents have less time and energy to devote to their children as well. However, the bond between a single parent and child may be strengthened because of the amount of intimacy available in a dyad compared to a triad (see chapter 2).

These dynamics may disproportionately affect some minority groups because some family demographics vary by race. According to the 2000 U.S. Census, African Americans, for example, have larger families on average than the overall population, and they are also more likely to be single-parent households (McKinnon and Bennett 2005). Hence, if family structure affects life outcomes, then children in those families may be affected to a greater degree than other members of society.

Class, Race, and Gender in Families. A family's social class position is another important structural dimension affecting socialization processes. Income differences not only influence the resources available to raise children, but they can also actually affect socialization processes themselves (Gecas 1992; Kohn 1969). Compared to working-class families, middle-class families differ in the values and behaviors taught to children as well as how they teach them those things. Middle-class families tend to stress autonomy and individual development over conformity. In addition, middle-class families are less likely to use punitive child-rearing practices than their counterparts in the working class. Middle-class children, as a result, are more likely to value independence later in life than working-class children.

The family can also be a source of **racial socialization,** learning about one's ethnic and racial identity in a given culture. Families may pass on their cultural heritage to their children in the form of racial or ethnic pride, history, and heritage. Minority parents can also help prepare their children for racial bias in the future (Hughes 2003; Hughes and Johnson 2001). Racial socialization is important because a strong ethnic identity is associated with greater psychological well-being (Yip 2005).

Families are essential to **gender socialization,** the learning of expectations about how to behave related to one's gender (Gecas 1992) (see "doing gender" in chapter 5). How children come to appropriate thoughts, feelings, and behaviors associated with age, gender, or other roles is not completely understood. On one level, children simply model the behavior of their parents. We know that mothers continue to do more housework than men, and men work more outside of the home (Bianchi et al. 2006; Robinson and Godbey 1997). These differences can have long-lasting consequences for gendered behavior. Cunningham (2001), for instance, found that fathers' participation in routine housework when their children were very young had a positive effect on their sons' later participation in housework whereas mothers' employment during their daughters' formative years decreased the relative contributions of daughters later in life. Hence, teaching gender-role attitudes may influence future behavior, but so do parental characteristics and behaviors.

Recent research has attempted to understand how children conceive of gender roles at different developmental stages. Milkie and colleagues (1997) analyzed over 3,000 essays in which children were asked to explain why their parent is the "best" mother or father. They studied children's responses in these essays, finding patterns in how children conceive of their parents. Their results generally support findings that show the significance traditional gender roles play in family relationships. However, they also found that children generally downplayed the significance of father's labor force participation. Comparing essays written in 1979 and 1980 with those written in the early 1990s, however, they found that the latter cohort of children deemphasized the parent as a caretaker role, moving toward a more recreational role, especially for fathers. Hence, children's perceptions of family roles change over time.

Families are also a place to learn fundamental beliefs about the world. The transmission of values from generation to generation seems obvious: Our parents tell us right from wrong, and we generally accept those things to be true. However, children often modify their parents' values or adopt altogether new ones. Glass and her colleagues (Glass, Bengston, and Dunham 1986) studied the transmission of gender, political, and religious ideology among members of three-generation families (youth, parents, and grandparents). They found very little convergence of parent–child attitudes. Rather, they found that status inheritance—the maintenance of class position—was the primary means of maintaining attitude similarities. Hence, families not only teach and model values to their children, they also impart their social positions, which ultimately produces similar values and beliefs.

Socialization of values and beliefs can occur on multiple levels at the same time. For instance, family influences can be observed in the context of larger social forces, including peers, the media, or other social institutions. Kelley and De Graaf (1997) studied religious beliefs in the context of family upbringing and nation's religious environments. They found that people in more religious nations adopt more orthodox values than those living in more secular nations. However, they also found that family religiosity had a stronger effect than national religiosity on children's religiosity in secular nations; the converse is true in orthodox nations. Thus, the socialization processes found among friends and family can be influenced by larger social and cultural contexts.

Adults in Families. The life-course perspective makes it clear that children are not the only ones who are socialized. As young adults move from their childhood family into forming families of their own, they must learn to adapt to adult family roles such as spouse or parent. It is not just a passive adapting to roles; rather, people make choices about when and how to enter into different roles. One of the great challenges for adults trying to craft a meaningful life is to attempt to weave together important roles such as being a husband or wife, a mother or father, and a paid work role. Life-course sociologists study what happens when people enter into or exit from various roles, and how that affects future sequencing of their life paths. We are aware, for example, that becoming a parent as a teenager greatly affects the kind of education and work roles that women enter. Life-course sociologists also are concerned with the mental health consequences of family–work trajectories. Nomaguchi and Milkie (2003) found that entering parenthood affects well-being, but its effects vary by gender and marital status. For married women, those becoming parents had a better profile than those who remained childless; for unmarried men, those who became fathers over the five-year time frame were more depressed than nonfathers.

School Contexts

Schools are a second major agent of socialization, representing the institution of education. The classroom serves as an intermediary place between family and work. Although technically designed to impart knowledge about many subjects, the classroom is also a place to learn norms of behavior. Children are placed in large, homogeneous classrooms in which peer influences dominate the social context, above and beyond the effects of families.

Children are entering day care and school at earlier ages and staying in those institutions until adulthood. Hence, the influence of schooling on socialization has become more pronounced through the late 20th and early 21st centuries. It is difficult to know if these relational changes, emphasizing peer-group relationships over parent–child interactions, are beneficial for child development, but the socialization processes in schools will likely become even more influential over time.

Classroom Structure and Socialization Processes. Much like the family group structures children's lives at the earliest ages, the classroom represents a group, albeit a much larger one, from which children learn about the world. Because one or two adults typically attend to classes of 20 or 30 children, classroom settings are less intimate and provide children less exposure to adult behavior than home settings. Classrooms are also unique in that they are composed of the same age group and are divided relatively equally by sex, at least in Western nations (Gecas 1992). Hence, classrooms have less direct adult–child interaction than home environments and more competition for attention and resources among children.

Classrooms are also bureaucratically structured in a way that limits child–adult bonds (children leave a teacher after the successful completion of one school year) and emphasizing rationalization and competition among similar age groups (Gecas 1992). The large status gap between students and teachers may influence the development of a student subculture in which the students form a homogeneous subgroup relative to their higher-status teachers. Much like the division of labor in families, school bureaucracies and hierarchies may contribute to the socialization of rationality and order associated with Western culture.

We can apply the same socialization processes found in the family to school contexts. However, schools have different structural features that affect those processes. For instance, obedience to rules becomes paramount in bureaucratic settings such as schools. In addition, teachers and administrators have formal rewards and punishments available, such as grades and detentions, to encourage the maintenance of social order in the classroom. Because students are in large homogeneous groups, they are also influenced by peer pressure to a greater degree than in family contexts.

The increased emphasis on peers, as well as the notion of adults as "outsiders" who merely impose rules and restrictions, may help to explain the development of popular media portrayals of a rebellious student culture. The film *Fast Times at Ridgemont High* (1982) portrayed a California high school almost devoid of any supervision. Students had a subculture in which parents and other adults were outsiders while students developed a social hierarchy within the school structure. Actor Sean Penn played a character, Jeff Spicoli, a drug-using surfer on the fringe of society. This position in the high-school subculture made him one of the cool people in the film, someone who did not live by society's norms and values. Similar portrayals of student life are seen in movies such as *Mean Girls* (2004) which humorously details the sometimes viscious competition between teenage girls, and *American Pie* (1999), a film about four young men who vow to lose their virginity before prom night.

Class, Race, and the Pygmalion Effect. Teachers' interactions with children affect the values and beliefs of children much the same as parents' interactions. However, teachers do not share the same relationships with their students as do the students' parents. For instance, if you are reading this book as part of a class, your parents probably care more about your grade in the class than does your professor. The social distance between teachers and students can open the door to subtle forms of bias, some negative and some positive.

In a classic study, *Pygmalion in the Classroom*, researchers Robert Rosenthal and Lenore Jacobson (1968) gave a group of elementary students an intelligence test at the beginning of the school year. They then randomly selected a small percentage of the students and told teachers that these were the students who should be expected to "bloom" intellectually over the coming year. The researchers' statements were not true, but the teachers believed that the randomly selected students possessed great potential. Rosenthal and Jacobson then retested the students at the end of the year. They found that those students who were randomly deemed to be "bloomers" at the beginning of the year showed a 12-point average improvement in their intelligence test scores compared to an 8-point average improvement among students who had not been labeled. Hence, teacher expectations can influence students' intellectual development. This dynamic is often called the **Pygmalion effect.**

The ramifications of the Pygmalion study can be applied to processes that occur in relation to other types of labels and categorizations of students. Students deemed "slow learners" at a young age may be influenced by expectations in the classroom that limit their academic responsibilities or generally expect less from them. Similarly, children from racial minorities and other disadvantaged groups may find additional hurdles to their intellectual development because of potentially biased interactions with teachers and other important cultural gatekeepers (Alexander, Entwisle, and Thompson 1987; Cooper and Allen 1998).

Being a member of a minority group may influence classroom processes in other ways. According to the U.S. Census Bureau, in 2005 African Americans represented about 13% of the American population. Hence, a fully integrated classroom of 20 students may have only two or three African Americans. Although classrooms may be homogeneous in terms of age, the minority members of the classroom may feel strain in the face of their differences from majority members. In other words, these students stand out from the rest of the class. Rosenberg (see Elliott 2001; Rosenberg 1986) called this feeling **contextual dissonance.** Minority students feel many of the same peer pressures found in more homogeneous classrooms but also must cope with the feeling that they stand apart from other students. Rosenberg's research shows that the result of this dissonance, whether based on class, race, or ability, is a reduction of students' sense of self-esteem.

Peer Culture

Most of our discussion of socialization agents has emphasized the passive nature of child development: children learn social expectations by modeling family and teacher behavior. School adds the influence of peers to socialization processes, but most research continues to emphasize children as recipients of some formal developmental goals. More recent research and theory has started to examine how children actively participate in the socialization process (Corsaro 2005; Jencks 1996). Much of this work has emphasized children's peer cultures.

Peer-Group Structures. The most important difference between school and peer-group culture is the voluntary nature of peer-group affiliation. Children have more freedom of thought and behavior in a peer-group context than they do inside the classroom. They may also choose to structure their relationships to include like-minded others. In addition, children can choose to leave the group, unlike their family and school groups (Corsaro 2005; Gecas 1992; Jencks 1996). In some sense, peer groups serve to teach children how to think more independently from institutional and adult constraints. Much of our adult life is spent navigating formal and informal contexts, including work, school, family, and friends. The increasing influence of peer groups into the teen years prepares children to manage complex role relationships with guidance not often found in their immediate families.

In one sense, children's peer culture is more egalitarian because it is free of institutional restraints. However, research shows that children learn to stratify at very young ages. Adler and Adler (Adler 1996; Adler and Adler 1998) conducted an extensive study of elementary children to understand children's hierarchies, using both interview data and personal observations. Their research showed that children form friendship cliques that represent their relative status in children's culture, largely derived from the larger adult culture. These cliques can be divided into four major groups:

1. The popular clique
2. The wannabes
3. Middle friendship circles
4. Social isolates

The **popular clique** includes children with an active social life and with the largest number of friends. They also have the most control of the rest of children's culture. That is, the kids among the popular crowd had more say in the activities and the definition of cool than children in other cliques. It is estimated that the popular clique represents about a third of children (Adler and Adler 1998).

The **wannabes** represent children that want to be popular but do not quite get accepted into this group. Although they are occasionally accepted into the popular clique's activities, they never sustain that status in the group. This group represents about 10% of children. The **middle friendship circles,** in contrast, represent about half of children. This group forms smaller circles of friends and is less hierarchical than the two previous groups. They do not seek popularity but obtain social comfort from their small circles of friends and family.

The final group, the **social isolates,** represent less than 10% of children. This group has trouble establishing any relationships with kids in the other cliques.

These children may have behavioral problems or simply have trouble relating to other children. Adler and Adler (1998) observed that many of these children turned to each other as a source of comfort, although this method was not always successful because many isolates want to avoid the stigma associated with being an isolate (Kless 1992). Many of them simply spent time alone, drifting around the playgrounds, watching the other children play.

Peer-Group Socialization Processes. Gecas (1992) argued that peer-group socialization includes three areas of child development:

- The development and validation of the self
- The development of competence in the presentation of self
- The acquisition of knowledge not provided by parents or schools

The development of the self certainly starts in family contexts. As we discussed earlier in this chapter, children first learn their sense of mastery and self-worth from family members, especially parents. Peers provide additional information from which to evaluate our sense of worth. This process can occur through informal interactions, through the remarks and reactions our friends make about our behaviors. Because peer associations are more voluntary than family and school contexts, rewards and punishments offered by peers can have a particularly powerful effect on individual self-evaluations.

Children must also learn subtle aspects of social life. They must learn how to interact in different social contexts. A small part of this "act" is related to manners of behavior, such as the appropriate fork to use at the dinner table. It also includes appropriate greetings and salutations and things to do to avoid causing a fight. Although some of these things are learned at home, many of them fall in the purview of peer relationships. Peer groups provide knowledge unique to a given age group or generation. In other words, parental norms may not be appropriate for same-aged peer groups. Hence, peers construct and provide different norms of behavior than families and schools. Examples of conflict between family and peer-group norms are numerous. Think about a time when you wanted to wear a particular piece of clothing or jewelry when you were living with your parents. Your choices may have been driven by the latest fashion or fad. Another example is a teenager who is given a pair of jeans with the word, "Squeeze" at the backside of the waistline. The teenager sees nothing wrong with this word as she accepts the jeans from her friend, only to find out that the choice of jeans is seen as inappropriate by her parents. She argues that "all of the kids are doing it," leading her parents to investigate. The parents talk to other parents and find that their daughter is correct—many of the kids are wearing this style at school! The girl's parents' standard of dress diverged from that of her peers. The girl is left to battle over these two different standards, much like you probably did.

Finally, peers also help individuals develop knowledge about the world that they tend not to get from traditional sources. One example is the transmission of knowledge about sexual behavior. Parents and teachers may share some rudimentary information about the process of having sex and its consequences. However, these sources of information do not always review the more subtle aspects of sexual behavior, what "turns on" the other person, what activities are deemed "normal," and so on. Individuals may feel more comfortable discussing such topics with their peers than with their parents or teachers. Peer discussions and interactions also give people an opportunity to think and decide about such things in a less-stressful environment.

Other Socializing Agents: The Role of Media

There are almost certainly other agents of socialization in your life that we have not discussed. You may have been influenced by a small town community, a religious group, or some other group unique to your life. Different cultures may adopt other agents of socialization. The media is a particularly good example in the Western world and is a growing influence on the rest of the world. Americans spend about 15 hours a week on average watching television (Robinson and Godbey 1997). A major way that agents of socialization affect us is merely through observation and adaptation: We watch other people do things and adopt those behaviors over time. Hence, watching people on television may provide role models for our own behavior. If we see racism and sexism on television, we may feel that these behaviors are acceptable and even adapt them into our own repertoire of attitudes. Alternatively, watching people live out alternative lifestyles on television may engender more "tolerance" toward these behaviors. Indeed one of the most important influences of the media is as a pervasive presence throughout society in helping to define what is "normal" (Milkie 1999).

You can probably think of other agents of socialization in society. Different cultures may use alternative means to pass on their culture to their children. Some forms of socialization are more explicit than others. For instance, schools are designed to prepare students to work in the larger economic structure of a given society. However, schools socialize children to more subtle aspects of our culture, such as attitudes toward different issues and topics. Similarly, your search for additional agents of socialization will likely show you other explicit and subtle ways that society is maintained over time.

Section Summary

This section of the chapter applied the social structure and personality perspective to answer the questions: What are the four elements of life-course sociology? What are agents of socialization, and how do they affect our lives? The life-course perspective incorporates the effects of historical times, timing in our lives, linked lives, and human agency to understand individual development. Specifically, it examines how historical conditions affect people's selves, the relationships we have with significant others, and our ability to make decisions about our trajectories. Agents of socialization include the family, schools, and peers. These and other agents of socialization play important roles in the socialization process because they give the individual different contexts for learning about society.

GP Group Processes and Socialization

I took the GREs [Graduate Record Exam] twice but I can't seem to get the score I want. Am I a dumb person? Why is it that people around me seem to be doing so well but I am not? Maybe I have a learning disability. I don't know.

—Rich, senior Sociology major

Rich's question may seem pretty straightforward—the test probably reflects his actual abilities. He took the test twice, verifying its findings. But these test scores are relative in two ways. First, Rich's score is relative to other people who took the test. Compared to the highest score, his score may seem low. However, a large number of people likely scored lower than Rich. In addition, aptitude tests may reflect cultural biases that make it difficult to assess real ability. Work in the group processes perspective tries to assess how these biases can be manifested in group contexts.

Finding Socialization in Group Processes

Most theories in the group processes tradition are tested through experiments. We discussed the experimental method in chapter 3. In a typical experiment, two groups of people experience conditions that are identical except for one element that is varied by the researchers. Experimentalists assign groups to different levels of an independent variable before measuring a dependent variable. For example, a researcher interested in the effects of violent television (the independent variable) on aggressive behavior (the dependent variable) might randomly assign one group to watch television with violence and another to watch television without violence and then measure levels of aggression in the two groups. In this way, the researcher can determine the effect of violent television on aggressive behavior.

Although the described study represents the introduction of a socialization experience, sociologists are usually interested in more long-term socialization experiences that can last over periods of up to several years. For that reason, experiments usually are not well suited to examine socialization processes. How could we use socialization as an independent variable in an experiment? Because socialization is a lifelong process, whereas the typical experiment lasts no longer than an hour or two, researchers could not give one group a certain socialization experience and another group a different one. Time, money, and a number of other factors make it impossible to give people a meaningful socialization experience in a laboratory.

One way around the problem of socializing people in an experiment lies in the fact that people from different groups experience different socialization processes. So, experimental researchers might assign people to groups based on their socialization experiences. Male and female participants, for example, could be assigned to different experimental groups. Doing that, however, would take away the major strength of experiments—random assignment. We can't randomly assign people to be men or women in an experiment. Without random assignment, we could not know that any differences between men and women in the study were due to socialization and not something else; biological differences, for example.

Although socialization is not well suited to experimental investigations, experimental work in the group processes tradition has nonetheless contributed to our understanding of socialization processes.

Recall the discussion of status characteristics theory from chapter 4. The status characteristics theory describes the process through which the characteristics that people possess lead to inequalities in groups. According to the theory, and supported by hundreds of studies, people (often unconsciously) develop expectations for the performances of people in groups based on their characteristics. People expected to perform at a higher level talk more in the group, are evaluated more highly, and have more influence over group decisions.

Status characteristics theory helps us understand how the contributions of women and minority group members become devalued in our society, and it is probably the most successful theory in the group processes tradition. Importantly, however, status characteristics theory has no propositions and makes no predictions about race, gender, or any other characteristics. In other words, status characteristics theory does not propose that women will tend to talk less and have less influence in groups than men. Instead, status characteristics theory lays out the process that will occur *if* something is acting as a status characteristic in a group.

One way to think about this is that the events explained by status characteristics theory begin *after* people have been socialized. Suppose, for example, that people in our society have been socialized to value the contributions of men more than the contributions of women. Gender, in other words, is a status characteristic. Status characteristics theory then explains how gender will affect what happens when people interact in task groups. Again, the theory doesn't tell us *what* characteristics are status characteristics—it tells us what will happen *if* something is a status characteristic.

Whenever people get together in a group, they do so in the context of the larger society of which they are a part. For example, we would expect the dominant norms and values of the United States to guide the behaviors of people working in a task group within the United States. Status characteristics theory defines **referential beliefs** as beliefs held in common by people about the usual relationships between particular status characteristics and reward levels. The source of referential beliefs is the larger society within which a group operates, and the way that we all come to have common referential beliefs is through socialization processes.

Research in status characteristics theory can tell us about socialization processes by telling us about the referential beliefs that guide people in groups. If a particular characteristic is consistently found to act as a status characteristic, for example, then we will have evidence that people hold referential beliefs associated with the characteristic. Moreover, we will have insight into how people are socialized to view the characteristic.

In the case of gender, overwhelming evidence from research in status characteristics theory indicates that the contributions of women are devalued in our society relative to the contributions of men (e.g., Hopcroft, Funk, and Clay-Warner 1998; Troyer 2001; Wagner and Berger 1997). In other words, performances by women are rated lower than the same performances by men. There is also evidence that these gender differences appear to be becoming less pronounced (e.g., Foschi and Lapointe 2002). Through all these experimental studies, we can see that people in our society are socialized to value contributions from women less than contributions from men, but also that this tendency may be moving in the direction of a situation in which both men and women receive proper recognition for their performances.

Assessing the Effects of Socialization

Group processes experiments also have the capacity to explain the consequences of socialization processes. One area in which they have contributed is in understanding group differences in tests of mental ability. As a college student, you have almost certainly confronted the important role that standardized tests play in our society. For one thing, your scores on standardized tests such as the SAT or ACT probably influenced the colleges to which you considered applying and may be the ones to which you were admitted.

An important issue is whether standardized tests accurately measure ability. Studies find that African Americans score lower on average than Whites on standard ability tests such as IQ tests or the SAT. On tests of Intelligence Quotients (IQ), the average difference between Whites and African Americans is somewhere around 10 to 12 IQ points (Herrnstein and Murray 1994). Social scientists are left with the task of determining why Whites tend to score higher.

Michael Lovaglia and his colleagues (Lovaglia, Lucas, Houser, Thye, and Markovsky 1998) proposed that status characteristics theory might contribute to explaining the gap in test scores between African Americans and European Americans. If you recall the discussion of status characteristics theory from chapter 4, the theory applies to groups formed for the purpose of completing a task, not to individual performances on tests. Lovaglia and his colleagues extended the theory by proposing that status processes affect individual performances when those performances are likely to affect the status of the individual in the future.

Research in status characteristics theory has shown that race operates as a status characteristic in American society, with the contributions of European Americans valued more than the contributions of other group members (Cohen and Roper 1972; Webster and Driskell 1978). In other words, people in the United States hold referential beliefs that link European Americans to high status, and people (perhaps unconsciously) expect higher performances from European Americans.

Lovaglia and his colleagues (1998) used this information to develop a theory to explain the race difference in standardized test scores. First, European Americans are higher in status than African Americans. Second, standardized tests have implications for the future status of people who take them. Third, people are rewarded for performing at levels comparable with their status and punished for performances that contradict their status positions. The Pygmalion study discussed earlier in this chapter, for example, found that intellectual ability was punished when it violated expectations. Lovaglia and colleagues proposed that these factors may combine to lead to lower scores on standardized tests for African-American test takers.

The next step was for Lovaglia and his colleagues to test their theory. One way to do it would be to take samples of European-American and African-American students similar in grade point average (GPA), socioeconomic status, and other factors. The researchers could then tell the European-American test takers that they are expected to do very well and the African-American test takers that they are expected to do less well. The researchers could then have participants take a standardized test and measure whether scores differed between the two groups. The problem with this design is that it runs into the problem of random assignment. If there were differences in test scores between the two groups, how would we know that it was due to the status created by the researchers and not to something else that varies with race, such as differences in socialization experiences? Because it would not allow for random assignment, there is no way to include race as an independent variable in an experimental study without producing results that are difficult to interpret.

Lovaglia and his colleagues solved this problem by creating a new status characteristic and then randomly assigning participants to conditions based on that characteristic. When participants arrived for the study, they were asked if they were left- or right-handed. The researchers then placed a bright wristband on the wrist of the preferred hand. Half of the participants in the study were placed in a high-status condition and half in a low-status condition. If a participant was right-handed and in a high-status condition, she was told that right-handedness was associated with a number of positive personal traits (e.g., rationality and organized thinking) and that left-handedness was associated with a number of negative traits (e.g., impulsiveness and inattention). Right-handed low-status participants were told a number of positive traits for left-handers (e.g., creativity) and negative traits for right-handers (e.g., rigid thinking).

In these ways, the researchers created a status characteristic in the laboratory. As with race, people expected higher performances for members in one category of the characteristic than from members in another category. Further linking their created status characteristic with experiences based on race, the researchers told participants in the two groups that they could expect different rewards based on their performances: High-status participants were told that they would receive greater rewards for good performances than would low-status participants. Because most people in society do not actually expect more or less competent performances from left- or right-handed people, the researchers were able to randomly assign people to status conditions. They would not have been able to do this if they had looked directly at race.

After learning that they were either high or low in status based on their handedness, participants took a standard test of mental ability. Lovaglia and his colleagues found that participants in the high-status condition, on average, scored significantly higher on the IQ test than did participants in the low-status condition. The difference they found was almost as large as the average difference in scores between Whites and African Americans.

The research of Lovaglia and his colleagues indicates that socialization processes significantly affect how people perform on tests, over and above their individual ability. Remarkably, the study carried out by Lovaglia and his colleagues created status differences in about 15 minutes of computerized instructions. This was enough to create significant differences in test scores. Imagine how much greater the effects might be of a lifetime of socialization in a culture that values contributions from some groups more than those from others.

Section Summary

The last section of this chapter addressed the question: How do group processes researchers study socialization? Group processes researchers often focus on the effects of socialization after it occurs. Specifically, status characteristics theory can tell us about socialization processes by shedding light on the referential beliefs that guide people in groups. If a particular characteristic is consistently found to act as a status characteristic, for example, then we will have evidence for socialization that advantages one category or characteristic over another.

Bringing It All Together

I really like to read biographies. I think that if you REALLY want to learn about someone, you need to study ALL of the factors that affected their lives—historical, family, and anything else that influenced their lives.

—Ken, senior History major

In this chapter, we applied the three perspectives in sociological social psychology to understand how society shapes how we are socialized. If we want to know how people came to be the way they are, Ken seems to think that biographies are the only way to go. But the three perspectives in social psychology show that there are some similarities in the ways individuals manage personal and social events in their lives; hence, we can go beyond biographies to understand human growth and change over time.

From an interactionist perspective, most children learn to relate by adapting adult roles and practicing them before become independent members of society. We also examined socialization processes among children's peer cultures, how children have the ability to adapt and transform adult roles in their interaction with other children. The social structure and personality perspective was applied in the form of life course sociology and reviewing the role of agents of socialization (e.g., family and peers) in how we learn about the world. Finally, the group processes perspective was used to understand the effects of socialization on group processes, how the effects of socialization can be seen in the ways that groups consistantly organize themselves.

Summary

1. Sociologists study socialization processes at every stage of development from childhood to late adulthood. The self develops through a symbolic process. An essential aspect of self-development is the ability to take the role of the other.

2. The sociology of childhood focuses on how children are active participants in creating culture.

3. Life-course sociology is based on the notion that humans adapt to different situations based on their social and historical location relative to different events and cultural "moments." Four major themes in life-course sociology include historical context, timing, linked lives, and agency.

4. Sociologists view agents of socialization as mediators of the larger society rather than direct causes of socialization. The family is considered the first or primary agent of socialization because children are raised from infancy with their parents and siblings. Schools and peers are two other important agents of socializations.

5. The group processes perspective often examines the role of socialization after it has occurred, reviewing, for instance, how expectations about gender or race affect group interactions.

Key Terms and Concepts

Agency: An aspect of life-coure sociology referring to our ability to make decisions and control our destiny.

Agents of socialization: Individuals or groups most influential in the process of teaching children the norms and values of a particular culture.

Birth cohort: A group of people born around the same time period.

Children's cultural routines: A stable set of activities or routines, artifacts, values, and concerns that kids produce and share in interaction with each other.

Contextual dissonance: A feeling that minority members of a group feel because they are different from the majority members.

Game stage: The third stage of self-development in which children are capable of managing several different roles.

Gender socialization: Learning expectations about how to behave related to one's gender.

Generalized other: The attitudes of the whole community.

Historical context: An aspect of life-course sociology referring to how historic events affect development for different birth cohorts.

Idiocultures: A system of knowledge, beliefs, behaviors, and customs shared by an interacting group to which members refer and employ as a basis of further interaction.

Life course: The process of personal change from infancy to late adulthood resulting from personal and societal events and from transitions into and out of social roles.

Life events: Any event that causes significant changes in the course of our lives.

Linked lives: An aspect of life-course sociology referring to our relationships with other people.

Looking-glass self: The reliance on responses of others in the development of the self.

Middle friendship circles: Smaller circles of friends that are less hierarchical.

Play stage: Second stage of self-development in which children begin to use language to make-believe as they play others' roles.

Popular clique: Children with an active social life and with the largest number of friends.

Preparatory stage: First stage of self-development in which children simply mimic the attitudes and behaviors of their parents and caretakers.

Pygmalion effect: When children develop according to expectations of a group or society.

Racial socialization: Learning about one's ethnic and racial identity in a given culture.

Referential beliefs: In status characteristics theory, beliefs held in common by people about the usual relationships between particular status characteristics and reward levels.

Social isolates: Children that have trouble establishing any relationships with those in other cliques.

Socialization: The ways in which individuals attempt to align their own thoughts, feelings, and behavior to fit into a group or society.

Timing: An aspect of life-course sociology referring to incidence, duration, and sequence of roles, and to the relevant expectations and beliefs based on age.

Turning point: When the "normal trajectory" of our lives is altered by a life event or role change.

Wannabes: Children that want to be popular but do not quite get accepted into this group.

1. Have you ever interacted with a group of small children? Can you see the socialization processes as reviewed at the beginning of the chapter (e.g., playing adult roles)?

2. Did any major life event affect your development in some way? How did it affect you? Do you think most people would have reacted to that event in a similar way?

3. Which agent or agents of socialization, if any, had the greatest effect on you? What ways did it affect you? How do you know?

4. Describe a status characteristic that may affect how other people relate to you. Have you noticed this before? When?

PART 3

Areas of Social Life

At this point in your social-psychological journey, you have reviewed the major perspectives and methods in the field and applied them to your understanding of stratification processes, the self and identity, and socialization. The next several chapters will apply those approaches to understand different areas of social life. We start with the social psychology of deviance by examining the ways that people break the rules of social life. Most of the literature we have reviewed thus far focuses on how individuals develop and follow social conventions. But when do people decide *not* to follow those rules? Most of the work in this area focuses on understanding crime and delinquency but it can easily be applied to other forms of deviance such as talking back to an authority or violating social norms. We follow this chapter with social psychological research on mental health, often considered a type of deviance. That is, deviance includes any thoughts, feelings, or behaviors that significantly differ from the people around you, no matter the cause. We also examine the social psychology of attitudes and behavior in chapters 9 and emotions in chapter 10, followed by a review of collective behavior in the last chapter. These chapters cover a plethora of research specialties in the field of sociological social psychology but all of them share the application of the essential perspectives and methods reviewed in the first section of the book.

The Social Psychology of Deviance

Chapter 7

Why do people have to hurt each other anyway? Why do people take things from other people? Criminals are stupid!

—Carlos, senior Business major

The term *deviance* typically brings to mind behaviors that we view as immoral or are illegal. Social psychologists define the concept more broadly than this and without an attached moral judgment. **Deviance,** in social psychology, refers to any thought, feeling, or behavior that departs from accepted practices in a society or group. Many deviant behaviors are of course illegal—murder, for instance. Other deviant behaviors, however, are not illegal—singing loudly along with an MP3 player while walking on a public street, for example. In some cases, behaviors mandated by laws can themselves be deviant—such as driving *only* the speed limit on some highways. Deviance, then, goes beyond the legal code of a society. In simple terms, it refers to any behavior that violates the norms of a group.

Carlos's statement reflects a resentment of lawbreakers. His feelings emphasize the breaking of formal norms and values that are encoded into law. Many laws represent what anthropologists call **mores.** Mores refer to widely held beliefs in society, so widely held that many of them are formalized into law, thereafter invoking both deep sentiments and harsh punishments for breaking them. Mores are contrasted with **folkways,** less-serious rules of behavior in a group or society. Mores may include rules against incest or child molestation, whereas folkways are violations such as poor manners.

Most social psychology textbooks that cover deviance tend to focus on theories and research associated with criminal deviance. The goal of criminology is to understand the processes that lead people to break laws. That is what Carlos wants to understand at the beginning of this section. However, from an interactionist point of view, the role of *deviance* in society is a bit more complicated. In fact, interactionists generally view deviance as a normal part of the symbolic interaction process. Structural and group-centered views of deviance tend to focus on the social conditions that increase the likelihood of breaking laws. These views come from the larger sociological specialty of criminology. We emphasize the broader sense of deviance in everyday life before reviewing traditional theories and research on criminal forms of deviance, answering the following questions:

- How do we define what is normal or deviant?
- How does the construction of deviant labels contribute to the development of deviant lifestyles?
- What structural conditions influence individuals' decisions to commit deviant acts?
- How do group relationships influence the development of deviance and perceptions of deviance?

SI   Interactionist Approaches to Deviance

At first it felt a little weird. I was always told to stay away from drugs. But I always seemed to find myself hanging out with the "wrong crowd" in high school. I let my hair grow long and smoked a little weed. People would call me a "hippy-freak" because I looked like the typical 60s hippy. Maybe I was, I don't know. It bothered me at first, then I got used to it. I guess you can say that I am proud of it really. The 1960s were a time of liberation and change. I am all about that. . . .

—Steve, sophomore Undeclared

In some sense, deviance is a necessary part of the symbolic interaction process of negotiating social reality. Interactionism assumes that individuals decide to maintain (or break) social norms and standards during every interaction. When you talk with a friend, you will likely look her in the eye and maintain an appropriate and comfortable distance between the two of you. Further, the depth of intimacy in the discussion will correlate with the closeness of your friendship. But how do friendships develop over time? Friends must share more intimate aspects of their lives over time to feel a sense of closeness. Intimacy assumes that one person is willing to share details about herself to the other. Most relationships start with low levels of intimacy but progress toward more intimate levels through successive self-disclosures of personal information. In the beginning, however, one person must decide to deviate from the norm of acquaintance talk—the relationship cannot progress into something more meaningful unless someone breaks the rules. Hence, individuals must deviate from their previous relationship with the other person to change it. Small deviations in social norms are necessary for the development of relationships. You might have felt some anxiety related to this type of deviance when trying to decide whether to say the words "I love you" to a special romantic partner before she had said it to you.

Deviance is traditionally applied to larger breaks with social conventions. The process by which Steve decided to experiment with drugs and change his values and beliefs (as well as the length of his hair) suggests a gradual acceptance of alternative norms. At first, Steve seemed a little hesitant to be associated with the 1960s hippie movement. Over time, he came to accept the label and the stereotypes associated with it. He actually came to embrace the new title, believing that his new values, although different from conventional society, are good and true. In this sense, deviance is also about identity formation, how people come to see themselves as deviant (Herman-Kinney 2003).

The interactionist approach to deviance views it as a manifestation of social interactions, like any other thought, feeling, or behavior. When an individual decides to deviate from the norms of a group, she will likely incur penalties for making such a decision. If it is a mild infraction, belching in public for instance, it may only receive a few raised eyebrows or a mild statement such as, "Excuse me!" A more serious infraction, such as pushing someone in your way, may get a few stern statements like, "Hey, watch where you are going!" or some physical response, perhaps pushing you back.

The symbolic interaction process allows us to study deviance at different levels. Ethnomethodology helps us to understand smaller forms of deviance in everyday life. Alternatively, labeling theory is traditionally applied to understand how individuals come to deviate from more serious rules and laws in society.

Ethnomethodology and Deviance

Ethnomethodology was introduced in chapter 1 as a theory designed to link individual-level interactions with the broader society. Ethnomethodology can be considered an extension of symbolic interactionism that emphasizes how individuals account for what is happening in social interaction. However, ethnomethodologists do not assume that there is shared meaning in a given interaction. Rather, individuals enter and leave interactions with somewhat different interpretations of those interactions. Ethnomethodology emphasizes how individuals construct and defend their views of social reality (Pfohl 1985). Thus, individuals have different sets of boundaries regarding acceptable and unacceptable behavior. People who can provide better accounts of a situation can convince others of those accounts, thereby controlling the meaning of good and bad, or deviance and conformity, in society.

In an effort to maintain efficiency in interaction, individuals index thoughts, feelings, and behaviors from their own perspectives, a process called **indexicality.** The meaning of a given behavior may be defined as deviant to one person but not to another person. For instance, smoking a cigarette may be considered normal to most people in a bar but quite abnormal (i.e., deviant) in a formal office setting. In addition, a teenager experimenting with smoking may see it as novel or sexy, whereas someone older who is trying to quit may see it as a dangerous and expensive habit.

Reflexivity is the process by which individuals think about a behavior within its social context and give meaning to it. At some point, a person's behavior may come to be labeled as deviant to one or more people in a given situation. An individual drinking alcohol in an office environment, for example, will reflect on that behavior. If others view the behavior as deviant, the individual decides whether she concurs with the label. If the label is accepted, the individual may categorize herself accordingly, potentially drinking even more often in public as she comes to think of herself as "a drunk." Alternatively, the individual can react against the deviant label and stop the behavior.

A product of this interaction process is the documentary interpretation of actions, using evidence of the deviant behavior to infer meaning and motive in the behavior of the deviant person (Pfohl 1985). Because we can't read the minds of other people, we rely on their behaviors as our guide to their motives. People are especially likely to use the documentary interpretation of actions when inferring the motives behind deviant behavior because they don't trust deviants, compared to nondeviants, to give honest accounts of their motivations.

Labeling Theory of Deviance

Ethnomethodological perspectives help to elaborate the basic processes by which individuals come to be defined (and define themselves) as deviant in the first place. Labeling theory is more formally applied to the study of these processes from the interactionist perspective. **Labeling theory** argues that deviance is a consequence of a social process in which a negative characteristic becomes an element of an individual's identity. In short, an individual becomes a deviant through the acceptance of a deviant label. That label may be the result of an external force such as friends or family, or formal social control agency such as police or doctors. The labels are especially likely to be applied to those with little power in the society, such as ethnic minorities. Once the label is applied to us, we then continue to use this identity in interactions, like we would any other aspect of our identity. The result can be a self-fulfilling prophecy in which we act according to our label, ensuring that we live up to the expectations that are set for us. In sum, labeling theory argues that people who are labeled as deviant become more likely to commit deviant acts in the future, much as the "drunk" in the preceding example.

The roots of labeling theory stem from symbolic interactionism's focus on the social construction of the self found in the work of Mead and Cooley. Cooley's (1922) "looking-glass self" (see chapter 5) refers to how individuals come to understand their identities based on others' reflections of them. We give meaning to ourselves based on how people react to us and on our judgments of those reactions. If we behave according to social standards of a given group, we may be thought of as "normal" and come to understand ourselves as such. Alternatively,

Labeling theory emphasizes the effects of early interactions with law enforcement on the development of deviant identities in adulthood.

if we act in ways that appear to others to be odd or weird, we may rethink our sense of self to include others' designations of us as deviant.

Types of Deviance

The explicit connection of interactionist principles to the study of deviance can be found in the work of Frank Tannenbaum (1938). Tannenbaum began some of the earliest research in labeling theory by focusing on the process by which juvenile delinquents are "tagged" as deviants by conventional society, leading these individuals to fall into patterns of deviance. He argued that the process of defining a person as bad or evil starts with the definition of his or her acts. First, other people (e.g., friends, family, or authorities) define a person's act as bad or evil. Second, these people then ascribe the act to the individual (rather than the situation), gradually defining the individual as bad. Finally, a change in the self-concept takes place when the person committing the deviant act applies the label of deviance to herself, beginning to think of herself as bad.

Edwin Lemert (1951) extended Tannenbaum's work by arguing that there are two forms of deviance in the labeling process. **Primary deviance** refers to the initial act that causes others to label the individual a deviant. The first arrest of a drug user may lead people to believe a person is a deviant. **Secondary deviance** occurs

Box 7.1   **Lemert's Stages Leading to Secondary Deviance**

Lemert (1951) argued that it takes multiple attempts at deviance before it moves from primary to secondary. The following stages show the process by which individuals' interaction with other people may lead them to accept the deviant label. It is not as simple as accepting a label on the completion of a single deviant act.

1. Primary deviance

2. Social penalties

3. Further primary deviation

4. Stronger penalties and rejections

5. Further deviation

6. Crisis reached in the tolerance of such deviance acceptable by a community

7. Strengthening of the deviant conduct as a reaction to penalties

8. Ultimate acceptance of the deviant social status

Lemert's work focuses on the continual interaction between the individual and her social environments, a major interactionist approach to all social development, including deviant behavior and identities. Hence, interaction and meaning-making processes are involved in the development of deviance like any other identity formation.

---

after an individual accepts the deviant label and continues to commit deviant acts, thus supporting the initial label (see Box 7.1).

The acceptance of the deviant label may be a result of a number of different processes. An individual may accept the label as a means of dealing with the consequences of some deviant behavior. When an individual acts in a deviant manner, others usually label her as deviant. Infractions of social order cause the newly defined deviant to account for her behavior simply to restore order by either accepting the indexing process reviewed earlier or providing another account or reason for the behavior. Indexing may lead to an individual to be categorized as deviant. Social order is then restored by applying new sets of rules and expectations for the newly labeled individual, giving her a new set of behavioral guidelines.

A typical example of this process is the behavior and reactions involved in high-school pranks. For instance, a group of students may decide to illegally enter a high-school quad after hours and proceed to douse the trees with streams of toilet paper for a bit of fun. Upon being caught, the teenagers are told to account for their actions in the face of punishment. Ultimately, all of them will be asked to provide motivations for their behaviors. Accepting the act as part of one's identity (i.e., identifying oneself as a deviant), is only one of the possible ways to account for those acts. The students can alternatively account for their behaviors by arguing that they felt peer pressure to do it or say that they simply "didn't know" it was bad.

Most deviance research focuses on more serious infractions of norms or of the law in which police, the courts, medical doctors, and other agents of social control must adjudicate deviant behavior. **Agents of social control** represent the state's attempts to maintain social order, to enforce the mores of society. Some laws are accepted more readily than others. Murder is almost universally accepted as a form of deviance to be punished, whereas drinking and drug laws vary widely by nation. Of course, infractions viewed as more serious are associated with the strongest penalties. It is not surprising that murder and robbery get more attention by agents of social control than theft. More people commit less-serious offenses than the more-serious ones (see Figure 7.1). Hence, some of the least-perpetrated types of deviance (e.g., murder) are considered the most important types of deviance to control.

Using Lemert's (1951) framework, the role of the larger society is most present during secondary deviance, when the individual comes to identify herself as a deviant. According to labeling theorists, although society does not directly cause primary deviance to occur, it contributes to the labeling process when agents of social control label an act and the person committing the act (i.e., secondary deviance). A self-fulfilling process develops in which individuals reflect on their deviant behaviors based on the reactions of agents of social control, leading them to commit further deviant acts to support the label.

Many studies support the basic labeling process. In one classic example, William Chambliss (1973) followed the lives of two sets of boys in a small Midwestern town; he called them the Saints and the Roughnecks. The Saints were middle-class, college-bound boys, whereas the Roughnecks came from the working class. Both

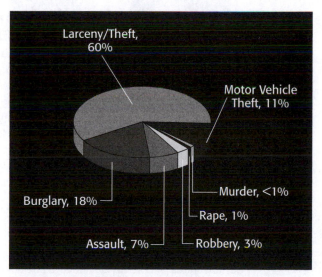

Figure 7.1   Distribution of U.S. Crimes
Source: Adapted from 2003 Uniformed Crime Report.

groups participated in a series of delinquent behaviors: drinking, stealing, and vandalism, among other things. However, none of the Saints were ever arrested, but the Roughnecks were often in trouble with law enforcement officers. Chambliss wanted to know why.

Chambliss (1973) found that the Saints, in terms of the absolute number of delinquent acts, were more deviant than the Roughnecks. They engaged in more truancy and drank more regularly than the Roughnecks. However, the Roughnecks' behavior caused more damage than that of the Saints, and they were more likely to engage in violent behavior. Chambliss concluded that the Roughnecks shared a larger portion of law enforcement (an agent of social control) attention for three reasons. First was differential visibility as a result of economic standing in the community. Because the Saints had more access to private transportation in the form of cars, they could easily evade detection from police and other enforcers or engage in delinquency away from their homes. The Roughnecks had to hang out in public spaces more often, in full view of police. Second, the Saints interacted with authorities differently than the Roughnecks. The Saints would act penitent even when they believed that they had done no wrong (a form of "cultural capital" they acquired in interactions with middle-class people), whereas the Roughnecks would act belligerent to the end. Finally, the agents of social control showed a clear bias for the Saints and against the Roughnecks. Chambliss found that the police interpreted transgressions by the two groups differently: In the eyes of the police, the Saints were simply "sowing wild oats," whereas the economically deprived Roughnecks were "up to no good." Once labeled delinquents, the Roughnecks were much more scrutinized in all their behaviors—hence, their deviance was more often noticed than that of the Saints, promoting a self-fulfilling prophecy.

Moral Careers and Deviant Subcultures

In his famous work, *Outsiders: Studies in the Sociology of Deviance*, Howard Becker (1973), a prominent labeling theorist, extended the basic premises of labeling theory by elaborating the processes through which primary deviance leads to secondary deviance and the importance of deviant subcultures in maintaining the deviant self-image. His study followed the development of marijuana laws and the recreational use of drugs (see Box 7.2). He also used participant observation of Chicago musicians to illustrate the social life of deviant subcultures. In his book, **outsiders** refer to people labeled as deviants who accept the deviant labels. Outsiders accept their deviant label and see themselves outside conventional society.

Becker (1973) described a three-stage process by which individuals become outsiders:

1. An individual commits a deviant act (primary deviance).
2. The person is caught doing the act by someone else and begins to accept the deviant status (secondary deviance). The deviance becomes a part of her master status, one that affects all other aspects of her life, the life of an outsider.
3. The deviant joins a deviant subculture, thereby solidifying her deviant status.

Box 7.2   Becoming a Marijuana User

Howard Becker was famous for his analysis of how individuals come to use mind-altering drugs and how they interpret those experiences. Becker was writing at a time when other researchers, such as the famous psychologist Timothy Leary, were studying drugs as a way of "consciousness raising." Meanwhile, government officials warned of the negative side effects of these drugs. Although drug use may represent a physiological/chemical reaction in the body, Becker argued that subjective reactions to drugs can only be studied through observation and interviews. Drug reactions can be subjective because individuals can focus on any one of a number of physiological effects and interpret those effects differently (e.g., as good or bad).

Becker's observation of drug users found that reactions to drug use depended on the group being studied. When a new user was in the presence of experienced users, he could rely on them to help him focus on more positive aspects of the experience. Alternatively, a nonuser may highlight the more disconcerting aspects of the drug experience simply out of inexperience with the drug. The drug culture provides the user the tools necessary to interpret and enjoy the drug experience. The result is a negative or positive association with the experience. Becker's work shows that social interpretations are an important part of deviant experiences.

In this final stage, the individual starts on a **moral career** in which she comes to live a deviant lifestyle.

Stigma, Passing, and Covering

Thus far, most of our discussion of deviance has focused on social behavior, or criminal behavior more specifically. However, symbolic interactionists believe that deviance can take on many forms. Erving Goffman (1963) defined **stigma** as "an attribute that is deeply discrediting" in interaction (3). Stigma includes any form of deviance associated with an individual: physical, emotional, or social. Specifically, stigma can take three forms:

1. A physical deformity or "abominations of the body"

2. Being part of an undesirable social group, such as a racial or religious minority

3. A character flaw, including mental disorders, addictions, or a criminal record

The first form of stigma is most noticeable and the most difficult to cover up. The last form of stigma is usually the least noticeable. In Goffman's work, he tried to find ways that individuals attempt to manage stigma. He found that individuals try to pass and cover their deviance to interact in everyday life. **Passing** refers to ways that people try to make themselves look like "normal" people, whereas **covering** includes ways of concealing their problems from people. In the first form of deviance, physical abominations, is probably difficult to "pass" as normal because these deviations are usually readily apparent to other people. However, addictions to drugs and alcohol may be covered by only drinking alone or concealing the alcohol by pouring it in other drinks when other people are not looking.

There are many other ways that individuals may choose to manage their deviant identities. Heckert and Best (1997) interviewed 20 White redheaded women to examine the stereotypes associated with being a redhead in U.S. society: being labeled as hot-tempered, wild, and otherwise quirky. Although the authors did find that many of these women were stigmatized as a result of their hair color, they also found that they were able to transform their negative experiences into something positive about their hair color and their senses of self. Hence, self-indication can help individuals manipulate the labeling process to produce positive interpretations of stigma.

When individuals choose to accept their stigmas, it may produce a self-fulfilling prophecy. Schur (1971) argued that this process may lead to a retrospective interpretation of the person's life to find support for the deviant label. **Retrospective interpretations** refer to reinterpretations of past behaviors in light of the person's new role as a deviant. People, including the deviant herself, begin to reanalyze past behaviors in light of her new status. The courts can contribute to this process by examining past behaviors to help assess current motives. Once a person is accused of a crime, for example, her past behaviors that at the time seemed innocent may be reevaluated as early signs of future criminal behavior. Much like the self-indication process reviewed in chapter 5, then, the deviant identity is constantly being negotiated and renegotiated both internally (i.e., self-indication) and socially.

Section Summary

The first section of this chapter applied the interactionist perspective to answer the questions: How do we define what is normal or deviant? How does the construction of deviant labels contribute to the development of deviant lifestyles? First, we applied enthnomethodology to understand the processes of indexicality and reflexivity in making decisions about what thoughts, feelings, and behaviors are deemed normal or undesirably different. Labeling theory extends this perspective of deviance by examining how being labeled deviant leads to subsequent deviant behavior through the development of a self-fulfilling prophecy in which primary acts of deviance produce secondary acts of deviance under certain conditions.

SSP | Social Structure and Deviant Behavior

My great uncle used to tell me a story about growing up in communist Poland. He said that the people there would simply take things from the local construction sites to work on their own homes. People made so little money, it was just "understood" that people would take things to get by. They never called it stealing. In fact, they considered "state" property to be the people's property since it was a communist country at the time. They did it just to get by. It really wasn't stealing according to my uncle.

—Jim, senior Criminal Justice major

From a macrosociological perspective, crime is not simply an individual decision. Deviant behavior may be a choice, but those choices are made in context of a larger set of factors. Our choices are constrained by the information and resources we have available to cope with our situation. In addition, larger societal norms create limitations on how we can achieve legitimate goals in life. We may all want a nice car but must limit our desires based on what we can afford at any given time in our lives. Some people are able to obtain such things quite readily, whereas the rest of us must wait until we receive enough income from work or other sources to acquire them. We may choose to find alternative ways of obtaining these goals. Perhaps we could find a higher-paying job. We could also simply take a vehicle without paying for it. However, the latter alternative is not sanctioned by the state. Hence, structural conditions provide some limitations to our decision-making processes.

Jim described a situation in which alternative sets of norms developed in communist Poland. Poland was a communist regime through much of the 20th century. Communist governments of the Eastern Block (as it was called) produced a society in which individuals had very little wealth, and the state maintained complete control of the economy. At times this led to shortages in many areas of life. Jim's uncle described the way that citizens began to cope with shortages in building supplies by obtaining them from local construction sites. To obtain needed items, they redefined the act of taking property as normal. They later justified their acts based on the limitations induced by a communist economy.

For Jim's uncle, socio-historical conditions influenced the types, levels, and justification for stealing. Structural theories of deviance tend to focus on the social-structural conditions that affect deviance levels. These theories either emphasize the social conditions that make deviance more likely to occur or the role of individuals' immediate environments that influence their decisions to take on a deviant career.

Anomie and Social Strain

Emile Durkheim is a major figure of the macrosociological perspective called functionalism, describing society as a system of self-regulating parts held together via social bonds. Durkheim argued that individuals can lose their sense of place in society, especially in times of great social change when norms and values become less clear. Under these conditions, individuals may develop a sense of **anomie** or "normlessness," where there is little consensus about what is right and wrong. Without a clear sense of right and wrong, individuals lack the guidance to make clear decisions in life.

The concept of anomie was applied to the study of deviance by the sociologist Robert Merton. Merton (1968) believed that deviance is a natural outcome of social conditions in which socially acceptable goals cannot be obtained through legitimate means, serving as the basis of **strain theory.** The story of Jim's uncle shows the Polish people in a situation in which they could not legitimately obtain the items they needed, forcing them to resort to alternative methods.

Although Jim's case may be useful to understand the theft of needed goods, how do we explain the stealing of less-needed items, such as radios and televisions? Strain theory simply argues that these are "legitimate" things in our society; they are socially acceptable, thereby making these items legitimate goals for most people. The American dream of having a nice house and car seems reasonable to most people. But what about people who cannot obtain these goals through conventional means? Should they limit their desires to obtainable goals like a ramshackle apartment and public transportation? Statistics show that most lower-income people do choose to limit their goals, thus avoiding crime. However, people with lower incomes see the same advertisements as their middle- and upper-class peers. Their limited access to education and their lower-paying jobs, however, stifle their abilities to get these things.

Merton (1968) developed a typology to outline the relationship between society's goals and individual deviance (Table 7.1). Under this typology, individuals in society fit into one of five categories. **Conformists** represent the comparison group, people who try to obtain the goals of society through accepted means. Going to school and finding a good job that pays well is a common way for Westerners to be conformists. **Innovators** share the goals of society with conformists but they employ illegitimate means to obtain those goals. You may want a nice car like everyone else. If you do not have the money to obtain that goal, you may rely on alternative means. For instance, you may decide to steal the car, cheat on your taxes to get enough money to put a down payment on the car, or sell illegal drugs.

Table 7.1	Merton's Typology of Deviance	
	Adoption of culturally approved means	Acceptance of culturally approved goals
(a) Conformist	+	+
(b) Innovation	–	+
(c) Ritualism	+	–
(d) Retreatism	–	–
(e) Rebellion	+ or –	+ or –

Ritualists are people who change their attitudes toward success in their lives. They give up trying to achieve wealth and prestige but continue to accept culturally accepted norms of behavior. A ritualist lives with the philosophy, "Don't aim high and you won't be disappointed." Merton associated this pattern of life with lower-middle-class families emphasizing the importance of social control and accepting one's place in the world, whereas poorer and richer families may be more likely to encourage breaking rules in one way or another. Hence, ritualists do not break laws, but they also recognize that they cannot obtain some of the things valued in society. They are ritualistic because they continue to live traditional lives, perhaps working a regular job and taking care of their families, but give up trying to achieve wealth and other societal goals. Alternatively, the **retreatist** neither accepts the goals of the larger society nor the means to achieve those goals. Essentially, retreatists give up on the American dream *and* lifestyle. In the movie *Mosquito Coast* (1986), Harrison Ford plays a character who gets fed up with the middle-class American lifestyle and takes his family to Central America to set himself free. He neither accepts America's goals (e.g., nice house and car) nor the way that Americans go about achieving those goals (e.g., a white-collar job). He simply tries to opt out of the system. In reality, we find most retreatists in the form of vagrants, when people wander from place to place with no regular employment.

Finally, **rebellion** occurs when individuals seek to challenge either the traditional goals or the accepted means of achieving those goals. In short, rebels try to change society in some way. The 1960s were associated with a lot of rethinking of middle-class values and goals. Is a nice house and car really that important in life? Maybe we should focus on relationships more than our material well-being. Alternatively, rebels may try to change the way people obtain some of the traditional goals. Can we find a way to obtain a nice house and car without working 60 plus hours a week? The rebel challenges us to rethink our goals and values.

Strain theory has been revised over the years to include other forms of strains that may lead to deviance. Robert Agnew (1985, 2001), for instance, argued that strain may result from the blockage of pain-avoidance behavior. Individuals seek to obtain rewards from society but also want to avoid punishment. Deviance may reflect strains at both ends of the spectrum. Specifically, frustration may result from not being able to obtain our goals (rewards) or from trying to escape pain (punishment). If our ability to avoid pain is blocked, Agnew argued, individuals will use deviance to either escape the source of pain or remove the source of aversion.

This revised version of strain theory extends the concept of strain to include a range of social conditions. For instance, in a study of Chinese middle- and high-school students, researchers examined how strains at home and school (e.g., negative relations with family, friends, and teachers) affected rates of delinquency in the form of violence and property crimes (Bao, Haas, and Pi 2004). They found negative relations with family and friends to be associated with delinquent behavior, partly because these strains led to negative emotions such as anger or resentment, ultimately leading to delinquency. Similar research has been done on other forms of strain such as racial discrimination (Simons, Chen, Steward, and Brody 2003) and negative life events (Sharp, Terling-Watt, Atkins, Gilliam, and Sanders 2001).

Social Control Theory

Another structural approach to the study of deviance is social control theory developed by Travis Hirschi (1969). Unlike other theories of deviance, Hirschi tried to understand why people choose *not* to commit criminal acts. Under Merton's typology, one might expect most of us to be innovators because we cannot obtain many societal goals. We may be able to legitimately obtain a car but not necessarily the car we want. Hirschi wanted to know why individuals do not choose illegitimate means to attain such goals. If you really want a Corvette and do not have a job that pays enough to buy that Corvette, why not just go down to the local dealer and steal it after hours?

Clearly, fear of criminal prosecutions stops many people from attempting to take things that do not belong to them. But other factors may limit our willingness to obtain things illegally. What would your mother think of you if you got caught? What if the neighbors found out about your transgression? According to **social control theory,** deviance results when individuals' bonds with conventional society are weakened in some way. In other words, strong ties tend to breed conformity in groups. When those ties are weakened, people feel free to deviate from norms because they are not concerned with how other people will respond to their offenses.

Social control theory is based on the principles of the social structure and personality perspective, particularly the proximity principle (see chapter 2). The proximity principle states that individuals are affected by social structure through their immediate social environments. We feel the effects of society through our friends and family, our work and social lives. Social control theory extends this idea by stating that when the bonds between the individual and her immediate social environment (i.e., friends and family) are not well established, she is less motivated to live by the rules.

Social control theory proposes four ways that individuals are bonded to society: attachment, commitment, involvement, and belief. **Attachment** refers to emotional bonds with other people. Strong attachments to friends and family help individuals internalize the norms and values of the larger society. They also provide an incentive to follow the rules; knowing that your delinquent behavior may offend someone close to you may make you think twice about committing a crime.

Commitment is the rational component of conformity, that is the decision to follow the rules (Hirschi 1969). Much like Merton's strain theory, social control theory proposes that people may choose to accept societal goals and means to obtain them or not. If people do decide to accept them, they may become less likely to break the law because the consequences of law breaking (such as jail time) can interfere with the ability to obtain many of society's accepted goals (such as a home life with a partner and children). In addition, she may lose her investment (e.g., time spent on education) in the system. (See Box 7.3.) **Involvement** refers to people's participation in acceptable social activities such as clubs, churches, and other organizations. Being involved in these activities limits peo-

Box 7.3   **Studies in Conformity**

Psychological social psychologists are also interested in the social conditions that influence conformity within groups. In a famous study by Solomon Asch, subjects were asked to match the length of a line to three other ones. Each subject was placed last in a series of seven or more other people, confederates who were instructed to choose the wrong line. A third or more of the subjects would choose a line that was clearly a different size than the original one, conforming to the confederates' incorrect choices. Asch found that the conformists would either question their own judgment of the line or simply "go along to get along" with the group.

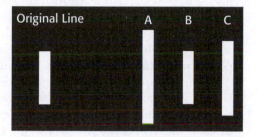

Conformity is a natural part of human social life, making it hard to deviate from the norms and values of other people. If six people before you said that line C was the closest in length to the original line, which line would you choose? These types of studies help us to see the power that other people have in our decision making—both consciously and unconsciously. These processes lead us to "go along to get along."

ple's ability to commit crime and provides additional attachments to people. The final component of social control theory is belief. **Belief** refers to people's respect for law and order in society.

Social control theory is based on the simple logic that people more vested in society have more to gain from the social system than people who have little connection with society. If you view society as something of value, then you are less likely to act out against it. Laws represent collective beliefs. Breaking laws is of less consequence if you do not believe them to be part of your identity. Similarly, if you are not concerned with what other people think about your behavior, then there is less reason to inhibit it. In short, our emotional connections with other people help defer gratification and control our impulses for the short-term rewards of crime.

The basic premises of social control theory were tested in Hirschi's (1969) famous book, *Causes of Delinquency*. Hirschi used self-reported delinquent behavior in a youth survey conducted in 1965. His data showed that the number of self-reported delinquent acts went down as communication levels increased between fathers and sons. Students who were more concerned with their teachers' opinions were significantly less likely to commit delinquent acts than students who did not much care what their teachers thought of them. Students who were more involved in school also reported lower levels of delinquency, supporting the idea that involvement in legitimate activities is associated with less deviance. Finally, Hirschi studied commitment by examining subjects' educational aspirations (their desire to go on to college) and found that as educational aspirations increased, levels of delinquency went down.

More recent research has challenged some of the Hirschi's initial findings. Greenberg (1999) reanalyzed Hirschi's data using modern statistical techniques. He found that many of the initial findings were accurate, but the strength of those finding were substantially lower than Hirschi had assumed. He also found some evidence supporting structural strain theory; greater educational strain, when educational aspirations could not be achieved through legitimate means, was associated with higher delinquency rates. In fact, Greenberg stated that the findings supporting strain theory are as strong as the findings supporting social control theory.

Other research continues to support some of the basic elements of social control theory. Sampson and Laub (1990; Laub and Sampson 1993), for instance, combined the life-course perspective (see chapter 6) and social control theory to examine the lives of two groups of youths (ages 10 to 17) growing up in Boston. Five hundred of the youths had no prior record of delinquency, and another 500 youths were sampled from two correctional facilities. Sampson and Laub used the data to examine the role of adult social bonds in mediating the impact of past deviant behavior on adult criminal behavior. Their findings showed that the delinquent sample was much more likely to lead a life of crime in adulthood than the youths in the nondelinquent sample. However, delinquents who developed strong ties to work and family were much less likely to develop a deviant career than those with fewer ties, even after controlling for important background factors. The authors argued that social bonds can influence levels of criminality, even for people brought up in harsh social environments that limit their abilities to lead more traditional lives.

Section Summary

A structuralist approach is applied to answer the question: What structural conditions influence individuals' decisions to commit deviant acts? Social strain and social control theories assume that societal conditions provide the context for committing deviance, mostly in the form of delinquency and crime. Social strain theory, for instance, argues that society provides both the goals and the means to obtain those goals. If people lack the ability to achieve societal goals through legitimate means, they may turn to illegitimate means to obtain them. Social control theory incorporates the role of social bonds in the decision to commit deviance; individuals with stronger connections to society are less likely to commit deviant acts than people with fewer bonds.

I will never forget the e-mail I got from this student, trying to extol the virtues of polygamy. He sent me this link to a Web site for some sort of on-line magazine. The articles revolved around this idea that Americans are too uptight about sex and should open their worlds to accepting multiple spouses and partners. I really don't have much of a problem with that except that I started noticing that all of the authors of these articles were men! I think it may take some time for this set of values to catch on with other groups in society!

—Daniel, Family Studies instructor

The beginning of this text was dedicated to the social construction of society and the subsequent adoption of societal norms and values by individuals. Although criminologists tend to view deviance as a problem that needs to be addressed, interactionists are more likely to view rule production and subsequent breaking as part of a larger process. By extension, the fundamental processes involved in the creation of deviance occur in group contexts. However, groups may vary in acceptable rules and standards, even in the same society. Some Americans attend conservative churches or temples, whereas others attend more liberal-minded congregations or none at all. The groups we spend time with provide the context for deciding what is right and wrong. Some people may appear to be deviating from societal norms simply because they are following the norms of their peers. Their peers, however, may have different norms and values than the larger society. Ironically, then, conforming to our peer groups' norms may lead to deviance from the larger society.

Daniel's example focuses on a movement to normalize polygamy in the United States. The United States—like many nations in the world—has a norm of pair bonding in which two people form some sort of union, often for the purposes of raising children. Polygamy is legal in a number of countries as well. This group wishes to change American norms to include polygamy. However, Daniel notices that the authors of the Web site are decidedly male. The authors seem to suggest that people should be open to multiple partners, a view encouraging males to "spread their seed" to as many females as possible. As a result, Daniel begins to doubt whether the motives of the group are representative of women's views on the matter. Regardless, although the pro-polygamists' perspectives deviate from the larger culture, they are clearly supported by other group members. These alternative norms are "right" and "good" to these men.

The idea that people can simply choose a deviant pathway such as polygamy in a similar way that most of us choose among traditional roads is very similar to interactionist approaches to deviance. However, it adds the idea of behavioralist theories in psychology that emphasize the role of operant conditioning and imitation. In behavioral psychology's approach, people learn behaviors based on the rewards and punishments associated with them (i.e., people will learn to continue behaviors that are rewarded and discontinue behaviors that are punished). **Differential association theory** states the deviance is learned through interaction with others. Individuals who associate with deviant people are more likely to learn deviant behavior than those who do not spend time with deviant others. In other words, we learn deviance like we learn what is normal and good, through family, friends, and schooling.

The Principles of Differential Association Theory

Differential association theory was developed by Edwin H. Sutherland and colleagues. Sutherland's goal was to introduce a theory that would explain the social causes of deviance. The theory is based on nine principles (Sutherland and Cressey 1999: 241–242):

1. Criminal behavior is learned.
2. Criminal behavior is learned in interaction with other persons in a process of communication.
3. The principle part of the learning of criminal behavior occurs within intimate personal groups.
4. When criminal behavior is learned, the learning includes techniques of committing the crime as well as motives, drives, rationalizations, and attitudes.
5. The specific direction of motives and drives is learned from definitions of the legal codes as favorable or unfavorable.
6. A person begins delinquent behavior when she has an excess of definitions favorable to violation of law over definitions unfavorable to violation of the law.
7. Differential associations may vary in frequency, duration, priority, and intensity.
8. The process of learning criminal behavior by association with criminal and anticriminal patterns involves all the mechanisms that are involved in any other learning.
9. Although criminal behavior is an expression of general needs and values, it is not explained by those general needs and values, because noncriminal behavior is an expression of the same needs and values.

The key component of this theory is that learning occurs in groups. Other group members provide both the motives and the knowledge necessary to commit crime (principle #4). The context of the group is also important: We must be interacting with people to whom we feel close (principle #3). In addition, we learn criminal attitudes and behaviors like any other attitudes and behaviors, through communication and exchange of meaning (principle #2).

The latter principles emphasize the decision-making processes that occur in groups. We may learn how to deviate from a group but choose to do otherwise. Why would one choose to deviate from society? Sutherland argued that individuals balance the costs and benefits of deviant behavior like any other decisions in life (principles #6 and #8). If we believe that deviance provides a better alternative than other options, we will choose to be deviant.

Think about a situation in which a poor man is trying to get to a job interview. He has a car but almost no gas. The interview could mean the difference between a stable income or just getting by in life. His friends share a story in which they pumped gas and then left without paying, providing him basic techniques for stealing gas that limit the possibility of being caught (e.g., covering the license plate). Although that behavior may produce an arrest, he also knows how to minimize this risk. Further, the loss of this interview may make life almost as unbearable as prison. The costs of not acting on the advice of his peers may outweigh the risk of going to prison.

The deviant's decision to commit the act is similar to any other cost-benefit analysis, but it is still a decision. However, that decision employs the use of advice and input from friends, family, and acquaintances. Association with deviant others provides both the information and motives to commit deviant acts. Sutherland and Cressey (1999) described two situations, one with a sociable, active, athletic young boy and the other a person with "psychopathic" tendencies. They suggested that if the former begins spending time with delinquent boys, he will become a delinquent. Alternatively, in the latter case, if the psychopathic boy stays isolated and introverted, he is less likely to become delinquent than he would otherwise because he lacks the interaction with delinquent others. Hence, our social surroundings influence the direction and outcomes of our disposition.

Differential Association, Gender, and the Culture of Honor

Research using differential association theory is generally conducted by examining deviants' relationships with other people. Studies may ask individuals to indicate the types of people they spend the most time with, assessing the deviance of their peers. Research generally supports the idea that people who spend more time with deviants are more likely to support and conduct deviant behavior themselves. For instance, in a study of French boys and girls, Hartjen and Priyadarsini (2003) found measures of differential association strongly related to delinquency for both boys and girls. However, other research shows that the role of differential association may be stronger among boys than girls (Piquero, Gover, Macdonald, and Piquero 2005). That is, the delinquent peer associations seem to be better predictors of delinquency among boys than girls. It is difficult to understand this relationship, but it is important because gender is one of the strongest independent predictors of delinquency with boys being more likely than girls to engage in most forms of deviance.

Differential association can also be used to explain why certain regions of the country tend to have higher rates of violence than other areas. Richard Nisbett (1993; Nisbett, Polly, and Lang 1995), a psychologist, completed an extensive study of violence in the southern United States. Southerners are statistically more likely to commit violent crimes than people in any other region of the United

States. Nisbett showed that although Southerners generally do not endorse violence any more than Northerners, they are significantly more likely to support certain types of violence—in cases of self-defense and in response to insults—than Northerners. Hence, under some conditions, there is a culture of honor in the South, a place in which violence is more acceptable as a matter of honor. Being raised in such a culture increases the likelihood of using violence as a legitimate response to provocation.

Nisbett (1993) traced the South's culture of honor to its early herding economy. He argued that herding is a much more fragile industry than farming because of the amount of time and money put into each animal being raised. Although the loss of a few plants would not reduce the overall value of a yield of corn, the loss of even one animal represents many years of feeding and maintenance. The image of the tough cattle herder may simply reflect individuals' focus on keeping a tight reign on expensive property. Being portrayed as weak may give potential thieves the idea that a person is unable to protect his or her herd. To reduce the possibility of theft, many herders may have adopted a policy of hypervigilance toward outsiders, thus leading to a culture of honor.

There are a number of problems trying to study violence rates in the South. The prevalence of many crimes is associated with poverty, minority race, and other factors such as warm weather, all of which exist disproportionately in the Southern United States. Nesbitt focused on crimes perpetrated by Whites only, comparing rates of crime relative to city size, among other factors. He found homicide rates in more rural areas of the South, where a culture of honor is more likely to exist, to be higher than in urbanized areas, where it is less likely to exist. Further, he found that areas categorized as having a history of herding had significantly higher rates of violence than those areas deemed farming communities. These findings continue after controlling for a host of other factors generally associated with violent behavior. In this case, the culture of honor helps show the importance group norms and values may play in our decisions to commit deviant acts.

White-Collar Crime

Differential association theory is useful to understanding how people can rationalize almost any form of deviant behavior. The differences between the Saints and the Roughnecks described earlier in this chapter suggest a bias against lower-status perpetrators. Upper middle- and upper-class offenders show up as perpetrators in different types of crimes, usually associated with less stigma than working-class crimes of passion. Typical examples of middle- and upper-class **white-collar crimes** include embezzlement, cheating, and laundering money, among others. These are crimes that are associated with higher-status individuals in the course of their work (Sutherland 1940).

White-collar crime may appear to be less serious than other forms of deviance like rape or murder, but it can have a large impact on society, as government and private industry lose millions of dollars as a result of fraud and other such crimes. In Donald Cressey's (1971) social-psychological study of embezzlement behavior,

The white-collar crimes of former Enron executives like Kenneth Lay cost millions of dollars in losses for stockholders and the pensions of many employees after the demise of the company.

he argued that perpetrators try to find ways to justify their crimes, to make them appear less serious. Rather than accepting the behavior as deviant, embezzlers talk about their behavior in legitimate terms such as "borrowing" rather than "taking" other people's money. These findings can apply to similar forms of deviance among the middle and upper classes. In a large-scale study of cheating behavior among college students, for example, over two-thirds indicated that they had cheated at some time as an undergraduate student (McCabe 1992). Most of the cheaters defended their cheating by denial of responsibility (e.g., an unfair workload) (61%), condemnation of the teacher or assignment (28%), an appeal to higher authorities (e.g., peer pressure) (7%), and denial of injury (e.g., cheating was harmless) (4%). Hence, social conditions influence interpretations of white-collar deviance.

Studying Deviance in a Lab

In chapter 6, we said that experimental work in the group processes tradition typically does not address socialization because socialization cannot be manipulated in a laboratory. Experimentalists face similar issues when answering questions about deviance. As you learned in reading the earlier sections of this chapter, most social psychological theory and research on deviance represents efforts to understand criminal behavior. Criminal behavior, like socialization, is difficult to measure in a laboratory setting. Nevertheless, as with socialization, group processes researchers have furthered our understanding of criminal behavior in experimental studies by testing theories of basic social processes that have relevance to crime in the real world.

One important criminological issue that has received a great deal of attention in recent years is the high incidence of procedural errors in the prosecution of serious crimes. With the advancement of DNA testing, numerous criminal convictions have been overturned. Moreover, most of these overturned convictions are for serious crimes. For example, although less than 2% of convictions are for homicides, about 50% of known wrongful convictions have been for homicides.

There are a number of possible explanations for why so many erroneous convictions have been made for serious crimes. One is that prosecuting attorneys, when faced with significant pressure to convict, may be more likely to engage in misconduct in order to obtain convictions in more serious cases. It also might be that there are not more erroneous convictions for serious crimes, but only that more erroneous convictions are *found* for more serious crimes. More media attention is focused on cases involving serious crimes, and more time and money are spent trying to discover errors in these cases. For example, a thorough appeal process is mandated in death penalty cases. This process would probably be more likely to uncover errors than would appeals in cases that are less severe.

Lucas and his colleagues (Lucas, Graif, and Lovaglia 2006) developed a theory with the potential to contribute to our understanding of why so many wrongful convictions are in cases involving serious crimes. The theory, which they developed from extensive literatures in sociology and psychology, has three parts:

1. Prosecutors will become more likely to think that defendants are guilty as crimes are more severe.
2. Prosecutors will view attaining a conviction as more important when they hold a stronger belief in the defendant's guilt.
3. Prosecutorial misconduct to obtain a conviction will increase as perceptions of guilt and perceived importance of attaining a conviction increase.

The theory, then, proposes that if there are two trials for different crimes, both with identical evidence against the defendant, then prosecutors will be more likely to think the person charged with the more-serious crime is guilty than the person charged with the less-serious crime. Further, the theory says we should expect prosecutors to view obtaining a conviction as more important and to be more likely to engage in misconduct when the crime is more serious.

Think about trying to test the theory above. How might you go about it? One option could be to interview prosecutors and ask their opinions about the guilt of defendants and about their misconduct in criminal trials. A problem with this approach would be that prosecutors might be motivated to be less than forthcoming. Also, even if they were completely honest, our memories often don't accurately line up with our previous actions, and the prosecutors' answers might not match what actually happened.

A second strategy could be to look back through case files and to determine whether more incidences of misconduct have been found for more serious than for less serious crimes. This has in fact been done: More misconduct is found for more serious crimes than for less serious crimes. However, this is difficult to interpret because, again, more effort is spent trying to find errors in more serious cases.

The theory also might be tested through an experiment. The experiment could have two conditions with different levels of severity of crime and then measure perceptions of guilt, perceived importance of obtaining a conviction, and misconduct. A reasonable question one might ask about this experiment is what it might tell us about misconduct in the real world. The answer is that it would tell us nothing about what goes on in the real world. At least not directly. Experiments are not conducted to inform us about things that go on in the real world. Instead, experiments test theories that are about the real world. If experimental tests support theories, then we have evidence that the theory might accurately predict events that occur in the real world.

To test their theory, Lucas and colleagues (2006) created an experiment in which students acted as prosecuting attorneys in a mock criminal trial. Participants believed that other people in the study were acting as defense attorneys and judges. Participants were told that their job in the study was to go through a file for a criminal case, turn over relevant materials to a defense attorney, and construct a case for a judge. Their goal was to try to get the judge to return a conviction against the defendant.

Every participant in the study received a case with the exact same evidence against a defendant. The study, however, had two conditions. In one condition, the victim of the crime fully recovered within a few days. In the other condition, the victim died from injuries he sustained during the crime.

Participants in the two conditions went through case materials. They were told that all materials that might bear on the guilt or innocence of the defendant must be turned over to the defense attorney. To create an opportunity for misconduct, the researchers constructed the materials so that most of it pointed to the defendant as the most likely suspect, but some pointed to a different person as a potential suspect. They measured misconduct as whether participants withheld questions from the defense that pointed to a different suspect.

After participants turned over materials to the defense attorney, they put together a case to present to the judge. They then answered a number of questionnaire items, including ones asking how important it was to them to get a conviction and how likely they thought it was that the defendant was guilty.

In support of their theory, Lucas and colleagues (2006) found that participants prosecuting the more-severe crime, compared to those prosecuting the less-severe crime, were more likely to believe that the defendant was guilty, said that obtaining a conviction was more important to them, and were more likely to withhold relevant information from the defense.

Again, this study does not directly tell us anything about the likelihood that actual working prosecutors will engage in misconduct. It does, however, demonstrate a process capable of increasing misconduct in the prosecution of more severe crimes. Whether that process produces more misconduct when actual prosecutors handle more serious cases is an open question. Safeguards in the criminal justice system, such as the rigorous training that prosecutors receive, might limit these processes. Other factors, such as increased pressure to convict in more serious cases, may make them more likely. What the research of Lucas and his colleagues (2006) does provide is a compelling reason to investigate misconduct among actual prosecutors of serious criminal cases.

Section Summary

This section applied the group processes perspective to answer the question: How do group relationships influence the development of deviance and perceptions of deviance? Here, groups provide the context for decision making about deviant behaviors, both our own and other people's behavior. Differential association theory assumes that we learn deviant behavior like any other behavior, from other people. Groups can also influence our decisions about whether others' behavior is deviant or not.

Bringing It All Together

Crime, to me, is the number one problem in the world today. It seems like we keep putting more police on the street and developing programs to "fix" the problem but we never seem to get rid of it. How can social psychology fix the problem?

—Carol, senior Accounting major

Carol's query assumes that social psychologists believe that deviance is a bad thing that needs to be eliminated in society. At the beginning of this chapter we defined deviance as any behavior that departs from accepted practices in a society or group. Because accepted practices may vary in time and space, the nature of deviance changes too. From an interactionist perspective, we create deviance and then label some people as deviant. From this perspective, deviance is maintained through social interactions in and around the court system. "Fixing" the problems of deviance and crime requires a change in how we relate to deviant people. More structural approaches found in social strain and control theories would suggest that large-scale changes in society like reducing economic inequalities are required if we want to eliminate some forms of deviance. Finally, from a group processes perspective—differential association theory specifically—we need to change who people affiliate with to change someone's delinquent behavior. All these perspectives help to show the complex nature of deviance and how it is manifested in society.

Summary

1. From a social-psychological perspective, deviance is a necessary part of the symbolic interaction process of negotiating social reality. Interactionism assumes that individuals decide to maintain (or break) social norms and standards during every interaction. Deviance allows for change in relationships and society as a whole.

2. Ethnomethodological perspectives of deviance emphasize how individuals construct and defend their views of social reality, the "real" boundaries of social life. People who can provide better accounts can convince others of those accounts, thus controlling the meaning of good and bad—deviance and conformity in society.

3. Labeling theory is a major interactionist perspective of deviance. It is based on the notion that deviance is a consequence of a social process in which a negative characteristic becomes an element of an individual's identity.

4. Strain and social control theories apply macrosociological perspectives of deviant behavior, arguing that deviance results from a larger set of societal conditions. Societal norms create limitations to how we can achieve legitimate goals in life. They also give goals that are unattainable for some people.

5. Groups provide both the motives and the knowledge necessary to commit crime. Differential association theory states that deviance is learned through interaction with others. This theory may help explain how and why people rationalize deviant behavior, especially crimes committed by middle- and upper-class people called white-collar crimes.

Key Terms and Concepts

Agents of social control: The state's attempts to maintain social order through police and courts and other representatives of the state.

Anomie: A sense of "normlessness," where there is little consensus about what is right and wrong.

Attachment: Component of social control theory referring to emotional bonds with other people in society.

Belief: Component of social control theory referring to people's respect for law and order in society.

Commitment: Component of social control theory referring to an individual's desire to obtain societal goals through legitimate means.

Conformists: People who try to obtain the goals of society through accepted means.

Covering: Attempts to conceal a stigma.

Deviance: Refers to any behavior that departs from accepted practices in a society or group.

Differential association theory: Theory that deviance is learned through interaction with others.

Folkways: Less-serious rules of behavior in a group or society.

Indexicality: The process by which individuals index thoughts, feelings, and behaviors from their own perspective.

Innovators: People who share the goals of society with conformists but employ illegitimate means to obtain those goals.

Involvement: Component of social control theory referring to people's participation in acceptable social activities such as clubs, churches and other organizations.

Labeling theory: Theory that argues deviance is a consequence of a social process in which a negative characteristic becomes an element of an individual's identity.

Moral career: When a deviant lifestyle becomes a normal part of an individual's life.

Mores: Widely held values and beliefs in a society.

Outsiders: People labeled as deviants who accept the deviant labels.

Passing: Attempts to hide stigma by looking normal.

Primary deviance: The initial deviant act that causes other people to label the individual a deviant.

Rebellion: When individuals seek to challenge either the traditional goals or the accepted means of achieving those goals.

Reflexivity: The process by which individuals think about a behavior within its social context and give meaning to it.

Retreatist: People who neither accept the goals of the larger society nor the means to achieve those goals.

Retrospective interpretations: Reinterpretations of past behaviors in light of the person's new role as a deviant.

Ritualist: Someone who approves of the ways people should live their lives but give up trying to obtain societal goals.

Secondary deviance: Additional deviant acts that support the initial deviant label.

Social control theory: Theory that deviance results when individuals' bonds with conventional society are weakened in some way.

Stigma: An attribute that is deeply discrediting.

Strain theory: Theory that argues that people choose to commit deviance as a natural outcome of social conditions in which socially acceptable goals can not be obtained through legitimate means.

White-collar crimes: Crimes typically associated with middle- and upper-class individuals such as embezzlement, cheating, and laundering money.

Discussion Questions

1. Think about forms of deviance that do not apply to crime and delinquency. How might an individual incorporate deviance as part of their identity? To produce social change?

2. Have you ever been considered a deviant? If so, how do the deviance theories apply to your situation?

3. How do you think your attitudes toward deviance and deviant behavior relate to your position or location in society?

Mental Health and Illness

Chapter 8

My first semester of college was rough. I mean, I was always depressed! I would just sit in my room, maybe surf the net or something but I would never study. My grades were terrible, and it only made me feel more depressed. My roommate kept bugging me—wanting me to go to a club meeting with her. I really did not want to go but she guilted me into it. So I went. I did not think much of it at first but it got me out talking to people. After a couple of days, I found myself going to class again. Then, I joined another group at a church here. I started to study some more and my grades went up. It is funny how just one club meeting seemed to change so many other aspects of my life!

—Sandy, sophomore Political Science major

Sandy's experience is similar to what a lot of students go through in their first year of college. Most students feel a little anxious and awkward as they begin to experience an entirely different way of life. Students no longer have their routines from high school. Most important, many students are separated from the people with whom they used to interact on a regular basis in their hometowns. This separation cuts off many of the support mechanisms we all need to get through the day—people we turn to for help to get things done as well as people with whom we talk just for fun and for verifying our views of the world. When these supports are taken away from us, we lose a major source of emotional connection in the world. Most of us get over this problem without much trouble by finding new sources of support. But some become depressed or anxious enough that it impairs their daily functioning.

Many people believe that mental illness is an individual's problem reflecting internal dilemmas and issues. The sociological view of mental health and illness lies in stark contrast to this perspective and provides an alternative to biological and psychological models of mental illness. In short, sociologists argue that some of the fundamental causes of psychological problems are social. The **sociology of mental health** is the study of the social arrangements that affect mental illness and its consequences (Aneshensel and Phelan 1999).

Sigmund Freud and other psychoanalytic psychologists emphasized internal processes, often stemming from childhood relationships, that lead to mental illness and are processed unconsciously. Biologists and neurologists examine the role of physiological aspects of mental illness. Although sociologists do not necessarily discount biology and psychology in trying to understand mental illness, they believe that a social lens is critical to gaining the whole picture of mental illness.

The three areas of sociological social psychology each make unique contributions to the study of mental health and illness: symbolic interaction to the *construction*; social structure and personality to *causation*; and group processes to some *consequences* of mental illness. Symbolic interactionists focus on how meanings of mental illness change over time and across cultures. Essentially, meanings about mental illness, like any other thing, are created through interactions within particular cultures—and as cultures differ, so do ways we approach this kind of deviance. Social structural and personality theorists examine the social statuses and conditions that cause depression, anxiety, substance abuse, and the like. Group processes scholars help us understand how the status of being mentally ill can be stigmatized and may affect interactions between people. Once you read about these sociological perspectives, you may rethink what it means to have psychological problems.

We will address the following questions in this chapter:

- What does it mean to be mentally healthy? How do we construct the meaning of mental illness?

- What are the structural conditions in society that contribute to distress?

- How does our mental health influence our sense of identity and our interactions with other people?

SI The Social Construction of Mental Health

In second grade, my uncle Trent was a little wild. His second grade teacher actually tied him to a chair with a rope in order to keep him calm and focused on his work. Uncle Trent claims it was just a strict school that kept him from expressing his free spirited ways. But he was thought of as a bad kid for quite a while. I got to thinking that my neighbor Nick, who is now in 1st grade and is also rambunctious, could never be tied to a chair. It's just not allowed anymore. Instead, his teacher suggested he be evaluated for Attention Deficit Disorder and maybe even medicated. It makes me wonder about this new illness and whether it is the right thing to do with Nick. Is ADHD real?

—Simone, junior Sociology major

In this vignette, Simone begins to question what it means to be "mentally ill." Her young neighbor displays the same kind of behavior as did her uncle, but the two were treated very differently by adults. In an earlier era, her uncle was considered bad, but her neighbor is considered "ill." How can we make sense of this? Perhaps these maladies have always been around but were unnamed until scientists labeled them as such. Alternatively, societies may construct new illnesses and label people who have traits thought to reflect those labels.

In Simone's case, an older family member had trouble managing behavior in the classroom and was labeled as a deviant and treated as such. Her neighbor today is treated like a "sick" person who needs treatment more than punishment. This example reflects a philosophical debate regarding the line between criminal and medical deviance. Are people different because they choose to act differently, or do these differences reflect physiological problems that need treatment, like any malady? Interactionists examine the ways deviance is constructed and how mental health is treated when it is identified as a malady.

Defining Mental Illness

An interesting feature of mental conditions with which people can be diagnosed is that many of these categories are quite new. ADHD was virtually unknown when Simone's Uncle Trent was a boy—it did not exist! Societies have always had some people who act somewhat different or seemingly strange, exhibiting an array of symptoms that do not necessarily make sense to others. Several sociologists focus on the socially constructed nature of what we call "mental illness." They emphasize historical changes that have led to a redefinition of mental illness or current-day examples of how groups work together to create new labels for mental illnesses.

Madness and Civilization

Michel Foucault (1965) was a French social philosopher who studied the meaning of mental illness through history. He examined the ways that Western society viewed the role of madness from the Middle Ages to the present, emphasizing the 17th, 18th, and 19th centuries. He said that 1656 was an important date in the history of madness because that is the year that the "Hôpital General" opened in Paris, marking the start of the "great confinement" in which the insane and other deviants were housed together and separated from the rest of society. The mad were set aside from the masses, much like the lepers had been in past generations. For the first time in the West, madness formally became something to keep away from society for its protection.

The "Hôpital General" and other places of confinement housed both sane and insane individuals who deviated from social norms and laws. Criminals were kept with people who, by today's standards, would be considered sick and in need of medical attention. Hence, deviance was the primary distinction between residents and nonresidents of the Hôpital General. The meaning of being sick changed dramatically after the Middle Ages. Foucault (1965) attributed this change to a number of societal-level changes going on in Europe during this period. He argued that the increased focus on reason made unreason unfathomable. In addition, new economic developments led to new attitudes toward the vagabond and the idle. Being idle was a scourge to society, something that must be hidden away from the marketplace.

Ideas about madness changed over time as reform movements emerged to purify these houses of confinement. Foucault (1965) argued that "unreasonable" people in society began to be more accepted, just as the physical sciences were beginning to assert that the universe does not necessarily operate under easily identifiable rules, laws, and principles. Therefore, separating "unreasonable" people made less sense to state leaders and intellectuals in later eras. In addition, economic conditions changed in a way that made the insane more useful. Developing economies included jobs that required cheap labor, thus giving stigmatized mental patients something to do on their release from confinement.

The reform movements of the 18th and 19th centuries also led to the separation of criminals from the insane. The insane started receiving medical treatment instead of punishment. Although both groups were still considered deviant, only the prisoners continued to be confined en masse. The mentally ill started receiving treatment to fix their maladies. Some would remain in asylums but many of them were set free—restrained only by therapy and social stigma. Hence, criminal and mental deviants were separated but treated as undesirably different from the rest of society.

The Medicalization of Deviance and Social Problems

Foucault's work focused on historical analysis of the way society has come to label and treat mental illness. He took a social-constructionist perspective on this form of deviance. Modern researchers with a constructionist perspective focus on the **medicalization of deviance,** referring to ways in which social problems—including mental health problems—have come under the boundaries of medicine (Conrad and Potter 2000). Historically, there have been three forces driving what aspects of social life become medicalized (Conrad 2005):

1. The power and authority of the medical profession
2. Activities of social movements and interest groups
3. Directed organizational on professional activities

The role of medical professionals in labeling a behavior or condition a medical problem, number 1 above is straightforward. Doctors serve as gatekeepers in the

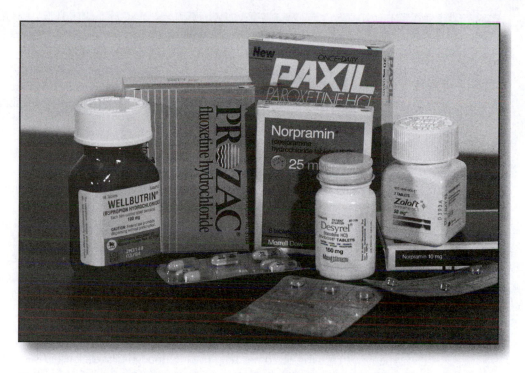

Pharmaceutical companies have great impact on the marketing of psychotropic drugs to the general public. Drug advertisements present a biological explanation of mental illnesses.

medical industry, with the power to label something under the purview of medical science. Labeling is the first step in developing treatment for a disease or medical problem. It also makes a problem more than just a social issue but stresses the biological aspects of the problem, requiring a medical solution to resolve it.

Conrad (2005) also pointed out that there are different types of groups who have sought to define problems as medical to legitimize their problems or seek treatments for them, such as organizations of medical professionals. Other groups can initiate social movements (medical or not) with the sole purpose of medicalizing an issue. A classic example of this process is the role of organizations in medicalizing posttraumatic stress disorder (PTSD). The basic premise of PTSD has been around since the inception of war. Soldiers who suffer mental-health problems as a result of their exposure to combat have been labeled "shell-shocked" (WWI) or as "battle fatigued" (WWII), but none of these disorders were included in the first edition of the *Diagnostic and Statistical Manual* (DSM-I, 1952) by the American Psychiatric Association (APA), the primary guidebook for diagnosing mental-health disorders (see Box 8.1). Rather, this condition was treated as a reaction to stress that was temporary in nature (Scott 1990). The second edition of the *DSM* appeared in 1968, also with no reference to the problem. Things changed as the United States moved into the final stages of the Vietnam War. Although there

Box 8.1   The Diagnostic and Statistical Manual

Most psychological and psychiatric treatment of mental illnesses is guided by the *Diagnostic and Statistical Manual* (DSM). First developed in the 1950s, the *DSM* has gone through several revisions. With each revision, new information is added to the manual and some diagnoses change. The *DSM* currently has five axes:

1. **Axis I:** Clinical disorders such as depression, anxiety, and attention-deficit disorder.

2. **Axis II:** Developmental and personality disorders such as antisocial disorder and mental retardation.

3. **Axis III:** Medical conditions that may influence mental disorders (e.g., HIV/AIDS may produce mental illnesses).

4. **Axis IV:** Psychosocial stressors that may influence mental disorders (e.g., death of a loved one).

5. **Axis V:** Global assessment of functioning—a scale used to assess how the first four axes are affecting patients.

The *DSM* is designed as a repository of diagnoses for hundreds of mental disorders. It can be criticized for treating mental illness like physical illness, linking specific treatments with positive outcomes (e.g., healing) though this relationship is less clear for mental-health conditions. More recent versions (e.g., the *DSM-IV-TR,* 2000) have begun to recognize the important role of social conditions that may affect diagnoses and treatment of mental illnesses.

---

was no plan to add a category for PTSD to the third edition of the *DSM,* several psychiatrists, social workers, and lawyers pushed the APA to add the category. These efforts led the development of a working group that gathered data in support of the development of a category of disorder related to traumatic stress, one that could apply to people exposed to combat or other major stresses. The 1980 *DSM-III* was released with a category of "posttraumatic stress disorder" among its listing of over 200 other disorders.

Modern interest groups influencing the medicalization process are more economic than social in nature (Conrad 2005). These include health maintenance organizations (HMOs), the pharmaceutical industry, and consumers. HMOs commonly limit the types of treatments for which they will pay. For instance, the use of medicines to treat mental illness has increased, whereas repayment for psychotherapies has declined. This shift has influenced how people define their problems, moving from social to biological explanations. Pharmaceutical companies play a role in this process by determining the direction of research, emphasizing some treatments more than others and appealing directly to consumers to buy their products. For instance, pharmaceutical advertisers spend as much money marketing directly to consumers today as they spend marketing to doctors, and spending on television advertising of pharmaceuticals increased sixfold between 1996 and 2000.

Finally, the growth of professional and health services organizations has contributed to an effort to codify and design specific treatments for mental diseases (Horwitz 2002). If psychologists and psychiatrists were to compete with "real" medical doctors, then they would need to treat "real" diseases and report "real" outcomes. We can see a broken arm through certain devices and determine whether or not that arm has been healed after treatment. The same thing is not true for most mental illnesses. The move for more precision in the mental health industry is shown by the increasing specificity in its labeling. For example, the number of disorders listed in the *DSM* more than doubled between the third and fourth editions, a span of 14 years. The medicalization of a disorder also helps to separate the disease from individuals' identity and control. Instead of being a "crazy person," you can be described as a person with a mental illness. This same process is true with physical illnesses. We are not likely to be described as "a broken-armed person," but instead as a person with a broken arm.

Labeling Theory and the Social Control of Deviance

Although there has been a move to better codify mental disorders in the DSM, it is still difficult to label and treat them because they cannot be studied as a physical object that can be observed, such as a torn ligament or broken leg. Thomas Szasz (1968, 1974) argued that mental illness is a myth, that it is socially constructed like any other aspect of social life. Further, psychoanalysis, a major form of treatment for some mental illnesses, is a moral not a medical activity (Szasz 2003). From this perspective, mental illness is simply a form of deviance; rather than being fined or punished for deviant illegal behavior, mental-health deviants are "treated" to resolve their deviant tendencies. In addition, this process is largely controlled by the client, they have more choice in seeking and acting on treatment, whereas criminal deviance is controlled by the state.

Labeling theory was introduced in Chapter 7 to help explain the social causes of criminal deviance. If mental health problems are viewed as a form of deviance, labeling theory can also be applied to study mental illnesses. Labeling theory emphasizes the processes by which an individual comes to accept a negative characteristic as part of her identity. In the case of medical deviance, this process may include accepting the labels associated with the *DSM*, such as being depressed, an alcoholic, or someone with ADHD. Once the label is accepted, it encourages others to expect the behavior from an individual. The individual then begins to view her own behavior in relationship to the label.

As applied to mental health, labeling theory emphasizes different agents of social control employed to segregate and label criminal versus ill groups. Foucault outlined the break between these two groups in France when the police, prisons, and courts began managing criminal deviance, whereas doctors and mental health practitioners managed the mentally ill. The challenge of studying these processes is that the system of defining what is normal and obtaining conformity varies by society (Scheff 1999). Each group has its own point at which deviance arouses enough indignation that perpetrators are segregated and labeled by their deviance. This perspective moves away from the individual-level explanations about why people commit deviant acts and focuses more on social conditions surrounding the act. Individual-level explanations of deviance focus on the following questions.

1. What are the causes of deviance?
2. How can it be stopped?

Social explanations of deviance focus on larger questions such as: Why does a particular society define a behavior as deviant that others do not? Modern uses of labeling theory are not completely at odds with other explanations but instead try to help researchers understand the larger context of deviance. Moreover, those taking a social constructionist approach examine why certain groups might get certain labels. We will examine some of this kind of research in the next section.

Section Summary

The first section of this chapter applied the interactionist perspective to respond to the question: What does it mean to be mentally healthy? How do we construct the meaning of mental illness? We examined how the meaning of deviant behaviors has changed over time in the Western world, moving from a form of deviance akin to criminal deviance, to a form of malady that should be treated. Labeling theory is also applied to mental illness to understand how individuals and groups contribute to the social construction of some mental illnesses.

(SSP) Social Causes of Stress

> *I saw a woman on a bus that makes a stop at the University. She had two little kids with her; one was handicapped. She was wearing a wrinkled janitor's uniform so she must have been dropping them off at child care somewhere before she went to work. I felt so sad for her and wanted to help. It was very clear from the way she looked that she was really depressed. The older kid kept talking to her but it was like she did not hear him. Obviously life was overwhelming to her.*
>
> —Don, sophomore Marketing major

Although specific individuals feel the mental bruises and jolts associated with daily life in different ways, sociologists focus on the patterns that recur when we look closely at social patterns in mental health. Those using the social structure and personality approach have identified a number of patterns related to stress.

First, our social statuses are strongly related to experiencing stressors. We will review research that shows that people of lower social class status experience the most stressors and most mental health problems, for example. There are also other patterns by ethnicity, gender, and age, but economic status is critical. Don notices a lower-income woman who has many chronic strains in her life—the lack of private transportation, a young child's extensive demands that are associated with his special needs, and so on. These conditions seem to manifest themselves in the health and well-being of this woman.

There are regularities to the outcomes people experience when they are exposed to terrible events or chronic strains that arise in their roles. The **stress process** model attempts to help us understand the social connections among stressful events and strains, the resources people bring to deal with problems, and the outcomes they experience.

The basic components of the stress process include stressors, outcomes (distress), moderators, mediators, and SES characteristics (Pearlin 1989; Pearlin, Menaghan, Lieberman, and Mullan 1981) (see Figure 8.1). Distress can be manifested in a person in a number of ways. People may show signs of depression or anxiety or they may act out their distress through alcoholism or antisocial behavior (see, for example, Aneshensel, Rutter, and Lachenbruch 1991; Serido, Almeida, and Wethington 2004; Turner and Kopiec 2006; Turner, Taylor, and Van Gundy 2004; Umberson, Wortman, and Kessler 1992).

The stress process model emphasizes the social structural conditions by which individuals manifest mental health problems. Hence, from a social structural and personality perspective, mental health, in part, is produced by social conditions.

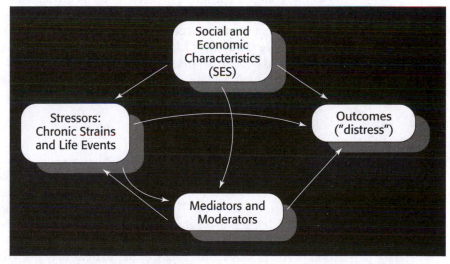

Figure 8.1   The Stress Process Model.

Source: Adapted from Pearlin, Menaghan, Lieberman, and Mullan (1981).

Social conditions both influence the problems we have and our access to resources necessary to manage those problems. In the example of the janitor on the bus, Don understood her problems as social in nature: The expectations to be a good mother, the resources available to cope with stress, and the opportunity for stress relief are found in the prevailing social conditions surrounding her. She may have lacked the resources to cope with her difficult life circumstances.

Stressors and Outcomes

Stressors can come in at least two forms: negative life events and chronic strain. **Negative life events** include any events deemed unwanted or stressful to an individual. Exposure to negative life events leads to distress (Aneshensel 1992; Lantz, House, Mero, and Williams 2005; Pearlin et al. 1981). Negative life events can include things such as the death of a loved one or marital separation (Gotlib and Wheaton 1997). **Chronic strain** include regular strains within our social roles that may cause mental health problems over time by the accumulation of small amounts of stress rather than a single event. Chronic stressors or daily hassles may have even more influence on individuals compared with events that only occur infrequently. Another way that a stressor can affect people is through the creation of other conditions ("secondary stressors" because they occur after the initial ones) that may exacerbate the initial stressor. For instance, job loss, stressful in itself, may also affect marriage negatively, further exacerbating other anxieties.

What kind of stressors do you think college students experience the most? The answer to that question will help explain the types and levels of mental health outcomes that college students experience in school. Most of the stressors that college students are exposed to are an accumulation of unique strains (e.g., adjustment problems, roommate situations, and problems with an overwhelming number of school demands) (Jackson and Finney 2002). Some students do experience the death of a loved one or loss of a job, but these experiences are less likely to occur than in other groups simply because of students' age and length of time in school (4 to 5 years). The stresses they do experience may be manifested in excessive drinking or clinical depression, both considered mental health problems.

Stressors can lead to many kinds of difficulties. A common mental health problem is depression. Most measures of depression and other mental health measures rely on the patient's ability to indicate her emotional state. For instance, the Center for Epidemiological Study measures depression by asking how often the patient has experienced feelings, such as "I did not feel like eating" or "I felt depressed" in the last week. The important aspect of this measure is that it includes a series of thoughts and behaviors associated with feeling depressed. A simpler one-item assessment would not be very robust because it only includes one dimension of the problem. For instance, the patient may not know how to define "depressed" and rely on whatever she happens to know about it. Another patient may have a more technical definition of the word *depression*, leading to a more accurate answer to the question.

Table 8.1 CES-Depression Scale

Instructions: Using the scale below, please circle the number before each statement that best describes how often you felt or behaved this way DURING THE PAST WEEK:

During the past week:	Rarely or none of the time (less than 1 day)	Some or a little of the time (1–2 days)	Occasionally or a moderate amount of time (3–4 days)	Most or all of the time (5–7 days)
1. I was bothered by things that usually don't bother me.	0	1	2	3
2. I did not feel like eating; my appetite was poor.	0	1	2	3
3. I felt that I could not shake off the blues, even with help from my family or friends.	0	1	2	3
4. I felt that I was just as good as other people.	0	1	2	3
5. I had trouble keeping my mind on what I was doing.	0	1	2	3
6. I felt depressed.	0	1	2	3
7. I felt that everything I did was an effort.	0	1	2	3
8. I felt hopeful about the future.	0	1	2	3
9. I thought my life had been a failure.	0	1	2	3
10. I felt fearful.	0	1	2	3
11. My sleep was restless.	0	1	2	3
12. I was happy.	0	1	2	3
13. I talked less than usual.	0	1	2	3
14. I felt lonely.	0	1	2	3
15. People were unfriendly.	0	1	2	3

(continued on next page)

| Table 8.1 | CES-Depression Scale (continued) |

	Rarely or none of the time (less than 1 day)	Some or a little of the time (1–2 days)	Occasionally or a moderate amount of time (3–4 days)	Most or all of the time (5–7 days)
16. I enjoyed life.	0	1	2	3
17. I had crying spells.	0	1	2	3
18. I felt sad.	0	1	2	3
19. I felt that people disliked me.	0	1	2	3
20. I could not get going.	0	1	2	3

Scoring: Items are summed after reverse scoring item 4, 8, 12, and 16. Total CES-D scores range from 0–60, with higher scores reflecting higher levels of depression.

Source: Adapted from Radloff (1977). Copyright 1977 West Publishing Company/Applied Psychological Measurement Inc. Reproduced by permission.

Mediating and Moderating Conditions

Although many studies have found a direct relationship between stressors and mental health outcomes, the relationship is usually small (Cockerham 2003; Turner and Roszell 1994). As a result, researchers have tried to determine how and why people differentially respond to the same stressors. According to the stress process model, people have different capacities or resources with which to manage stressful events; thus, variations in resources should explain differences in how people react to stressors (Aneshensel 1992; Pearlin 1989; Pearlin et al. 1981). It is in this sense that people are thought to process stressful events, using various resources to cope with them.

Personal and Social Resources

Resources employed to manage stressors can take two forms. **Personal resources** include elements of our self-concept that may be beneficial in managing events. People who feel that they have greater control over what happens to them (mastery) tend to deal with life's problems better than those who feel little sense of control (Turner and Roszell 1994). It may be that those with high levels of mastery feel they are able to manage problems but it may also be that they are able to avoid problems or stressors more easily. Similarly, people with more positive self-images (self-esteem) seem to be able to cope with stressful events better than those with low self-esteem. Perhaps those with higher senses of self-esteem do not see negative events in terms of their self-worth; thus, they are less concerned about the long-term consequences of events to the self (Pearlin and Schooler 1978; Turner and Roszell 1994).

People also turn to their friends and family for help during difficult times. Access to people to whom you can turn in a time of need is called **social support or social resources.** Social supports can take a variety of forms. It may simply take the form of a companion to share your troubles, giving you an opportunity to vent your frustrations to someone else. Access to and use of other people or groups and organizations in dealing with difficult situations has been found to reduce the distress associated with stressful events (Cockerham 2003; Pearlin 1989). In some cases perceived support—perceptions of received support irrespective of actual support—has been found to have the same (or stronger) effects as actual support (Sarason, Pierce, and Sarason 1994). These findings make sense given the nature of many stressful events. If someone becomes distressed from losing a job, then feeling that someone else is available to provide food, clothing, and comfort may relieve some of the concerns associated with job loss and act as both mediators and motivators.

Personal and social resources fit under the general category of **moderators** in the stress process; they affect the direction or strength of the relationship between a stressor and mental health (Baron and Kenny 1986; Pearlin et al. 1981). Imagine a situation in which two people lose their jobs. One person is very confident that she can find another job, whereas the other person has no such feelings of security. Under these conditions, the first person is likely to react to the job loss differently than the second person. Both may develop a sense of anxiety over the news, but the strength of the stressor, job loss, is going to be significantly stronger for the second person. In this case, the individual's sense of mastery moderates the relationship between job loss and mental health.

Social or personal resources can also act as **mediators.** A mediator is a variable that can explain the relationship between the stressor and outcome (Baron and Kenny 1986). That is, a mediator connects the stressor to the outcome. First, the stressor causes a change in the mediating variable, then the mediator affects the outcome variable. For instance, losing a job can be linked to mental health *through* loss of mastery: The loss of a job erodes a sense of control which creates distress. Thus, job loss affects on mental health through loss of mastery.

Gender and Social Support

Social resources can influence individuals by providing more access to instrumental and emotional support in times of need (Pearlin 1989). However, social support is not distributed evenly across the population (Turner and Marino 1994). Research shows that men have larger, less close networks of relationships than women, whereas women have closer relationships with fewer people. These differences may reflect structural differences in men's and women's lives with men's networks associated with employment and women's networks associated with kin

(Moore 1990; Pugliesi and Shook 1998). Under this schema, men have the advantage of having more weak ties to find work (see chapter 4), but women have the advantage of strong social supports to help cope with stressful life circumstances (Umberson, Chen, House, Hopkins, and Slaten 1996). Other research suggests that support differences reflect socialization patterns such that boys and girls are taught to seek different levels and types of support from other people. In one study, researchers found that levels of feminity and masculinity were associated with seeking and receiving emotional support. Specifically, being more feminine—among both males and females—was associated with seeking and receiving emotional support, whereas masculinity was associated with seeking more tangible support (Reevy and Maslach 2001).

The stress process helps social scientists understand differential outcomes of negative life events and chronic strains. People have different personal and social resources with which to manage stressors. We have reviewed some of the ways in which social position influences the availability of resources that help people cope with life events. But our structural position also determines the number and type of stressful conditions that influence our mental health. The following section examines the social distribution of mental health, or how status influences the distribution of mental health problems.

Socioeconomic Characteristics: The Epidemiology of Mental Health

The last component of the stress-process model involves individuals' socioeconomic characteristics. The **epidemiology of mental health** emphasizes the distribution of mental health conditions in society. Different socioeconomic characteristics are associated with different levels of mental health problems. Research in this area is important because it highlights the effects of societal positions on health and well-being. For example, women report higher levels of depression and anxiety than men do, whereas men generally have more substance abuse problems than women (Aneshensel, Rutter, and Lachenbruch 1991; Mirowsky and Ross 1995; Turner, Wheaton, and Lloyd 1995). Other important characteristics associated with different mental health outcomes are marital status and social class, with married people reporting lower levels of distress than singles (Turner et al. 1995) and people of lower socioeconomic status (SES) reporting higher levels of distress than those of higher SES, largely because they experience more negative life events (Aneshensel 1992; Aneshensel and Sucoff 1996).

Class, Race, and Mental Health

The prevalence of mental health disorders is inversely related to economic status: As income goes up, the prevalence of disorders goes down. This finding is generally true of most types of disorders, including affective disorders such as depression, as well as schizophrenia and personality disorders. In a famous study, Robert Faris and H. Warren Dunham (Faris and Dunham 1960, originally 1939) used Chicago city maps to trace the addresses of over 30,000 people who had received psychiatric treatment from mental hospitals. They found that a significant number of schizophrenic patients lived in poorer areas of the city. This was one of the first studies to show a relationship between class position and well-being.

Modern studies generally support Faris and Dunham's (1960) findings. Measuring class in terms of education, for instance, Robins, Locke, and Regier (1991) found that high-school graduates were significantly less likely to be diagnosed with a disorder than people without a high-school degree (30% to 36%). Similarly, almost half (47%) of people on welfare or receiving disability payments had a disorder at some point, and a third (31%) had active symptoms. Men working in unskilled jobs also had more disorders than those in better jobs.

The relationship between class and disorder becomes salient when comparing the prevalence of disorder among racial categories because income is unevenly distributed across these groups. Some research shows that African Americans are more prone to mental illness than European Americans and Latino Americans (Robins et al. 1991). These differences may be due to stresses associated with racism in society. However, it may also be due to the higher concentration of Blacks in poverty; that is, race differences reflect class differences (Cockerham 1990). Hence, racial differences in mental health may simply reflect the relatively lower socioeconomic position of African Americans in U.S. society. However, a number of studies continue to show that some minorities, particularly African Americans, are more vulnerable than Whites, controlling for income and other factors (George and Lynch 2003; Kessler and Neighbors 1986; Ulbrich, Warheit, and Zimmerman 1989). One study, though, using a sample of Canadians, found that some minorities, including Black Canadians, reported *better* mental health than English (White) Canadians (Wu, Noh, Kaspar, and Schimmele 2003). In another study, using a sample of Americans, researchers found lower-SES white males reported *higher* rates of psychiatric disorders than their black counterparts (Williams, Takeuchi, and Adair 1992). Thus, although race is related to mental health outcomes, this relationship becomes more complex with the introduction of economic and cultural factors.

Racial stereotypes may also contribute to the disproportionate diagnoses of certain mental illnesses among African-American patients. Loring and Powell (1988) conducted a study in which 290 psychiatrists were given two case studies to diagnose, manipulating the race (African American or Caucasian) and gender of the patient. The researchers found similar diagnoses among psychiatrists when the sex and race of the patient was absent from the records and when the race and sex of the psychiatrist and patient coincided with one another. Caucasian and African-American psychiatrists, however, were more likely to diagnose African-American male subjects with aggressive disorders compared with other groups (given the same description), under-scoring the pervasiveness of cultural stereotypes. More recent research shows that African Americans are less likely to be diagnosed with bipolar disorder and more likely to be diagnosed with schizophrenia than Caucasians (Neighbors, Trierweiler, Ford, and Muroff 2003). However, the research found no racial differences in diagnoses of depression, the most common disorder.

Gender, Family, and Well-Being

Marital status is another characteristic associated with mental health and well-being. Married people are generally happier, healthier, and financially better off than single, divorced, and widowed people (Diener, Gohm, Suh, and Oishi 2000; Kim and McKenry 2003; Simon 2002; Waite and Gallagher 2000). Married people on average report higher levels of life satisfaction, lower levels of distress, and better physical health than their single counterparts. Married people report better sex lives too.

The positive effects of marriage on health and well-being may reflect access to social support or the committed nature of marital relationships. For instance, cohabiting is associated with higher levels of well-being than being single—reflecting access to regular social support. However, being married continues to have a stronger effect on well-being than being single or cohabiting, and the positive effects of marriage continue after controlling for relationship quality (Dush and Amato 2005; Kim and McKenry 2003).

There are also gender differences in mental health. Studies consistently show that women report higher levels of depression and other emotional disorders than

Men and women tend to manifest mental-health problems in different ways with men reporting more issues of substance abuse than women.

men. However, men are more likely to exhibit behavioral disorders such as alcoholism, drug addiction, and aggression. Hence, overall levels of mental health are probably comparable between men and women, but the disorders are manifested in different ways (Aneshensel, Rutter, and Lachenbruch 1991; Mirowsky and Ross 1995; Turner, Wheaton, and Lloyd 1995).

It is difficult to determine exactly why we would find mental health differences between men and women. Perhaps women are taught to release their stress emotionally, whereas men are taught to resist crying and encouraged to act on their emotions. Women may also be more open to sharing about their emotional problems with researchers or professionals than are men. Hence, women may be more likely to admit and seek treatment for affective disorders than men. Loring and Powell's (1988) research mentioned earlier found that male clinicians tend to overestimate the prevalence of depression in women. However, Mirowsky and Ross (1995) found that although women are more expressive than men, this difference did not explain the differences in distress levels between men and women. Women reported higher levels of most emotions, including sadness, anxiety, and anger, an emotion traditionally associated with men. Mirowsky and Ross (1995) argued that women's less-powerful positions in society simply produce more stressors, leading to more distress.

Community and Neighborhood Contexts

A significant amount of research over the last decade has tried to link larger, social-structural conditions of a community to personal outcomes. Some of this work emphasizes cultural differences between regions. Much of it also emphasizes how consistent patterns of macro-social life affect individuals. Several studies examine the effects of neighborhood conditions on their residents, much like Elijah Anderson's (1999) research of Philadelphia's inner-city life discussed in Chapter 4. Communities and neighborhoods represent a set of environmental and social conditions that affect most or all their residents (McLeod and Lively 2003).

Rural and urban communities represent different worlds and expectations for individuals. Rural areas may have less stimulation and a slower pace of life than urban environments. Conversely, urban areas may have more activities but more stressful living conditions.

You might expect that urban areas expose people to more stress and strain than rural ones, leading to speculation that people will be better off in rural areas than in urban ones. People in urban environments are exposed to a lot of stimulating activity, but must also face overcrowding and a stressful pace of life. Research addressing the link between urban or rural life to mental health has not been consistent. Counter to what we might expect, there is some evidence that there is a **malaise** or psychological state of unhappiness associated with living conditions in particularly rural or urban areas (Fischer 1973). Moreover, this finding may be worldwide, that rural areas in most parts of the world produce this kind of malaise. The rural malaise may reflect the lack of stimulation associated with a routine lifestyle found in many rural places, whereas urban malaise tends to be restricted to central areas of larger cities generally associated with poor living conditions.

How do poor economic conditions produce poor mental health? Aneshensel and Sucoff (1996) found that people in poorer neighborhoods report higher levels of distress, probably because there are more "ambient hazards" in their living area. **Ambient hazards** can include exposure to crime, poor living conditions, and lack of services. Thus, poor economic conditions associated with urban life may affect mental health by producing different numbers and kinds of stressful conditions.

The place in which we live can also influence our well-being through the availability of work. Losing a job and living in areas with high unemployment is associated with higher distress than being unemployed and living in a more economically vibrant area (Dooley et. al 1988; Dooley et al. 1994).

Community contexts may also influence access to the social resources necessary to manage stressful life events. People in rural areas tend to live farther apart from one another than in urban areas, possibly making face-to-face contact with friends and family more difficult. Hence, access to social networks may be more limited. In one study, Amato (1993) found that urbanites both find and give more help to friends than people living in more rural areas. Urbanites also report expecting more help from friends than people in more rural areas. Amato argued that urban dwellers tend to live farther from their families than rural people; hence, they are more likely to turn to friends for help.

Section Summary

In this section, we applied the social structure and personality perspective to answer the question: What are the structural conditions in society that contribute to distress? Here, we apply the stress process model to study how social conditions such as negative life events or chronic strains affect us, ultimately leading to mental health outcomes like depression and anxiety. We also examined how social and personal resources protect us from the effects of negative events; for instance, higher sense of mastery and access to social support helps to reduce the effects of negative life events. Finally, we examined how exposure to events and access to resources vary by socioeconomic status.

GP | Mental Health as a Status Characteristic

> *I was diagnosed with ADD [Attention Deficit Disorder] when I was twelve. I remember it pretty clearly because it had a big impact on my relationships with my friends. Some of my friends' parents did not like them hanging out with me. I think that they thought that ADD was contagious or something. Anyway, I just noticed the parents would talk to me differently than before. It made them nervous somehow. . . .*
>
> —John, freshman Biology major

One of the ways that mental disorders differ from physical disorders is that they are more often difficult to notice in a public venue. Erving Goffman's (1963) work on stigma addresses this issue by indicating that people are sometimes better able to pass or cover as "normal" with mental disorders than physical ones such as being immobilized in a wheelchair. However, when a mental disorder is known to other people, it serves as a status characteristic affecting interactions in ways similar to other aspects of our self.

John's story tells about being diagnosed and treated for attention deficit disorder (ADD). He noticed that people around him started treating him differently as a result of his diagnosis. He lost some friends because parents were not comfortable with his condition. He was deemed different even though there were no physical indications of his stigma. People were not sure how to relate to him anymore, perhaps making them nervous or uncomfortable.

According to the group processes perspective, people set up different expectations of individuals' performance depending on their status characteristics. This idea is the basis of expectation-states theory (see chapter 4). Diffuse status characteristics influence other people's expectations of how well we can perform in almost any social situation.

Wagner (1993), a scholar in the group processes perspective, addressed whether mental illness likely acts as a diffuse status characteristic. He argued that three properties are required for a mental condition to be considered a diffuse status characteristic. First, the illness must be considered something that is unwanted or less desirable than other states. Like other characteristics, it has to be something that can be ranked as better or worse than something else. The fact that mental illness is labeled an "illness" suggests that it is a condition that people are trying to relieve or separate from themselves. Experts are paid to help in these efforts, further classifying individuals as sick or well, in better or worse conditions.

Second, mental illness must also be associated with other characteristics that are tied to the illness. Mentally ill people, for example, may be considered less stable, more aggressive, or unpredictable than "normal" people. Hence, the mentally ill label is negative in and of itself and is also associated with other negative attributes. Finally, there must be general expectations associated with a person's ability to perform in a group. There must be an expectation that the mentally ill are less capable than "normal" people.

These expectations can affect group transactions in similar ways as other status characteristics. Individuals who are mentally ill may be less likely to contribute to a group task because they believe that they are less capable than other group members. Other group members may devalue the contributions made by the mentally ill individual because of her status in the group and the negative assumptions associated with mental illness (Wagner 1993). The result of this process is that stigmatized individuals will likely have less influence on their social worlds than those who are not stigmatized, partly because of the limitations placed on them by the other group members and partly from their own belief in their limitations. Having less status in social situations may then perpetuate the original status-organizing processes that led to negative expectations associated with the stereotype. Although Wagner's work details how mental illness likely acts as a status characteristic, little research in the group processes tradition has examined the status consequences of mental illness. Given the limited research from this perspective, we apply related research from the symbolic interaction perspective to this section of the chapter.

Mental Health and Selfhood

One of the more famous sociologists to study deviance and mental health was Erving Goffman. Goffman became famous for his study of the presentation of the self (see chapter 5). Much of his work focuses on how individuals maintain a healthy image of themselves over time and in interactions with other people. If roles give us direction for our thoughts, feelings, and behavior, then disobeying such guidelines may be defined as defiance, at best, or irrationality at worst. Hence, Goffman's conception of deviance incorporates everything from criminal behavior (see chapter 7) to physical deformities and mental health problems.

Box 8.2   **Parson's Sick Role**

Talcott Parsons (1951) applied elements of role theory (chapter 2) to explain the importance of role expectations in "being sick." He argued that sick people have expectations for behavior, above and beyond the physical ramifications of the ailment itself. Specifically, he said that sick people have certain rights and responsibilities. Their rights include being exempt from normal social life (e.g., missing work) and the right to be taken care of by other people. However, sick people are responsible to try and get well, seeking out professional help to treat their malady. Ignoring these expectations may lead to rebukes from friends and family, like any other role violation. Parson's analysis of the sick role was one of the first attempts to apply sociological perspectives to health and illness. Can you see how this work applies to people with mental illnesses?

Stigma and Mental Illness

In the last chapter we defined stigma as an attribute that is deeply discrediting. Stigma may include attributes associated with mental illness (Goffman 1963). Much like other forms of stigma, people labeled with mental illness can react by using techniques such as passing and covering (see chapter 7), making oneself appear "normal" to other people (passing) or trying to conceal an illness (covering). (See Box 8.2). Using this schema, emotional disorders may be most easily concealed, whereas others, such as drug addictions, may have physical manifestations that make it difficult to hide the illness.

Passing and covering are ways in which individuals manage their self-concepts in public venues. However, people with stigmas must cope with attributes deemed unacceptable and thus must find alternative ways of managing these differences. Some of those differences are more difficult to pass and cover than others. From this perspective, many mental illnessess can be covered quite well because they have no physical manifestations. However, it also makes it difficult to determine how "well" an individual is. Patients with broken legs can say that they are healed when they are able to use their legs without pain. A depressed patient may not be able to make the same determination about their condition without some guidance from a mental health professional.

The Career of the Mental Patient

Asylums and prisons serve as the last resort for people who will not or cannot conform to the standards of conduct in society. Goffman (1961) described the ways in which individuals adapt to their captivity in his book, *Asylums: Essays on the Social Situation of Mental Patients*. He described mental institutions as **total institutions,** places where individuals are required to isolate themselves from the rest of society. Other total institutions can include monasteries, prisons, and boarding schools. The goal of the asylum, according to Goffman, is to force the patient to adjust her sense of self to the rules and regulations of the institution. He noted that inmates of asylums are subjected to a series of humiliations and debasements to induce this change.

The change that is supposed to occur in asylums is associated with the presentation of self in society. When individuals are not capable of maintaining appropriate behaviors, their behavior must be adjusted to meet societal standards. But Goffman's (1961) research also shows that individuals resist changes to the self when they become institutionalized. During their confinement, patients find small ways to rebel against the system. A patient may try to steal some extra food or sneak something from the outside world into the asylum. Patients also try to develop senses of individuality by designating different spaces as "out-of-bounds" to others, thereby giving them a small sense of control over their lives.

Goffman (1961) also described the different ways that patients manage to cope with their confinement. Some patients, for instance, adapt to the institution by **conversion,** living up to the expectations of the staff and doctors. Alternatively, patients may try **intransigence,** rebelling against the staff expectations. In between these two extremes are forms of **withdrawal,** curtailing interaction with others at the asylum, or **colonization,** when patients use experiences of life from the outside world to show that the asylum is a desirable place to live. Goffman's work on asylums shows that individuals do not conform to any single set of behaviors or attitudes toward the system. Some patients try to accept their transformations of the self to being "normal," whereas others fight to maintain independent senses of self.

These coping techniques are illustrated in the film, *One Flew over the Cuckoo's Nest* (1975). Actor Jack Nicholson plays a prisoner sent to an insane asylum, where he starts a small, subtle rebellion among the patients against the staff. In doing so, he gives patients a sense of hope and meaning. We see a series of characters using different techniques to manage their asylum, ranging from Nicholson's intransigence to conversion from other patients. The audience is challenged to assess whether the main character is truly insane or if powerful agents of the state merely deem people mentally ill as a way to keep them under control.

Thus having the status of mental illness significantly affects an individual's life in community settings and in institutions. The most amazing thing that group process and symbolic-interactionist researchers show us is how a label can completely change how others view us. Even if two people are behaving identically, the one with a stigmatized status will likely be treated more negatively and with different responses than the one without such a label. Being aware of this can help us to question our assumptions when we have opportunities to deal with labeled people.

Section Summary

The last section of this chapter addressed the question: How does our mental health influence our sense of identity and our interactions with other people? Traditional research in group processes does not address mental health per se, but groups play a major role in the definition and reactions to people with mental health problems. First, mental health conditions may be status characteristics that individuals in groups use as a basis of further interaction. Second, the stigma associated with some mental illnesses affects interactions in the larger society, especially when managing deviant identities in total institutions, when patients are confined to asylums for treatment.

Bringing It All Together

> When my son with diagnosed with depression, I really did not take it seriously. I mean, I did not buy it—I really think too many diagnosis are made falsely, and people are over medicated. But he just never got his homework done, he seemed so listless. I decided to give the drugs a chance. I remember one day, after being on the antidepressant for a couple of weeks, he told me that he could literally "feel" the drug wearing off on the way home from school one day. I don't know, maybe there is something going on there.
>
> —Beth, nontraditional student

This chapter addresses the social conditions that affect our mental health and well-being. Symbolic interactionists tend to focus on how we construct mental illness, whereas researchers using the social structure and personality perspective study the impact of social conditions on our well-being. Group processes emphasizes mental illness as a status characteristic that may influence group dynamics.

Although we focus on the social conditions that influence mental health and well-being, our chapter does not discount that there may be some biological roots to mental disorders. The nontraditional student, Beth, is skeptical of mental health diagnoses and treatment at first, but starts to rethink her position when her son starts taking an antidepressant drug. The two general perspectives—the social and biological causes of mental illness—are not exclusive. Most importantly, social stressors like role strains and overloads can interact with individual factors like predisposition toward certain disorders. Moreover, the experience of taking a drug itself may be influenced by social conditions. Ultimately, biological factors may be important, but social factors create patterns of mental health outcomes that are fascinating—and critical to examine.

Summary

1. The history of madness and civilization shows that the meaning and treatment of mental illness has changed dramatically over the centuries. In Europe, mental illness was considered similar to other forms of deviance such as criminality into the 17th century.

2. Sociologists view many manifestations of mental illness to be the result of social conditions that tax individuals' capacity to manage her life. The stress process is a model to help understand the relationship of negative life events and chronic strains to our mental health and well-being, focusing also on the resources we use to manage those stressors.

3. Social and economic characteristics are associated with different levels of mental health outcomes, with men and women reporting different types of mental health disorders. Other important social characteristics that are implicated in well-being include marital status, age, and social class.

4. According to the group processes perspective, people set up different expectations of individuals' performance depending on their status characteristics. Mental illness may be considered a negative status characteristic that influences members' expectations of the mentally ill in a group setting as well as the contributions made by those members.

5. Mental illness may be a form of stigma for individuals, an attribute that is deeply discrediting. Patients housed in total institutions like insane asylums try to cope with their concealment in many different ways, including conversion, intransigence, and forms of withdrawal and colonization.

Key Terms and Concepts

Ambient hazards: Exposure to poor community conditions such as crime, poor living conditions, and lack of services.

Chronic strain: Day-to-day role strains that may cause mental health problems over time by the accumulation of small amounts of stress.

Colonization: A way in which patients manage institutionalization by showing that their institution is a desirable place to live.

Conversion: A way in which patients manage institutionalization by living up to the expectations of the staff and doctors.

Epidemiology of mental health: The study of the distribution of mental health conditions in society.

Intransigence: A way in which patients manage institutionalization by rebelling against the staff expectations.

Malaise: A psychological state of unhappiness associated with living conditions in particularly rural or urban areas.

Mediators: Part of the stress process referring to variables that intervene between a stressor and an outcome.

Medicalization of deviance: Ways in which social problems—including mental health—have come under medical boundaries.

Moderators: Part of the stress process that includes the personal and social resources that affect the direction or strength of the relationship between a stressor and mental health.

Negative life events: Part of the stress process referring to any event deemed unwanted or stressful to an individual.

Personal resources: Part of the stress process referring to elements of our self-concept that may be beneficial in managing events.

Social support or social resources: Access to friends and family available to help during stressful or difficult times.

Sociology of mental health: The study of the social arrangements that affect mental illness and its consequences.

Stress process: A model that outlines the relationships among social statuses, stressful experiences, the resources people bring to deal with problems, and the outcomes they experience.

Total institutions: Places where individuals are isolated from the rest of society.

Withdrawal: A way of managing life in an asylum involving the curtailing of interaction with others.

Discussion Questions

1. Have you ever been diagnosed with a cognitive, emotional, or behavioral problem? If so, how did other people reaction to your condition? Do you know someone who has been diagnosed with a mental health condition? How did your relationship change, if at all, with this person?

2. If certain mental health conditions are affected by our position in society, how might we change social policies to help those most in need?

3. There is great debate about the institutionalization of people with severe mental illnesses. Do you think people with such problems should be institutionalized? Why or why not?

Attitudes, Values, and Behaviors

Chapter 9

My dad was always very clear when we were little. All people of all races and religions are to be treated with respect and are considered equal. I really thought that was an important part of the way he was raising us. Then my little sister started dating someone of a different race. He did not exactly freak out, nor did he forbid the relationship, but you just knew that all of his negative comments were because this kid was Black. He couldn't stand it and seemed very stressed out for seven months until they broke up.

—Melinda, senior Physical Education major

An **attitude** is a positive or negative evaluation of an object, a person or group, or an idea. Although political scientists, psychologists, and sociologists study attitudes, they approach the field in different ways. Political scientists study attitudes in the form of political polls measuring people's evaluations of government policies or politicians. Psychologists tend to focus on the nature and formation of attitudes. Sociologists examine how our position in society affects attitude formation, emphasizing the role of our race, class, and gender in how we develop and maintain our attitudes about the world around us (Schuman 1995).

The social psychological study of attitudes seeks to explain how social forces affect individuals' attitudes and how these attitudes in turn relate to behavior. One of the interesting things you will learn in this chapter is that our attitudes or conscious thoughts about the world are not necessarily linked with parallel behaviors. Melinda's experience with her father shows just that. Connections that seem quite clear, that positive attitudes toward something will lead to positive behaviors toward that object, simply don't reflect what happens in the real world. Although attitudes are sometimes correlated with behaviors, the relationship is complex. First, the relationship between our attitudes and behavior are often quite weak—our attitude toward an object does not necessarily lead to behaviors toward that object. Second, general attitudes do not necessarily lead to specific behaviors—you may have a positive attitude about exercise but find that you never set aside time to work out. Finally, people can change certain attitudes somewhat readily, thus making the relationship between attitudes and behavior difficult to study.

The goal of this chapter is to examine sociological research on attitudes and behaviors. We focused on our self-attitude, or our sense of self, which is symbolic interactionists' main focus, in chapter 5. In this chapter, after discussing how attitudes are conceptualized, we will emphasize three areas of study within sociological social psychology. First, we will examine the nature of attitudes and behavior in the context of theory and research associated with the social construction of attitudes from an interactionist perspective. Second, we will examine how attitudes vary by social location. Finally, we will apply the group processes perspective on attitudes, specifically related to attitudes toward other people in groups. Specifically, this chapter will address the following questions:

- What is the nature of an attitude? How do researchers study attitudes and behaviors?
- How do people construct attitudes?
- How do attitudes vary across social groups? Do attitudes change over time?
- How do attitudes toward other people form in group contexts?

SI The Construction of Attitudes

I never really thought much about drugs or marijuana until I joined the fraternity. I had seen all of the advertisements about how bad drugs are but then my friends kept telling me it was OK. Of course, they were all doing it. I gave it a shot. It wasn't so bad. I guess I would be for legalizing it. . . .

—Darnell, junior Economics major

The interactionist perspective views attitudes like any other aspect of social life: They are continually being constructed based on our interactions with other people. Contemporary research suggests that direct experience with specific people or objects may have as strong or stronger effect on our attitude development than our preexisting values and beliefs, supporting elements of the interactionist and group processes perspectives reviewed earlier in this book (Maio, Olson, Bernard, and Luke 2003). These findings probably reflect the fact that values and beliefs are largely derived from indirect experience, whereas direct exposure to a person or an object provides tangible information from which to form attitudes about an object.

Darnell's experience with marijuana reflects these research findings: Despite all the advertising against the use of drugs, he tries it and decides that it is not so bad after all. Of course, his friends have a lot to do with his attitude change, providing additional arguments in support of the drug. The positive experience he derives from using the drug probably influences his opinion on the matter too. The goal of this section is to review the basic components of attitudes, the major interactionist perspectives on attitude construction and the relationship between attitudes and behavior.

Dimensions of Attitudes

We have defined attitudes as positive or negative evaluations of an object, person, or group. Attitudes can be malleable in nature, changing quite readily. However, people have more enduring thoughts and feelings about objects as well. We also ponder what other people think about the topics that concern us. The role of larger norms and values come into play in complex ways. **Values** and **beliefs** refer to strongly held, relatively stable sets of attitudes. Values may be produced through socialization in families and school, as well as in society at large. However they are formed, values are considered in the context of how attitudes are formed and shaped over time.

Attitudes are composed of several dimensions. First, there are "thinking" *and* "feeling" components of our attitudes toward any object. The cognitive or "thinking" aspect of an attitude is formally called an **opinion.** This distinction is important because people can think about a person or object in one way but then *feel* very different about that same object. You may cognitively think that homosexuality is okay but still feel uneasy among a group of gay men. Hence, if you simply ask for an opinion, you may not get a true sense of that person because you will only capture one aspect of it. Most public attitude opinion polls focus on our cognitions about a particular topic.

In addition to dividing attitudes into thinking and feeling components, attitudes can be measured in terms of direction and strength:

- Direction—separating negative or positive attitudes about an object.
- Strength—the level of positive or negative response to that object.

In short, attitudes are positive or negative evaluations of an object. In addition, you can have a strong or weak opinion on the object. You may have a negative evaluation of an object but not care much about it. These dimensions determine how you may act toward the attitude object. For instance, you may have a positive evaluation of a political candidate but not care enough to actually go out and vote for that person in an election.

Modern perspectives on attitudes incorporate the idea that there are situations in which attitudes do not exist or in which someone has mixed feelings about an object. That is, it is possible to have a **nonattitude** toward an object, when you do not care either way about something. For instance, you may have no opinion about a political candidate simply because you do not have enough information to form a view. Alternatively, you may have both negative and positive attitudes toward the person; you may dislike the way that she dresses but appreciate her beliefs on a topic. Such complexities make it difficult to use public opinion as a representative of people's "real" beliefs on a topic. However, some research suggests that people will give you an attitude or opinion of a person or issue, even when they have limited or no information about the topic (Converse and Presser 1986; Fletcher and Chalmers 1991; Schuman and Presser 1980).

Studying Behavior: How People Use their Time

The study of human behavior through time diaries has become a popular research approach in recent decades. In a way, this kind of research complements attitudinal studies. We know that attitudes do not necessarily correlate highly with behavior. **Time-use** researchers try to determine exactly what people do on a day-to-day basis as a way to really *know* what people value, regardless of what they say.

Time-use researchers examine productive and free time, as well as personal care time. **Productive time** refers to paid work, housework and child care, and traveling associated with productive work (i.e., commuting to work). **Free time** refers to leisure activities such as reading, watching television, listening to the radio and other activities that we do for our own pleasure. Researchers have tried to assess individuals' use of time by either asking them how much time they spend in various activities each week using a survey, or by using a time diary. The diary method has people write down what they are doing and how much time they spend doing each activity, beginning at midnight and continuing over a 24-hour period.

John Robinson and Geoffrey Godbey's (1997) study of time illuminates how most Americans use their time and compares these findings over time and with other countries in the world. Their research shows that the average American spends over 120 hours a week on productive activities, including work, family care, and personal care . The rest of their time is "free time," time spent on activities such as watching television or socializing, two of the most popular uses of free time. Table 9.1 uses similar data collected by the Bureau of Labor Statistics American Time Use Survey to give specific breakdowns of the "average" American in 2003.

Surveys continue to show that people believe they have less time than they actually do. Robinson and Godbey's (1997) work shows a gap between the free time people believe they have and the actual free time available to them. There seems to be a growing number of people who feel rushed despite the fact that we have more free time, on average, and work less than in the past. This sense of having less time has led people toward **time deepening** behavior, in which people may do more with the time that they have available to them. Time deepening can occur in four ways:

- Attempting to speed up an activity.
- Substituting a shorter activity for a longer one (e.g., playing 9 holes of golf instead of 18).

Table 9.1	The Average Week of an American	
		Total Hours per Week
Productive Time		
	Work hours*	25.6
	Family care	23.0
	Personal care	76.5
	Subtotal	125.2
Free Time		
	Television	18.2
	Home communication	8.7
	Entertainment	5.3
	Education	4.4
	Recreation	3.8
	Organizations	2.4
	Subtotal	42.8
	Total	**168**

* Work hours include both working and nonworking people in the U.S., 25 to 64 years old.

Source: American Time Use Survey, 2003-2004.

- Doing more than one activity at once (multitasking).
- Maintaining a schedule for activities.

Each of these techniques allows people to do more things in the same time period. The result of time deepening may be positive, allowing people to do more things, but it also may give people a sense of frustration and stress. People may feel that they have less time than they actually do.

Linking Attitudes and Behavior

One of the reasons people study attitudes is to predict their behaviors. However, the relationship between attitudes and behavior is not always clear. That is, how is knowing something about someone's attitude useful in predicting her behavior? (See Box 9.1.) One of the earliest uses of polling was to predict election results,

| Box 9.1 | Ajzen's Theory of Planned Behavior |

The most prominent theory linking attitudes and behavior comes from two psychologists, Icek Ajzen and Martin Fishbein. Ajzen and Fishbein tried to understand how our attitudes interact with our larger sets of beliefs and social norms in our decision-making processes. They argued that one of the reasons we do not find large correlations between attitudes and behavior is that we must incorporate social norms into our predictive models. In addition, our attitudes only predict our intention to act toward an object rather than the actual behavior. For instance, you may dislike someone (attitude) and plan to cause them harm (intention), but that does not necessarily mean that you will actually harm them (behavior).

The following model is one of the most recent versions of the model. It includes individuals' attitudes toward a behavior but also includes the idea that people consider the likelihood of their actions having the intended effect (perceived behavioral control) before acting. Using the previous example, the intention to hurt someone may be curbed if you believe that you are not capable of producing harm to the other person.

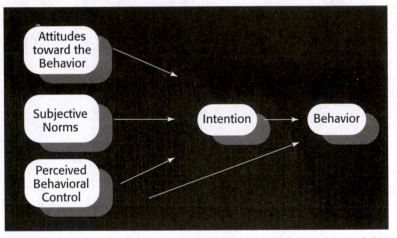

Source: Based on Icek Ajzen's Web site accessed at http://www.people.umass.edu/~aizen/. See also Ajzen, I. (1991).

The Theory of Planned Behavior (also known as the Theory of Reasoned Action) also incorporates our beliefs about what other people would think about the behavior under the heading "subjective norms." If we believe that other people will support the behavior, we are much more likely to act on an attitude than we would if they do not support it. Hence, this model recognizes the importance of social relationships in deciding whether to act on an attitude, helping to explain why some attitudes lead people to act in some cases and not others.

Box 9.2   The Weighted Average Model in Psychology

The weighted average model assumes that we process information such as attitudes in the same way as adding new numbers to a pool of existing numbers, with new numbers getting averaged into the existing set of numbers. Hence, if you have a negative opinion about someone and learn that she did something nice, you will not immediately develop a favorable opinion of her. Instead, you will average the new positive information with the existing data that says that she is not a good person. Your new image of the person may be less negative but still negative overall.

The model does not assume that all information is equally assessed. Some information will have more power over your assessment than other information. We bias information about a person or an object based on the person who is giving us the new information as well as the nature of the information. For instance, you will probably weight information from trustworthy resources, such as family and friends, more than information from strangers or acquaintances. Further, we tend to weight early information (e.g., first impressions) more than subsequent information. This dynamic is called the primacy effect. However some research shows that a recency effect can also occur, when the most recent information is weighted more than other information. The recency effect is particularly likely when much time has passed since the first impression.

The weighted average model incorporates interactionist conceptions of the relationship between agency and interaction—that people take information about the world and process it before making any conclusions. That is, people are not simply empty vessels being manipulated by outside forces but active participants in attitudinal processes.

---

using public opinion surveys to predict how people would actually vote. Polls successfully predicted that Theodore Roosevelt would beat Alfred Landon in the 1936 presidential race (Sudman, Bradburn, and Schwarz 1996). Polls became increasingly used for predicting election results. However, pollsters failed to predict Harry Truman's victory over Thomas Dewey in 1948, causing many to question the ability to use polling to predict how people will act in the voting booths.

The relationship between our attitudes and behavior is typically small, with an average correlation of about .38 (Kraus 1995). This means that for every one unit change in an attitude toward an object there is, on average, only a .38 change in the behavioral unit. For instance, if military recruiters relied on this figure, it would mean that for every 100 persons who said that they intended to join the military, only 35 to 40 of them would actually end up serving in the armed forces. This information is not terribly useful when planning future recruiting efforts. A number of issues affect whether researchers will find a relationship between a measured attitude and a particular behavior. (See Box 9.2.)

The small relationship between attitudes and behavior—and between attitudes and other attitudes—may simply reflect poor measurement of attitudes and/or behaviors (Raden 1985; Schuman 1995). Several conditions increase the likelihood that researchers will find relationships between attitudes and behaviors or between attitudes and other attitudes. First, researchers need to be very specific about the attitudes and behaviors in question. Asking respondents their attitude about abortion generally, for example, will sometimes elicit different responses than when asking about abortion in which the life of the mother is at risk. In addition, general attitudes are often called on when people are unaware of the specificities associated with a particular issue. For instance, if you want to ask people their opinion toward building a nuclear power plant in their town, they may have very little knowledge of the costs and benefits of nuclear power for their town, leaving them to rely on their general attitudes toward the environment and nuclear power to make their decision. Hence, most people will provide an opinion on a topic, but some people are more informed about the topic than others, making their responses more reliable and consistent over time than people with less knowledge.

Prejudicial Attitudes and Behavior

One major application of symbolic interaction to the study of attitudes and behaviors is the understanding of **prejudice,** an attitude of dislike or active hostility toward a particular group in society. Much of the work using the symbolic interactionist framework emphasizes the causes of prejudicial attitudes toward different racial and ethnic groups. One of the earliest writers on American racial prejudice was W. E. B. Du Bois. Du Bois made very frank observations of the poor relationships between African Americans and Whites in the United States and Europe more broadly. In a work originally published in 1920, he wrote,

> The discovery of whiteness among the world's peoples is a very modern thing—nineteenth and twentieth century matter, indeed. The ancient world would have laughed at such distinction. . . . Today we have changed all that, and the world in a sudden, emotional conversion has discovered that it is white and by that token, wonderful! This assumption that of all hues of God whiteness alone is inherently and obviously better than brownness or tan leads to curious acts. . . . (Du Bois 2003, originally 1920, p. 44)

Du Bois considered the subtle and not-so-subtle ways that prejudice manifests itself in society, through both words and deeds, ranging from acts of violence such as lynching to the way two people may interact in a way that shows their social position relative to race. In the same article about white people he wrote:

> (W)hite faces . . . I see again and again, often and still more often, a writing of human hatred, a deep and passionate hatred, vast by the vagueness of its expression . . . I have seen a man—an educated gentleman—grow

livid with anger because a little, silent, black woman is sitting by herself in a Pullman car. I have seen a great grown man curse a little child, who had wandered into the wrong waiting room. (Du Bois 2003, originally 1920, pp. 46–47)

Although many Western cultures have changed since Du Bois' observations, prejudice is still commonplace and researchers continue to study prejudicial attitudes, examining how and why they develop and how they relate to specific behaviors.

Prejudicial attitudes are reflected in many ways in society, some more clearly than others. These attitudes help to maintain group boundaries.

Blumer's Theory of Group Position

Herbert Blumer was one of the most influential interactionists in the study of racial prejudice (Williams and Correa 2003). Blumer (1958) argued that prejudice is largely a group phenomenon rather than an individual attribute because it defines a group characteristic, one's race. According to the **theory of group position,** prejudicial attitudes reflect a group's relative position in society. Negative attitudes are defined to maintain a group's relative position in society. Specifically, among the dominant group, themes of group superiority (toward oneself) and inferiority (toward the minority group) help to sustain one's higher status in society. These two factors influence the development of the feeling of entitlement among the dominant group, believing they deserve their position, and fear of the lower-status group. Ultimately, it establishes antipathy between the groups.

Although Blumer's work was focused on African-American/White relationships in America, it can also be applied to other ethnic groups (Williams and Correa 2003). Race serves as a source of identity relevant to other groups in society who compete for limited resources. Greater competition between groups increases hostility between groups, both vying for relative position (Bobo and Hutchings 1996). Prejudicial attitudes are linked to groups that are seen as a threat to economic and cultural interests of another group, leading to the development of negative attitudes toward those groups.

The Study of Social Distance

Another important way that social psychologists have studied prejudicial attitudes is through the study of social distance. **Social distance** refers to how close we feel to other people. The strength of attitudes toward people in other groups may reflect our prejudices toward people in those groups. Emory Borgardus (1882–1973) (1958) developed an instrument called the social distance scale to assess individuals' sense of social distance to people of other ethnic and racial groups. The original social distance scale asked respondents the most that they were willing to do with a person from each of the racial or ethnic groups listed in the survey. The statements included the following activities:

1. Would marry
2. Would have as close friends
3. Would have as neighbor
4. Would have as co-worker
5. Would have as speaking acquaintances only
6. Would have as visitors only to my nation
7. Would bar from my country

The highest score for attitudes toward people from a particular group would be a 1 (would marry) and lowest score would be a 7 (would bar from my country). The average score for each group represents the average social distance people feel toward those groups.

Findings from 40 years' worth of research in the United States through the middle of the 20th century using this scale shows that among college and university students, respondents felt "closest" to "Canadians," "Americans," and "English" (see Table 9.2). (Owen, Eisner, and McFaul 1981). Groups with the worst scores included Asians and Blacks. The worst scores rarely exceed four, suggesting that respondents' prejudicial attitudes were usually centered around intimate friendships and family relationships.

More recent attempts to study social distance attitudes have shown the scale to be reliable. Parrillo and Donoghue (2005) found similar levels of social distance in a national study of college students conducted in 2001 with an overall score of 1.45 among 30 groups. As with the earlier studies, European Americans received the lowest scores. The highest scores included Arabs (1.94), Muslims (1.88), and Vietnamese (1.69). Consistent with earlier findings, women appear to be more tolerant than men. The authors also pointed out that overall distance scores and the spread between social groups have both decreased over the years, suggesting that attitudes have generally become more tolerant toward people of different racial and ethnic backgrounds. The social distance scale has been adapted to study racial and ethnic attitudes in places as diverse as Canada (Weinfurt and Moghaddam 2001), the Czech Republic (Rysavy 2003), and Ukraine (Panina 2004).

LaPiere's Study of Prejudice

Prejudicial attitudes and social distance do not necessarily lead to aggressive or hostile behavior between groups. That is, just because you feel prejudice toward an individual—or people from a particular race, class, or gender—does not mean that

Table 9.2   Research Using the Bogardus Social Distance Scale

Rank	1926 Group	Score	1946 Group	Score	1956 Group	Score	1966 Group	Score
1	English	1.06	Americans	1.04	Americans	1.08	Americans	1.07
2	Americans	1.10	Canadians	1.11	Canadians	1.16	English	1.14
3	Canadians	1.13	English	1.13	English	1.23	Canadians	1.15
4	Scots	1.13	Irish	1.24	French	1.47	French	1.36
5	Irish	1.30	Scots	1.26	Irish	1.56	Irish	1.40
26	Negroes	3.28	Japanese Am	2.90	Japanese	2.70	Turks	2.48
27	Turks	3.30	Koreans	3.05	Negroes	2.74	Koreans	2.51
28	Chinese	3.36	Indians, Asia	3.43	Mexicans	2.79	Mexicans	2.56
29	Koreans	3.60	Negroes	3.60	Indians, Asia	2.80	Negroes	2.56
30	Indians, Asia	3.91	Japanese	3.61	Koreans	2.83	Indians, Asia	2.62

Source: Adapted from Owen and colleagues (1981).

you will necessarily act on those attitudes. In a famous study, Richard T. LaPiere (1934) spent two years traveling extensively with a Chinese couple in the United States, staying at various hotels and eating at local restaurants. His work was being conducted during a time in the United States when racial segregation was still considered acceptable by many people. He wanted to know if people's attitudes toward different races coincided with the treatment of people of those races. To study this relationship, he conducted a survey of racial attitudes from the owners of the establishments he had visited during his travels with the couple as well as some restaurants and hotels he did not visit over that period of time.

LaPiere's (1934) primary survey question was: "Will you accept members of the Chinese race as guests in your establishment?" He then compared their verbal responses to their actual experiences at those establishments. One hundred and twenty-eight hotels and restaurants that had been visited responded to the survey. Of those that responded, 92% indicated that they would not give service to Chinese people. Only one of the respondents said that they would provide service to this group. The rest were undecided. However, their actual experiences differed markedly from the attitudes expressed in the survey. Of the 251 hotel and restaurant visits (both accompanied and unaccompanied by the author), only one hotel refused service to the Chinese couple. In fact, almost 40% of the visits were coded as being "very much better than [the] investigator would expect to have received (himself) . . ." (235). A summary of his findings can be found in Table 9.3.

Table 9.3	Summary of LaPiere's Attitude-Behavior Experiment	
	Responses to Survey about Service to Chinese People*	Actual Experience with Service at the Same Hotels and Restaurants
Would not provide service to Chinese patrons or Undecided	127	1
Would provide service to Chinese patrons	1	250

*Based on responses to the question: "Will you accept members of the Chinese race as guests in your establishment?" Only 128 hotels and restaurants visited responded to the survey.

Source: Adapted from LaPiere (1934).

LaPiere's (1934) study was one of the first to show that attitudinal research is limited in its ability to predict individuals' behaviors. According to LaPiere, attitudes exist as symbolic representations in the mind of an individual. What individuals do with those symbolic representations is highly dependent on the social conditions surrounding those individuals, especially when confronted with real people and tangible physical conditions.

A more recent study tried to link attitudes and behaviors surrounding the hiring of minorities. Pager and Quillian (2005) compared employers' self-reports about their willingness to hire Black and White ex-offenders and their actual hiring behavior in a creative field experiment. Although there were no differences in employers' statements about hiring ex-offenders of either race, the study showed that White ex-offender candidates were more likely to get callbacks from employers than Black ex-offenders who presented the exact same resumes. The results suggest that employers consciously or unconsciously acted against their stated attitudes.

These studies show the prevalence of prejudice in society and the challenges associated with assessing how those prejudices influence our behaviors. Sometimes we are aware of these prejudices and do not act on them, as in LaPiere's study, and sometimes we think (or report that) we are not prejudiced, when in fact we act in prejudicial ways. These contradictions make it difficult to fully address issues of prejudice and discrimination in society.

Section Summary

The first section of this chapter addresses the questions: What is the nature of an attitude? How do researchers study attitudes and behaviors? How do people construct attitudes? Here, we reviewed the cognitive and emotional dimensions of attitudes and the use of time diaries to track individuals' behaviors. Specifically, we analyzed the development of prejudicial attitudes and behavior, assessing the role of group position in developing negative attitudes toward minority groups. We also examined how prejudicial attitudes do not always lead to prejudicial behaviors.

SSP | Social Structure, Attitudes, and Behavior

I really don't think I have "values" per se. I take things as they come. I guess you could say that I am a "renaissance" man in that I base my decisions on what is rational. I see all of my religious friends making bad decisions about society based on a bunch of unfounded beliefs and values that they memorize from their parents and churches. I am beyond all of that. . . . Maybe that is why I am a science major.

—Mike, junior Biology major

Most of us think that we develop our attitudes and values using rational decision-making processes. Mike certainly believes that this is the case. He generally believes that he is above religious and family influences on his decision-making processes, relying more on rationality than systems of beliefs represented in religious doctrines. However, his decisions may actually be based on American cultural views of rationality and science. He probably spends a lot of time with groups that espouse his values. Although he does not filter ideas through a religious doctrine, he may be filtering them through a science-based paradigm popular in Western cultures. Like many of us, Mike may not be aware of the norms and values that govern his decision-making processes. In this section we will review structural conditions that influence our attitudes, including the role of agents of socialization and our social position in the form of race, gender, and age.

Attitudes and Agents of Socialization

From a structural point of view, individuals rely on their primary agents of socialization (e.g., family, school, and peers) for initial sets of values and beliefs that govern attitude processes. Exposure to different aspects of life allows us to form new attitudes toward those things, using information gained from direct experience. However, people who are unable to gain such exposures may simply rely on the information they have gained through formal socialization processes.

Primary agents of socialization serve as a basis by which we make decisions about future social issues. Indeed, the values and attitudes of our parents have a strong influence on our values and attitudes later in life. Figure 9.1 demonstrates that there is a 70% overlap between teens' political ideologies (conservative, liberal, or moderate) and their parents' ideologies.

Families transmit attitudes in at least two ways. First, families generally produce offspring of similar status in society, and status is associated with attitude

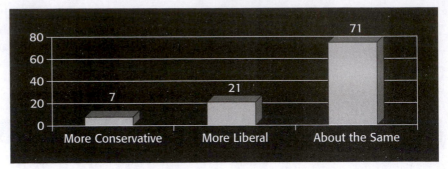

Figure 9.1   Passing on Values and Attitudes

Based on the question: "Thinking about social and political issues, how do your views compare to those of your parents? Are your views more conservative, more liberal, or about the same?

Source: Adapted from Lyons (2005).

similarity. Second, families may simply socialize or teach their children their values and beliefs (Glass, Bengsten, and Dunham 1986). Some families do this better than others. In one longitudinal study of parents and children, researchers found that parent–adolescent attitudes were most similar in families in which adolescents were involved in decision making and had warm relationships with their parents (Brody, Moore, and Glei 1994). Hence, attitude similarity remained strongest among warm, loving families.

Families not only transmit attitudes but behaviors too. In a study of student activism during the Persian Gulf War, Duncan and Stewart (1995) found that students' reports of their parents' activities during the Vietnam War were strongly related to their children's activist behaviors during the Persian Gulf War. They also found that parents' behavior indirectly affected students' activism through the development of attitudes toward war, ultimately affecting the likelihood of activism.

Gender, Attitudes, and Behavior

Few pollsters would conduct a survey or poll without including a series of questions about socioeconomic characteristics such as race, income, and gender. These variables have become essential to understanding attitudes because the responses to other survey questions vary by such characteristics. Social structure and personality researchers are also interested in how social statuses affect attitudes. And they do. For instance, about 37% of Americans identify themselves as "very conservative" or "conservative," 23% say they are "liberal" or "very liberal," and 38% say they are "moderate" on social issues (Carlson 2003). Hence, on average, Americans' political attitudes can be defined as moderate to conservative. However, these values vary by region and social location, with Westerners and women reporting to be more liberal than Southerners and men. Further, married people tend to be more conservative than singles. Race is also important with more non-Whites identifying themselves as liberal than Whites.

The relationship between gender and attitudes depends on the topic. Women, for instance, were less supportive of invading Iraq with U.S. ground troops than men (Moore 2002). The biggest support gap occurred in November 2001, when 80% of men but only 68% of women supported the invasion of Iraq. Similarly, Smith (1984) found women to be less supportive of the use of force or violence in an array of law enforcement situations. However, gender difference on some topics, such as race attitudes, have been limited (Hughes and Tuch, 2003). Hence, gender may be more salient for understanding some attitudes than others.

Behavioral differences between men and women are quite clear. Men and women continue to spend different amounts of time with their children (with women doing more child care than men). Women's time with children has stabilized, whereas men's time with children has increased in the last 30 years (Bianchi 2000) (see Figure 9.2). Women's time in child care has remained consistent despite the increases in time spent in the paid labor force over the last century, largely due to many fewer hours in housework and to more multitasking (Bianchi, Robinson, and Milkie 2006).

These data show that women are adopting men's role behaviors at a faster pace than the converse. Bianchi and her colleagues (2006), for instance, show that the percentage of mothers in the workforce has gone from 45% in 1975 to 70% in 2000 and that parents'—fathers and mothers—total workload (paid and unpaid) has increased in the last 30 years, though women continue to do more housework than men. They estimate that parents average a 9- to $9\frac{1}{2}$-hour workday, 7 days a

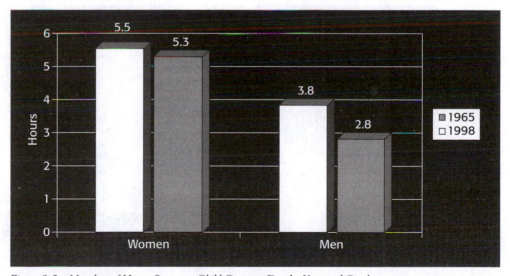

Figure 9.2   *Number of Hours Spent on Child Care per Day by Year and Gender*

Source: Adapted from Bianchi, Robinson, and Milkie (2006).

week when unpaid work in the home and paid work outside the home are combined.

Race and Attitudes

Polls and studies regularly show that African Americans and Whites often disagree on a number of social issues. Specifically, African Americans tend to be more supportive of public policies related to civil rights (Wolf 1998), including gay civil liberties (Lewis 2003; Wolf 1998) and affirmative action (Bobo 1998). These differences may reflect structural positions of African Americans in U.S. society who share a history of discrimination and lack of entitlements (Wolf 1998). Alternatively, races may reflect different cultural identities and beliefs, an issue that will be addressed in more detail under the rubric of social identity theory later in this chapter.

Group Affiliations and Complexity of Attitudes

Because individuals have multiple statuses, understanding attitudes requires examining all of people's characteristics simultaneously. For instance, both men and Whites in the United States have generally supported the use of the death penalty more than women and African Americans (see Figure 9.3). The greatest differences are between African Americans and Whites, with 71% of Whites but only 44% of African Americans favoring the death penalty (Carroll 2004).

Do some of our group memberships have more power over our attitude formation than others? One way to study these relationships is to examine multiple

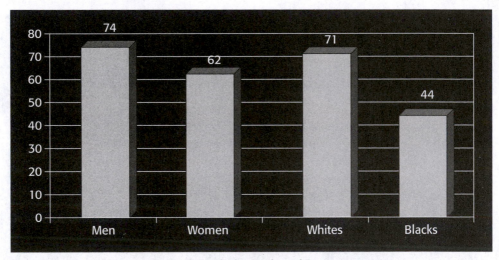

Figure 9.3   *Percent Favoring the Death Penalty by Gender and Race*

Based on the question: "Are you in favor of the death penalty for a person convicted of murder?"

Source: Adapted from Carroll 2004.

affiliations at the same time. In a study of support for the Iraq War, for instance, Rohall and his colleagues (Rohall, Ender, and Matthews 2006) found that military academy and ROTC students were significantly more supportive of the war than civilian students. Traditionally, these differences have been explained by arguing that military personnel are socialized to be more accepting of war than their civilian counterparts, creating a culture of war. However, almost half of the effects of military affiliation on attitudes toward war was explained by the disproportionate number of males associated with the military—men (both military and civilian) are generally more supportive of these war efforts than women. In this case, gender had a greater effect on attitudes toward war than military affiliation.

Attitudes across the Life Course

If later cohorts are more liberal, they make the average American (or Canadian or whatever group is being examined) more liberal when they replace the earlier, more conservative cohorts. Social structure and personality researchers study cohort replacement by comparing attitudes toward social issues based on the birth cohort, or generation, to which people belong.

Attitude Stability and Change

Americans' attitudes toward social issues have changed in a number of ways over the years. Duane Alwin (Alwin 2002, p. 43) cited several examples, including the following:

- In 1977, 66% of Americans said that it is better if the man works and the woman stays home; in 2000, only 35% did.
- In 1972, 48% said that sex before marriage is wrong; in 2000, 36% did.
- In 1972, 39% said that there should be a law against interracial marriage; in 2000, 12% did.
- In 1958, 78% said that one could trust the government in Washington to do right; in 2000, only 44% did.

Historical experiences can affect some groups of people, whereas other groups are left relatively unaffected, much like the Great Depression discussed in chapter 6. Thus, many of the social changes that have occurred in the United States occurred unevenly across groups.

The study of attitude change is complicated by the fact that trends in support for an issue can change without much of a change in the overall level of support for it. For instance, attitudes toward penalties for the possession of marijuana have changed since the 1970s, but the majority of Americans do not support its legalization (Rohall 2003) (see Figure 9.4). Only 12% of Americans believed that marijuana should be legalized in 1970; that percentage had increased to 34% in 2002. Despite support for the legalization of marijuana over the last 30 years, it is clear

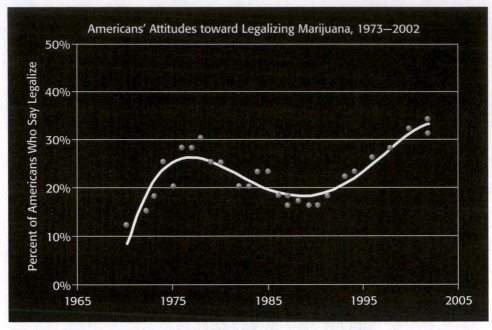

Figure 9.4   Attitudes toward Legalizing Marijuana over Time

Source: General Social Survey and Gallup Polls; graph adapted from Rohall (2003).

that Americans are not ready to make the drug legal. Hence, in one sense, opinions about illegal drugs have changed dramatically over the last 30 years. On the other hand, Americans, as a whole, continue to think that it should remain illegal. In essence, we should care about both the trends in and the overall levels of support for various issues.

Cohort Differences over Time

In chapter 6, we examined the effects of generational differences in exposure to life events on our senses of self. From the interactionist perspective, generations should develop different attitudes based on their different social interactions and experiences over time (see Box 9.3). More recent cohorts, for example, tend to be more ideologically liberal in terms of their political affiliation than earlier generations (Carlson 2003).

One area of generational research is the study of continuity and change associated with attitudes toward sex and sexual relations. Americans have generally become more liberal in their attitudes toward gender roles and sexual behavior since the 1970s (Bolzendahl and Myers 2004; Harding and Jencks 2003; Smith 1992). However, much of these changes occured in the 1960s and the 1980s, showing some leveling off in the 1990s (Hardings & Jencks 2003). Hence, attitudes vary by generation, but these changes may ot be linear or consistent over time.

Box 9.3   **Balance and Cognitive Dissonance Theories**

Psychologists have long been interested in how individuals process information. Attitudes are not developed or changed without using existing cognitive resources to interpret new information. This information may come from interactions with other people, reading, or watching television. How do people manage so many different sources of information? How does this knowledge affect how we act in the world?

Fritz Heider (1896–1988), a psychologist, developed balance theory to explain how individuals manage opinions with the people around them. The basic model consists of three parts: (1) the person, (2) another person, and (3) an attitude object.

A State of Balance

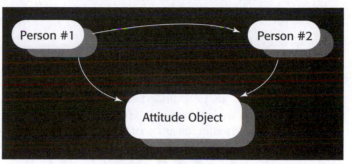

To achieve balance, the attitude of person #1 toward the attitude object must be in sync with her attitude toward the other person and that person's attitude toward the object. If you are prochoice and your friend is prolife, this is considered an imbalanced state, because you have a positive relationship with your friend. Ways to resolve this situation include changing your opinion toward abortion, changing your friend's opinion of abortion, or no longer being friends with the person.

Cognitive dissonance theory was developed by Leon Festinger (1919–1989) in the 1950s. The theory extends balance theory by incorporating individuals' behaviors into their attitude processes. Festinger argued that individuals must assess their attitudes relative to their behaviors. If we act in a way that conflicts with our beliefs, this disjunction produces a sense of dissonance, or psychological tension. We can reduce this dissonance by changing our beliefs about the behavior or by changing our behavior. For example, you might consider yourself easygoing but find yourself blowing up over what you realize, on reflection, were minor incidents. You would probably feel dissonance over these events. According to cognitive dissonance theory, you would likely reduce the dissonance by either changing your attitudes (deciding you are a little bit high strung) or by changing your behavior (blowing up less often).

Section Summary

The second section of this chapter applied the social structure and personality perspective to answer the questions: How do attitudes vary across social groups? Do attitudes change over time? Here, we examine how attitudes are passed on among family members, effectively socializing us to the values and beliefs of our parents. We also see that attitudes vary in society based on group affiliation with men and women, and different racial and age groups varying in their beliefs about various social issues. Finally, we applied the life-course paradigm to understand the ways that attitudes change over time.

GP | Group Processes and Attitudes

Let's face it, some people have it, some people don't. People either follow you or they don't. Leaders are born, not made. . . .

—Frank, sophomore English major

The interactionist and social structure and personality perspectives on attitudes place attitude formation and development in the context of the groups with which we affiliate. Group-processes scholars continue this by examining how group processes shape attitude formation. Frank clearly believes people are born to be liked or lead other people. Group processes work shows that interactions in groups affect attitudes toward people inside and outside of the group.

Status Construction Theory

Ridgeway and Balkwell (1997) (also see Berger, Ridgeway, and Zelditch 2002) combined elements of the symbolic interactionism and group processes perspectives in the development of status construction theory. **Status construction theory** posits that individuals develop status value in face-to-face interactions through three principle linkages:

1. Structural characteristics of society constrain interactions among individuals.
2. These interactions encourage actors to develop status beliefs about individual differences.
3. Interactions teach these beliefs to other people in the group.

This theory asserts that attitudes about individuals in groups form as a result of both direct experience in the group and larger cultural information contained in the status of the individuals. Hence, the theory combines macro- and microstructural conditions that affect our attitudes toward other people. We bring expectations about other individuals' statuses in society into day-to-day interactions. These expectations serve as a basis for attitudinal development in those groups. Direct experience adds to our attitude development, serving to support our expectations or not.

Race and ethnicity serve as status characteristics that can impact interactions in a variety of social settings.

In one experiment, Ridgeway and her colleagues (1998) had students team up in groups of two, each with a confederate (individuals who participants believed were fellow research subjects but were in fact part of the research team). The researchers studied interaction between two sets of groups: those deemed to have more resources (high-resource group) and those with fewer resources (low-resource group). They also assessed participants' attitudes toward other group members after a series of activities. Research dating to the 1930s has shown that individuals have biases toward their own groups and negative biases against people in other groups (see Box 9.4). However, Ridgeway and colleagues found that individuals in both the low- and high-resource groups developed positive biases toward the high-resource group. People in the high-resource group were judged to be higher in status, more respectable, and more competent than people in the disadvantaged group. These positive attitudes may make it easier for both groups to get what they want from the other group: Dominant groups get compliance from the subordinate group, whereas subordinates receive positive sentiment and some support. Subordinate groups give their positive attitudes toward dominant groups in exchange for the dominate groups' agreement to provide support in some way.

The applications of status construction theory to day-to-day life are clear. If you have the opportunity to interact with a disadvantaged person, you may treat

Box 9.4   **The Robbers' Cave Experiment in Psychology**

In a classic psychological study conducted in the 1950s, Muzafer Sherif and his colleagues (1988, originally 1954) conducted a field experiment with 22 White, 11-year-old boys, none of whom knew each other prior to the experiment. The boys were sent to a remote summer camp in Oklahoma at Robbers' Cave State Park. The boys were randomly assigned to one of two groups: The Eagles or the Rattlers. Sherif had the groups participate in a series of competitions over a four-day period. He found that prejudicial attitudes started to develop as the competitions continued. These prejudices continued despite the introduction of meetings designed to ease tensions between the groups. It was only when the groups had a "superordinate" goal, a problem that required the groups to work together, that the groups dropped some of their negative attitudes toward one another.

This study shows the power that groups have in constructing opinions about other people. In particular we make distinctions between "in-groups" and "out-groups"—people we identify with versus those we do not. Sherif easily manipulated the boys' attitudes toward members of the outside group by creating tension and conflict between the groups through competition.

her differently than someone who shows some sign of wealth and prosperity. Moreover, this bias will likely lead to differential evaluation of people from these groups. Your attitude toward other people will be constructed from both your direct experience with the person and their social position, or the traits and resources they bring to the situation, such as race, gender, income or appearance. Further, if you are a lower-status person, you are likely to share positive biases toward individuals who show signs of being prosperous in the world.

Social Identity Theory and Attitudes

One of the fundamental aspects of social identity theory is that people have a tendency to categorize themselves into groups and use those categorizations as a reference point for their attitudes toward members of other groups in society (see Chapter 5). The groups we identify with are considered to be **in-groups,** whereas the groups with which we do not identify are called **out-groups.** In addition, threats to groups serve to magnify the effects of group identity. When a group is threatened by another group, the first group will likely form tighter bonds while developing a stronger animosity toward the out-group.

Nationality represents one type of group affiliation. Canadians differentiate themselves from Americans, for example, and Americans differentiate themselves from Canadians. Such group designations serve as major aspects of our identity (see Chapter 5). Groups also serve as a source of information about other groups. Threats serve to heighten our identity with the in-group, in this case our national identity.

The terrorist attacks against the United States on September 11, 2001, provided a natural experiment to see how social identity affected Americans' attitudes. Robb Willer (2004) used public opinion data on Americans' attitudes toward President George W. Bush and the number of terror warnings issued by the federal government. He found that government-issued terror warnings led to increases in approval ratings for the president. Attitudes toward the president became more positive as fears of outsiders increased. These findings are attributed to the tendency to view members of our in-group more positively when the group is threatened. In this case, the terrorist alerts served as a sign of potential threat against the United States.

In another study employing social identity theory, Burn and colleagues (2000) analyzed support for feminism among men and women. The researchers found that women who rated high on gender self-esteem (feeling positive about women) were more likely to show support for feminism than those who reported lower group self-esteem. In addition, women were more supportive of feminism than men, suggesting that in-group members (women), especially those who strongly identify with this group, are more supportive of in-group ideologies.

These studies show the importance of group contexts in developing our attitudes. These contexts can include our gender, racial, and status groups, among others. Being a member of a group, particularly if that group identity is salient to you, influences your interpretation of information given to you and your attitudes toward external objects—the people and things around you.

Section Summary

The last section of this chapter applied theories and research from the group processes perspective to address the question: How do attitudes toward other people form in group contexts? According to status construction theory, beliefs about individuals in groups form through interaction in group contexts. Individuals bring in expectations of group members based on societal biases that affect future interpretations of performance in the group. Social identity theory helps us to understand how our group identities affect attitudes toward people within our group and toward outsiders. From this perspective, group contexts provide a venue to evaluate our attitudes and behavior toward other people in the world.

Bringing It All Together

I just don't understand why there is so much hate in the world. We've got people bombing innocent civilians, hate groups killing just about everybody. Why can't we all just get along?

—Dennis, freshman Undeclared

Dennis has a legitimate concern. One of the reasons we study attitudes and behaviors is to understand how to make the world a better place. If we can find the root causes of anger and hatred between people, maybe we could stop the violence between them. In this chapter, we applied the three social psychological perspectives to provide insights into attitude processes more generally and prejudicial attitudes specifically.

The symbolic interactionist perspective was applied to understand the nature of attitudes and behavior. Here, we examined the multidimensional nature of attitudes, that they can have both rational and evaluative components, and the social construction of prejudice. Using the social structure and personality perspective, we found out that attitudes vary based on the social groups we belong to, notably our race and gender. Finally, research and theory from the group processes perspective shows that beliefs about others are informed by our position in a group and our group memberships in general. The research and theories employed in this chapter will not end prejudice and hatred in society, but we hope that they may inform you on how to understand those attitudes when they occur.

Summary

1. Attitudes incorporate emotional, intellectual, and behavioral dimensions—how we feel, think, and behave toward an object. Attitudes are measured in terms of their direction and strength, though people can also have nonattitudes toward objects. Behaviors can be characterized as either productive time like work and family care or free time, including activities like watching television or socializing.

2. The relationship of attitudes and behavior, on average, is typically very small with an average correlation of .38. The small relationship between attitudes and behavior—and other attitudes—may reflect poor measurement of attitudes or the complexities of attitudes themselves.

3. Interactionist perspectives view attitudes like any other aspect of social life: They are constantly being constructed based on our interactions with other people. Our group memberships in society can have a large influence in our attitudes toward people in other groups based on the relative standing of those groups.

4. Some attitudes and opinions have been found to vary directly with our social status in society. Men and women regularly report different attitudes toward some social issues, as do African Americans and Whites. Many attitudes toward major social issues have changed over the last half century.

5. Status construction theory posits that individuals develop status value through face-to-face interaction as well as from larger societal prejudices. Social identify theory emphasizes the role of in-groups and out-groups in our attitude development.

Key Terms and Concepts

Attitude: A positive or negative evaluation of an object, a person or group, or an idea.

Free time: Time used for leisure activities like reading, exercising, watching television, listening to the radio, and other activities that we do for our own pleasure.

In-groups: Groups with whom we identify.

Nonattitude: When you do not care either way about something.

Opinion: The cognitive or "thinking" aspect of an attitude.

Out-groups: Groups with which we do not identify.

Prejudice: An attitude of dislike or active hostility toward a particular group in society.

Productive time: Time used for paid work, housework and child care, and traveling associated with productive work (i.e., commuting to work).

Social distance: How close we feel to other people.

Status construction theory: Group processes theory that posits that individuals develop status value in face-to-face interactions with other people.

Theory of group position: Theory that prejudicial attitudes reflect a group's position in society.

Time deepening: When people do more with the time that they have available to them.

Time use: The study of what people do on a day-to-day basis.

Values and beliefs: Strongly held, relatively stable sets of attitudes.

Discussion Questions

1. Think about some of your values and beliefs. How do you think they would be different if you lived in another place or were of a different gender or race?

2. Think about your upbringing. What aspects of your life affected the values and beliefs you have today? What factors influence your decisions on a day-to-day basis?

3. How is your average day similar or different from those of other people? How do you manage your free and productive time?

4. Can you think of a situation in which you were judged incorrectly in a group setting? What caused that misperception?

The Sociology of Sentiment and Emotion

I always feel embarrassed when I think about it—my grand-mother's funeral, that is. I could not stop laughing. I loved the woman, but I just couldn't stop the laughter.

—Janet, freshman Psychology major

I magine that one of your professors has scheduled an exam covering difficult course material. The exam will significantly affect your course grade, and you have spent days mastering the material. You are sure that you will ace the test. When the day of the exam arrives, your professor notifies the class that she has decided to drop the test and is instead assigning a 20-page course paper. How do you think you would respond to this? Would you be angry? Would you let go with a stream of obscenities? Do you think that you would hit, kick, or break things?

How you answer the preceding questions would likely depend in large part on where you were when you learned the information. If you read the information in an e-mail in your apartment or dorm room, you would probably react very differently than if the professor announced it in class. It is much more likely, for example, that you would kick over a chair in your dorm room than in your classroom. How we express our emotions, then, is affected by social conditions. It is not just our reactions, how-ever, that are affected by the setting. Our emotions themselves can be determined by characteristics of our social environment.

We tend to think of our emotions as things over which we have little control. We do not choose to cry during sad movies or to become angry with annoying family members. Instead, we see emotions as carrying us away. Consider a professional, male baseball player who charges the pitcher after he is hit by a pitch. On some level, the player must know as soon as he starts running toward the pitcher that he is facing a suspension, a fine, and public condemnation. But he continues nonetheless. His emotions seem to carry him away, and his only goal becomes to hurt this other person.

We often think that emotions override rational thought. In fact, discussions often treat rationality and emotion as though they are opposite ends of some spectrum. Acting emotionally, to some, means abandoning reason. If we look more closely, however, we can see that there is at least some rational calculation involved in even those actions that seem completely driven by emotion. Consider the baseball player who loses control and charges the pitcher. What is the one thing that essentially every baseball player who charges the pitcher does before he takes off to the mound? He puts down his bat. The player seems intent on hurting this other person, but he puts down something that would give him a big advantage in the fight he is about to start! Just as the player knows at some level that charging the mound will lead to trouble, he knows that bringing the bat will lead to *big* trouble—likely the difference between a suspension from his job and felony assault charges.

Social interactions are associated with different emotional responses such as crying at a funeral, leading sociologists to study the social conditions that produce particular emotions.

The sociology of emotion does not disregard the biology or psychology of emotion. Rather, sociologists are interested in how people interpret their physical sensations, the social conditions that are likely to produce physiological stimulation, and how structural conditions influence both of these processes. In short, sociologists want to know how society affects our feelings and our emotional expressions.

Although emotions may be to some extent hardwired into our biological systems, our emotions are also affected by social conditions. Under most social conditions, we follow the rules, laughing when it is appropriate to laugh and crying when we should cry. However, there are times when we cannot—or choose not to—follow these rules. Janet's story highlights some of these issues. She questions whether people should naturally feel bad at funerals. What makes a death something to be mourned in the first place? Janet knows that it is inappropriate to laugh at a funeral yet finds it impossible to stop herself from doing so.

The **cybernetic approach** to the study of emotion asserts that social conditions shape our emotions, and in turn, our emotions act to maintain social structures (Franks 2003). Like much of sociological social psychology, the approach views social interaction as both shaping and being shaped by society. Although social conditions give rise to different emotions, emotions are also essential to the maintenance of social organization. This chapter will start by reviewing how sociologists study the upward movement of emotions in the creation of society and the social construction of emotions more generally. It will also review the structured nature of emotions, how society shapes the scope and expression of emotions. Other important topics will be addressed by answering the following questions:

- What are emotions? What are the components of emotions?
- How do people learn emotions?
- How is identity related to emotions?
- How does our status in society affect our use of emotions?
- What norms govern the use of emotions in different social settings?
- How do group settings affect our emotions?

 ## Constructing and Using Sentiment and Emotions

I always thought that emotions are hardwired. I read in psychology class that some emotions are "hardwired" in that researchers have found them to exist in most countries in the world today. Doesn't that mean that they exist outside of any influence of culture?

—Francis, sophomore Computer Science major

One of the earliest sociological writings about emotions comes from Charles Horton Cooley, who defined **sentiment** as a feeling that has been given meaning by society (Stets 2003). In short, sentiments give meaning to stimuli occurring in the body. For example, you may feel pain and decide if it is good or bad, strong or mild, among other things. Alternatively, you may wonder whether a feeling you have for someone else is love or sexual attraction. Society helps individuals develop meaning for each of these biological feelings. Languages provide hundreds of terms that can be applied to a range of feelings.

Francis's beliefs about the biological foundations of emotions are well founded. Many scholars in sociology, psychology, and anthropology argue that some emotions are based on biologically founded instinct, developing over tens of thousands of years of evolution. Fear, for example, may result from humans' desire to avoid dangerous situations. From a purely social constructionist point of view, even basic instincts are learned through social interaction, through primary agents of socialization, and then the larger society (see chapter 6). Still other scholars accept that some emotions may be instinctual but then vary by social context. Simply put, emotions have different values and meaning depending on one's culture.

The Dimensions and Components of Emotions

We defined sentiment as a feeling that has been given meaning by society. Sociologists often use sentiment and emotion interchangeably. In contrast, Peggy Thoits (1989) treats emotions and sentiment as distinct and argues that **emotions** have four dimensions:

1. Situational cues
2. Physiological changes
3. Expressive gestures
4. An emotion label

Hence, emotions are a compilation of feelings, social conditions, and labels. **Situational cues** tell when and what emotion is appropriate in a given social interaction, ultimately producing changes in our body, **physiological changes,** that reflect what is going on in the situation, such as happiness, anger, or fear. **Expressive gestures** are usually associated with a particular emotion that "goes" with a particular label. A child given a present at a birthday party is using the cue of the gift to stimulate happiness and excitement. These feelings are expressed with a smile or some other gesture. We give an **emotional label** to her feelings of happiness, giving us some indication that she is happy. All these conditions do not have to occur simultaneously for an emotion to exist or be recognized by another person. Thoits uses the examples of being afraid without knowing why and notes that children can get emotional without having the words to express their feelings.

Many other terms are associated with the concept of emotion. **Affect** is an evaluative component of an emotion, whether good or bad (Smith-Lovin 1995), whereas **mood** refers to more diffuse emotional states that last a relatively long period of time. Finally, **feelings** may be referred to as internal states associated with a particular

Box 10.1 **Universal Expressions of Emotion**

Some sociologists and psychologists believe that there are "primary emotions" that have evolved through evolutionary processes and thus can be recognized in every culture around the world. Paul Ekman and his colleagues have conducted extensive research on the meaning of facial expressions in cultures as diverse as Sumatra, Japan, Germany, and Greece. The researchers show subjects a series of pictures of people with various facial expressions designed to represent emotions such as anger, disgust, fear, and happiness, among others. The researchers find a tremendous amount of agreement about the meaning of these facial expressions across cultures. In particular, five emotions can be recognized in both literate and non-literate cultures: anger, fear, happiness, sadness, and disgust. Note that four out of five of these emotions are negative, suggesting that emotions developed for survival purposes, to protect us against danger by preparing for attack (anger or disgust) or fleeing from it (fear).

emotion (Stets 2003). Sentiments, then, are societies' imprint on our feelings, moods, affect, and emotions—the constructed meanings associated with them.

Kemper (1987) argued that emotions occur on two levels. **Primary emotions** refer to physiologically grounded emotions that we inherit through evolutionary processes, including anger, fear, and depression (see also Box 10.1). **Secondary emotions** derive from primary emotions when we attach varying meanings to primary emotions. Secondary emotions are most similar to sentiments and are learned through socialization. Guilt, for example, is a response to the arousal of the primary emotion of fear. Sociologists tend to focus on secondary emotions where meaning is derived from social interactions. That is, according to Kemper, society may have more impact on the formation and meaning of secondary emotions than on primary ones. Secondary emotions are sometimes called "social emotions."

Symbolic interactionism is premised on the construction and interaction of symbols, typically associated with cognitive, thinking processes. Interactionists also believe that emotions are important to these symbolic processes, even though we may not always be conscious of them (Franks 2003). There are three ways that emotions contribute to social interactions:

1. Emotions can serve as the basis of our thought processes.
2. Emotions can give meaning to different physical and social conditions.
3. Emotions are directly linked to our decision-making processes.

As an illustration of these principles, consider how a sense of embarrassment may influence the way we act in a public setting, making us decide to act more reserved so as to not call attention to ourselves. The feelings of embarrassment may be a result of someone putting us in our place. Knowing this information, we can decide how to act on the insult, perhaps leaving the group setting or retaliating in some way. Regardless of these processes, we take emotional states to inform our decision about the best way to interact with the people around us.

In a study of emotional management among wheelchair users, Spencer Cahill and Robin Eggleston (1994) found that emotions played an important role in the behaviors of their subjects. Simply deciding whether to venture out in public was associated with mixed feelings of fear, embarrassment, and excitement—the excitement of being in public places mixed with the fears associated with being handicapped, tied to access to various facilities or the embarrassment of standing out among "stand-up people" (302). The researchers found that, once out in public, wheelchair users regularly managed the challenges of being handicapped with different emotions. Humor is an important asset to interactions between wheelchair users and stand-up people, allaying the anxiety resulting from the accidents that inevitably resulted from crowded stores and streets. A wheelchair user, for instance, would fall down and use humor to keep witnesses from being too anxious about the incident. This example shows the importance of emotions in initiating decisions (e.g., whether to leave home) and how people use them during interactions (e.g., employing humor to divert other feelings).

Socialization of Emotions

Symbolic interactionists view the learning of emotions like any aspect of social life. We develop meaning—whether a cognitive or affective meaning—of an object or person through interaction with other people. We use this meaning to help guide our behavior in day-to-day life. The **sociocentric model of emotional socialization** argues that the primary means of learning about emotions comes from social instruction, primarily from family, friends, and schooling (Pollack and Thoits 1989). Agents of socialization interpret and label childrens' emotions during their interactions, helping them recognize the causes and consequences of their feelings.

In a study of disturbed three- to five-year-old children in a therapeutic school, Pollak and Thoits (1989) studied at least two dimensions of the emotion-learning process. First, instructors tried to identify and explain children's emotions. Typically, instructors would associate an emotion word (e.g., anger or frustration) with a situational cause. The authors provided the following example (26):

GIRL [SEVERAL TIMES]: My mom is late.

STAFF MEMBER: Does that make you mad?

GIRL: Yes.

STAFF MEMBER: Sometimes kids get mad when their moms are late to pick them up.

In this example, the child is taught to associate her emotion (anger) with an appropriate cause (being late). In short, the emotion is labeled and connected to a specific cause.

Children are also taught appropriate ways to express their emotions. Pollak and Thoits (1989) found that songs were often employed to help students make the connection between emotions and expressions, such as: "If you're happy and you know it, clap your hands" (29). Instructors would rely on statements such as "most children" as a way of letting children know how their behavior fits in the larger context of society. The researchers made it clear that the goal was not to control students' internal feelings but rather their outward expressions, notably expressions of anger and aggression. They concluded that simply labeling an emotion is not enough to teach children how to develop their emotional lives. Rather, children need a much more elaborate socialization process that explicitly links situational conditions, expression of the emotion, and words to identity the feeling.

Identity, Interactions, and Emotions

Once learned, emotions work very much like symbols. We use them in our day-to-day interactions as a way of communicating with other people. We may pass someone in the hallway and give a nod and smile, indicating that we mean no harm or wish to make a connection. Emotions also help us to better understand ourselves (see chapter 5). Emotions provide information about how well we are maintaining our self as well as our presentation of that self. These processes are what we defined in chapter 7 as reflexivity, the process in which individuals reflect back on and give meaning to an object, including our senses of self. In the case of emotions, Rosenberg (1990) argued that people use reflexive processes to identify, display, and experience emotions. Hence, individuals try to produce emotional states in themselves and others.

Affect Control Theory

In chapter 5 we learned about affect control theory. Applied to our identities, affect control theory argues that people use emotions as signals about how well they are performing their roles or identities in a given situation. Affect control theory (ACT) includes an analysis of the role of emotions in interactions more generally. It is based on three basic principles (Heise 2002):

1. Individuals create events to confirm the sentiments that they have about themselves and others in the current situation.

2. If events don't work to maintain sentiments, then individuals reidentify themselves and others.

3. In the process of building events to confirm sentiments, individuals perform the social roles that are fundamental to society.

These premises simply indicate that people use emotions in their day-to-day interactions to help them get along with other people. Anger may serve as a sign that something is not going right between you and your partner. Similarly, a feeling of joy or love may have the opposite effect. Feelings or emotions may serve as better indicators about our relationships with other people than rational thinking processes. If something does not feel right in a situation, a person often has the option of changing her definition of the situation or herself.

Affect control theory (Heise 1999, 2002; Lively and Heise 2004; see also Osgood 1962) proposes that there are three aspects of sentiment toward an object:

1. **Evaluation**—its goodness or badness
2. **Potency**—its powerfulness or powerlessness
3. **Activity**—its liveliness or quietness

Together, these form the EPA dimensions of emotions. Affect control theory proposes that we can respond to anything—ourselves, other people, and objects—along the EPA dimensions, rating these objects relative to one another. Essentially, EPA ratings provide a sense of how good, powerful, and active an object is to a person. These ratings can be applied to people, objects, or events. (See Table 10.1.)

Fundamental sentiments refer to enduring emotional meanings in a given society. We can all probably conjure up feelings associated with our friends and enemies, as well as the meanings associated with ice cream and candy. Different cultures may develop different EPA readings for the same object. For instance, Heise (2002) found that the Japanese evaluate family members less positively than people in other cultures (e.g., the United States and Canada), whereas Chinese people evaluate family most positively using these EPA readings.

Individuals may also develop **transient sentiments** during specific interactions, sentiments unique to particular interactions between people. These sentiments may confirm fundamental sentiments about an object or not. For instance, in the United States, a patient may go see a doctor, believing that she is fundamentally good (evaluation), powerful (potency), and neither lively nor still (activity) (Heise 2002). If the doctor lives up to the fundamental sentiment, giving clear, concise advice in a neutral way, the patient's transient sentiments concur with the fundamental sentiment, producing feelings of ease and gratefulness. Alternatively, if the doctor does not live up to these expectations, perhaps waffling in her diagnoses (less powerful), the fundamental and transient sentiments conflict, leaving the patient with negative feelings about the doctor and the interaction.

Table 10.1	The Three Aspects of Affect Control Theory	
Evaluation	**Potency**	**Activity**
Nice vs. Awful	Big vs. Little	Fast vs. Slow
Good vs. Bad	Powerful vs. Powerless	Noisy vs. Quiet
		Active vs. Inactive

Source: Adapted from Web site: www.indiana.edu/~socpsy/Act

Dramaturgy and Emotion

Under the ACT framework, individuals can help each other recover from situations in which transient and fundamental sentiments conflict (Heise 2002). In this way, we actively align our emotions, attitudes, and behaviors with other people through impression management—using emotions as cues to our identity. Erving Goffman's work on impression formation (see chapter 5) relies heavily on the idea that emotions help us develop and maintain our impressions presented to other people. If we attempt to present a front that includes being intelligent or "cool" and fail at this impression, it will likely be embarrassing for ourselves and the other people (perhaps our friends and family). Hence, emotions serve as signals about our impressions. Emotions also provide motivation to restore our impressions; sympathy helps others to contribute to this restoration process. Believe it or not, other people want to quickly help you to *not* look so foolish. It is uncomfortable for everyone. Spilling a drink in public will likely be met with help from a number of people to both assist you in cleaning the mess as well as to make you feel less awkward about the accident; one of the helpers might make a quick joke about the incident or provide examples when she did something similar in the past.

Louis Zurcher (1982) employed the principles of impression management to study emotional performances of fans, coaches, and players at a college football game. He found that each of these groups follow **emotional scripts,** expectations about when and how to display certain emotions—excitement or anger, for instance. The winning pass is associated with joy. Crowds are expected to act with applause in this case. In addition, certain emotional cues provoke rapidly changing emotional expressions. That is, under some conditions, individuals must know when to change their emotions rather quickly, to keep pace with the events at a game. **Emotional cues** give people information about when and what emotions are appropriate in a given social setting. A football player, for instance, may raise his two arms in the air, trying to arouse the crowd to cheer on the other players, hence motivating them to play better. Scripts and cues help people guide the development and expression of emotion, suggesting that people make rules for their emotions in the same way as norms and values.

Society and Emotions

We often think of emotions as very personal. We learn them through socialization and incorporate them into our identities, but emotions also have important social consequences. Emotions contribute to the maintenance of society. At one level, friends and family may conjure up positive feelings, helping us stay committed to the institution of the family. But what motivates us to stay committed to our country, religion, and work?

There are at least two ways that our emotions help maintain societal bonds. First, emotions are a source of satisfaction, a reason to stay committed to a job or a religious group. In this sense, emotions serve as motivators to maintain relationships over the long haul. Pride may help us stay connected to our school or our country. Second, emotions make us feel bad when we do not live up to societal standards. The campaign against "deadbeat dads," for instance, was designed to make fathers think about their financial and emotional responsibilities to their children—and feel bad when failing at them.

Shame and Society

Religious groups, employers, and family members, representing three major social institutions, can all elicit negative emotions, making us angry with the rules of our church, poor working conditions, or bad family relationships. Scheff (1990) argued that negative emotions such as shame help us to conform to the rules of society. When we decide not to conform, this may produce a bad feeling, making us turn that feeling into pride by "following the rules." If social order exists through the laws and rules a society has created, then emotions such as shame and guilt are important emotions in maintaining that order. Self-control over our emotions also helps us to suppress our wants and desires for the good of a higher order, for society. Thus, a major way that society influences conformity to rules is the use of shame and other negative emotions such as fear and concern over the consequences of rule breaking.

Interaction Ritual Chains

Randall Collins's (1981, 2004) **theory of interaction ritual chains** extends symbol interaction theory to incorporate the role of emotions in the interaction process. The theory focuses on the **interaction ritual** as the unit of analysis, the exchange of symbols and emotion between individuals (see also Goffman 1967). **Emotional energy** serves as the basis of these interactions, referring to a heightened sense of excitement produced by a feeling of belonging. Emotional energy is important because it gives people the motivation to carry on the ritual process—to participate in society. Collins (2004) describes the role of emotions in the interaction process as "charg[ing] up symbol objects with significance" (38). In other words, emotions make attitude objects (i.e., people, events, or objects) worth talking about or interacting with, explaining why people attach themselves to the interaction process in the first place.

According to this theory, emotions are present in any social interaction. It goes further to state that individuals in social settings seek to develop a common mood, a generalized feeling. In other words, they seek to share a similar feeling. For instance, you may be meeting with other students to discuss a professor. Individuals may provide different sentiments on the issue, but members will likely seek a common feeling about the teacher. This emotional coordination produces a sense of solidarity, a connection between the individual and the group. If you leave with a strong sense of solidarity, it will give you higher levels of emotional energy, giving you confidence in the interaction process, the basis of society. Alternatively, you may leave feeling no connection with the other group members, leaving you to feel low emotional energy, manifested by feelings of depression and low self-esteem. Emotional energy is necessary in the development of solidarity. It also gives us a sense that we contribute to the groups we belong to, and helps us make decisions about how to behave during interaction rituals.

Section Summary

In this section of the chapter, we applied the interactionist perspective to answer the questions: What are emotions? What are the components of emotions? How do people learn emotions? How is identity related to emotions? Here we examined the physiological, social, and behavioral components of emotions. Emotions include simple sensations as well as more consistent emotional states of being or moods. Interactionists generally believe that emotions are constructed like any other aspect of social life, through interaction with other people. In addition, emotions are important in developing and maintaining our identities, serving as a cue for when we are playing our roles appropriately, and they help to motivate people to participate in society in the first place.

SSP ❙ Structural Conditions Affecting Emotions

I don't know . . . there is just something about the guy. Maybe it was the way that he spoke at the convention. He really cares about people. I mean, a man with all of that experience. He is so smart. Even if he does not win the election, I will support him in whatever he does. He is a great guy.

—Jason, senior Marketing major

The cybernetic approach to emotions argues that emotions go from being created in microsocial interactions "up" to contributing to the construction of society. They also go "downward"; once society is created, it can influence the development of emotions in a group or population. Social structural conditions that typically influence individuals in society include norms, statuses, and positions (see chapter 2). Sociological social psychology focuses on how our position in society affects our emotions and the emotions that we elicit from other people.

Jason's feelings about a civic leader show the importance of emotion in maintaining status structures in society. His affection for this leader makes Jason want to follow him, even if he does not win the election. We discussed the importance of class position in developing favorable opinions of powerful people and groups in society in chapter 9. Similar research and theory is applied to emotions because attitudes can include feelings about a person or an object.

Power, Status, and Emotions

Collins's (1981, 2004) work on the role of emotions in the development of society shows the importance of social position in these processes. In short, our emotional competence may influence our position in a group. Once that position is established, however, it also contributes to future emotional displays of group members. Theodore Kemper (1991) argued that power and status serve as universal emotion elicitors. That is, power and status are the primary causes of emotions in our day-to-day life.

Kemper's theory is called the **power-status approach** to emotions. The theorem is that "a very large class of human emotions results from real, anticipated, imagined, or recollection of outcomes of social relations" (Kemper 1991: 333). Power is defined as the ability to obtain what you want from other people despite resistance, whereas status refers to voluntary compliance to an individual based on her position in a group. Although other aspects of our lives are important to the development and expression of emotion, Kemper argued that power and status are the most important structural determinants of our emotional lives.

Using this approach, higher-status people in society should experience and express different emotions than lower-status people. Research, for instance, suggests that high-power individuals seem to express more anger and contempt, whereas submissive individuals express more fear and surprise—and other people expect those groups to elicit such emotions (Mondillon, Niedenthal, Brauer, Rohmann, Dalle, and Uchida 2005). Higher-status people should also experience more positive emotions such as happiness and security as a result of their positions. The loss and gain of power can also elicit emotions in people (Kemper 1991), a topic that will be addressed in more detail later in this chapter.

A person's gender is an indication of relative status in society. Because women typically have lower status than men, they would be expected to report more negative emotions. In addition, a typical American stereotype is that women are more emotional and emotionally expressive than men. There is some evidence that boys and girls are socialized to express different types of emotion, with boys punished and girls encouraged to express feelings of sadness and fear (Garside and Klimes-Dougan 2002). Mental health research also shows that women are more likely than men to be diagnosed with emotional disorders such as depression (Aneshensel, Rutter, and Lachenbruch 1991; Mirowsky and Ross 1995; Turner, Wheaton, and Lloyd 1995). But other research shows very little difference in the types of intensity of emotion expressed by men and women. Simon and Nath (2004), for instance, found no difference in the frequency with which men and women report anger or shame, though they did find that women report more sadness than men. The disparities in these findings may simply reflect the specific types of emotions being studied (with women reporting more of some emotions and not others) or reflect a labeling process such that women are assumed to be more emotional than men, regardless of their actual feelings.

Feeling Rules and Norms

Power and status are only two ways in which societal conditions affect our day-to-day lives. Like other aspects of social life, there are norms or expectations about how to feel in different situations. Arlie Russell Hochschild (1983) called the norms that govern our emotional lives "feeling rules." **Feeling rules** tell us how we *should* feel in different social interactions. Feeling rules are different than behavioral rules because they are rarely codified. We may say that some behaviors, such as robbery or murder, are inappropriate for people to do and thus codify these behavioral boundaries into a law. The same is not done in the arena of emotions.

Although we do not codify rules regarding emotional expectations, Hochschild (1983) argued that we can discover these rules in a variety of ways. Much like the breaching experiments discussed in chapter 2, the best way to know when feeling rules exist is to attempt to break those rules. We may receive "rule reminders" from friends and family when we do not "feel" appropriately. For instance, if you act depressed at your college graduation, someone might say, "You should be happy today! Most people feel a sense of pride when they accomplish something like this," reminding you that you are not feeling what most people (are thought to) feel in similar situations. Another way that people give rule reminders is to assume how you are feeling in a particular situation. You may be at a school football game that is going particularly well for your team when a friend from another school approaches you and says, "You must be totally excited for your team!" Many women are told when they give birth to a baby, "This is so wonderful!" and "Congratulations!" Yet it can be a time of fear and anxiety, exhaustion, and generally negative emotions. Although the comments are well meaning and certainly make sense when we consider them within the context of American culture, where motherhood is highly valued, they may fuel new mothers' anxieties that they don't feel the "right" emotions of joy and excitement.

Emotion Work

Hochschild (1983) also proposed that certain jobs in our economy require **emotion work,** the generation of prescribed emotion to meet the demands of a job. Emotion work is particularly prevalent in service jobs such as flight attendants, nurses, and other professions in which workers are expected to feel and display certain emotions toward their clients or customers. For instance, nurses are expected to feel sympathy toward their patients, and attendants are expected to act positively toward customers. Feeling rules associated with emotion work often conflict with people's actual feelings, producing a sense of strain, especially if they blame themselves for the deviance. This conflict is similar to having differences in societal norms and our own personal values in a given situation, suggesting both attitudinal and emotional outcomes are structured in society.

The commodification of emotions is associated with a concept called **McDonaldization,** the process of hyperrationality of the service workforce, applying assembly-line techniques to interpersonal work (Ritzer 1993). Although all jobs probably require some sort of emotion work, modern Western economies rely heavily on service work, interaction between people rather than producing goods in factories. Consider a well-paid marketing expert. She may be a professional, but she must deal with clients (confident and positive) while submitting proposals and results to her boss (compliant) and colleagues (friendly and helpful). Emotion work is essential to achieving success in the modern professional world, leading one psychologist to argue that emotional intelligence, or our ability to control and employ emotions in our social environments, is as important as intellectual abilities on the job (Goleman 1997).

The Socioemotional Economy

Candace Clark (1987) extended the concept of feeling rules by arguing that there is a socioemotional economy governed by feeling rules. The **socioemotional economy** is a system for regulating emotional resources among people. This economy links individuals into larger networks of people. Sympathy may seem to be a natural process, but Clark's research highlights the amazing social fabric underlying the exchange of sympathy between people. She argued that sympathy, like many emotions, requires at least two people, a sympathizer and a sympathizee, someone to give the sympathy and someone to receive it.

Clark found that there are different expectations of the sympathizer and the sympathizee, depending on the social situation. There are two basic principles of sympathy etiquette. First, you give sympathy only when it is appropriate. The person must be worthy of sympathy, and you must be the appropriate person to provide sympathy. For instance, if you work at a local grocery store, it may not be appropriate to send flowers to the company's chief executive officer after hearing

People are not only expected to give but also receive sympathy from the people around them, producing a socioemotional economy.

Chapter 10: The Sociology of Sentiment and Emotion

of the death of her son. Second, sympathy should be reciprocated. If someone is nice to you during a difficult time, you are expected to reciprocate that sympathy to them if the appropriate situation arises.

Clark's research established four rules of sympathy etiquette:

1. Do not make false claims to sympathy.
2. Do not claim too much sympathy.
3. Claim some sympathy.
4. Reciprocate to others for the gift of sympathy.

The first rule of sympathy makes sense: Do not try to claim sympathy when you do not deserve it. Perhaps you work with someone who is always complaining about a problem but later learn that she is being dishonest about the problem, perhaps to get attention. This type of behavior empties her **sympathy account,** the amount of sympathy that a person can expect from other people.

Similar to the first rule, the second rule states that a person should not claim too much sympathy. In the previous example, even if she had been honest about all her problems, she may run the risk of using up all of the sympathy credits stored in her account. People may decide to ignore the coworker over time, at best, or make fun of her, at worst.

The third sympathy rule assumes that people should accept some sympathy. If a colleague displays sympathy for some loss you have had, you should admit to the loss and accept her sympathy, perhaps by providing some thanks for her expression of sympathy. On the other hand, you will be expected to return that sympathy to that person in the future, initiating the fourth rule, that sympathy needs to be reciprocated. Some people may try to avoid sympathy from friends and colleagues because they are concerned about having to repay others for their kindness.

Emotion Culture

Emotion culture refers to a society's expectation about how to experience different emotions (see Stearns and Stearns 1986). It represents the fact that individuals in a society learn to experience feelings in a similar way, as our thoughts and behavior. Lofland (1985) studied the cultural conception of grief, arguing that the intensity and duration of grief in a society depends on:

1. How much particular relationships are invested with significance.
2. The mortality rates of the group.
3. How much feelings are controlled.
4. How much individuals are physically isolated from others.

These factors are predicted to interrelate differently in each society over time. For example, some cultures may have high mortality rates, making people invest less emotional energy in a child (because they fear imminent loss). In contrast, in the contemporary United States, which has a relatively low infant mortality rate and few children per family compared with the past, children are viewed as emotionally priceless (Zelizer 1985).

Sociologists have also tried to understand the cultural context of emotions. Ann Swidler (2001), for instance, studied how Americans conceive of love and relationships. To Swidler, culture is like a "tool kit" that people use to help decide how to act. For example, people use their culture to define love and what it means to be in a good relationship. Swidler's research showed that Americans continue to hold two conflicting views of love, one that focuses on the mythic aspects of love found in novels and movies and another view of love that emphasizes the realistic aspects of relationships. Love is also seen as something voluntary and free, a matter of individual choice, making commitment difficult for people because they do not feel constrained by culture norms to stay in relationships. She found that Americans use the mythic view of love to initiate and end relationships, such as deciding when to marry and when to divorce someone. However, people use the realistic view of love to maintain committed relationships on a day-to-day basis. That is, if we want to marry someone, we might focus on the great feelings that are produced in the presence of the other person. Similarly, we may argue that those feelings have disappeared as we explain to our friends the reasons for a divorce.

Section Summary

The second section of this chapter applied the social structure and personality perspective to answer the questions: How does our status in society affect our use of emotions? What norms govern the use of emotions in different social settings? First, emotions are affected by our positions in society in that people with higher positions possess the ability to express different types of emotions than people in lower positions. Second, there are a number of feeling rules and norms about the appropriate expression of emotion. Hence, the social structure and personality perspective emphasizes how society structures the type of emotions individuals express at any given time.

GP | Group Processes and Emotions

Man, that really made me mad. I worked my tail off on that group paper but only got a B. That's just not fair; I worked harder on that paper than the other guys, and they got Bs too!

—Justine, junior Physics major

The group processes perspective seeks to study the development of emotion in group contexts. Like symbolic interactionism, group processes theory and research views emotions as stemming from interactions between individuals. Group processes scholars also incorporate the importance of statuses and norms in the development and expression of emotions among people. Some of the earliest work on group processes found that group interaction requires some level of socio-emotional leadership to achieve its goals (Bales 1965).

In Justine's case, a sense of unfairness produces feelings of anger. Her desire for parity is an essential component of the exchange processes reviewed in previous chapters. We are not only motivated to maintain a balance between what we contribute to a group and what we get out of it, but a host of emotions are also associated with these processes. Group processes work on emotions tries to uncover the conditions under which different emotions are produced during interactions between people.

Feelings and Social Exchange

Imagine a situation in which you have competed in a race only to lose narrowly to another runner. At first, you congratulate the runner and then go on to receive the second place award. However, you later receive news that the winner had cheated in some way. How do you think that this news will make you feel? You will most likely see the loss as unfair, perhaps generating a sense of disgust and anger. If you cannot change the ruling of the race, that may also introduce a sense of frustration.

We reviewed social exchange theory in chapter 4. One of the primary principles of social exchange theory is that individuals expect reciprocity in their interaction with other people. If we help other people, we expect about the same level of help some time in the future. Researchers using social exchange theory study the effects of exchange processes on individuals' emotions. In particular, exchange researchers want to know people's emotional reactions when they get too much or too little out of a series of exchanges. They also try to determine how the rules of the exchange, the procedure by which rewards are given in a group, influence our emotional reactions to an interaction. In other words, it is not only who wins the game but also how the game is played.

A basic proposition of exchange theory is that emotions are affected by what people get out of their social interactions (Molm 1991) (see Box 10.2). In general, we are more satisfied when we get more than when we get less. Trying to predict the emotions people will feel based on the rewards they get, however, becomes more complex than simply saying that those who get more will feel more positive emotions. Imagine going to court for a speeding ticket and learning that the fine has been dropped. Now imagine working eight hours one day at a job, only to have your boss tell you at the end of the day that he has decided not to pay you for your time. Your reaction to an outcome of "nothing" in those two situations would likely be very different—happy in the first situation, furious in the second. Social exchange theory proposes that our emotions are based on what we actually get in a situation as compared to some comparison referent. That comparison might be what we expected to get, what we think we should get, or what other people in similar situations have gotten. These comparisons are often a matter of fairness, or justice (Jasso 1980).

Box 10.2	Aggression and Love in Psychology

Two traditional areas of research in psychological social psychology are love and aggression. One popular psychology theory argues that love has several different forms. Robert Sternberg developed the Triangular Theory of Love. This theory suggests that love has three basic components that can be combined to form eight types of love. The three basic components of love are intimacy (emotional closeness), passion (physical arousal), and commitment (the promise to maintain the relationship). Nonlove is when all three of these factors are not present in a relationship. This model is important because it can be applied to many different types of relationships, including family, friends, and lovers.

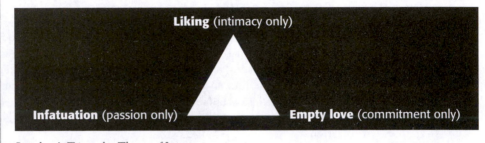

Sternberg's Triangular Theory of Love

Aggression refers to the intentional harm of one person by another. One traditional explanation of aggression is the frustration–aggression hypothesis that argues that all aggression results from frustration that results from the blocking of a goal. Hence, if you are driving to work and someone cuts you off, thus blocking your goal of getting to work, it will likely cause you a sense of frustration, leading you to act aggressively to resolve this emotion. This aggression may also be displaced on an individual other than the one who obstructed your plans.

These theories of love and aggression emphasize individual processes. They also assume a universal quality that can be applied to love and aggression in different cultures and at different times. Some sociologists may agree with these models, but others, notably interactionists, focus on the fluid nature of emotions, that they are constructed over time. Hence, the meaning of love may vary by place and time.

Justice and Emotion

Social exchange research often occurs in settings in which members of a group contribute to a group effort and are rewarded for their efforts. For instance, you may be asked to solve problems for your group. If you are particularly good at solving those problems, you might think you should be rewarded more than someone who has produced less for the group. Traditionally, exchange theorists propose that any imbalanced exchange should produce a negative emotion. Getting less reward for your work than you deserve may be met with anger, whereas getting more than you deserve may produce a sense of guilt.

There are at least two ways in which the fairness of exchange processes may affect your emotions. Beliefs about the fairness of what people get is called **distributive justice.** If you believe that the amount of money you and your coworkers make is fair, then you feel that there is distributive justice. However, people may also be concerned about the procedures used to decide the distribution of goods. You may think that the outcomes are fair but that the procedures used to decide the outcomes are suspect. Beliefs about the fairness of the methods used to make distributions is called **procedure justice.**

In terms of distributive justice, research shows that people get angry when they give more than they get out of an exchange (Smith-Lovin 1995). Guilt is generally expected when people get more out of an exchange than they contribute, but research in this area has been inconsistent, sometimes showing guilt and sometimes not (Hegtvedt and Killian 1990; Homans 1974). In some cases, people may feel a positive emotion as a result of getting more out of an interaction than they contribute (Hegtvedt 1990; Smith-Lovin 1995). In other cases, people feel guilty when they get more than their contributions merit. Finally, perceived fairness regarding procedural justice generally produces positive feelings about negotiations and helps relieve negative emotions about the outcomes of the exchanges between people (Hegtvedt and Killian 1999).

Status and Emotion

Earlier in this chapter we discussed the importance of power and status on our emotions. People who gain status develop a sense of pride, whereas losing status creates shame. Expectation states theory (see chapter 4) focuses on the role of status in group relationships. If exchange processes represent the fundamental way in which individuals interact with one another, our status in a group influences those exchange processes.

The discussion of expectation states theory in chapter 4 made clear that group interactions go differently for high-status group members than for low-status group members. Individuals with high status in groups talk more, have their performances evaluated more highly, are asked more for their inputs, and have more influence over group decisions. In short, high status comes with perks. One outcome of this is that high-status group members experience more positive emotions. Lucas (1999) carried out a study in which he randomly assigned some high-performing workers in groups to high-status positions by giving them titles indicating their competence. He found that the high performers who received the high-status titles enjoyed future interactions more than did those high performers who did not receive the titles. Other research (e.g., Kemper 1991; Lovaglia and Houser 1996) supports this basic finding: High-status group members experience more positive emotion than do low-status group members.

High- and low-status group members differ not only in their emotional experiences, but also in their emotional expressions. Although group members of all statuses experience emotions, these emotions can be either suppressed or expressed. High-status group members, compared to low-status members, are freer to openly express their negative emotions (Ridgeway and Johnson 1990). In this way, social structure constrains the expression of emotion, with low-status group members facing pressure to not display the negative emotions they are more likely to feel.

Power and Emotion

As we discussed, emotion is affected by what we get from our social interactions. In general, people who receive more feel more positive emotion than people who get less. Power is the ability to get what we want, even if other people want to stop us from getting it. As a result, we should expect power to affect emotional reactions.

Power comes from a different source than does status. Status in a group is based on esteem or respect. For example, you will likely defer to a doctor on medical matters because you respect her judgment. People with power might be respected, but they can get what they want even when they are not. Suppose that your boss at work tells you to do something. You may not like your boss, and you may not want to comply with her request, but if you don't do it, she has the power to fire you.

Power in exchange comes from being structurally positioned to essentially demand compliance from other people. Edward Lawler and his colleagues (Lawler 2001; Lawyer, Thye, and Yoon 2000; Lawler and Yoon 1993) have developed a program of theory and research on the emotions that result from exchange relationships. They proposed that people feel positive emotion in exchange relationships when they feel a sense of control in those relationships.

Imagine that three students—Jorge, Susan, and Michael—are all in the same difficult class. The students sometimes share notes and discuss the class. However, of the three, only Susan has a clear understanding of the material. As a result, Jorge and Michael depend on her more than she does on either of them, and Susan will likely feel a greater sense of control. The work of Lawler and his colleagues suggests that she will experience more positive emotions in the interactions than will Jorge and Michael.

A question that is of fundamental interest to group processes scholars, and to sociologists more generally, is what binds people to their social relationships. If we can understand what keeps people in their exchange relationships with others, then we will have solved a basic problem of social order: We will better understand why societies and the groups in them form and remain stable.

The work of Lawler and his colleagues shows that positive emotions bind people to their social relationships. In other words, when people feel positive emotions in their relationships with other people, they become committed to those relationships. Moreover, Lawler and colleagues have shown that relationships characterized by equal power are especially likely to engender positive emotion and commitment. Imagine what would likely happen in the study group example—Susan knows the material much better than Jorge or Michael. If the students are only tied to each other based on being in the same class, would you expect their study relationship to continue throughout the semester? Probably not. Susan would likely resent giving more than her fair share to the group, and Jorge and Michael might feel guilty about not contributing.

Now imagine a group of two students who both have a pretty good understanding of the course material. These students meet regularly to discuss the course, share notes, and so on. Would you expect the students to continue meeting throughout the semester? Probably. The students have equal power, and they derive equal benefits from the relationship. According to Lawler and his colleagues, they would likely feel positive emotion and develop a sense of commitment to the relationship.

Section Summary

Group processes research was applied in this section to answer the question: How do group settings affect our emotions? Group contexts are important to understanding emotions in two ways. First, the principles of social exchange theory suggest that individuals in groups seek justice and fairness. If people do not perceive justice, especially if they feel underrewarded, negative emotions result. Second, our position in groups can affect our emotions. More-powerful people, for instance, experience more-positive emotions because of their ability to control group interactions. Positive emotions also help to sustain group interactions.

Bringing It All Together

Without love, you really don't have anything when you think about it. Your friends and family don't mean anything to you and you have no reason not to hurt someone else. Even your job becomes a bore without some liking for it.

—Janelle, sophomore Anthropology major

We have applied the three perspectives of sociological social psychology to understand the role of emotions in society. Emotions can be used as barriers to civil societies, a fuel for feuds and disputes among people. However, we have also seen the important role that emotions can play in the development of society. Janelle's analysis of love reflects the positive impact of emotions in our lives—giving people and activities purpose and meaning. A considerable amount of work using the symbolic interactionist perspective focuses on the social construction of emotional states. From this perspective, emotions serve to help construct and maintain society by providing cues for how to behave during interactions and as a motivation to participate in society.

The social structure and personality perspective shows that emotions are not necessarily irrational. Research and theory from this perspective emphasizes the way that emotional outcomes are structured by social arrangements with positions and social norms governing the type and degree to which emotions are expressed. Finally, the group processes perspectives studies emotions in group contexts, showing how emotions both reflect group position and affect relationships between group members. Together, these perspectives tie individuals' emotional expressions to larger social conditions.

Summary

1. Sociological perspectives on emotion emphasize the cybernetic approach to the study of emotion, that emotions radiate upward from individual-level interactions to maintain social structures as well as downward, when social structure helps to shape our emotions.

2. Symbolic interactionists view the learning of emotions like any aspect of social life, through interaction with other people. The sociocentric model of emotional socialization argues that the primary means of learning about emotions comes from social instruction, whereas affect control theory argues that people use emotions as signals as to how well they are performing their role in a given situation.

3. People use emotional scripts and cues to help use emotions in day-to-day life. The theory of interaction ritual chains emphasizes the role of emotions in maintaining macrosociological social institutions.

4. The power-status approach to emotions says that emotions result from real, anticipated, imagined, or recollection of outcomes from social interactions. The gain or loss of power and status are primary ways in which our position affects our emotional life.

5. The norms that govern our emotional lives are called feeling rules. We may receive "rule reminders" from friends and family when we do not "feel" appropriately. Emotion work refers to the generation of prescribed emotion to meet the demands of a job. The commodification of emotions is associated with a concept called *McDonaldization*.

6. The socioemotional economy is a system for regulating emotional resources among people that links individuals into larger networks of people. Sympathy is an important example of this economy. Emotion culture refers to a society's expectation about how to experience different emotions.

7. According to the group processes perspective, there are at least two ways in which exchange processes may affect your emotions: the concern over getting what is fair out of the group and the way in which distributions are made in a group.

8. Emotions can also affect status relationships in group exchanges such that higher-status people are freer to express certain emotions than lower status people.

Activity: Element of affect control theory referring to how a person's sentiment toward an object is lively or quiet.

Affect: An evaluative component of an emotion.

Cybernetic approach: The study of emotion that assumes that social conditions shape our emotions, and in turn, our emotions act to maintain social structures.

Distributive justice: In exchange theory, it is the beliefs about the fairness of what people get.

Emotion culture: A society's expectation about how to experience different emotions.

Emotion work: The generation of prescribed emotion in order to meet the demands of a job.

Emotional cues: Information about when and what emotions are appropriate in a given social setting.

Emotional energies: A heightened sense of excitement produced by a feeling of belonging in society.

Emotional label: Element of emotion referring to the terms we use to label our feelings.

Emotional scripts: Expectations about when and how to act excited or angry, or any other emotion.

Emotions: Feelings that incorporate situational cues, physiological changes, expressive gestures, and an emotion label.

Evaluation: Element of affect control theory referring to how a person's sentiment toward an object is good or bad.

Expressive gestures: Element of an emotion referring to the indications we give of the emotion we are experiencing.

Feeling rules: Tell us how we should feel in different social interactions.

Feelings: Internal states associated with a particular emotion.

Fundamental sentiments: Enduring emotional meanings in a given society.

Interaction ritual: The exchange of symbols and emotion between individuals essential to maintaining society.

McDonaldization: The process of hyperrationality of the service workforce, applying assembly-line techniques to interpersonal work.

Mood: A diffuse emotional state that lasts a relatively long period of time.

Physiological changes: Element of emotion referring to the changes in our body that reflect the emotion in a given situation.

Power-status approach: The study of emotions based on the idea that human emotions result from real, anticipated, imagined, or recollected outcomes of social relations.

Potency: Element of affect control theory referring to how a person's sentiment toward an object is powerful or powerless.

Primary emotions: Physiologically grounded emotions that we inherit through evolutionary processes, including anger, fear, depression, and satisfaction.

Procedure justice: In exchange theory, it is the beliefs about the fairness of the methods used to make distributions.

Secondary emotions: Emotions that derive from primary emotions when we attach varying meanings to primary emotions.

Sentiment: A feeling that has been given meaning by society.

Situational cues: Element of emotion that tells when and what emotion is appropriate in a given social interaction.

Sociocentric model of emotional socialization: Theory that argues that the primary means of learning about emotions comes from social instruction, primarily through family, friends, and schooling.

Socioemotional economy: A system for regulating emotional resources among people.

Sympathy account: The amount of sympathy that a person can expect from other people.

Theory of interaction ritual chains: Theory that emphasizes the role of emotions in maintaining macrosociological institutions.

Transient sentiments: Sentiments unique to specific interactions.

Discussion Questions

1. How many different words can you come up with to describe the emotions of love, frustration, or anger? That is, how many different dimensions of a "feeling" can you come up with?

2. Think of a social situation in which an emotion was present (e.g., a funeral or party). How do you think other people would have reacted if you acted with no emotion?

3. To what degree do you think that emotions are innate or learned? Why?

4. Discuss some of the ways you have felt when someone treated you unfairly. What were some of things you did, if anything, to manage your feelings?

Collective Behavior

I knew almost nothing about basketball. I was not even sure how many players are on a basketball team. Nonetheless, when my daughters were playing high school basketball in rural Illinois "basketball country," I shouted, cheered, and booed along with hundreds of other fans in steamy gyms on many cold winter nights in spite of the fact that I know so little about the game! I felt strong allegiance with the parents of our players and I also began to feel animosity toward the opposing fans. I often left the gym with sore hands from clapping loudly with others to try to urge our team on to victory.

—Steve, nontraditional student

Most of the earlier chapters focused on the influence of groups and society on individuals. In this chapter, we will review social psychological theories and research that try to explain large group behavior. Steve reflects on how engrossed he became while watching his daughters' basketball games. Steve was not a basketball fan outside the stadium. However, when he was at the game, he could not resist succumbing to the exaggerated emotions of the crowd. What drove this change in his thoughts and feelings? Of course he was motivated to support his daughters. But what other social processes were going on that could account for his "basketball fever"?

Sociologists have studied sports crowds and many other types of collective events, including celebrations, ceremonies, riots, fads, disasters, demonstrations, and social movements. This chapter will provide you with a brief overview of the theories and research associated with the study of collective behavior. Earlier we defined collective behavior as action or behavior of people in groups or crowds, usually as a reaction to an event or to express a common sentiment (Rohlinger and Snow 2003). This behavior typically includes situations in which individuals act differently in group contexts than they would in ordinary environments. Collective behavior can take the form of protests, riots, or panics. It may also include fads and trends in which large numbers of people become obsessed with an object or idea for a period of time.

The term *collective behavior* came into use in the 1920s when William Henry Prince (1920) discussed "collective behavior" in his study of the great Halifax, Nova Scotia explosion of 1917. The first introductory sociology text ever published, Park and Burgess's *Introduction to the Science of Sociology* (1921) also included a chapter on collective behavior. Although crowds are viewed by sociologists as a form of collective behavior, one of the earliest books written about crowds, Charles Mackay's (1852) *Memoirs of Extraordinary Popular Delusions and the Madness of Crowds,* never used the term *collective behavior.* Likewise, Gustave LeBon (1960, originally 1895), who is often credited as the "father of collective behavior," never used the term when he wrote his book *The Crowd.* The early work of Mackay and LeBon focused on crowd excitement and included many discussions of the fickleness, sentimentality, mania, and amorality of crowds. This treatment of crowds as irrational entities came to dominate most of the first century of sociological writing about the crowd and collective behavior.

In 1968, Carl Couch challenged these views when he suggested crowds are no more or no less bizarre than other social systems (Couch 1968). Evidence to support his view was soon forthcoming. Researchers working through the newly established Disaster Research Center at Ohio State University began to regularly find that survivors of disasters were capable of caring for themselves and others and restoring order to their communities rather quickly; they did not stampede from danger or become helpless because of emotional shock, as earlier stereotypes suggested.

In the 1970s Clark McPhail led teams of observers to demonstrations, civil disorders, sporting events, and shopping malls to systematically observe crowds. McPhail's teams utilized multimedia data collection techniques. They first used notepads and check sheets for recording data manually and later augmented these with film and video cameras. Simultaneous observations were made at several locations in or near crowds. After studying and comparing data from hundreds of events, McPhail concluded that much of what had been previously written about crowds and collective behavior was not accurate (Miller 2000). To distinguish his work from earlier treatments, he began to refer to crowds as gatherings and to write about collective action within gatherings. By the 1980s, sociologists generally began to use the term **collective action** to reflect the seemingly purposive nature of people's behavior when they collectively celebrate, mourn, worship, protest, compete in athletics, or confront disasters.

Another concept related to collective behavior and action is social movements. Blumer (1972) defined **social movements** as collective action designed to produce new social orders. Hence, collective action may turn into a social movement, but social movements incorporate large-scale goals and plans that often exceed the temporary nature of most other forms of collective behavior or action. This chapter will review theories and research related to the concepts of collective behavior, collective action, and social movements. Specifically, we will address the following questions:

- Do people act differently in large groups than when they are alone? How do crowds contribute to the development of mass hysteria?

- What theories explain individuals' rational behavior in large groups?

- What structural conditions affect crowd behaviors?

- What are the phases of collective behavior found in large social movements? What kinds of behavior actually occur during a period of collective behavior?

- How do group and individual motivations interact in social movements?

SI | Constructing Collective Behavior

It will be remarked that among the special characteristics of crowds there are several— such as impulsiveness, irritability, incapacity to reason, the absence of judgment, and of the critical spirit, the exaggeration of the sentiments, and others besides— which are almost always observed in beings belonging to inferior forms of evolution—in women, savages, and children, for instance.

—Gustave LeBon (1960, originally 1895:36)

The French Revolution (1789–1794) is associated with some of the most ghastly behavior by groups in the history of humankind. Mobs of French citizens would go through the streets of Paris, collecting people to be killed in the name of the Revolution. A state of paranoia existed in France at the time. Although LeBon lived after the French Revolution, he sought to understand why such "cultured" people could become like dogs killing their victims in packs. The French went from being among the most "developed" and "civilized" peoples of the world to individuals willing to commit the most barbaric acts.

Since LeBon's writings, social scientists have tried to understand the social conditions that produce such changes in individuals. Some contemporary perspectives stem from LeBon's early work, emphasizing the emotional changes in people as a result of being in a crowd. Other people emphasize the rational aspects of crowd behavior. The first part of this chapter will examine ways in which crowds have been shown to transform individuals' thoughts, feelings, and behavior. Later sections will review current research on crowd behavior.

Mass Hysteria Theory

Everyday life is composed of a wide variety of collective events, such as high school basketball games, that are characterized by the joined expression of intense feeling. Early writers such as Mackay (1852) found such "crowd madness" a worthy subject

Traditional research on collective behavior emphasizes the irrational behaviors in protest groups and riots.

for pioneering work. LeBon was struck by the even more spectacular, emotion-laden events that were part of revolutions that overthrew the monarchies of Europe. The concern for collectively experienced and expressed emotion is the basis of the earliest general theory in the field of collective behavior.

LeBon probed the workings of crowds, representative forms of government, and social movements throughout his writing career. In bold terms, LeBon frequently wrote that all crowds exert an inherently negative influence on people. This thinking is the basis of **mass hysteria theory** (also called contagion theory), in which individuals in crowds lose their ability to think and act rationally. LeBon describes groups' influence on their members as a rapidly transmitted, **contagious mental unity,** a sense of a shared emotional bond that emerges whenever people interact in a group—be it a revolutionary street crowd or a parliament—making individuals act more on animalist emotions than reason. For LeBon, contagious mental unity was the root cause of the horrors he witnessed during the Paris riots of 1871, referring to situations in which people are overcome with a shared emotion in a crowd.

Like other writers of his time, LeBon freely adopted terminology drawn from Darwin's essays on biological evolution. LeBon stated that the contagious mental unity of crowds reduces the mental capacity of enlightened and cultured people to the level of "those inferior forms of evolution," such as "women, savages, and children." The three main ingredients of contagion theory are

1. **Intensity of behavior**—situations in crowds in which people quickly lose their inhibitions to act, and the tempo of their behavior increases.

2. **Homogeneity of mood and action**—people in crowds exhibit a shared willingness to follow suggestions, as in a hypnotic trance.

3. **Irrational behavior**—when people within crowds act without reason; they are incapable of respect for social standards, conventions, and institutions.

With these three ingredients, the crowd is unable to sustain focus and moves rapidly from one object or idea to another. Increased intensity is accompanied by homogeneity of mood and action in which people exhibit a shared willingness to follow suggestions, which LeBon described as similar to a hypnotic trance. Finally, the result of these processes, according to mass hysteria theory, is that this contagious mental unity overcomes individuals' rational capabilities. People in the crowd do not reflect on outcomes of their action; perceptions are distorted, and feelings of power emerge that become the basis of attacks on authorities or unfortunate victims. Mass hysteria theory proposes that without critical ability and powers of reflection, people within crowds are incapable of respect for social standards, conventions, and institutions—irrational behavior, when people act without reason, is characteristic of the crowd.

LeBon warned that he saw society entering an "age of crowds" that would be like a new Dark Ages. He cautioned against revolutionary crowds rioting in the streets and called our attention to special types of crowds: criminal juries, electoral bodies, and parliamentary assemblies. In LeBon's France, the dispensing of justice had once been the sole responsibility of magistrates appointed by the king. After the French Revolution, criminal juries were part of the judicial system, and unlike a magistrate or judge, the jury, in LeBon's view, displayed "suggestibility" and had only a "slight capacity for reasoning." Intellectuals or tradesmen—it made no difference—were each likely to deliver faulty verdicts.

LeBon argued that voters, or electoral crowds, now invested with the power to elect people to office, had a pronounced absence of critical spirit and aptitude for reasoning. Voters in this view responded best to flattery and fantastic promises. For LeBon, universal suffrage brought society's "inferior elements" into the political process.

From LeBon's point of view, the work of parliaments is always inferior to that of isolated statesmen and specialists. The parliamentary assemblies of different nations produce strikingly similar debates, votes, and ill-conceived decisions. He argued that all parliaments have an unavoidable tendency to produce financial waste and to destroy individual liberty. For LeBon, juries, electorates, and parliaments have the power of tyrants but the wisdom of fools.

Although LeBon described the effects of contagious mental unity, he did not explain how this mental unity emerges in crowds. For this reason, the famous sociologist Robert K. Merton (1960) characterized LeBon as a problem finder rather than a problem solver. Sigmund Freud, a contemporary and critic of LeBon, attempted to explain contagious mental unity as the result of crowd members' unconscious love of the crowd leader. This psychoanalytic explanation, set forth in *Group Psychology and the Analysis of the Ego* (Freud 1945, originally 1921), has had relatively little impact within the field of collective behavior, but there have been other attempts to account for contagious mental unity.

Herbert Blumer and Circular Reaction

In 1934, 39 years after *The Crowd* was published, symbolic interactionist Herbert Blumer wrote an essay titled "Outline of Collective Behavior" (Blumer 1972). Blumer's "Outline" is not as value laden as LeBon's *The Crowd*. For example, contagious mental unity is not described as similar to the mental processes of "inferior forms of evolution." Unlike *The Crowd*, Blumer's "Outline" is an objective classification and analysis of crowd-related phenomena. More so than LeBon, Blumer attempted to describe social-psychological mechanisms through which mental unity develops. Blumer also classified different types of crowds.

Remarkable events, such as the destruction of the World Trade Center and Pentagon on September 11, 2001, create tensions that dispose people to gather together and then to anxiously move about in a seemingly aimless and random fashion. Blumer (1972) called such apprehensive behavior **milling.** Blumer pointed out that milling is not a feature of all crowds, and that milling can vary in intensity.

According to Blumer, intense milling can transform human interaction in a fundamental way. He stated that there is ordinarily a largely covert, **interpretive phase** to human interaction; that is, people respond to one another by interpreting the other's gestures and remarks, rehearsing or visualizing a possible response, and then conveying a response. This phase of interaction acts as a buffer that lengthens the time between stimulus and response, thus allowing people to differentiate themselves from others by composing responses rather than mirroring, in a simple stimulus–response fashion, the other's action. Finally, it is within the interpretive phase of interaction that rationality resides, where outcomes of action are envisioned, and where alternative lines of action are compared.

Under conditions of intense milling, the interpretive phase of the act is disrupted; in some situations, such as a crowded gym during a game, it may become so noisy that people cannot "hear themselves think." As the interpretive phase of interaction deteriorates, the buffer effect is lost, and behavior becomes intense and rapid, differentiation becomes more difficult, and people act alike—unanimity in mood and action prevails. Finally, with the interpretive phase of interaction gone, people become suggestible and irrational. Blumer described this state as **circular reaction** and called it a natural mechanism of collective behavior.

For LeBon, crowds are inclined toward destruction and foolishness. Blumer (1972) presented a more elaborate classification of crowds based on focus and internal cohesiveness. **Acting crowds** develop a focus, or goal, and act with unity to achieve the goal. An example of the acting crowd is a throng of townspeople who assemble a brass band and hastily build a speaker's platform in anticipation of a surprise visit from their governor. An **expressive crowd** lacks a goal and is primarily just a setting for tension release, often through rhythmical action such as applause, dancing, or singing. An audience offering a standing ovation at the end of a concert, for example, is an expressive crowd.

Blumer stated that aggregates of people dispersed over large geographic areas can, under conditions of social unrest, assume some of the characteristics of compact acting and expressive crowds. A **public** is an aggregate of people, often from the same social class, who are concerned with a specific issue. A public discusses ways to meet the issue, such as a community deciding on a school bond referendum. A **mass** is composed of anonymous individuals from many social strata; it is loosely organized and does not engage in discussion or interaction. Blumer cited the California gold rush of 1849 and other human migrations as examples of mass behavior.

Blumer (1972) emphasized how collective behavior evolves into new forms of group and institutional conduct. Within crowds, publics, and masses appear new expectations, values, conceptions of rights and obligations, tastes, and moods on which new social systems are founded. For LeBon, crowds bring about the downfall of civilizations; for Blumer, crowds play an important part in the development of new forms of social life.

Collective Identity

One underlying assumption of the crowd-transformation perspective is that there is some sort of connection between group members making people in a crowd less individualistic than in other social settings. This sense of "oneness" is important to understanding why people join and continue to participate in collective activity (Rohlinger and Snow 2003). Although we no longer speak of "contagious mental unity," the basic idea continues to be an important aspect of research in collective behavior. **Collective identity** refers to an individual's sense of connection with a larger community or group (Polletta and Jasper 2001).

Collective identity is important in every stage of collective behavior. First, movements may emerge because individuals from varying backgrounds develop a sense of connection resulting from shared frustration over an issue (Polletta and Jasper 2001). For instance, you may have a strong concern over environmental or gay-rights issues, drawing you to affiliate with people who have similar convictions. These types of social movements have been dubbed **new social movements,** those movements that center around specific issues rather than class-based political mobilizations (e.g., workers' rights). Our sense of collective identity may also help in the recruitment and commitment to a cause. Members of a movement may use this sense of connection—this collective identity—to motivate others to join the cause. It may also serve to motivate current members to become more active in the movement. A member may share his or her experience helping to change policy, giving people a sense of hope in achieving their goals.

Collective identities also help movement leaders make choices regarding the direction and goals of a movement (Polletta and Jasper 2001). Collective identities help define "who we are." A pacifist group, for instance, will likely choose a nonviolent sit-in as a protest rather than aggressive tactics to maintain congruence between their goals and methods. Finally, identities play a role in the outcomes of social movements, either as a part of the movement itself (e.g., self-help movements) or as a way of transforming the culture, giving greater legitimacy to the movement or the activists' senses of self over time. Hence, collective identities can serve to transform a group's members and the larger culture.

Applications and Critiques of Mass Hysteria Theory

Mackay's *Memoirs of Extraordinary Popular Delusions and the Madness of Crowds* and LeBon's *The Crowd* are compelling reading and have been in print almost continuously since they were first published. Each portrays crowds, and the people that comprise them, in a negative light. At best, crowds are seen as creating states of madness or euphoria. At its worst, people in crowds are seen as prone to violence and ready to attack anyone or anything that thwarts their aims, however transitory. This negative view of the crowd has greatly influenced the sociological study of the crowd to the present day. Researchers have used the terms "contagious mental unity," "social contagion," and "circular reaction," as well as the more popular term "mass hysteria," to refer to the theoretical approach that guides their studies. Today, sociologists are likely to use terms such as "mass psychogenic illness," "mass sociogenic illness," and "deindividuation" to refer to negative emotional transformation in the crowd (Miller 2000). McPhail (1991) identified this approach to the study of the crowd and collective behavior as the "transformation perspective." What do decades of research from the transformation perspective tell us about the crowd? A brief summary follows.

First, the transformation approach to the study of the crowd has yielded surprisingly few empirical studies of crowds. Most sociological studies or accounts of mass hysteria, on examination, turn out to be reports of events that were first identified as hysteria by police, firefighters, health-care workers, or journalists. Sociologists later used these sources to support their discussion of crowds and hysteria (Miller 2000).

An extensive search of sociological sources yields only nine empirical studies of mass hysteria, none of which were designed to directly observe milling or circular reaction during the event (Miller 2000). One of the earliest studies examined peoples' reaction to the 1938 *War of the Worlds* Halloween radio broadcast in which radio broadcasters portrayed an invasion of Earth by Martians (Cantril 1940, 1966). The broadcast was designed to sound realistic, using real places and street names. Media accounts of the broadcast suggested that residents fled New York en masse, to escape the alien invasion. Careful study of public reaction, however, showed very little mass hysteria among city residents. Virtually all the listeners who became frightened by the broadcast tuned in about 12 minutes into the broadcast, when the studio actors enacted a realistic-sounding news report from where the spaceship supposedly landed. But only a very small group of residents became panic-stricken by the event. Even those who fled the city primarily got in their cars and went to the homes of friends and family.

Box 11.1   The Case of the Stairway of the Stars Concert

A dozen police cars, fire trucks, and ambulances were parked on the lawn of the Santa Monica Civic Auditorium late on Thursday evening, April 13, 1989. Their flashing lights illuminated the faces of hundreds of people moving about the vehicles. Many of the faces were young, some showed fear, some were crying. Police, firefighters, and paramedics moved among the people on the lawn. Near a medical tent, there were rows of stretchers, and many of them were occupied. It was not an earthquake or a terrorist bomb that had forced one of the largest evacuations in Santa Monica history. The Civic Auditorium had been emptied by what was to be later identified as "mass hysteria."

Nearly a thousand young musicians and singers of the Santa Monica-Malibu Unified School District had rehearsed since ten o'clock that morning for the 40th Annual Stairway of the Stars concert. This was the big concert of the year for band, orchestra, and chorus students in grades four through high school. None of the musicians, or their teachers and parents, had expected this gala event to end in this fashion.

During the afternoon rehearsals, however, students and teachers had complained that the auditorium was hot, stuffy, and "smelled funny." Many students said they had to sit and rest during the day because they had headaches and felt dizzy. At least two students fainted during the day, and several students had been unable to complete rehearsal because of nausea and fever. Even though rehearsals had been difficult and uncomfortable, the classical music concert started on time.

During the concert, however, students continued to experience many flulike symptoms, including headaches, dizziness, weakness, abdominal pains, nausea, and shortness of breath. Spectators also reported experiencing similar discomforts. Toward the end of the Stairway of the Stars program, some performers had collapsed or fainted, and many others were too ill to continue. School officials called an early end to the concert and ordered the evacuation of the auditorium.

Did the students experience a major epidemic or simply some sort of mass hysteria? This incident led many to believe that a mild form of hysteria occurred in which students transferred some physiological symptoms to other people. In other words, people began to believe that they were sick, even when they had no real ailments.

A more recent application of mass hysteria theory is a study of the outbreak of fainting and illness at a large, high school band concert in 1989 (Small, Propper, Randolph, and Spencer 1991). (See Box 11.1 for more information about this event.) Like most studies of mass hysteria, data were obtained by participants and witnesses by using interviews and questionnaires days or weeks after the event. Musicians and spectators at the concert began to complain of various illnesses, including dizziness, abdominal pain, and shortness of breath. In all, of the four to five thousand people present at the concert, about 200 to 250 people became ill. Researchers found that the best predictor of the development of symptoms was observing a friend becoming ill, implying a contagion effect. However, it should be noted that only a small percentage of people in this crowd actually became ill.

Is contagious mental unity sufficient to make excited people believe that Earth is being invaded or to make people physically ill? Can the crowd transform normally rational people into believers that their car windshields are being pitted by radioactive fallout, or that a "mad gasser" is prowling their neighborhood by night? Many people make such claims. However, a critical examination of the data from these studies shows that hysterical symptoms are not very widespread. In some instances less than 1% of potential "victims" reported symptoms, and in no instance did a majority report symptoms. Although mass hysteria studies fail to substantiate the widespread prevalence of hysterical symptoms during these episodes, the studies have shown that there is nearly complete dissemination of information or stories about the symptoms throughout the communities in which these events occur. This general preoccupation, or dissemination of quite unique information throughout a community, does not necessarily reflect the workings of hysteria, nor does it seem to make a later recurrence of such incidents more likely.

Rational Choice in Collective Behavior: Emergent Norm Theory

The challenge of studying collective behavior is that both highly charged, emotional behavior as well as calm, rational behavior can occur in groups. Blumer (1972) tried to address this combination in his theory of circular reaction in which heightened emotions result from lack of communication, not psychosis, in such groups. More recently, theorists have focused on the rational side of behavior in large groups. These researchers tend to call this behavior "collective action" rather than collective behavior (Miller 2000). The idea is that people in groups are purposive in their decisions and actions in everyday life, including larger group events. Several theories and research studies have addressed this topic.

In their book, *Collective Behavior*, Ralph Turner and Lewis Killian (1972) argued that groups constrain their members more than producing some sort of contagious emotional reaction. In short, the **emergent norm theory** of collective behavior focuses on how individuals come to accept the constraints imposed by a group. These norms are conveyed using a variety of techniques, including gestures and verbal statements. This perspective also assumes that individuals enter groups with unique attitudes and perspectives, and they may not act in unison, a feature of the crowd called **differential expression.**

Individuals may change their attitudes as members of a group over time, but this process is relatively rational compared to the contagion models discussed earlier in this chapter. Most group interactions are rational simply because cultures have learned ways to manage those events. Funerals, weddings, and other such events have prescribed roles and norms that govern how people should act in those situations. However, some groups may face situations in which there are no norms to guide individual behavior. Protests and rallies often lack clear guidelines for how members should act. In these cases, behavior may seem irrational because the group has not had the time to develop norms for its members. However, rationality is the norm; that is, groups move toward rationality when possible and fall into irrationality only under conditions that limit the ability of group members to communicate behavioral guidelines.

In one application of emergent norm theory, researchers interviewed over 400 tenants of New York's World Trade Center after the 1993 bombing to assess evacuation behaviors (Aguirre, Wenger, and Vigo 1998). The explosion occurred around noon on February 26, killing six people. Thousands of tenants from the two 110-story buildings had to be evacuated amid fire and smoke-filled stairways. (Electrical power was lost, leaving elevators, lighting, and public address systems inoperable.) The researchers studied the milling behavior of evacuees, assessing the effects of group size and social relationships on their evacuation patterns. They found that most people were in groups, and about half of those groups were large groups with 20 or more people. A considerable amount of milling occurred in these groups, largely rational behavior such as seeking information about the event and advice about what to do. Most found the people around them to be helpful during the event. Less than 10% of the tenants fled the scene without engaging in confirmatory behavior. Hence, even under very threatening conditions, the symbolic interaction (i.e., meaning-making) processes among coworkers were used to help shape appropriate evacuation procedures.

Turner and Killian (1972) also described different types of crowd participants. People bring different backgrounds and resources to an event that may affect their responses. These types include:

1. **Ego-involved participant**—person who participates in a crowd activity because of a strong personal commitment to the issue with which the group is involved.
2. **Concerned participant**—a crowd participant motivated by concern over a group's goal or issue who does not incorporate the issue into her or his identity.
3. **Insecure participant**—a participant looking for direction from the group.
4. **Curiosity seeker**—crowd participant motivated by curiosity about the group or event.

First, there is the type of person who feels a strong personal commitment to the issue with which the group is involved (ego-involved participant). Second, there are people who are not directly involved with a group's goal but participate out of concern over an issue, the concerned participant. The third type of person is insecure, participating merely for the sense of connection with the group. Finally, the fourth type of person participates in the group out of curiosity, the curiosity seeker.

Consider the men who went to the Million Man March in 1995. Some of these men, such as the March's leader, Louis Farrakhan, may have been there because the March represented an important part of who they were. Being an African American is an important aspect of their lives, shaping their thoughts and opinions about the world. There may also have been participants who shared the leaders' concerns over issues facing African-American men, but who did not incorporate the movement into their own senses of self. A third group included people who were looking for a sense of identity in the march; by participating it, they hoped to gain a better sense of who they were as African-American men and fathers. These men can be referred to as insecure participants. Finally, the curiosity seekers simply wanted to know what the march was all about and what the leaders had to say.

Turner and Killian's (1972) work can be referred to as a "dispositional approach" to the study of collective behavior because it emphasizes that individuals may be more or less susceptible to crowd influences, depending on their relationship to the crowd or social movement (Rohlinger and Snow 2003). People more connected to a movement may be more influenced by crowd behavior than those who are simply there out of curiosity.

Value-Added Theory

Another major theoretical perspective in the study of collective behavior is **value-added theory,** associated with Neil Smelser (Miller 2000). From this perspective, there are different types of collective behavior and several social-structural determinants of collective behavior. Hence, to fully understand the causes of a particular event or events, according to the value-added theory, we need to distinguish the type of collective behavior in question and the social conditions surrounding it.

Types of Collective Behavior

According to value-added theory, there are five types of collective behavior: the panic, the craze, the hostile outburst, the norm-oriented social movement, and the value-oriented social movement. One of the reasons it is difficult to predict behaviors in a crowd setting is that the people may be gathered for very different reasons, producing different kinds of outcomes. People in these different types of groupings have different goals and expectations.

Value-added theory emphasizes five different types of crowd settings, ultimately leading to different outcomes:

1. **Panic**—when large numbers of people are overwhelmed with a common fear.
2. **Craze**—when large numbers of people become obsessed with a product, behavior, or idea.
3. **Hostile outbursts**—any type of mass violence or killings.
4. **Norm-oriented social movements**—movements to change the way things are regulated in society.
5. **Value-oriented social movements**—attempts to change the social order of society.

A panic refers to a situation in which large numbers of people are overwhelmed with a common fear. The 1929 stock market crash is often used as an example of a wide-scale panic. A craze simply refers to when large numbers of people become obsessed with something, such as the purchase of a product (e.g., hula hoops) or an activity (e.g., disco dancing). Hostile outbursts include any type of mass violence or killings, such as the Rwandan genocide in the 1990s. Norm-oriented social movements include movements to change the way things are regulated in society, such as the Temperance Movement in the United States during the 1920s. Finally, value-oriented social movements include attempts to change the social order of society—replacing a religious government with a secular democracy, for instance.

From the value-added approach, the role of emotion in collective behavior depends, in part, on the type of group behavior being considered. We would expect the most rational behavior to occur in social movements (both norm- and value-oriented) because they require some level of coordination and communication to succeed. Alternatively, panics, by definition, are based on emotion. Hence, we would predict more emotional behavior in those cases than during social movements.

Determinants of Collective Behavior

According to value-added theory, there are five determinants of collective behavior.

1. There must be **structural conduciveness**—a society must be in a condition amenable to the formation of movements.
2. There must be some level of **structural strain** in society over some issue or problem, the driving force of a collective behavior that provides a motivation to reduce strain.
3. There must be a **generalized belief,** a shared view of the problem and how to resolve the tension.
4. There must be some sort of **mobilization for action,** individuals' reaction to an immediate threat.
5. The **action of social control,** how authorities react to the behavior, determines how an event will be manifested in society.

Specifically, the social control agents in society—such as the government and police—can relieve or instigate fears and anxieties by modifying any of the previous components. For instance, the government may produce a press release to tell citizens not to panic during a crisis event.

According to value-added theory, each determinant of collective behavior must be present for collective action to take place. For instance, the stock market crash of 1929 could not occur in a small hunting-and-gathering society without an advanced economy (structural conduciveness) nor in a society that had not inflated the stock market in a way that required a large-scale shift to correct itself (structural strain). Investors shared the same idea about how to fix the problem: Get out of the market before losing all of their investments (generalized belief).

In the case of the stock market crash, investors reacted to the lack of information available to make investment decisions (mobilization for action), causing them to fear for their financial lives. Finally, the inaction of financial and government leaders to the crisis left people to act on their worst fears (action of social control). The compilation of these determinants led to wide-scale panic producing the worst financial downturns in American history.

Perception Control Theory

Another rational choice approach to collective behavior is perception control theory. **Perception control theory** is based on the premise that people must be able to monitor and interpret one another's behavior in order for collective action to occur. In short, people adjust their actions to make them congruent with what is expected of them. According to McPhail (1994), there are three sources of perception control input:

1. **Independent instructions**—individual decisions.
2. **Interdependent instruction**—assumes that individuals work together to make decisions.
3. **Organizational instruction**—information provided by a movement's leadership or some other outside force.

Each form of instruction occurs naturally in different types and stages of collective behavior. The latter form of instruction is probably most necessary in larger demonstrations where coordination is more difficult to maintain than in smaller groups. Interdependent instruction is important amid the crowd members themselves, turning to each other for assistance and cooperation during an event. This perspective is supported by the finding that most violence and looting in riots occurs sporadically and in small groups rather than en masse (the larger group) (McPhail 1994). Perception control theory extends rational views of collective behavior by narrowing the range of interaction between people, helping to examine the ways people try to maintain order in groups. As in Blumer's theory of circular reaction, however, these communication lines, regardless of their form, often break down, leading to confusion, perhaps explaining both rational (when communication lines are intact) and irrational (when they break down) behaviors.

Section Summary

The first section of this chapter applied the interactionist perspective to address the questions: Do people act differently in large groups than when they are alone? How do crowds contribute to the development of mass hysteria? What theories explain individuals' rational behavior in large groups? Traditional interactionist approaches to the study of collective behavior focus on the ways that groups produce hysteria among their members, a result of the normlessness that often comes from the lack of communication among group members during collective events. However, groups also form new norms to manage such events, despite the tendency toward hysteria. Hence, collective events can produce both rational and irrational behaviors, depending on the type of group and the participants involved in a given collective event.

SSP The Structure of Crowds and Social Movements

I guess you can say that I am a committed activist. I think if people want to change things, they just need to get up and start doing it. If more people did that, we would have a better place! First, you have to change yourself, then you change the system. If you get people together, you can get the whole society to change.

—Dustin, senior History major

Dustin's perspective emphasizes the importance of the individual in the transformation of society; he believes that if individuals want to change the world, they just need to get up and do it. This process starts from a personal change and then includes getting other people together to assert changes in society. In contrast to Dustin's perspective, a more structural position would argue that society includes strains such as poverty that lead people to want change. But society also gives some people more access to the resources necessary to change society (e.g., money to send out flyers or access to elites who have more control over resources), and there are other groups who have alternative agendas for society. Society, in other words, provides strains, resources, and limitations that help or limit individuals' ability to change the system through social movements (Snow, Soule, and Cress 2005). We will examine two structural perspectives on social movements in society, followed by an examination of research on protest behaviors.

Social Structure and Social Movements

Most of our discussion in this chapter has emphasized collective behavior and action. The study of social movements incorporates elements of these concepts but also examines the social structural conditions that may lead people into social movements. Interactionist perspectives of social movements do not preclude the importance of structural conditions in explaining behavior and outcomes of those movements but see structure as a source of interaction. That is, social structural conditions provide a reason to initiate social movements as well as the context in which individuals make decisions during such movements (Snow 2003).

What are the structural conditions that lead people to initiate social movements? According to **resource mobilization theory,** movements are a product of the interaction between the social conditions that lead people to want change and resources available to make those changes (Zald and Ash 1964; Snow 2003). Social movements often reflect reactions to inequality in societies, such as the women's suffrage movement in the United States or movements based on the desire to obtain better living conditions. They may also reflect responses to social change. Van Dyke and Soule (2002), for instance, studied the growth of the patriot/militia movement in the 1990s, showing a relationship between the decline of manufacturing jobs and family farms associated with the mobilization of these groups. In these cases, mobilization of the movements was considered a response to a threat produced by structural changes in society.

This theory emphasizes how groups (rather than individuals) interact to produce social movements in society. Individuals may formalize groups to bring about social change. These groups are referred to as **social movement organizations.** Once formed, they must negotiate for social change given resources available to them. In support of the theory, research shows that environmental social movement organizations (McLaughlin and Marwan 2000) and the feminist movement (Soule, McAdam, McCarthy, and Su 1999) tended to prosper during periods of economic prosperity.

Another approach that examines group-level interactions in the development of social movements is the political process or "opportunity" theory. The **political process theory** examines the interaction of competing interests and opportunity structures in groups' decisions and ability to produce social change (Gamson 1990; Lipsky 1968). A group may want to produce some change in society and have the resources to help make those changes but must compete with other groups with dissimilar interests. Alternatively, some groups may seek and obtain social change with little or no resources. Under this schema, researchers must incorporate multiple social conditions—and multiple groups—that influence the development or decline in social movements (Jenkins, Jacobs, and Agnone 2003).

Behavior during Collective Events

Collective behavior is often associated with panics—people running helplessly toward the door of a burning building, for example. These forms of collective behavior are the ones you see the most prominently highlighted in the media. But some aspects of collective behavior and social movements can be predictable and even rational. Research coming out of the 1970s and 1980s has given us an idea about the size, scope, and behaviors occurring in modern social movements. Here, we examine patterns of behavior within social movements—how many people show up to specific events, what they do while they are there, and social conditions that influence behavior at events.

Phases of Collective Behavior

Research in social movements has developed to the point where we can divide social processes into phases (McPhail and Tucker 2003):

1. **Assembling Phase**—factors that bring people together into the same place at the same time.

2. **Gathering Phase**—behaviors occurring during a social movement.

3. **Dispersal Phase**—behaviors leading to the end of a social movement gathering.

The processes and behaviors in each of these phases have been studied extensively. The former phase focuses on the conditions that lead people to enter social movements. The dispersal phase emphasizes the behaviors occurring when people leave a movement. Finally, there is research in what happens during the collective behavior. What exactly do people in a crowd of 500,000 do?

The assembling phase refers to the factors that bring people together into the same place at the same time. Research shows that most people learn about social movements from their friends, family, and acquaintances, now probably occurring often through the Internet (McPhail and Tucker 2003). In fact, the best predictor of participating in a protest is simply being asked to attend the event (Schussman and Soule 2005). Our friends and family inform us on where to meet, when to be there, and what is going on. We learn what to expect when we show up. Not everyone who is informed about a gathering shows up to it. Generally, people who have no other obligations and have easy access to the site of the meeting are more likely to participate because there are no competing demands or limitations to their participation. Hence, images of students at a protest reflect people with flexible schedules. Someone working 9:00 AM to 5:00 PM is not likely to have the flexibility to leave her job to participate in a social movement at midday nor to travel across the country to a particular meeting site.

Imagine being in the middle of Washington, D.C., at the height of the 1960s protests. There are thousands of people around you. Most of the protests occur in the summer months when people have more time off from work and the weather is more hospitable for traveling. But it is also very humid and hot. You need access to facilities, water and food. As you look around, you don't know many people. In addition, you can barely hear any speakers. March leaders may not have detailed guides about what to do at each step of the movement. You rely on information from the people around you to get by.

The first important structural condition of such large gatherings is that they are actually comprised of small clusters of friends and family (McPhail and McCarthy 2004). Once in the crowd, individuals tend to form lines to access various services or events, such as the purchase of food and water or waiting for the use of facilities. Other behaviors include the development of an arc or ring around performers or speakers as well as the use of noises and gestures to evaluate such performances, usually in the form of cheers or jeers. Symbols are also very important to such gatherings, showing people a message about the meaning of the gathering can provide a sense of solidarity among its members.

There are many different forms of collective action. As a result, there are different ways in which people leave a gathering. The end of a protest march is going to produce a different behavior than a crowd trying to leave a burning building. A **routine dispersal** is one in which participants leave a gathering in a rational, orderly fashion (Miller 2000). The vast majority of gatherings end with a routine dispersal, partly because most gatherings are peaceful in nature. **Coerced dispersals** include situations in which a third party attempts to break up a group. This type of dispersal is often associated with police trying to end riots, for instance.

Emergency dispersals are those that occur during emergency situations such as fires or explosions. Research shows that even in these situations, people rarely act without reason; individuals do develop fear and anxiety, but it rarely leads to incapacitation or extreme behavior (McPhail and Tucker 2003). When such behaviors occur, they tend to be a result of the inability to see exits or limited access to them as masses of people attempt to leave through one exit point. Most businesses limit the number of people allowed in their buildings to avoid problems should a fire or other emergency require quick evacuation of the premises.

Here we see that there are certain patterns of crowd behavior, in the form of dispersal behaviors. In some cases, social conditions induce more emotional and random acts (e.g., emergency dispersals) than others. In other words, collective events largely produce routine, rational behavior—at least in the form of dispersal patterns—under most conditions.

Size and Media Coverage of Protests

Another aspect of collective behavior that has been studied extensively is the size and scope of different social movements over time. As the capital of the United States, Washington, D.C., has been a center of American protest movements. Protests and marches occur in other cities, but Washington, D.C., gives protestors access to lawmakers and political leaders, providing a unique venue for social movements. Researchers over the last 30 years have tried to assess the size and scope of these movements. However, the controversies over the actual number of participants at the Million Man March led to the prohibition of the U.S. Park Police from providing estimates of any such gathering.

The "gold standard" for estimating the size of a crowd or gathering is based on a simple formula that includes the percentage of a site occupied by people, the square footage of the site, and crowd density (McPhail and McCarthy 2004). An average of one person per five square feet is often used to estimate crowd sizes. To get a sense of proportion, there is about one person for two square feet in a crowded elevator. The density of the crowd varies by a person's position, with people in the front more close to one another than people in back and to the sides. The ratio of people to square feet continues to decrease as you move to the margins of group. Taking these differences into account is important in accurately assessing the size of crowds.

Differences in estimating crowd sizes cannot be overstated. McPhail and McCarthy (2004), for instance, used a formulaic approach to estimate the number of participants at the 2003 anti-Iraq war protests in Washington, D.C., using the dimensions of the area while accounting for differences in crowd density. They estimated that 50,000 people showed up at the rally compared to the 500,000 people estimated by the protest organizers!

Washington, D.C. has become the hub of protest activity in the United States.

Despite the controversies over counting large-scale protests, most protests and marches are small in nature. About a third of the demonstrations in Washington, D.C., are small pickets and vigils followed by another third representing larger marches and rallies (McPhail and Tucker 2003). Very few marches go over 100,000 participants, and most do not involve civil disobedience (Miller 2000). Unfortunately, there is a divergence between the types of gatherings that actually occur and what is reported by newspapers (see Table 11.1). McCarthy and colleagues (1996) compared the percentage of protests permitted in Washington, D.C., and those reported by any media source in 1981 and 1991. They show that only about 7% of protests actually get reported. Further, smaller protests are least likely to be reported, even though they represent the majority. Hence, there is a bias in the types of protests covered, leading to a skewed understanding of the size and scope of protests in the United States.

The nature of collective behavior and social movements make them more difficult to study than other aspects of social life. It would be challenging to create a lab experiment to study collective behavior of any size crowd. Natural experiments lack the control of lab experiments (see chapter 3), and it is challenging to truly motivate someone to participate in such activities. However, the field of collective behavior is unusual in its ability to bring together both qualitative and quantitative techniques in the study of social behavior.

Table 11.1	Differences in Permitted and Reported Demonstrations in Washington, D.C. (1991)		
Demonstration Size	N =	Percent of Demonstrations Permitted	Percent of Demonstrations Reported on by Media
Less than 26		53.4	3.3
26–100		20.8	7.7
101–1,000		20.7	11.9
1,001–10,000		4.1	29.8
10,001–100,000		1.0	37.5
Total percent		100.0	7.1
Number of demonstrations		1,856	133

Source: Adapted from McCarthy and colleagues (1996).

Section Summary

In this section, we focused on theory and research using a structural perspective to address the questions: What structural conditions affect crowd behavior? What are the phases of collective behavior found in large social movements? What kinds of behavior actually occur during a period of collective behavior? Here, we see that groups enter and act in some social movements like any other social act, seeking to address wants and needs of individuals and groups. Structural conditions produce strains that lead people to work together for change and resources necessary to carry-out desired changes. Although some group members may act irrationally, the movement as a whole generally results from the desire to obtain rational outcomes. Further, most collective events are quite small, and they tend to follow rational patterns with specific phases of assembling and dispersal.

GP   Group Processes and Collective Behavior

I sometimes feel that big business is working together to destroy the little guy. I am worried that there is a conspiracy in which the rich work together against the average Joe.

—Ricardo, junior Sociology major

Scholars in sociology's group processes tradition are particularly interested in collective action in terms of how it relates to structural power. In previous chapters, we discussed power as a position in a structure that allows actors to get what they want even when others resist. Whether or not Ricardo's concerns about big business are realistic, social science research indicates conditions under which such conspiracies might be likely to form and conditions that influence whether or not they will be effective. For example, suppose that some company, CompuGiant, specializes in selling a certain type of computer used in small businesses—we will call it the SBPro. CompuGiant is the only company in the world that sells this type of computer. Further suppose that there are three manufacturers that make SBPro's—MomAndPopSB, MiniSBSupply, and SmallPlayerSB. We could represent the relationship between these companies in a diagram that looks like that in Figure 11.1.

Suppose that each SBPro costs the manufacturers $1,000 to make. Also suppose that CompuGiant sells the SBPros for $3,000 each. It is not difficult to guess who will have the power in this situation. CompuGiant will be able to set the prices at which it buys the SBPros. As long as CompuGiant offers each supplier at least $1,000 per unit, the suppliers will be forced to sell their products. One or more of the manufacturers might resist at first, but as soon as one starts accepting the low price, the others will be forced to go along or face going out of business—they don't have any options other than CompuGiant.

In the long run, we would expect the manufacturers in this situation to operate at a level making just enough money to stay in business, whereas CompuGiant would make large profits as long as demand for the SBPros remained high. In this situation, CompuGiant is in a structurally powerful position. It can get what it wants (cheap computers) even when others (the manufacturers) resist.

Multiple social situations share characteristics with the example of companies involved in the manufacturing and sale of SBPros. People regularly interact in contexts in which some individuals have more power than others. The famous philosopher Bertrand Russell (1872–1970), in fact, called power the fundamental concept of the social sciences (Russell 1938). Collective action, however, has the ability to mitigate power differences that are based in structural positions.

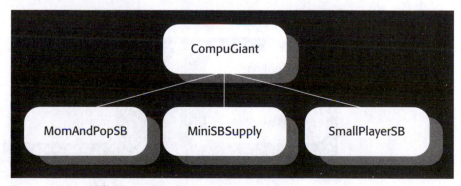

Figure 11.1   Model of Power Distribution

A **coalition** is an alliance of actors (i.e., people, organizations) formed for the purpose of achieving some goal. In the SBPro example, the manufacturers might band together and form a coalition in an effort to take CompuGiant's power away. The three manufacturers could collectively decide that none of them will sell their computers to CompGiant for less than $2,500, and they will share their profits with each other. As a result, we can draw a new diagram of the relationships between the companies to look like Figure 11.2.

In this scenario, CompuGiant's structural power has been taken away. By trading as a group, the three manufacturers have created a situation in which CompuGiant has no alternatives but to trade with the coalition. The ability that coalitions have to determine the power between positions is evidenced by the fact that a coalition such as the one in the SBPro example would be considered collusion and be illegal.

Research in the group processes tradition indicates that people will be likely to form coalitions when they are faced with large power disparities, and also that these coalitions can be successful. Coalitions, however, have their limitations. The biggest of these is the free-rider problem (Simpson and Macy 2004).

The **free-rider problem** occurs when some actors can reap the benefits of a group effort without incurring the costs. Public broadcasting represents a potential free-rider problem. Public broadcasting is supported by donations, but everyone, not just those who donate, can get the benefits of public broadcasting. As a result, there is an incentive to free ride—to listen to public broadcasting but to not contribute. This becomes a problem because if too many people free-ride, public broadcasting will go away.

The free-rider problem is an example of a social dilemma. A **social dilemma** is a situation whereby if every person (or company) acts in his or her own best interests, the results will be bad for the group. For example, think about major traffic delays caused by people who slow down to look at an accident that is off the road. These delays could be avoided if everyone would just continue driving and not slow down to look. Moreover, if you asked people stuck in traffic jams if they would be willing to give up being able to look at the accident to avoid a long traffic jam, we suspect that virtually everyone would say yes.

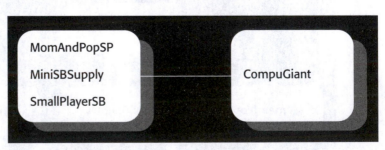

Figure 11.2   Model of a Coalition

Now suppose that you are stuck in a traffic jam because of people ahead of you rubbernecking at an accident off the road. You have traveled less than a mile in the last 30 minutes. You now reach the front of the line where the accident is off the road. Would you slow down to look? The best answer for the group is that you should not slow down and instead keep moving. Your most self-interested decision, however, would probably be to slow down and look at the accident. You already waited through the line, and you are about to accelerate away whether or not you slow down now. In this situation, everyone acting in her or his own self-interest leads to an outcome that is bad for the group.

Again, coalitions face the social dilemma that is known as the free-rider problem. Some people can get the benefits of coalitions without incurring the costs. In the preceding example, suppose that MomAndPopSB proposes a coalition to MiniSBSupply and SmallPlayerSB whereby they will share their profits and sell each unit for no less than $2,500. If MiniSBSupply agrees to the coalition, then SmallPlayerSB's best individual option becomes to free ride. SmallPlayer SB can take advantage of the coalition formed by the other two manufacturers and agree to sell CompuGiant computers for $2,400, undercutting the coalition and guaranteeing itself large profits.

Most coalition situations involve many more participants than the three in our example. Many, in fact, involve hundreds or thousands of people. One thing true of virtually all coalitions, however, is the possibility for free riders. If too many people free ride, a coalition will not be successful.

These dynamics are important to social movements and collective behavior more generally because they help explain behavior both within and between groups. Many group members act based on motives other than a group's goals, making it harder for a group to achieve its ends. In addition, motivations in such groups become confounded as people participate for both social and personal gain, making it difficult to predict how people will behave under the same conditions.

Section Summary

The last section of this chapter answered the question: How do group and individual motivations interact in social movements? Here we emphasize the importance of coalitions during collective behaviors and social movements. Individuals and groups bargain to gain control or access to resources. This process can instigate a series of dilemmas where individuals and groups must choose between their own welfare and that of the larger entity. Together, these concepts help us understand the complex interaction within and between groups during a social movement. Ultimately, group dynamics can influence the outcomes of social movements above and beyond the norms imposed by the collectivity reviewed in previous sections of this chapter.

I remember the first time I went to a rally on the mall (Washington, D.C.). I am not sure why I was there. I was afraid to ask anybody what to do. I stood around for awhile but even though there was tens of thousands of people, there was a LOT of space around me. I tried to listen to the speaker but I just couldn't hear him. I was hoping to get more out of it.

—Jackson, senior Sociology major

Jackson's experience is probably not uncommon for someone at a large rally. He went to a rally to change the world but felt a little let down. Despite all of the people around him, he did not feel as though he accomplished much. Like the hysteria theories discussed at the beginning of the chapter, he did experience heightened emotional arousal in the form of fear. But this fear was not transformed during his time at the event. Instead, it followed a pretty routine pattern. What would have happened if something would have provoked the crowd a bit, perhaps being instigated by poor police behavior? The initial emotions may have turned the crowd in another direction.

We have applied three perspectives to understand social movements and collective behaviors. From an interactionist perspective, large-group environments make it difficult to develop and follow norms, though most people eventually do so. Social structure and personality researchers emphasize how positions and resources affect participation in and outcomes of social movements. Finally, group processes research and theory helps to understand the role of group dynamics, especially the development of coalitions, to understanding why groups behave the way that they do during a social movement. Together, these perspectives provide a context for understanding why some social movements are associated with emotional outbursts, whereas others, indeed most, follow a fairly routine pattern.

Summary

1. Traditional theories of collective behavior, collective action, and social movements emphasize the ways in which crowds transform the individuals acting in them, turning them into irrational beings. Rational choice perspectives on collective action emphasize the idea that people in groups are purposive in their decisions and actions in everyday life, including group events.

2. Structural perspectives of social movements emphasize societal conditions that influence the development and success of such movements resulting from constraints associated with time and money.

3. Research on protests in the United States over the last 30 years has shown that most protests and marches are small in nature. Very few marches go over 100,000 participants, and very few involve civil disobedience. However, only the largest protests receive much media attention.

4. Research evidence in the group processes tradition indicates that people will be likely to form coalitions when they are faced with large power disparities. The free-rider problem and social dilemmas are typical problems found in behavior within and between groups.

Key Terms and Concepts

Acting crowds: Groups of people with a focus, or goal, who act with unity to achieve the goal.

Action of social control: Aspect of value-added theory referring to how authorities react to the behavior.

Assembling phase: Phase of collective behavior referring to the factors that bring people together into the same place at the same time.

Circular reaction: Process by which people become more and more suggestible and irrational after interactions become interrupted.

Coalition: An alliance of actors formed for the purpose of achieving some goal.

Coerced dispersals: Situations in which a third party attempts to break up a group.

Collective action: The purposive nature of people's behavior when they collectively celebrate, mourn, worship, protest, compete in athletics, or confront disasters.

Collective identity: An individual's sense of connection with a larger community or group.

Concerned participant: According to emergent norm theory, there are people who are not directly involved with a group's goal but participate out of concern over an issue.

Contagious mental unity: A sense of shared emotional bond that emerges whenever people interact in a group.

Craze: When large numbers of people become obsessed with something like the purchase of a product or an activity.

Curiosity seeker: According to emergent norm theory, it is the type of person who participates in the group out of curiosity.

Differential expression: Aspect of emergent norm theory that argues individuals enter groups with different attitudes and perspectives.

Dispersal phase: Phase of collective behavior referring to the behaviors leading to the end of a social movement gathering.

Ego-involved participant: According to emergent norm theory, it is the type of person who feels a strong personal commitment to the issue that the group is involved with.

Emergency dispersals: Crowd dispersals that occur during emergency situations like fires or explosions.

Emergent norm theory: Theory of collective behavior focusing on how individuals come to accept the constraints imposed by a group.

Expressive crowd: Crowd that lacks a goal and is primarily just a setting for tension release, often through rhythmical action such as applause, dancing, or singing.

Free-rider problem: When some actors can reap the benefits of a group effort without incurring the costs.

Gathering phase: Phase of collective behavior referring to the behaviors occurring during a social movement.

Generalized belief: Element of value-added theory that states group members must have a shared view of the problem and how to resolve tension.

Homogeneity of mood and action: According to mass hysteria theory, people in a crowd exhibit a shared willingness to follow suggestions.

Hostile outbursts: Any type of mass violence or killings.

Independent instructions: Aspect of perception control theory referring to individual decisions made during collective behavior.

Insecure participant: According to emergent norm theory, it is the person participating in a crowd merely for the sense of connection with the group.

Intensity of behavior: A key ingredient of contagious mental unity, referring to situations in which people lose their inhibitions to act and the tempo of their behavior increases.

Interdependent instruction: Aspect of perception control theory referring to when individuals in a group work together to make decisions.

Interpretive phase: Part of the circular reaction process in which people respond to one another by interpreting the other's gestures and remarks, rehearsing or visualizing a possible response, and then conveying a response.

Irrational behavior: An ingredient of mass hysteria theory referring to when people act without reason.

Mass: Anonymous individuals from many social strata that are loosely organized.

Mass hysteria theory or contagion theory: Theory based on the idea that individuals in crowds lose their ability to think and act rationally.

Milling: Part of the circular reaction process in which individuals at an event anxiously move about in a seemingly aimless and random fashion.

Mobilization for action: Element of value-added theory regarding individuals' reaction to an immediate threat.

New social movements: Those movements that center around specific issues rather than class-based political mobilizations (e.g., workers' rights).

Norm-oriented social movements: Movements to change the way things are regulated in society.

Organizational instruction: Aspect of perception control theory referring to when information is provided by a movement's leadership or some other outside force.

Panic: A situation in which large numbers of people are overwhelmed with a common fear.

Perception control theory: Theory based on the premise that people must be able to monitor and interpret one another's behavior for collective action to occur.

Political process theory: Examines the interaction of competing interests and opportunity structures in a group's ability to produce social change.

Public: An aggregate of people, often from the same social class, who are concerned with a specific issue.

Resource mobilization theory: Theory of collective action that views social movements as a product of the interaction between the social conditions that lead people to want change and resources available to make those changes.

Routine dispersal: A dispersal in which participants leave a gathering in a rational, orderly fashion.

Social dilemma: A situation whereby if every person acts in his or her own best interests, the results will be bad for the group.

Social movement organizations: When individuals formally organize into groups to bring about social change.

Social movements: Collective action designed to produce a new social order.

Structural conduciveness: Element of value-added theory that states society must be in a condition amenable to the formation of movements.

Structural strain: Element of value-added theory stating there must be some level of conflict over some issue or problem to initiate collective action.

Value-added theory: Theory based on the notion that to fully understand the causes of collective events, you need to distinguish the type of collective behavior in question and the social conditions surrounding it.

Value-oriented social movements: Attempts to change the social order of society.

1. Think about any large-group gathering that you have been in such as a sporting event. Did you feel any sense of arousal or cohesion with the group? Consider when the team is winning or losing, did that change the way you felt?

2. This chapter presented many theories and perspectives on how people act in large groups. Which theories did you find more useful in explaining collective behavior? Why?

3. How can the group processes research presented at the end of the chapter (e.g., coalitions and dilemmas in groups) help us understand larger collective behavior phenomenon?

References

Adler, Patricia A. 1996. "Preadolescent Clique Stratification and the Hierarchy of Identity." *Sociological Inquiry*:2: 111–142.

Adler, Patricia A. and Peter Adler. 1982. "Criminal Commitment among Drug Dealers." *Deviant Behavior* 3:117–135.

———. 1994. "Social Reproduction and the Corporate Other: The Institutionalization of Afterschool Activities." *The Sociological Quarterly* 35:309–328.

———. 1998. *Peer Power: Preadolescent Culture and Identity Formation*. New Brunswick, NJ: Rutgers University Press.

———. 1999. "The Ethnographers' Ball Revisited." *Journal of Contemporary Ethnography* 28:442–450.

———. 2003. "The Promise and Pitfalls of Going into the Field." *Contexts* 2:41–47.

Agnew, Robert. 1985. "A Revised Strain Theory of Delinquency." *Social Forces* 64:151–167.

———. 2001. "Building on the Foundation of General Strain Theory: Specifying the Types of Strain Most Likely to Lead to Crime and Delinquency." *Journal of Research in Crime and Delinquency* 38:319–361.

Aguirre, B. E., Dennis Wenger, and Gabriela Vigo. 1998. "A Test of the Emergent Norm Theory of Collective Behavior." *Sociological Forum* 13:301–320.

Ajzen, Icek. 1991. "The Theory of Planned Behavior." *Organizational Behavior and Human Decision Processes* 50:179–211.

Alexander, Karl L., Doris R. Entwisle, and Maxine S. Thompson. 1987. "School Performance, Status Relations, and the Structure of Sentiment: Bringing the Teacher Back In." *American Sociological Review* 52:665–682.

Alwin, Duane F. 2002. "Generations X, Y and Z: Are They Changing America?" *Contexts* 1:42–51.

Amato, Paul R. 1993. "Urban-Rural Differences in Helping Friends and Family Members." *Social Psychology Quarterly* 56:249–262.

Anderson, Elijah. 1999. *Code of the Streets: Decency, Violence, and the Moral Life of the Inner City*. New York: W.W. Norton.

Aneshensel, Carol S. 1992. "Social Stress: Theory and Research." *Journal of Health and Social Behavior* 18:15–38.

Aneshensel, Carol S. and J. C. Phelan. 1999. *Handbook of the Sociology of Mental Health*, edited by M. T. Hallinan. New York: Kluwer.

Aneshensel, Carol S., Carolyn M. Rutter, and Peter A. Lachenbruch. 1991. "Social Structure, Stress, and Mental Health." *American Sociological Review* 56:166–178.

Aneshensel, Carol S. and Clea A. Sucoff. 1996. "The Neighborhood Context of Adolescent Mental Health." *Journal of Health and Social Behavior* 37:293–310.

Aron, Raymond. 1965. *Main Currents in Sociological Thought I*. Translated by R. Howard and H. Weaver. New York: Doubleday.

Ausdale, Debra Van and Joe R. Feagin. 2002. *The First R: How Children Learn Race and Racism*. Lanham, MD: Rowman & Littlefield.

Babbie, Earl. 2002. *The Basics of Social Research*. Belmont, CA: Wadsworth.

Bales, Robert. 1965. "The Equilibrium Problem in Small Groups." Pp. 424–456 in *Small Groups: Studies in Social Interaction*, edited by P. Hare, E. F. Borgotta, and R. F. Bales. New York: Knopf.

Bao, Wan-Ning, Ain Haas, and Yijun Pi. 2004. "Life Strain, Negative Emotions, and Delinquency: An Empirical Test of General Strain Theory in the People's Republic of China." *International Journal of Offender Therapy and Comparative Criminology* 48:281–297.

Bandura, Albert. (1977). "Self Efficacy Towards a Unifying Theory of Behavioral Change." *Psychological Review*, 84(2): 191–215.

Bandura, Albert. 1997. *Self Efficacy: The Exercise of Control*. New York: W.H. Freeman Company.

Baron, Reuben M. and David A. Kenny. 1986. "The Moderator-Mediator Variable Distinction in Social Psychological Research: Conceptual, Strategic, and Statistical Considerations." *Journal of Personality and Social Psychology* 51:1173–1182.

Becker, Howard S. 1953. "Becoming a Marijuana User." *American Journal of Sociology* 59:235–242.

———. 1973. *Outsiders: Studies in the Sociology of Deviance*. New York: Free Press.

Berger, Joseph, Bernard P. Cohen, and Morris Zelditch, Jr. 1966. "Status Characteristics and Expectation States." Pp. 29–46 in *Sociological Theories in Progress*, Vol. 1, edited by J. Berger, M. Zelditch, Jr., and B. Anderson. Boston: Houghton Mifflin.

———. 1972. "Status Characteristics and Social Interaction." *American Sociological Review* 37:241–255.

Berger, Joseph, Cecilia L. Ridgeway, and Morris Zelditch. 2002. "Construction of Status and Referential Structures." *Sociological Theory* 20:157–179.

Berger, Joseph, Susan J. Rosenholtz, and Morris Zelditch, Jr. 1980. "Status Organizing Processes." *Annual Review of Sociology* 6:479–508.

Berger, Joseph, David G. Wagner, and Morris Zelditch, Jr. 1985. "Expectations States Theory: Review and Assessment." Pp. 1–72 in *Status, Rewards, and Influence: How Expectations Organize Behavior*, edited by J. Berger and M. Zelditch. San Francisco: Jossey-Bass.

Berger, Joseph, Murray Webster, Jr., Cecilia Ridgeway, and Susan J. Rosenholtz. 1993. "Status Cues, Expectations, and Behavior." Pp. 1–22 in *Social Psychology of Groups*, edited by E. Lawler and B. Markovsky. Greenwich, CT: JAI Press.

Berger, Peter. 1973. *Invitation to Sociology: A Humanistic Approach*. Woodstock, NY: Overlook Press.

Berger, Peter L. and Thomas Luckman. 1967. *The Social Construction of Reality: A Treatise on the Sociology of Knowledge*. Garden City, NY: Doubleday.

Bianchi, Suzanne M. 2000. "Maternal Employment and Time with Children: Dramatic Change or Surprising Continuity?" *Demography* 37:401–414.

Bianchi, Suzanne M., John P. Robinson, and Melissa A. Milkie. 2006. *Changing Rhythms of American Family Life*. Washington, D.C.: American Sociological Association.

Biddle, B. J. 1986. "Recent Developments in Role Theory." *Annual Review of Sociology* 12:67–92.

Blau, Peter M. 1964. *Exchange and Power in Social Life*. New York: John Wiley & Sons.

Blau, Peter M. and Otis Dudley Duncan. 1967. *The American Occupational Structure*. New York: Wiley.

Blumer, Herbert. 1958. "Race Prejudice as a Sense of Group Position." *Pacific Sociological Review* 58:3–7.

———. 1969. *Symbolic Interactionism: Perspective and Method*. Berkeley, Los Angeles, and London: University of California Press.

———. 1972. "Outline of Collective Behavior." Pp. 22–45 in *Readings in Collective Behavior*, edited by R. R. Evans. Chicago: Rand McNally.

Bobo, Lawrence. 1998. "Race, Interest, and Beliefs about Affirmative Action." *American Behavioral Scientist* 41:985–1003.

Bobo, Lawrence and Vincent Hutchings. 1996. "Perceptions of Racial Group Competition: Extending Blumer's Theory of Group Position to a Multiracial Social Context." *American Sociological Review* 61:951–972.

Bolzendahl, Catherine I. and Daniel J. Myers. 2004. "Feminist Attitudes and Support for Gender Equality: Opinion Change in Women and Men, 1974–1998." *Social Forces* 83:759–789.

Bonacich, Phillip. 1998. "A Behavioral Foundation for a Structural Theory of Power in Exchange Networks." *Social Psychology Quarterly* 61:185–198.

Borgardus, Emory S. 1958. "Racial Distance Changes in the United States during the Past Thirty Years." *Sociology and Social Research* 43:127–135.

Borgatta, Edgar F. and Robert F. Bales. 1953. "Interaction of Individuals in Reconstituted Groups." *Sociometry* 14:302–320.

Borgatta, Edgar F., Robert F. Bales, and Arthur S. Couch. 1954. "Some Findings Relevant to the Great Man Theory of Leadership." *American Sociological Review* 19:755–759.

Brody, Gene H., Kris Moore, and Dana Glei. 1994. "Family Processes during Adolescence as Predictors of Parent–Young Adult Attitude Similarity." *Family Relations* 43:369–373.

Bolzendahl, Catherine I. and Daniel J. Myers. 2004. "Feminist Attitudes and Support for Gender Equality: Opinion Change in Women and Men, 1974–1998." *Social Forces* 83:759–789.

Burke, Peter J. 1997. "An Identity Model of Network Exchange." *Social Psychology Quarterly* 62:134–150.

———. 2003. *Advances in Identity Theory and Research.* New York: Kluwer Academic/Plenum Publishers.

———. 2004. "Identities, Events, and Moods." *Advances in Group Processes* 21:25–49.

Burke, Peter J. and Jan E. Stets. 1999. "Trust and Commitment through Self-Verification." *Social Psychology Quarterly* 62:347–366.

Burn, Shawn Meghan, Roger Aboud, and Carey Moyles. 2000. "The Relationship between Gender Social Identity and Support for Feminism." *Sex Roles* 42:1081–1089.

Cahill, Spencer E. and Robin Eggleston. 1994. "Managing Emotions in Public: The Case of Wheelchair Users." *Social Psychology Quarterly* 57:300–312.

Cahill, Spencer E., William Distler, Cynthia Lachowetz, Andrea Meaney, Robyn Tarallo, and Teena Willard. 1985. "Meanwhile Backstage: Public Bathrooms and the Interaction Order." *Urban Life* 14:33–58.

Cahill, Spencer E. 2003. "Childhood." Pp. 857–874 in *Handbook of Symbolic Interactionism*, edited by L. T. Reynolds and N. J. Herman-Kinney. Lanham, MD: Rowman & Littlefield.

Cahill, Spencer E., Gary Alan Fine, and Linda Grant. 1995. "Dimensions of Qualitative Research." Pp. 605–629 in *Sociological Perspectives on Social Psychology*, edited by K. S. Cook, G. A. Fine, and J. S. H. House. Boston: Allyn & Bacon.

Cantril, Hadley. 1940. *The Invasion from Mars.* New York: Harper & Row.

———. 1966. *The Invasion from Mars: A Study in the Psychology of Panic.* New York: Harper & Row.

Caputo, Richard K. 2003. "The Effects of Socioeconomic Status, Perceived Discrimination and Mastery on Health Status in a Youth Cohort." *Social Work in Health Care* 37:17–42.

Carli, Linda L. 1991. "Gender, Status, and Influence." Pp. 89–114 in *Advances in Group Processes: Theory and Research,* edited by E. J. Lawler, B. Markovsky, C. Ridgeway and, H. A. Walker, Greenwich, CT: JAI Press.

Carlson, Darren K. 2003. "Americans Stake Out Ideological Ground." The Gallup Organization. Washington, D.C.

Carroll, Joseph. 2004. "Who Supports the Death Penalty?" The Gallup Organization. Washington, D.C.

Cast, Alicia D. 2003a. "Identities and Behavior." Pp. 41–53 in *Advances in Identity Theory and Research,* edited by P. J. Burke, T. J. Owens, R. Serpe, and P. A. Thoits. New York: Kluwer Academic/Plenum Publishers.

———. 2003b. "Power and the Ability to Define the Situation." *Social Psychology Quarterly* 66:185–201.

Chambliss, William J. 1973. "Race, Sex, and Gangs: The Saints and the Roughnecks." *Trans-Action* 11:24–31.

Cheung, Siu-Kau and Stephen Y. K. Sun. 2000. "Effects of Self-Efficacy and Social Support on the Mental Health Conditions of Mutual-Aid Organization Members." *Social Behavior and Personality* 28:413–422.

Clark, Candace. 1987. "Sympathy Biography and Sympathy Margin." *American Journal of Sociology* 93:290–321.

Cockerham, William C. 1990. "A Test of the Relationship between Race, Socioeconomic Status, and Psychological Distress." *Social Science and Medicine* 31:1321–1326.

———2003. *Sociology of Mental Disorder.* Upper Saddle River, NJ: Prentice Hall.

Cohen, Elizabeth G. and S. Roper. 1972. "Modification of Interracial Interaction Disability: Application of Status Characteristics Theory." *American Sociological Review* 37:643–655.

Coleman, James S. 1988. "Social Capital in the Creation of Human Capital." *American Journal of Sociology* 94:S95–S120.

Collins, Randall. 1981. "On the Microfoundations of Macrosociology." *American Journal of Sociology* 86:984–1014.

———. 1985. *Three Sociological Traditions.* New York and Oxford: Oxford University Press.

———. 2004. *Interaction Ritual Chains.* Princeton and Oxford: Princeton University Press.

Conrad, Peter. 2005. "The Shifting Engines of Medicalization." *Journal of Health and Social Behavior* 46:3–14.

Conrad, Peter and Deborah Potter. 2000. "From Hyperactive Children to ADHD Adults: Observations on the Expansion of Medical Categories." *Social Problems* 47:559–582.

Converse, Jean M. and Stanely Presser. 1986. *Survey Questions: Handcrafting the Standardized Questionnaire,* vol. 7, edited by M. S. Lewis-Beck. Newbury Park, CA: Sage.

Cook, Karen S., Richard M. Emerson, Mary R. Gillmore, and Toshio Yamagishi. 1983. "The Distribution of Power in Exchange Networks: Theory and Experimental Results." *American Journal of Sociology* 89:275–305.

Cook, Karen S. and Toshio Yamagishi. 1992. "Power in Exchange Networks: A Power-Dependence Formulation." *Social Networks* 14:245–265.

Cooley, Charles Horton. 1909. *Social Organization: A Study of the Larger Social Mind.* New York: Charles Scribner's Sons.

———. 1922. *Human Nature and the Social Order.* New York: Charles Scribner's Sons.

Copper, Erica and Mike Allen. 1998. "A Meta-Analytic Examination of the Impact of Student Race on Classroom Interaction." *Communication Research Reports* 15:151–161.

Correll, Shelley J. 2004. "Constraints into Preference: Gender, Status, and Emerging Career Aspirations." *American Sociological Review* 69:93–113.

Corsaro, William. A. (1992). "Interpretive Reproduction in Children's Peer Cultures." *Social Psychology Quarterly* 55(2): 160–177.

———. 2005. *The Sociology of Childhood.* Thousand Oaks, CA: Pine Forge.

Corsaro, William A. and Donna Eder. 1995. "Development and Socialization of Children and Adolescents." Pp. 421–451 in *Sociological Perspectives on Social Psychology*, edited by K. S. Cook, G. A. Fine, and J. S. House. Boston: Allyn and Bacon.

Corsaro, William A. and Laura Fingerson. 2003. "Development and Socialization in Childhood." Pp. 125–156 in *Handbook of Social Psychology*, edited by J. Delamater. New York: Kluwer Academic/Plenum Publishers.

Couch, Carl J. 1968. "Collective Behavior: An Examination of Some Stereotypes." *Social Problems* 15:310–322.

Cressey, Donald R. 1971. *Other People's Money: A Study in the Social Psychology of Embezzlement.* Belmont, CA: Wadsworth Publishing Company.

Crocker, Jennifer and Lora E. Park. 2003. "Seeking Self-Esteem: Construction, Maintenance, and Protection of Self-Worth." Pp. 291–313 in *Handbook of Self and Identity*, edited by M. R. Leary and J. P. Tangney. New York: Guilford Press.

Crosnoe, Robert and Glen H. Elder, Jr. 2004. "From Childhood to the Later Years: Pathways of Human Development." *Research on Aging* 26:623–654.

Cunningham, Mick. 2001. "Parental Influences on the Gendered Division of Housework." *American Sociological Review* 66:184–203.

Deaux, Kay and Daniela Martin. 2003. "Interpersonal Networks and Social Categories: Specifying Levels of Context in Identity Processes." *Social Psychology Quarterly* 66:101–117.

Deluca, Stefanie and James E. Rosenbaum. 2001. "Individual Agency and the Life Course: Do Low-SES Students Get Less Long-Term Payoff for Their School Efforts?" *Sociological Focus* 34:357–376.

Demo, David H. 1992. "Parent-Child Relations: Assessing Recent Changes." *Journal of Marriage and the Family* 54:104–117.

Denzin, Norman K. 1971. "Childhood as a Conversation of Gestures." *Sociological Symposium* 7:23–35.

———. 1977. *Childhood Socialization: Studies in the Development of Language, Social Behavior, and Identity.* San Francisco: Jossey-Bass.

Diekmann, Andreas and Kurt Schmidheiny. 2004. "Do Parents of Girls Have a Higher Risk of Divorce? An Eighteen-Country Study." *Journal of Marriage and Family* 66:651–660.

Diener, Ed, Carol L. Gohm, Eunkook Suh, and Shigehiro Oishi. 2000. "Similarity of the Relations between Marital Status and Subjective Well-Being across Cultures." *Journal of Cross-Cultural Psychology* 31:419–436.

Dooley, David, Ralph Catalano, and Karen S. Rook. 1988. "Personal and Aggregate Unemployment and Psychological Symptoms." *The Journal of Social Issues* 44:107–123.

Dooley, David, Ralph Catalano, and Georjeanna Wilson. 1994. "Depression and Unemployment: Panel Findings from the Epidemiologic Catchment Area Study." *American Journal of Community Psychology* 22:745–765.

Dooley, David and J. Prause. 1995. "Effect of Unemployment on School Leavers' Self-Esteem." *Journal of Occupational and Organizational Psychology* 68:177–192.

Du Bois, W. E. B. 2003. "The Souls of White Folk." *National Review* 55:44–58.

Duncan, Lauren E. and Abigail J. Stewart. 1995. "Still Bringing the Vietnam War Home: Sources of Contemporary Student Activism." *Personality and Social Psychology Bulletin* 21:914–924.

Durkheim, Emile. 1951. *Suicide: A Study in Sociology.* New York: Free Press.

Dush, Claire M. Kamp and Paul R. Amato. 2005. "Consequences of Relationship Status and Quality for Subjective Well-Being." *Journal of Social and Personal Relationships* 22: 607–627.

Elder, Glen H., Jr. 1987. "War Mobilization and the Life Course: A Cohort of World War II Veterans." *Sociological Forum* 2:449–472.

———. 1994. "Time, Human Agency, and Social Change: Perspectives on the Life Course." *Social Psychology Quarterly* 57:4–15.

———. 1999. *Children of the Great Depression*. Boulder, CO: Westview Press.

Elder, Glen H., Jr. and Rand D. Conger. 2000. *Children of the Land: Adversity and Success in Rural America*. Chicago: University of Chicago Press.

Elliott, Gregory C. 1986. "Self-Esteem and Self-Consistency: A Theoretical and Empirical Link between Two Primary Motivations." *Social Psychology Quarterly* 49:207–218.

———. 2001. "The Self as a Social Product and a Social Force: Morris Rosenberg and the Elaboration of a Deceptively Simple Effect." Pp. 10–28 in *Extending Self-Esteem Theory and Research: Sociological and Psychological Currents*, edited by T. J. Owens, S. Stryker, and N. Goodman. Cambridge, MA: Cambridge University Press.

Elliott, Gregory C., Melissa F. Colangelo, and Richard J. Gelles. 2005. "Mattering and Suicide Ideation: Establishing and Elaborating a Relationship." *Social Psychology Quarterly* 68:223–238.

Elliott, Gregory C., Suzanne Kao, and Ann-Marie Grant. 2004. "Mattering: Emperical Validation of a Social-Psychological Concept." *Self and Identity* 3:339–354.

Emerson, Richard M. 1992. "Social Exchange Theory." Pp. 30–65 in *Social Psychology: Sociological Perspectives*, edited by M. Rosenberg and R. H. Turner. New Brunswick, NJ: Transaction Publishers.

Faris, Robert E. and H. Warren Dunham. 1960. *Mental Disorders in Urban Areas: An Ecological Study of Schizophrenia and Other Psychoses*. New York: Hafner Publishing Co.

Ferguson, Kathy E. 1980. *Self, Society, and Womankind: The Dialectic of Liberation*. Westport, CT: Greenwood Press.

Fine, Gary Alan. 1979. "Small Groups and Culture Creation: The Idioculture of Little League Baseball Teams." *American Sociological Review* 44:733–745.

Fischer, Claude S. 1973. "Urban Malaise." *Social Forces* 52:221–235.

Fisek, M. Hamit, Joseph Berger, and Robert Z. Norman. 2005. "Status Cues and the Formation of Expectations." *Social Science Research* 34:80–102.

Fletcher, Joseph F. and Marie-Christine Chalmers. 1991. "Attitudes of Canadians toward Affirmative Action: Opposition, Value Pluralism, and Nonattitudes." *Political Behavior* 13:67–95.

Foschi, Martha. 1996. "Double Standards in the Evaluation of Men and Women." *Social Psychology Quarterly* 59:237–254.

———. 2000. "Double Standards for Competence: Theory and Research." *Annual Review of Sociology* 26:21–42.

Foschi, Martha and Vanessa Lapointe. 2002. "On Conditional Hypotheses and Gender as a Status Characteristic." *Social Psychology Quarterly* 65:146–162.

Foucault, Michel. 1965. *Madness and Civilization: A History of Insanity in the Age of Reason*. Translated by R. Howard. New York: Vintage Books.

Franks, David D. 2003. "Emotions." Pp. 787–809 in *Handbook of Symbolic Interactionism*, edited by L. T. Reynolds and N. J. Herman-Kinney. Lanham, MD: Rowman & Littlefield.

Freud, Sigmund. 1945. *Group Psychology and the Analysis of the Ego*. London: Hogarth.

Gamson, William. 1990. *The Strategy of Social Protest*. Homewood, IL: Dorsey.

Garfinkel, Harold. 1967. *Studies in Ethnomethodology*. Cambridge, MA: Polity Press.

Garside, Rula Bayrakdar and Bonnie Klimes-Dougan. 2002. "Socialization of Discrete Negative Emotions: Gender Differences and Links with Psychological Distress." *Sex Roles* 47:115–128.

Gecas, Viktor. 1982. "The Self-Concept." *Annual Review of Sociology* 8:1–33.

———. 1989. "The Social Psychology of Self-Efficacy." *Annual Review of Sociology* 15:291–316.

———. 1992. "Contexts of Socialization." Pp. 165–199 in *Social Psychology: Sociological Perspectives*, edited by M. Rosenberg and R. H. Turner. New Brunswick, NJ: Transaction Publishers.

———. 2001. "The Self as Social Force." Pp. 85–100 in *Extending Self-Esteem Theory and Research: Sociological and Psychological Currents*, edited by T. J. Owens, S. Stryker, and N. Goodman. Cambridge, MA: Cambridge University Press.

George, Linda K. and Scott M. Lynch. 2003. "Race Differences in Depressive Symptoms: A Dynamic Perspective on Stress Exposure and Vulnerability." *Journal of Health and Social Behavior* 44:353–369.

Gergen, Kenneth J. 2000. *The Saturated Self: Delimmas of Identity in Contemporary Life*. New York: Basic Books.

Glass, Jennifer, Vern L. Bengtson, and Charlotte Chorn Dunham. 1986. "Attitude Similarity in Three-Generation Families: Socialization, Status Inheritance, or Reciprocal Influence?" *American Sociological Review* 51:685–698.

Goffman, Erving. 1963. *Stigma: Notes on the Management of Spoiled Identity*. Englewood Cliffs, NJ: Prentice Hall.

———. 1959. *The Presentation of Self in Everyday Life*. Garden City, NY: Doubleday.

———. 1961. *Asylums*. New York: Anchor.

———. 1967. *Interaction Ritual Essays in Face to Face Behavior*. Chicago: Aldine.

Goleman, Daniel. 1997. *Emotional Intelligence*. New York: Bantam.

Gotlib, Ian H. and Blair Wheaton. 1997. *Stress and Adversity over the Life Course: Trajectories and Turning Points*. Cambridge, MA: Cambridge University Press.

Grace, Sherry L. and Kenneth L. Cramer. 2002. "Sense of Self in the New Millennium: Male and Female Student Responses to the TST." *Social Behavior and Personality* 30:271–280.

Granovetter, Mark S. 1973. "The Strength of Weak Ties." *American Journal of Sociology* 78:1360–1380.

———. 1995. *Getting a Job: A Study in Contacts and Careers*. Chicago: Chicago University Press.

Greenberg, David F. 1999. "The Weak Strength of Social Control Theory." *Crime and Delinquency* 45:66–81.

Harding, David J. and Christopher Jencks. 2003. "Changing Attitudes toward Premarital Sex: Cohort, Period, and Aging Effects." *Public Opinion Quarterly* 67:211–226.

Hartjen, Clayton A. and S. Priyadarsini. 2003. "Gender, Peers, and Delinquency: A Study of Boys and Girls in Rural France." *Youth & Society* 34:387–414.

Heath, Shirley Brice. 1983. *Ways with Words: Language, Life, and Work in Communities and Classrooms*. New York: Cambridge University Press.

Heckert, Druann Maria and Amy Best. 1997. "Ugly Duckling to Swan: Labeling Theory and the Stigmatization of Red." *Symbolic Interaction* 20:365–384.

Hegtvedt, Karen A. 1990. "The Effects of Relationship Structure on Emotional Responses to Inequity." *Social Psychology Quarterly* 53:214–228.

Hegtvedt, Karen A. and Caitlin Killian. 1999. "Fairness and Emotions: Reactions to the Process and Outcomes of Negotiations." *Social Forces* 78:269–303.

Heilman, Madeline E., Aaron S. Wallen, Daniella Fuchs, and Melinda Tamkins. 2004. "Penalties for Success: Reactions to Women Who Succeed at Male Gender-Typed Tasks." *Journal of Applied Psychology* 89:416–427.

Heise, David R. 1985. "Affect Control Theory: Respecification, Estimation, and Tests of the Formal Model." *Journal of Mathematical Sociology* 11:191–222.

———. 1999. "Controlling Affective Experience Interpersonally." *Social Psychology Quarterly* 62:1–16.

———. 2002. "Understanding Social Interaction with Affect Control Theory." Pp. 17–40 in *New Directions in Sociological Theory*, edited by J. Berger and M. Zelditch. Boulder, CO: Rowman & Littlefield.

Herman-Kinney, Nancy J. 2003. "Deviance." Pp. 695–720 in *Handbook of Symbolic Interactionism*, edited by L. T. Reynolds and N. J. Herman-Kinney. Lanham, MD: Rowman & Littlefield.

Herrnstein, R. J. and Charles Murray. 1994. *The Bell Curve: Intelligence and Class Structure in American Life*. New York: Free Press.

Hewitt, John P. 2003b. "Symbols, Objects, and Meanings." Pp. 307–348 in *Handbook of Symbolic Interactionism*, edited by L. T. Reynolds and N. J. Herman-Kinney. Lanham, MD: Rowman & Littlefield.

———. 2003a. *Self and Society: A Symbolic Interactionist Perspective*. Boston: Allyn and Bacon.

Hirschi, Travis. 1969. *Causes of Delinquency*. Berkeley: University of California Press.

Hochschild, Arlie Russell. 1983. *The Managed Heart: Commercialization of Human Feelings*. Berkeley: University of California Press.

Hogg, Michael A. and Cecilia Ridgeway. 2003. "Social Identity: Sociological and Social Psychological Perspectives." *Social Psychology Quarterly* 66:97–100.

Hogg, Michael A., Deborah J. Terry, and Katherine M. White. 1995. "A Tale of Two Theories: A Critical Comparison of Identity Theory with Social Identity Theory." *Social Psychology Quarterly* 58:255–269.

Hollander, Jocelyn A. and Judith A. Howard. 2000. "Social Psychological Theories on Social Inequalities." *Social Psychology Quarterly* 63:338–351.

Holstein, James A. and Jaber F. Gubrium. 2003. "The Life Course." Pp. 835–855 in *Handbook of Symbolic Interactionism*, edited by L. T. Reynolds and N. J. Herman-Kinney. Lanham, MD: Rowman & Littlefield.

Homans, George Caspar. 1946. "The Small Warship." *American Sociological Review* 11:294–300.

———. 1974. *Social Behavior: Its Elementary Forms*. New York: Harcourt, Brace, Jonanovich.

Hopcroft, Cathryn, Stephanie J. Funk, and Jody Clay-Warner. 1998. "Organizational Contexts and Conversation Patterns." *Social Psychology Quarterly* 61:361–371.

Horwitz, Alan V. 2002. *Creating Mental Illness*. Chicago: University of Chicago Press.

House, James S. 1977. "The Three Faces of Social Psychology." *Sociometry* 40:161–177.

———. 1992. "Social Structure and Personality." Pp. 525–561 in *Social Psychology: Sociological Perspectives*, edited by M. Rosenberg and R. H. Turner. New Brunswick, NJ: Transaction Publishers.

Hughes, Diane and Deborah Johnson. 2001. "Correlates in Children's Experiences of Parents' Racial Socialization Behaviors." *Journal of Marriage and the Family* 63:981–995.

Hughes, Diane, and Steven A. Tuch. 2003. "Gender Differences in Whites' Racial Attudes; Are Women's Attitudes Really More Favorable?" *Social Psychology Quarterly* 66(4): 384–401.

Hughes, Diane. 2003. "Correlates of African American and Latino Parents' Messages to Children about Ethnicity and Race: A Comparative Study of Racial Socialization." *American Journal of Community Psychology* 31:15–33.

Humphries, Laud. 1970. *Tearoom Trade: Impersonal Sex in Public Places*. Chicago: Aldine.

Hurh, Won Moo. 2003. *Personality in Culture and Society*. Dubuque, IA: Kendall/Hunt.

Ivie, Rachel L., Cynthia Gimbel, and Glen H. Elder, Jr. 1991. "Military Experience and Attitudes in Later Life Contextual Influences across Forty Years." *Journal of Political and Military Sociology* 19:101–117.

Jackson, Pamela Braboy and Montenique Finney. 2002. "Negative Life Events and Psychological Distress among Young Adults." *Social Psychology Quarterly* 65:186–201.

Jary, David and Julia Jary. 1991. *The Harper-Collins Dictionary of Sociology*. New York: HarperPerennial.

Jasso, Guillermina. 1980. "A New Theory of Distributive Justice." *American Sociological Review* 45:3–32.

Jasso, Guillermina and Murray Webster, Jr. 1999. "Assessing the Gender Gap in Just Earnings and its Underlying Mechanisms." *Social Psychology Quarterly* 62:367–380.

Jencks, Chris. 1996. *Childhood*. London: Taylor & Francis.

Jenkins, J. Craig, David Jacobs, and Jon Agnone. 2003. "Political Opportunities and African-American Protest." *American Journal of Sociology* 109:277–303.

Kalton, Graham. 1983. *Introduction to Survey Sampling*, vol. 35, edited by M. S. Lewis-Beck. Newbury Park, CA: Sage.

Kelley, Jonathan and Nan Dirk De Graaf. 1997. "National Context, Parental Socialization, and Religious Belief: Results from 15 Nations." *American Sociological Review* 62:639–659.

Kemper, Theodore D. 1987. "How Many Emotions Are There? Wedding the Social and Autonomic Components." *American Journal of Sociology* 93:263–289.

———. 1991. "Predicting Emotions from Social Relations." *Social Psychology Quarterly* 54:330–342.

Kerckhoff, Alan C. 1995. "Social Stratification and Mobility Processes: Interaction between Individuals and Social Structures." Pp. 476–496 in *Sociological Perspectives on Social Psychology*, edited by K. S. Cook, G. A. Fine, and J. S. House. Boston: Allyn & Bacon.

Kessler, Ronald C. and Harold W. Neighbors. 1986. "A New Perspective on the Relationships among Race, Social Class, and Psychological Distress." *Journal of Health and Social Behavior* 27:107–115.

Kim, Hyoun K. and Patrick C. McKenry. 2003. "The Relationship between Marriage and Psychological Well-Being: A Longitudinal Analysis." *Journal of Family Issues* 23:885–911.

Kless, Steven J. 1992. "The Attainment of Peer Status: Gender and Power Relationships in the Elementary School." *Sociological Studies of Child Development* 5:115–148.

Kohn, Melvin L. 1969. *Class and Conformity: A Study in Values*. Homewood, IL: The Dorsey Press.

Kohn, Melvin L. and Carmi Schooler. 1983. *Work and Personality: An Inquiry into the Impact of Social Stratification*. Norwood, NJ: Greenwood Publishing Company.

Kraus, Stephen J. 1995. "Attitudes and the Prediction of Behavior: A Meta-Analysis of the Empirical Literature." *Personality and Social Psychology Bulletin* 21:58–76.

Kuhn, Manford H. and Thomas S. McPartland. 1954. "An Emperical Investigation of Self-Attitudes." *American Sociological Review* 19:69–85.

Lantz, Paula M., James S. House, Richard P. Mero, and David R. Williams. 2005. "Stress, Life Events, and Socioeconomic Disparities in Health: Results from the Americans' Changing Lives Study." *Journal of Health and Social Behavior* 3:274–288.

LaPiere, Richard T. 1934. "Attitudes vs. Action." *Social Forces* 13:230–237.

Lareau, Annette. 2003. *Unequal Childhoods: Class, Race, and Family Life*. Berkeley: University of California Press.

Laub, John H., Daniel S. Nagin, and Robert J. Sampson. 1998. "Trajectories of Change in Criminal Offending: Good Marriages and the Desistance Process." *American Sociological Review* 63:225–238.

Laub, John H. and Robert J. Sampson. 1993. "Turning Points in the Life Course: Why Change Matters to the Study of Crime." *Criminology* 31:301–325.

Lawler, Edward J. 2001. "An Affect Theory of Social Exchange." *American Journal of Sociology* 107:321–352.

Lawler, Edward J., Shane R. Thye, and Jeongkoo Yoon. 2000. "Emotion and Group Cohesion in Productive Exchange." *American Journal of Sociology* 16:616–657.

Lawler, Edward J. and Jeongkoo Yoon. 1993. "Power and the Emergence of Commitment Behavior in Negotiated Exchange." *American Sociological Review* 58:465–481.

LeBon, Gustave. 1960. *The Crowd*. New York: Viking Press.

Leibow, Elliot. 1967. *Tally's Corner: A Study of Negro Streetcorner Men*. Boston: Little, Brown and Company.

Lemert, Edwin M. 1951. *Social Pathology: A Systematic Approach to the Theory of Sociopathic Behavior*. New York: McGraw-Hill.

Lewis, Gregory B. 2003. "Black-White Differences in Attitudes toward Homosexuality and Gay Rights." *Public Opinion Quarterly* 67:59–78.

Liebler, Carolyn A. and Gary D. Sandefur. 2002. "Gender Differences in the Exchange of Social Support with Friends, Neighbors, and Co-Workers at Midlife." *Social Science Research* 31:364–391.

Lipsky, Michael. 1968. "Protest as Political Resource." *American Political Science Review* 62:1144–1158.

Lively, Kathryn J. and David R. Heise. 2004. "Sociological Realms of Emotional Experience." *American Journal of Sociology* 109:1109–1136.

Lofland, Lyn H. 1985. "The Social Shaping of Emotion: The Case of Grief." *Symbolic Interaction* 8:171–190.

———. 1992. "Collective Behavior: The Elementary Forms." Pp. 411–446 in *Social Psychology: Sociological Perspectives*, edited by M. Rosenberg and R. H. Turner. New Brunswick, NJ: Transaction Publishers.

Loring, Marti and Brian Powell. 1988. "Gender, Race, and DSM-III: A Study of the Objectivity of Psychiatric Diagnostic Behavior." *Journal of Health and Social Behavior* 29:1–22.

Lovaglia, Michael J. 1995. "Power and Status: Exchange, Attribution, and Expectation States." *Small Group Research* 26:400–426.

Lovaglia, Michael J. and Jeffrey A. Houser. 1996. "Emotional Reactions and Status in Groups." *American Sociological Review* 61:867–883.

Lovaglia, Michael J., Jeffrey W. Lucas, Jeffrey A. Houser, Shane R. Thye, and Barry Markovsky. 1998. "Status Processes and Mental Ability Test Scores." *American Journal of Sociology* 68:464–480.

Lucas, Jeffrey W. 1999. "Behavioral and Emotional Outcomes of Leadership in Task Groups." *Social Forces* 78:747–778.

———. 2003. "Status Processes and the Institutionalization of Women as Leaders." *American Sociological Review* 68:464–480.

Lucas, Jeffrey W., Corina Graif, and Michael J. Lovaglia. 2006. "Misconduct in the Prosecution of Severe Crimes: Theory and Experimental Results." *Social Psychology Quarterly*, 69: 97–107.

Lyons, Linda. 2005. "Teens Stay True to Parents' Political Perspectives." The Gallup Organization. Washington, D.C.

Mackay, Charles. 1852. *Memoirs of Extraordinary Popular Delusions*. London: Office of the National Illustrated Library.

Mackie, Marlene. 1983. "The Domestication of Self: Gender Comparisons of Self-Imagery and Self-Esteem." *Social Psychology Quarterly* 46:343–350.

MacLeod, Jay. 1993. *Ain't No Makin' It; Aspirations & Attainment in a Low-Income Neighborhood*. Boulder, CO: Westview Press.

Maio, Gregory R., James M. Olson, Mark M. Bernard, and Michelle A. Luke. 2003. "Ideologies, Values, Attitudes, and Behavior." Pp. 283–308 in *Handbook of Social Psychology*, edited by J. Delamater. New York: Kluwer Academic/Plenum Publishers.

Markovsky, Barry. 1985. "Toward a Multilevel Distributive Justice Theory." *American Sociological Review* 50:822–839.

Markovsky, Barry, David Willer, and Travis Patton. 1988. "Power Relations in Exchange Networks." *American Sociological Review* 53:220–336.

May, Reuben A. Buford. 2001. " "The Sid Cartwright Incident and More": An African American Male's Interpretive Narrative of Interracial Encounters at the University of Chicago." *Symbolic Interaction* 24:75–100.

McCabe, Donald L. 1992. "The Influence of Situational Ethics on Cheating among College Students." *Sociological Inquiry* 62:365–374.

McCall, George J. 2003. "The Me and the Not-Me: Positive and Negative Poles of Identity." Pp. 11–26 in *Advances in Identity Theory and Research*. New York: Kluwer Academic/Plenum Publishers.

McCarthy, John D., Clark McPhail, and Jackie Smith. 1996. "Images of Protest: Dimensions of Selection Bias in Media Coverage of Washington Demonstrations, 1982–1991." *American Sociological Review* 61:478–499.

McKinnon, Jessie D. and Claudette E. Bennett. 2005. "We the People: Blacks in the United States." *Census 2000 Special Reports*. U.S. Census Bureau.

McLaughlin, Paul and Khawaja Marwan. 2000. "The Organizational Dynamics of the U.S. Environmental Movement: Legitimation, Resource Mobilization, and Political Opportunity." *Rural Sociology* 65:422–439.

McLeod, Jane D. and Katherine J. Lively. 2003. "Social Structure and Personality." Pp. 77–102 in *Handbook of Social Psychology*, edited by J. D. DeLamater. New York: Kluwer Academic/Plenum Publishers.

McPhail, Clark. 1991. *The Myth of the Maddening Crowd*. New York: Aldine De Gruyter.

———. 1994. "The Dark Side of Purpose: Individual and Collective Violence in Riots." *The Sociological Quarterly* 35:1–32.

McPhail, Clark and John McCarthy. 2004. "Who Counts and How: Estimating the Size of Protests." *Contexts* 3:12–18.

McPhail, Clark and Charles W. Tucker. 2003. "Collective Behavior." Pp. 721–742 in *Handbook of Symbolic Interactionism*, edited by L. T. Reynolds and N. J. Herman-Kinney. Lanham, MD: Rowman & Littlefield.

Mead, George Herbert. 1934. *Mind, Self, and Society from the Standpoint of a Social Behavioralist*. Chicago: Chicago University Press.

Meeker, Barbara Foley and Robert K. Leik. 1995. "Experimentation in Sociological Social Psychology." Pp. 630–649 in *Sociological Perspectives on Social Psychology*, edited by K. S. Cook, G. A. Fine, and J. S. H. House. Boston: Allyn & Bacon.

Merton, Robert K. 1960. *The Ambivalences of LeBon's The Crowd: Introduction to the Compass Edition of The Crowd*. New York: Viking Press.

———. 1968. *Social Theory and Social Structure*. New York: Free Press.

———. 1995. "The Thomas Theorem and the Matthew Effect." *Social Forces* 74:379–422.

Michael, Robert T., Edward O. Laumann, John H. Gagnon, and Gina Bari Kolata. 1995. *Sex in America: A Definitive Survey*. Clayton, Australia: Warner Books.

Milkie, Melissa A. 1999. "Social Comparisons, Reflected Appraisals, and Mass Media: The Impact of Pervasive Beauty Ideals on Black and White Girls' Self-Concepts." *Social Psychology Quarterly* 62:190–210.

Milkie, Melissa A., Robin W. Simon, and Brian Powell. 1997. "Through the Eyes of Children: Youth's Perceptions and Evaluations of Maternal and Paternal Roles." *Social Psychology Quarterly* 60:218–237.

Miller, David L. 2000. *Introduction to Collective Behavior and Collective Action*. Prospect Heights, IL: Waveland.

Mills, C. Wright. 1959. *The Sociological Imagination*. London: Oxford University Press.

———. 2002. *White Collar: The American Middle Classes*. Oxford: Oxford University Press.

Miner, Horace. 1956. "Body Ritual among the Nacirema." *American Anthropologist* 58:503–507.

Mirowsky, John and Catherine E. Ross. 1995. "Sex Differences in Distress: Real or Artifact?" *American Sociological Review* 60:449–468.

Molinsky, Andrew. 2005. "Language Fluency and the Evaluation of Cultural Faux Pas: Russians Interviewing for Jobs in the United States." *Social Psychology Quarterly* 68:103–120.

Molm, Linda D. 1991. "Affect and Social Exchange: Satisfaction in Power-Dependence Relations." *American Sociological Review* 56:475–493.

Molm, Linda D. and Karen S. Cook. 1995. "Social Exchange and Exchange Networks." pp. 209–235 in *Sociological Perspectives in Social Psychology*, edited by K. S. Cook, G. A. Fine, and J. S. House. Boston: Allyn & Bacon.

Mondillon, Laurie, Paula M. Niedenthal, Markus Brauer, Anette Rohmann, Nathalie Dalle, and Yukiko Uchida. 2005. "Beliefs about Power and Its Relation to Emotional Experience: A Comparison of Japan, France, Germany, and the United States." *Personality and Social Psychology Bulletin* 31:1112–1122.

Moore, David W. 2002. "Gender Gap Varies on Support for War." The Gallup Organization. Washington, D.C.

Moore, Gwen. 1990. "Structural Determinants of Men's and Women's Personal Networks." *American Sociological Review* 55:726–735.

Morgan, S. Philip. 2003. "Is Low Fertility a Twenty-First-Century Demographic Crisis?" *Demography* 40:589–603.

Mortimer, Jeylan T. and Roberta G. Simmons. 1978. "Adult Socialization." *Annual Review of Sociology* 4:421–454.

Musolf, Gil Richard. 2003b. *Structure and Agency in Everyday Life*. Lanham, MD: Rowman & Littlefield.
———. 2003a. "The Chicago School." Pp. 91–118 in *Handbook of Symbolic Interactionism*, edited by L. T. Reynolds and N. J. Herman-Kinney. Lanham, MD: Rowman & Littlefield.

Nagel, Joanne. 1995. "American Indian Ethnic Renewal: Politics and the Resurgence of Identity." *American Sociological Review* 60:947–965.

Nash, Jeffrey E. 2000. "Racism in the Ivory City: The Natural History of a Research Project." *Symbolic Interaction* 23:147–168.

Neighbors, Harold W., Steven J. Trierweiler, Briggett C. Ford, and Jordana R. Muroff. 2003. "Racial Differences in DSM Diagnosis Using a Semi-Structured Instrument: The Importance of Clinical Judgment in the Diagnosis of African Americans." *Journal of Health and Social Behavior* 44:237–256.

Nelson, Charles. 2005. *News Conference on 2004 Income, Poverty, and Health Insurance Estimates from the Current Population Survey*. Washington, DC: Census Bureau.

Neuman, W. Lawrence. 2004. *Basics of Social Research: Qualitative and Quantitative Approaches*. Boston: Pearson.

Nisbett, Richard E. 1993. "Violence and U.S. Regional Culture." *American Psychologist* 48:441–449.

Nisbett, Richard E., Gregory Polly, and Sylvia Lang. 1995. "Homicide and U.S. Regional Culture." Pp. 135–151 in *Interpersonal Violent Behaviors: Social and Cultural Aspects*, edited by R. B. Ruback and N. A. Weiner. New York: Springer.

Nolan, Patrick and Gerhard Lenski. 2004. *Human Societies: An Introduction to Macrosociology*. New York: Paradigm.

Nomaguchi, Kei M. and Melissa A. Milkie. 2003. "Costs and Rewards of Children: The Effects of Becoming a Parent on Adults' Lives." *Journal of Marriage and the Family* 65:356–374.

Oldmeadow, Julian A., Michael J. Platow, Margaret Foddy, and Donna Anderson. 2003. "Self-Categorization, Status, and Social Influence." *Social Psychology Quarterly* 66:138–153.

Osgood, Charles H. 1962. "Studies of the Generality of Affective Meaning Systems." *American Psychologist* 17: 10–28.

Owen, Carolyn A., Howard C. Eisner, and Thomas R. McFaul. 1981. "A Half-Century of Social Distance Research: National Replication of the Bogardus Studies." *Sociology and Social Research* 66:80–98.

Owens, Timothy J. and Sheldon Stryker. 2001. "The Future of Self-Esteem Research: An Introduction." Pp. 1–9 in *Extending Self-Esteem Theory and Research: Sociological and Psychological Currents*, edited by T. J. Owens, S. Stryker, and N. Goodman. Cambridge, MA: Cambridge University Press.

Pager, Devah and Lincoln Quillian. 2005. "Walking the Talk? What Employers Say Versus What They Do." *American Sociological Review* 70:355–380.

Pampel, Fred C. 2001. *The Institutional Context of Population Change: Patterns of Fertility and Mortality Across High-Income Nations*. Chicago: University of Chicago Press.

Panina, Natalia. 2004. "On the Measurement of Social Distance in the Research of Ethnic Toleration in Ukraine." *Studia Socjologiczne* 4:135–159.

Park, Robert E. and Ernest W. Burgess. 1921. *Introduction to the Science of Sociology*. Chicago: University of Chicago Press.

Parrillo, Vincent N. and Christopher Donoghue. 2005. "Updating the Bogardus Social Distance Studies: A New National Survey." *The Social Science Journal* 42:257–271.

Parsons, Talcott. 1951. *The Social System*. Glencoe, IL: Free Press.

Paules, Greta Foff. 1991. *Dishing It Out: Power and Resistance Among Waitresses in a New Jersey Restaurant*. Philadelphia: Temple University Press.

Pearlin, Leonard I. 1989. "The Sociological Study of Stress." *Journal of Health and Social Behavior* 30:240–256.

Pearlin, Leonard I. and Carmi Schooler. 1978. "The Structure of Coping." *Journal of Health and Social Behavior* 19:2–21.

Pearlin, Leonard I. and Allen J. LeBlanc. 2001. "Bereavement and the Loss of Mattering." Pp. 285–300 in *Extending Self-Esteem Theory and Research*, edited by N. Goodman, T. Owens, and S. Stryker. Cambridge, UK: Oxford University Press.

Pearlin, Leonard I., Elizabeth G. Menaghan, Morton A. Lieberman, and Joseph T. Mullan. 1981. "The Stress Process." *Journal of Health and Social Behavior* 22:337–356.

Peterson, Jean Treloggen. 1993. "Generalized Extended Family Exchange: A Case from the Philippines." *Journal of Marriage and the Family* 55:570–584.

Pfeffer, Jeffrey. 1993. *Managing with Power: Politics and Influence in Organizations*. Cambridge, MA: Harvard Business School.

Pfohl, Stephen J. 1985. *Images of Deviance and Social Control: A Sociological History*. New York: McGraw-Hill.

Piquero, Nicole Leeper, Angela R. Gover, John M. Macdonald, and Alex R. Piquero. 2005. "The Influence of Delinquent Peers on Delinquency: Does Gender Matter?" *Youth & Society* 36:251–275.

Pollack, Lauren Harte and Peggy A. Thoits. 1989. "Processes in Emotional Socialization." *Social Psychology Quarterly* 52:22–34.

Polletta, Francesca and James M. Jasper. 2001. "Collective Identity and Social Movements." *Annual Review of Sociology* 27:283–305.

Prince, Samuel Henry. 1920. *Catastrophe and Social Change*. New York: Columbia University.

Pugh, Meredith D. and Ralph Wahrmer. 1983. "Neutralizing Sexism in Mixed-Sex Groups: Do Women Have to Be Better than Men?" *American Journal of Sociology* 88:746–762.

Pugliesi, Karen and Scott L. Shook. 1998. "Gender, Ethnicity, and Network Characteristics: Variation in Social Support Resources." *Sex Roles* 38:215–238.

Putnam, Robert D. 2000. *Bowling Alone: The Collapse and Revival of American Community*. New York: Simon & Schuster.

Raden, David. 1985. "Strength-Related Attitude Dimensions." *Social Psychology Quarterly* 48:312–330.

Radloff, Lenore S. 1977. "The CES-D Scale: A Self-Report Depression Scale for Research in the General Population." *Applied Psychological Measurement* 1:385–401.

Rane, Thomas R. and Brent A. McBride. 2000. "Identity Theory as a Guide to Understanding Fathers' Involvement with Their Children." *Journal of Family Issues* 21:347–366.

Reevy, Gretchen M. and Christina Maslach. 2001. "Use of Social Support: Gender and Personality Differences." *Sex Roles* 44:437–459.

Reynolds, Larry T. 2003. "Intellectual Precursors." Pp. 39–58 in *Handbook of Symbolic Interactionism*, edited by L. T. Reynolds and N. J. Herman-Kinney. Lanham, MD: Rowman & Littlefield.

Reynolds, Larry T. and Nancy J. Herman-Kinney. 2003. *Handbook of Symbolic Interactionism*. Lanham, MD: Rowman & Littlefield.

Ridgeway, Cecilia L. 1982. "Status in Groups: The Importance of Motivation." *American Sociological Review* 47:76–88.

Ridgeway, Cecilia L. 2001. "Gender, Status, and Leadership." *The Journal of Social Issues* 57:637–655.

Ridgeway, Cecilia L. and James W. Balkwell. 1997. "Group Processes and the Diffusion of Status Beliefs." *Social Psychology Quarterly* 60:14–31.

Ridgeway, Cecilia L. and Joseph Berger. 1986. "Expectations, Legitimation, and Dominance Behavior in Task Groups." *American Sociological Review* 51:603–617.

Ridgeway, Cecilia L. and David Diekema. 1989. "Dominance and Collective Hierarchy Formation in Male and Female Task Groups." *American Sociological Review* 54:79–93.

Ridgeway, Cecilia L. and Cathryn Johnson. 1990. "What Is the Relationship between Socioemotional Behavior and Status in Task Groups?" *American Journal of Sociology* 95:1189–1212.

Ridgeway, Cecilia L., Kathy J. Kuipers, Elizabeth Heger Boyle, and Dawn T. Robinson. 1998. "How Do Status Beliefs Develop? The Role of Resources and Interactional Experience." *American Sociological Review* 63:331–350.

Ritzer, George. 1993. *The McDonaldization of Society: An Investigation into the Changing Character of Contemporary Social Life*. Newbury Park, CA: Pine Forge Press.

———. 1996. *Sociological Theory*. New York: McGraw-Hill.

Robins, Lee N., B. Z. Locke, and Darrel A. Regier. 1991. "An Overview of Psychiatric Disorders in America." Pp. 328–366 in *Psychiatric Disorders in America*, edited by L. N. Robins and D. A. Regier. New York: Free Press.

Robinson, John P. and Geoffrey Godbey. 1997. *Time for Life: Surprising Way Americans Use Their Time*. University Park: Pennsylvania State University.

Rohall, David E. 2003. "Illegal Drugs." *Contexts* 3:60.

Rohall, David E., Morten G. Ender, and Michael D. Matthews. 2006. "The Effects of Military Affiliation, Sex, and Political Ideology on Attitudes toward the Wars in Afghanistan and Iraq." *Armed Forces and Society* 59–77.

Rohlinger, Deana A. and David A. Snow. 2003. "Social Psychological Perspectives on Crowds and Social Movements." Pp. 503–528 in *Handbook of Symbolic Interactionism*, edited by L. T. Reynolds and N. J. Herman-Kinney. Lanham, MD: Rowman & Littlefield.

Roschelle, Anne R. and Peter Kaufman. 2004. "Fitting In and Fighting Back: Stigma Management Strategies among Homeless Kids." *Symbolic Interaction* 21:23–46.

Rose, Stephen J. 2000. *Social Stratification in the United States*. New York: The New Press.

Rosenberg, Morris. 1986. *Conceiving the Self*. Malabar, FL: Krieger.

———. 1990. "Reflexivity and Emotion." *Social Psychology Quarterly* 53:3–12.

Rosenberg, Morris and B. Claire McCullough. 1981. "Mattering: Inferred Significance and Mental Health among Adolescents." *Research in Community and Mental Health* 2:163–182.

Rosenberg, Morris and Leonard I. Pearlin. 1978. "Social Class and Self-Esteem among Children and Adults." *American Journal of Sociology* 84:53–78.

Rosenberg, Morris, Carmi Schooler, and Carrie Schoenbach. 1989. "Self-Esteem and Adolescent Problems: Modeling Reciprocal Effects." *American Sociological Review* 54:1004–1018.

Rosenthal, Robert and Lenore Jacobson. 1968. *Pygmalion in the Classroom: Teacher Expectation and Pupils' Intellectual Development*. New York: Holt, Rinehart and Winston.

Russell, Bertrand. 1938. *Power: A New Social Analysis*. New York: W.W. Norton.

Rysavy, Dan. 2003. "Social Distance toward the Roma. The Case of University Students." *Sociologicky Casopis* 39:55–77.

Sacks, Oliver. 1985. *The Man Who Mistook His Wife for a Hat and Other Clinical Tales*. New York: Summit Books.

Sampson, Robert J. and John H. Laub. 1990. "Crime and Deviance over the Life Course: The Salience of Adult Social Bonds." *American Sociological Review* 55:609–627.

———. 1996. "Socioeconomic Achievement in the Life Course of Disadvantaged Men: Military Service as a Turning Point, Circa 1940–1965." *American Sociological Review* 61:347–367.

Sarason, I. G., G. R. Pierce, and B. R. Sarason. 1994. "General and Specific Perceptions of Social Support." Pp. 151–177 in *Stress and Mental Health: Contemporary Issues and Prospects for the Future, Plenum Series on Stress and Coping*, edited by W. R. Avison and I. H. Gottlib. New York: Plenum.

Sauder, Michael. 2005. "Symbols and Contexts: An Interactionist Approach to the Study of Social Status." *The Sociological Quarterly* 46:279–298.

Scheff, Thomas J. 1990. *Microsociology: Discourse, Emotion, and Social Structure*. Chicago: University of Chicago Press.

———. 1999. *Being Mentally Ill: A Sociological Theory*. New York: Aldine de Gruyter.

Schieman, Scott, Tetyana Pudrovska, and Melissa A. Milkie. 2005. "The Sense of Divine Control and the Self-Concept: A Study of Race Differences in Later Life." *Research on Aging* 27:165–196.

Schieman, Scott and John Taylor. 2001. "Statuses, Roles, and the Sense of Mattering." *Sociological Perspectives* 44:469–484.

Schooler, Carmi. 1976. "Serfdom's Legacy: An Ethnic Continuum." *American Journal of Sociology* 81:1265–1286.

Schooler, Carmi and Gary Oates. 2001. "Self-Esteem and Work across the Life Course." Pp. 177–197 in *Extending Self-Esteem Theory and Research: Sociological and Psychological Currents*, edited by T. J. Owens, S. Stryker, and N. Goodman. Cambridge, MA: Cambridge University Press.

Schooler, Carmi, Mesfin Samuel Mulatu, and Gary Oates. 2004. "Occupational Self-Direction, Intellectual Functioning, and Self-Directed Orientation in Older Workers: Findings and Implications for Individuals and Societies." *American Journal of Sociology* 110:161–197.

Schuman, Howard. 1995. "Attitudes, Beliefs, and Behavior." Pp. 68–89 in *Sociological Perspectives on Social Psychology*, edited by K. S. Cook, G. A. Fine, and J. S. House. Boston: Allyn & Bacon.

Schuman, Howard and Stanley Presser. 1980. "Public Opinion and Public Ignorance: The Fine Line between Attitudes and Nonattitudes." *American Journal of Sociology* 85:1214–1225.

Schur, Edwin M. 1971. *Labeling Deviant Behavior: Its Sociological Implications*. New York: Harper & Row.

Schussman, Alan and Sarah A. Soule. 2005. "Process and Protest: Accounting for Individual Protest Participation." *Social Forces* 84:1083–1108.

Schwalbe, Michael L. and Clifford L. Staples. 1991. "Gender Differences in Sources of Self-Esteem." *Social Psychology Quarterly* 54:158–168.

Schweingruber, David and Nancy Berns. 2003. "Doing Money Work in a Door-to-Door Sales Organization." *Symbolic Interaction* 26:447–471.

Scott, Wilbur J. 1990. "PTSD in DSM III: A Case in the Politics of Diagnosis and Disease." *Social Problems* 37:294–310.

Serido, Joyce, David M. Almeida, and Elaine Wethington. 2004. "Chronic Stressors and Daily Hassles: Unique and Interactive Relationships with Psychological Distress." *Journal of Health and Social Behavior* 45:17–33.

Sewell, William H., Robert M. Hauser, Kristen W. Springer, and Taissa S. Hauser. 2003. "As We Age: A Review of the Wisconsin Longitudinal Study, 1957–2001." *Research in Stratification and Mobility* 20:3–111.

Shackelford, Susan, Wendy Wood, and Stephen Worchel. 1996. "Behavioral Styles and the Influences of Women in Mixed-Sex Groups." *Social Psychology Quarterly* 59:284–293.

Sharp, Susan F., Toni L. Terling-Watt, Leslie A. Atkins, Jay Trace Gilliam, and Anna Sanders. 2001. "Purging Behavior in a Sample of College Females: A Research Note on General Strain Theory and Female Deviance." *Deviant Behavior* 22:171–188.

Sherif, Muzafer, O. J. Harvey, B. Jack White, William R. Hood, and Carolyn W. Sherif. 1988. *Intergroup Conflict and Cooperation: The Robbers Cave Experiment*. Middletown, CT: Wesleyan University Press.

Shornack, Lawrence L. 1986. "Exchange Theory and the Family." *International Social Science Review* 61:51–60.

Simmel, Georg. 1950. *The Sociology of Georg Simmel*. Translated by K. H. Wolff. Glencoe, IL: Free Press.

Simon, Robin W. 2002. "Revisiting the Relationships among Gender, Marital Status, and Mental Health." *American Journal of Sociology* 107:1065–1096.

Simon, Robin W. and Leda E. Nath. 2004. "Gender and Emotion in the United States: Do Men and Women Differ in Self-Reports of Feelings and Expressive Behavior?" *American Journal of Sociology* 109:1137–1176.

Simons, Ronald L., Yi-Fu Chen, Eric A. Stewart, and Gene H. Brody. 2003. "Incidents of Discrimination and Risk for Delinquency: A Longitudinal Test of Strain Theory with an African American Sample." *Justice Quarterly* 20:827–854.

Simpson, Brent and Michael W. Macy. 2004. "Power, Identity, and Collective Action in Social Exchange." *Social Forces* 82:1373–1409.

Simpson, Eyler Newton. 1998. "Edward A. Ross and the Social Forces." *Sociological Origins* 1:27–32.

Small, Gary W., Michael W. Propper, Eugenia T. Randolph, and Eth Spencer. 1991. "Mass Hysteria among Student Performers: Social Relationship as a Symptom Predictor." *American Journal of Psychiatry* 148:1200–1205.

Smith-Lovin, Lynn. 1995. "The Sociology of Affect and Emotion." Pp. 118–148 in *Sociological Perspectives on Social Psychology*, edited by K. S. Cook, G. A. Fine, and J. S. H. House. Boston: Allyn & Bacon.

Smith-Lovin, Lynn and Linda D. Molm. 2000. "Introduction to the Millennium Special Issue on the State of Sociological Social Psychology." *Social Psychology Quarterly* 63:281–283.

Smith, Tom W. 1984. "The Polls: Gender and Attitudes toward Violence." *The Public Opinion Quarterly* 48:384–396.

Smith, Tom W. 1992. *Attitudes Towards Sexual Permissiveness: Trends, Correlations, and Behavioral Connections*. National Opinion Research Center, Chicago.

Snow, David A. 2003. "Social Movements." Pp. 811–833 in *Handbook of Symbolic Interactionism*, edited by L. T. Reynolds and N. J. Herman-Kinney. Lanham, MD: Rowman & Littlefield.

Snow, David A. and Cynthia L. Phillips. 1982. "The Changing Self-Orientations of College Students: From Institutions to Impulse." *Social Science Quarterly* 63:462–476.

Snow, David A., Sarah A. Soule, and Daniel M. Cress. 2005. "Identifying the Precipitants of Homeless Protest across 17 U.S. Cities, 1980–1990." *Social Forces* 83:1183–1211.

Soule, Sarah A., Doug McAdam, John McCarthy, and Yang Su. 1999. "Protest Events: Cause or Consequence of State Action? The U.S. Women's Movement and Federal Congressional Activities, 1956–1979." *Mobilization* 4:239–255.

Staples, Brent. 1995. *Parallel Time: Growing up in Black and White*. New York: Pantheon.

Stearns, Carol Zisowitz and Peter N. Stearns. 1986. *Anger: The Struggle for Emotional Control in America's History*. Chicago: University of Chicago Press.

Steele, Claude M. and Joshua Aronson. 1995. "Stereotype Threat and the Intellectual Test Performance of African Americans." *Journal of Personality and Social Psychology* 69:797–811.

Stets, Jan E. 2003. "Emotions and Sentiment." Pp. 309–338 in *Handbook of Social Psychology*, edited by J. Delamater. New York: Kluwer Academic/Plenum.

———. 2005 "Examining Emotions and Identity Theory." *Social Psychology Quarterly* 68:39–74.

Stets, Jan E. and Peter J. Burke. 1996. "Gender, Control, and Interaction." *Social Psychology Quarterly* 59:193–220.

———. 2005. "Identity Verification, Control, and Aggression in Marriages." *Social Psychology Quarterly* 68:160–178.

Stryker, Sheldon. 1992. "Symbolic Interactionism: Themes and Variations." Pp. 3–29 in *Social Psychology: Sociological Perspectives*, edited by M. Rosenberg and R. H. Turner. New Brunswick, NJ: Transaction Publishers.

———. 2002. *Symbolic Interactionism: A Social Structural Version*. Caldwell, NJ: Blackburn.

Stryker, Sheldon and Peter J. Burke. 2000. "The Past, Present, and Future of an Identity Theory." *Social Psychology Quarterly* 63:284–297.

Stryker, Sheldon and Kevin D. Vryan. 2003. "The Symbolic Interactionist Frame." Pp. 3–28 in *Handbook of Social Psychology*, edited by J. D. DeLamater. New York: Kluwer Academic/Plenum.

Sudman, Seymour, Norman M. Bradburn, and Norbert Schwarz. 1996. *Thinking about Answers: The Application of Cognitive Processes to Survey Methodology*. San Francisco: Jossey-Bass.

Sunshine, Jason and Tom Tyler. 2003. "Moral Solidarity, Identification with the Community, and Importance of Procedure Justice: The Police as Prototypical Representatives of a Group's Moral Values." *Social Psychology Quarterly* 66:153–164.

Sutherland, Edwin H. 1940. "White Collar Criminality." *American Sociological Review* 5:1–12.

Sutherland, Edwin H. and Donald R. Cressey. 1999. "The Theory of Differential Association." Pp. 237–243 in *Theories of Deviance*, edited by S. H. Traub and C. B. Little. Itasca, IL: F. E. Peacock.

Swidler, Ann. 2001. *Talk of Love: How Culture Matters*. Chicago: University of Chicago Press.

Szasz, Thomas S. 1968. "The Myth of Mental Illness." Pp. 222–281 in *The Social Control of Mental Illness*, edited by H. Silverstein. New York: Thomas Y. Crowell.

———. 1974. *The Myth of Mental Illness: Foundations of a Theory of Personal Conduct*. New York: Harper & Row.

———. 2003. "Cleansing the Modern Heart." *Society* 40:52–59.

Tajfel, Henri. 1982. "The Social Psychology of Interracial Relations." *Annual Review of Psychology* 33(1): 1–39.

Tannenbaum, Frank. 1938. *Crime and the Community*. Boston: Ginn and Company.

Taylor, John and R. Jay Turner. 2001. "A Longitudinal Study of the Role and Significance of Mattering to Others for Depressive Symptoms." *Journal of Health and Social Behavior* 42:310–325.

Thoits, Peggy A. 1989. "The Sociology of Emotions." *Annual Review of Sociology* 15:317–342.

———. 1991. "On Merging Identity Theory and Stress Research." *Social Psychology Quarterly* 57:101–112.

———. 1995. "Identity-Relevant Events and Psychological Symptoms: A Cautionary Tale." *Journal of Health and Social Behavior* 36:72–82.

Thomas, George M., Henry Walker, and Morris Zelditch. 1986. "Legitimacy and Collective Action." *Social Forces* 65:378–404.

Thomas, W. I. 1966. "The Relation of Research to the Social Process." Pp. 289–330 in *W. I. Thomas on Social Organization and Social Personality*, edited by M. Janowitz. Chicago: University of Chicago Press.

Thomas, William I. and Dorothy Swaine Thomas. 1928. *The Child in America: Behavior Problems and Programs*. New York: Knopf.

Thomas, William I. and Florian Znaniecki. 1958. *The Polish Peasant in Europe and America*. New York: Dover.

Thorne, Barrie. 1993. *Gender Play: Girls and Boys in School*. New Brunswick, NJ: Rutgers University Press.

Thye, Shane R. 2000. "A Status Value Theory of Power in Exchange Relations." *American Sociological Review* 65:477–508.

Troyer, Lisa. 2001. "Effects of Protocol Differences on the Study of Status and Social Influence." *Current Research in Social Psychology* 6:182–204.

Turner, Heather A. and Kathleen Kopiec. 2006. "Exposure to Interparental Conflict and Psychological Disorder among Young Adults." Journal of Family Issues 27(7): 131–158.

Turner, R. Jay, Blair Wheaton, and Donald A. Lloyd. 1995. "The Epidemiology of Social Stress." *American Sociological Review* 60:104–125.

Turner, R. Jay, Donald A. Lloyd, and Patricia Roszell. 1999. "Personal Resources and the Social Distribution of Depression." *American Journal of Community Psychology* 27:643–670.

Turner, R. Jay and Franco Marino. 1994. "Social Support and Social Structure: A Descriptive Epidemiology." *Journal of Health and Social Behavior* 35:193–212.

Turner, R. Jay and Patricia Roszell. 1994. "Psychosocial Resources and the Stress Process." Pp. 179–210 in *Stress and Mental Health: Contemporary Issues and Prospects for the Future, Plenum Series on Stress and Coping,* edited by W. R. Avison and I. H. Gottlib. New York: Plenum.

Turner, R. Jay, John Taylor, and Karen Van Gundy. 2004. "Personal Resources and Depression in the Transition to Adulthood: Ethnic Comparisons." *Journal of Health and Social Behavior* 45:34–52.

Turner, Ralph H. and Lewis M. Killian. 1972. *Collective Behavior*. Englewood Cliffs, NJ: Prentice Hall.

Ulbrich, Patricia M., George J. Warheit, and Rick S. Zimmerman. 1989. "Race, Socioeconomic Status, and Psychological Distress: An Examination of Differential Vulnerability." *Journal of Health and Social Behavior* 30:131–146.

Umberson, Debra, Meichu D. Chen, James S. House, Kristine Hopkins, and Ellen Slaten. 1996. "The Effect of Social Relationships on Psychological Well-Being: Are Men and Women Really So Different?" *American Sociological Review* 61:837–857.

Umberson, Debra, Camille B. Wortman, and Ronald C. Kessler. 1992. "Widowhood and Depression: Explaining Long-Term Gender Differences in Vulnerability." *Journal of Health and Social Behavior* 33:10–24.

Van Dyke, Nella and Sarah A. Soule. 2002. "Structural Social Change and the Mobilizing Effects of Threat: Explaining Levels of Patriot and Militia Organizing in the United States." *Social Problems* 49:497–520.

Wagner, David G. 1993. "The Labelling of Mental Illness as a Status Organizing Process." Pp. 51–68 in *Social Psychology of Groups: A Reader,* edited by E. J. Lawler and B. Markovsky. Greenwich, CT: JAI Press.

Wagner, David G. and Joseph Berger. 1993. "Status Characteristics Theory: The Growth of a Program." Pp. 23–63 in *Theoretical Research Programs: Studies in Theory Growth,* edited by J. Berger and M. Zelditch, Jr. Stanford, CA: Stanford University Press.

Wagner, David G. and Joseph Berger. 1997. "Gender and Interpersonal Task Behaviors: Status Expectation Accounts." *Sociological Perspectives* 40:1–32.

Waite, Linda J. and Maggie Gallagher. 2000. *The Case for Marriage: Why Married People are Happier,*

Healthier, and Better Off Financially. New York: Doubleday.

Walker, Henry A., George M. Thomas, and Morris Zelditch, Jr. 1986. "Legitimation, Endorsement, and Stability." *Social Forces* 64:620–643.

Warren, John Robert, Robert M. Hauser, and Jennifer T. Sheridan. 2002. "Occupational Stratification across the Life Course: Evidence from the Wisconsin Longitudinal Study." *American Sociological Review* 67:432–455.

Waters, Mary C. 1999. *Black Identities: West Indian Immigrant Dreams and American Realities:* Russell Sage.

Webster, Murray, Jr. and James E. Driskell. 1978. "Status Generalization: A Review and Some New Data." *American Sociological Review* 43:220–236.

Webster, Murray, Jr. and Martha Foschi. 1988. *Status Generalization.* Stanford, CA: Stanford University Press.

Webster, Murray, Jr. and Joseph M. Whitmeyer. 2002. "Modeling Second-Order Expectations." *Sociological Theory* 20:306–327.

Weinfurt, Kevin P. and Fathali M. Moghaddam. 2001. "Culture and Social Distance: A Case Study of Methodological Cautions." *Journal of Social Psychology* 141:101–110.

West, Candace and Don H. Zimmerman. 1987. "Doing Gender." *Gender and Society* 1:125–151.

Wilde, Melissa J. 2001. "From Excommunication to Nullification: Testing and Extending Supply-Side Theories of Religious Marketing with the Case of Catholic Marital Annulments." *Journal for the Scientific Study of Religion* 40:235–249.

Willer, David G. and Travis Patton. 1987. "The Development of Network Exchange Theory." Pp. 199–242 in *Advances in Group Processes*, vol. 4, edited by E. J. Lawler and B. Markovsky. Greenwich, CT: JAI.

Willer, Robb. 2004. "The Effects of Government-Issued Terror Warnings on Presidential Approval Ratings." *Current Research in Social Psychology* 10:1–12.

Williams, David R., David T. Takeuchi, and Russell K. Adair. 1992. "Socioeconomic Status and Psychiatric Disorder among Blacks and Whites." *Social Forces* 71:179–194.

Williams, Norma and Minerva Correa. 2003. "Race and Ethnic Relations." Pp. 743–760 in *Handbook of Symbolic Interactionism*, edited by L. T. Reynolds and N. J. Herman-Kinney. Lanham, MD: Rowman & Littlefield.

Wolf, Alan. 1998. *One Nation after All.* New York: Penguin.

Wu, Zheng, Samuel Noh, Violet Kaspar, and Christoph M. Schimmele. 2003. "Race, Ethnicity, and Depression in Canadian Society." *Journal of Health and Social Behavior* 44:426–444.

Yi, Zeng and Wu Deqing. 2000. "Regional Analysis of Divorce in China since 1980." *Demography* 37:215–219.

Yip, Tiffany. 2005. "Sources of Situational Variation in Ethnic Identity and Psychological Well-Being: A Palm Pilot Study of Chinese American Students." *Personality and Social Psychology Bulletin* 31:1603–1616.

Yodanis, Carrie. 2005. "Divorce Culture and Marital Gender Equality: A Cross-National Study." *Gender & Society* 19:644–659.

Zald, Mayer N. and Roberta Ash. 1964. "Social Movement Organizations: Growth, Decay, and Change." *Social Forces* 44:327–341.

Zelditch, Morris, Jr. 2001. "Processes of Legitimation: Recent Developments and New Directions." *Social Psychology Quarterly* 64:4–17.

Zelizer, Viviana A. Rotman. 1985. *Pricing the Priceless Child: The Changing Social Value of Children.* New York: Basic Books.

Zurcher, Louis. 1977. *The Mutable Self.* Beverly Hills, CA: Sage.

———. 1982. "The Staging of Emotion." *Symbolic Interaction* 5:1–22.

Index

Class, and mental health, 218–219
Close-ended questions, 72
Coalition, 300
Coerced dispersals, 296
Cognitive dissonance theories, 247
Collective action, 280
Collective behavior, 50, 281–293
   determinants of, 291–292
   group processes, 298–301
   mass hysteria theory, 281–288
   perception control theory, 292
   phases of, 294–296
   rational choice in, 288–290
   social structure and social movements, 293–294
   value-added theory, 290–292
Collective Behavior (Turner and Killian), 288
Collective identity, 285–286
Collins, R., 264
Colonization, 225
Commitment, 190
Community, and mental health, 221–222
Components principle, 38–41
Comte, A., 10, 11
Concrete operational stage, 146
Conformists, 188
Contagious mental unity, 282–283
Content analysis, 64
Contextual dissonance, 162
Control group, 69
Convenience sample, 59
Conversion, 225
Cooley, C. H., 11–12, 146
Couch, C., 280
Covering, 185–186
The Crowd (LeBon), 280, 284, 286
Culture, 20–22
   elements of, 21
Cybernetic approach, 257

D

Data analysis, 75
Dependent variables, 58–59
Deviance
   defined, 177
   and ethnomethodology, 179–180
   and group relationships, 193–200
   interactionist approaches to, 178–186

   labeling theory of, 180–181
   and social structure, 186–192
   studying in a lab, 197–200
   types of, 181–184
Diagnostic and Statistical Manual, 209, 210, 212
Differential association theory, 194–197
Differential expression, 288
Diffuse status characteristics, 103
Direct exchanges, 101
Dispersal phase, of collective behavior, 295
Distributive justice, 272
Doing gender, 88
Dramaturgical sociology, 123
DuBois, W. E. B., 10, 236
Dunham, H. W., 218
Durkheim, E., 9, 16, 38, 130, 187
Dyads, 48–49

E

Eggleston, R., 260
Ego, 120
Ekman, P., 259
Emergency dispersals, 296
Emergent norm theory, 288–290
Emotional arousal, 130
Emotional cues, 263
Emotional energy, 264
Emotional label, 258
Emotional scripts, 263
Emotion culture, 269–270
Emotions, 122–123
   dimensions and components of, 258–260
   and group processes, 270–275
   identity and interactions, 261–263
   socialization of, 260–261
   and society, 263–265
   structural conditions affecting, 265–270
Emotion work, 267–268
Empty love, 274
Epidemiology of mental health, 218–222
Equitable distribution, 46
Erikson, E., 156
Erikson's stages of social development, 156
Ethnicity, and identity, 135–136
Ethnograph, 75
Ethnographic study, 72
Ethnography, 62